ANTI-PRIMITIVISM
AND THE DECLINE OF THE WEST

The Social Cost of Cultural Ignorance

Volume One
The Primitive and the Supernatural

C. Stanley Urban
S. Thomas Urban

In Collaboration With
Jeff Urban

The Edwin Mellen Press
Lewiston/Queenston/Lampeter

Library of Congress Cataloging-in-Publication Data

Urban, C. Stanley.
    Anti-primitivism and the decline of the West : the social cost of
cultural ignorance / C. Stanley Urban, S. Thomas Urban in
collaboration with Jeff Urban.
        p.   cm.
    Includes bibliographical references and indexes.
    Contents: v. 1. The primitive and the supernatural -- v. 2. The
failure of Christianity, progress, and democracy.
    ISBN 0-7734-9855-9 (v. 1). -- ISBN 0-7734-9857-5 (v. 2)
    1. Progress--Religious aspects--Christianity. 2. Christianity-
-Controversial literature. 3. Christianity and other religions.
4. Religion, Primitive. 5. Ritual. I. Urban, S. Thomas.
II. Urban, Jeff. III. Title.
BR115.P77U73 1993
306--dc20   92-45203
                                                                 CIP

A CIP catalog record for this book
is available from the British Library.

The Edwin Mellen Press   The Edwin Mellen Press
        Box 450   Box 67
  Lewiston, New York   Queenston, Ontario
    USA 14092   CANADA L0S 1L0

                    Edwin Mellen Press, Ltd.
                    Lampeter, Dyfed, Wales
                    UNITED KINGDOM SA48 7DY

            Printed in the United States of America

To Rebecca
my life-long love
who,
like a good primitive,
has inspired and sustained
from
beyond the grave.

TABLE OF CONTENTS

PREFACE

This book is the result of an intensive dialogue of many years between two generations, father and son, scholars in different areas, history and sociology. Out of these divergent backgrounds, and the different points of view which they naturally engendered, eventually came a common product. It belongs to neither. It belongs to both. We, however, must acknowledge the contribution of younger son, Jeff. College graduate, and an avid student of serious literature on a half-dozen fronts, he often rendered valuable help. This was especially true with regard to volume two, the West. In reality it was something of a family enterprise. At any rate, this is the fourth version of writing which began with the presentation of a paper in an Honors seminar at Park College in the fall of 1981, entitled *THE TRINITY OF PRIMITIVE MAN: COSMOLOGY, RITUAL AND ART*. It was culled from a three-year research and a book as long as *War and Peace,* but one a lot less readable. Tom's participation dates from the spring of that year. From that time forward he became my guide and preceptor.

We soon became aware that, until World War II, anthropologists generally shared the West's contempt for so-called primitive cultures world-wide. (While few scholars are happy with that old term, we found nothing as meaningful to the general reader in our own culture. We never use it in a pejorative sense.) Meanwhile, those fragile cultures were happily sacrificed by us in the name of Christianity and the idea of progress.

While recent anthropologists deplored such ethnocentric attitudes, they have done so in scholarly monographs. This necessitated field studies in very limited areas. They remained skeptical concerning intellectual efforts to synthesize great masses of field studies across space and time. This is the task we set ourselves. Another innovation is this: after a lifetime spent as historian at small liberal arts colleges, teaching a great variety of courses through choice, I was psychologically prepared to view the so-called primitive through the perspective of 2,500 years of Western history.

Despite the obvious limitations of this method, it is our hope it best enables the general reader to understand and appreciate these "pure" and exotic cultures. We think it part of the Socratic challenge to Know Thyself. The present study of the cosmology, ritual and art of the primitive, therefore, may be regarded as a mirror in which we see ourselves and, therefore, better understand the human predicament. The so-called "modern" person behaves only rationally and systematically when he understands natural - not supernatural - causality. When he does not, he behaves in a manner quite similar to that of the primitive. His rules and regulations are not rational. Adherence to them is dictated by tradition and status roles rather than by scientific conclusions. Even at the highest levels, human behavior in such instances has more to do with magic than logic.

Meanwhile, save for the most rudimentary of cultures, cosmology, ritual and art harmoniously held native groups together, providing an élan vital. It was as fine an hour as conservatism ever enjoyed. It was the principal reason why the native everywhere did not need the introduction of Christianity to give him a good and virtuous life, capped by the promise of Salvation in the next.

Cosmology - or Genesis - was an imperative to allay the fears and anxieties of a naive people living in a frightening world. It served the same purpose for them as did the Old Testament for the ancient Hebrews. What is amazing, however, is the remarkable parallel between stories of the Creation, and the intimate relationship between God and man in both the Old and New Testaments, and those of the primitive world. Just as those virtually identical stories, or myths, confounded early Christian missionaries, so they destroyed among scholars the idea of Christianity as a unique religion.

As a consequence of this cosmology, the primitive lived in an ordered world, subject to law and controlled by unseen forces. This law was not physical, but moral. Since the primitive was given this law by the gods, right action was conformity with the law and anti-social action was contrary to it. If there were a single word to summarize the belief system, it was "order." It was zealously protected from both Socratic challenge within the tribe and outside erosion.

Cosmology used mythology to answer every crucial question about the remote, unknown and unknowable past the tribe needed to know, for example, "the fall of man" from a state of grace. All peoples were convinced, like the ancient Hebrews, that they lived at the vital center of all things, or that their temple and palace were the core of the world and the navel of the universe. Originally, man lived at peace with the animals and, most important, had easy access to Heaven for direct and inspiring encounters with the Creator. In this Garden of Eden man was innocent of suffering, work or death. But, then came the "fall" and the estrangement of the tribe from God, or the expulsion from Paradise. Because of this fact shamans and priests came into existence. It was only through these holy men that the sought-for intercourse between man and God could be resumed. Universal mythology assured one that eventually there would be Paradise Regained.

Myth and ritual were mutually dependent. Ritual gave the necessary present-day form or procedure to myth, something indispensable. Myth then invested that form with both antiquity and divinity with the purpose of rendering it immune from vulgar change or innovation. If myth were withdrawn from religion, it would probably be necessary to withdraw the rite also because frequently the latter is little more than myth put into action. For example, the Christian communion we have today is inseparable from the myth of the Last Supper.

Like the modern ritualist, best typified by Catholic ceremony, the primitive used ritual to preserve the invisible chain of prosperity which existed between the tribe and the supernatural world. Man celebrates ritual not only to remain knowledgeable and faithful to the spiritual past, but to bathe anew in the sacred pool of the gods. Although the roles of the priest in high primitive cultures and those of the West are similar, what captures our attention is the kinship in ecstasy and mysticism between the primitive shaman and the Old Testament prophet. Both were immersed in miracle, mystery and magic. Both anticipated those same elements in Christianity.

Perhaps the most significant of primitive rituals was that of the masculine puberty rites, or the epitome of a life force. The common thread binding them among a great many tribes the world over was the prevalence of the spectacular, the violent, the dramatic. On an earthly level, they ensured the domination of old men, keepers of esoteric and sacred knowledge. On a supernatural one, the ritual was adhered to even when knowledge of the meaning had been lost. It was sufficient to know that the ancestors understood, and that the gods alone remembered. Just as for the Hebrews in the Book of Job, man's salvation was not knowledge, but faith. The gods themselves were pleased with the unchanging and unchangeable ceremony. Thus, it was the greatest possible support for tribal conservation and the perpetuation of institutions. It not only subjected the present to the past, but the future as well.

As indicated, primitive societies postulated an order in the universe, refusing to submit to the idea of pure chance or chaos. This order, imposed upon the world by the supernatural, could not be perceived and rendered meaningful simply by observation and experiment. It could only succumb to emotion, intuition, and mysticism. This accounted for the virtual universal prevalence of what we term Platonic Idealism in primitive art. It conveyed the idea that the summit of aesthetic perfection, or beauty, transcended human experience and was unchanging and unchangeable. This meant it was alien to human values and unaffected by both history and cultural evolution. This philosophy helped explain how, despite the daily prevalence of what we call naturalistic art, the primitive almost invariably moved into the geometric and abstract varieties to express his idea of the sacred. Primitive art had its finest hour when devoted to supernatural ends. Here it was truly functional. It enabled the tribe to speak with ancestors, ghosts, and gods who controlled an energy source which might do the tribe either infinite good or harm.

To the historian there exists a remarkable parallel between the ancient Greek rites celebrating the pagan god, Dionysus, and such primitive tribes as the Cubeo in the Amazon river basin. The common aim was to dramatize the whole range of human emotions, proceeding from the calm to the frenzied in order that the entire community experience a catharsis. Both the followers of Dionysus and the primitive throughout the world understood the mysterious, but beneficial, effects which came to the community after the death of human *katharma* or *pharmakos*. Willingly or not, the victim acted as a surrogate sacrifice for the entire community, draining away any impurities. The ritual and drama of the cults merged god and man because the Dionysian belief system immortalized both. Finally, its principle attribute was violence because its patron saint taught that wisdom followed after, and because of emotional excess.

In many respects the Christian drama parallels the Dionysian scene. First, God and man truly merged in the person of Jesus who was fully God and fully man. As was the case with all such heroes and gods, Jesus had the gift of prophecy. He forsaw his own bloody demise and the traitors within his own ranks. His lingering and painful death on the cross was sufficient to satisfy the blood lust of the Dionysian orders. And what was the significance of this great and willing sacrifice but to efface original sin, or the act of wiping out collective guilt? Lastly, because of pagan sin and guilt, Christian wisdom followed and triumphed. Ever since, the followers of Jesus have been ceremonially partaking of his flesh and blood. The catharsis of the entire community follows as a direct consequence.

Art, therefore, was the indispensable vehicle in the Trinity of the primitive. Through ritual and prayer, the tribe was made perpetually aware of its cosmology and mythology, involving Creation of the universe and the First Man, its direct ancestor, and the original Social Contract between him and the gods. If we imagine Cosmology and Ritual as the arms of the Cross, or the laterals, the vertical pole uniting them is Art. These three elements provided the navel of the universe, or that point where the tribe lived, the dramatic interaction between man and his gods, and, finally, purpose, which was to live up to the terms of the Social Contract between man and the supernatural. Thus, every tribe was armed with the same comfortable assurances about past, present and future as were the ancient Hebrews with the concept of Jehovah.

The perpetuation of this "historical" drama acted as a Passion Play for the primitive in precisely the same sense that the medieval Christians used the drama of the life, death, and resurrection of Jesus for the benefit of the faithful.

One irresistible conclusion drawn from this study was awareness of the mutual dependency between a people and its supernatural authorities. While a tribe's dependence upon its gods is quickly manifest, the reverse is much less obvious. But, when a people forget and cease to worship, the god or gods die. The Hebrew author of Psalm 137, one written in Babylonian captivity, recognized the religious duty of forgetting neither Israel nor its God.

Of course the genius of the primitive lay in his grasp of the relationship between the tribe and nature. Instead of regarding it as an adversary, but one made to conform to man's needs, the primitive saw himself as a brother to all the animals. He, like them, had to conform to the dictates of nature if the tribe was to remain in harmony with the supernatural. The waste of nature's resources was forbidden. One killed only out of need, not for sport. Animals which the tribe depended upon for food or clothing were usually worshipped. Thus, daily living occurred within a spirit of religiosity. Population was carefully adjusted to what nature would support in the leanest years. Stasis, not change, not progress, was life's aim. Philosophically speaking, this meant satisfaction with one's being, and not perpetually, and generally futilely, striving for one's becoming.

But, while primitive ideologies were independent of the Christian one, they proved quite vulnerable to technology in the form of tools, goods, food and medicine, and, finally, to the military organization and weapons system of the West. Where and when Christianity came in the wake of technological conquest, its universal elements were blurred in the process. Parochialism eventually triumphed.

To sum up, the price primitive peoples pay for being seduced or conquered by white civilizations is that a once homogeneous culture is transformed into a schizophrenic one. We do not believe that it is either wise or virtuous to attempt to impose ethnocentric absolutes upon those with entirely different cultural backgrounds and social needs. When that happens, the results have been uniformly disastrous involving the loss of tribal self-respect and the will to live. Even when given more time and good counsel, primitive peoples demonstrated a seeming inability to understand or appreciate Western values when applied to their daily lives. Therefore, they should be encouraged to develop the potential of their own culture which has a relative value equal to ours.

A final, but extremely significant, departure from the anthropological norm is contained in volume two; we examine traditional Western assumptions as to the superiority of Christianity and progress. To obtain objectivity, it is necessary to approach these subjects as if we were anthropologists amid an alien people. However, cutting loose from one's own cultural moorings insures unpredictable results. Chapter X. of this volume contains a summary of the controversial arguments advanced in the next one.

While none object when we employ this method on the Soviet Union, certain volatile quarters are liable to resent its usage upon our own society when it is consistently perceived in less than flattering terms. Generally speaking, these are the same individuals who apparently think that in all crucial issues it is the duty of Americans to give voice to no unpopular thoughts. (See Louis Wirth's "Preface" to Karl Mannheim, *Ideology and Utopia. An Introduction to the Sociology of Knowledge* (New York, Harcourt-Brace, 1940, xvii).

As for us, while we lay no claims to truth, we consciously and persistently pursued it. Thus, we believe the end product, however strange and exotic, deserves a hearing and some reflection upon it. Let it, as Thomas Jefferson observed, enter the market place of ideas.

Curiously, even before its publication, the work had a limited impact. Tom says it was his emphasis upon our interpretation of the demise of Soviet communism which enabled him to receive the Kosciuszko Foundation grant for summer study in 1992 at Jagiellonian University in Cracow, Poland. It is the oldest university in central Europe. The Yale International Scholar award came as a consequence. (Incidentally, at the same time Tom was in Poland, Jeff toured Russia).

Acknowledgements

From scholarly sources on a national scale, we are indebted to Dr. Charles Wagley, Director of the Center for Latin American Studies at the University of Florida in Gainsville, Dr. Al Reis, chairman of the department of Sociology at Yale, and Dr. Donald Shields, department of Speech and Communications at the University of Missouri at St. Louis.

Locally, Dr. Ron Brecke of the Political Science department, read and gave valuable commentaries on every chapter of the two volumes. Dr. Jerzy Hauptmann, chairman of that department, originated the seminar in which this volume first took form in 1981. Resource professors included Al Dusing, John Gore, John Jamara, Merrill Proudfoot, John Hamilton, John Patton, Ron Miriani, E. M. Fleming, Michael DuMaine, Emily Hauptmann, and Janet McClellan.

Betty Dusing of our Library staff acted as my invaluable proofreader and much more on the last two versions of the piece. Betty Vestal procured much needed interlibrary loan materials. Camille Lloyd was the word processor in each instance.

Local off-campus people who assisted were Phil A. Koury, author and master of prose, and two former neighbors from Weatherby Lake, Barbara Bowman and Neva Jean Kitterman.

The attractive page design and typesetting were provided by Diane Hume . Carole Bosch was my helpful and efficient editor.

Chapter I

THE PRIMITIVE AND THE ANTHROPOLOGICAL DILEMMA:
Historical Perspective

Why did Western scholarship, especially anthropologists, do such a questionable job over a long period of time in the reporting and interpretation of aboriginal life? In retrospect, one sees it as virtually inevitable. The conquering West sent explorers, missionaries and anthropologists to the colonies, along with its political and military administrators, during the lush period of imperialism from 1870 to 1914. Despite the terrible, internecine conflict between and among the white man in World War I, this unequal position among the races persisted until World War II. By virtue of race, nationality, religion, age, sex and the like, these interlopers saw what they were conditioned to see. They generally felt a social distance factor prevailed in their favor. While professionally they sought a dispassionate report on exotic peoples, subjectively they often felt that the latter should not stand in the way of history, progress and Christianity. Occasionally, however, romanticists claimed to have discovered the "noble savage" in action. Here one repeats the inevitability theme. When, in history, has the intelligensia of the conquering peoples done a fair and accurate reporting job on the life and customs of the conquered? The truth of the matter is that the more obviously different the latter are from the former, the more difficult, if not impossible, the task becomes. The position of observation is simply too limited.

This chapter has clear limits and limitations for it does not pretend to be the history of a discipline (anthropology) but rather that of a discipline in history. We shall examine its nineteenth century origins, its self-defined mission, and its elements of human subjectivity, whether perceived or not. The same conflict between scientific aspirations of observation and reporting versus unconscious bias featured twentieth century anthropology in its heyday. There follows an analysis of the abrupt changes forced upon Western anthropology after World War II. Finally, while its traditional subject matter was primitive, or "primitive," tribesmen, a definition of this proved another matter.

From the outset its focus was upon the study of distant, isolated, very small and nonliterate, but exotic populations. These were the so-called primitive peoples who, technologically speaking, were undeveloped. A presumption shared by many was that a Western science could eventually be distilled out of a great many such studies and thus the behavior of man in a universal sense would no longer be a mystery.[1] That purpose remained a constant factor. Prior to World War I the philosophy and techniques were fully developed for the participant observer—invariably a Westerner—to study and report on these different and intriguing cultures.[2] Such practices persisted until the virtual disappearance of such peoples as subject matter, or shortly after World War II.

If the search for the primitive is motivated by our desire to discover or rediscover the nature of human nature, or the nature of man,[3] then one must add that the effort itself bears no relationship to the numerical numbers, vigor and importance of the existing primitives at any time. We do it because the problem exists in our own mind, if not in the world itself. If we find that these cultures are already lost or destroyed as a result of our own actions, then that discovery only makes us more zealous to ascertain the nature of that which civilization virtually effaced or perverted. In brief, the scholarly effort is both compulsive and necessary to those who seek to understand themselves and their societies better through a study of primitive behavior. However, they do this mindful of the caveat of other anthropologists who questioned the assumption that primitive man was necessarily closer in human traits and characteristics to prehistoric or primordial man than was so-called advanced or civilized peoples.[4] Such a failure among social anthropologists to agree upon the purpose of the mission, while typical of the internal dissent among scholars at every critical juncture, may well be due to the perplexities and ambiguities of the subject matter itself.

The initial research difficulty lay in the fact that, contrary to one's expectations, the meaning of the term primitive itself was far from self-evident; instead it has had an almost constantly shifting academic perspective ever since the shaky start of nineteenth century anthropologists. These scholars labored under certain social limitations: they were all men; all had a middle class background, and they were evangelical Christians, especially the English. Consequently, they shared an overweening pride in their own culture which caused them, for example, to misunderstand the position of women.[5] The same scholarly prejudices in nineteenth century America were noted by Franz Boas.[6] On a larger scale, anthropologists erred in their assumption that these societies never underwent changes of a profound nature in space and time.[7] As devotees of economic determinism, some assumed that the physical environment always shaped and molded tribal history and culture.[8] Another fallacy widely current was the notion that a

4

primitive society was one which was simple in its forms and aspects.[9] Laura Thompson had another and larger objection to the work of much of the early anthropologists and one which encompassed many of the limitations described above. She felt that the static models of the diffusion and linkage of culture were largely due to the remoteness of the researcher from the scene. Instead it was a library-oriented or museum-oriented affair, often being based on samples of material culture, which resulted in a rigid and mechanistic product. Not until the anthropologists actually invaded the field did they discover the necessity to substitute more dynamic models in an environmental context.[10]

However, in retrospect, the most serious error committed by early anthropologists and other scholars was when they disparaged these cultures as of but little worth. This persistent prejudice was an integral part of our Christian heritage.[11] It affected the outlook of the earliest anthropologists, like Edward B. Tylor and Lewis Henry Morgan, who believed Indians to be a savage and inferior people.[12] This perception was sometimes carried to the extreme by the affirmation that primitives were incapable of reasoning logically.[13] As a result of his travels in the Australian bush in the early eighteen-nineties, a German naturalist concluded that the natives not only belonged to inferior human races but had a rather low rank among these. The intelligence of the aborigine of Australia, he lamented, was far behind that of any other primitives he had observed.[14] Reporting on the life pattern of the Shoshoni Indians of the Great Salt Lake basin, the historian Hubert Howie Bancroft thought there was little if any difference between them and the brutes, no missing link for example.[15] In 1912, the Negritos of Northern Luzon in the Philippines were described in almost identical fashion.[16]

It would appear that, taking two prominent nineteenth century students of the American Indian as examples, many prejudices against the aborigine were based on an uncritical acceptance of the idea of progress. It also dominated their contemporaries in the Western world. Since progress toward perfectibility was an ideal goal, then it was relatively easy to postulate a rank order at that endeavor. As always, the elite was quick to despise or pity those who were obviously lower down on the totem pole.[17] Savage man, insisted Lewis H. Morgan, was inferior to the modern man on both mental and moral levels. This could be demonstrated both by cave art and archaeological remains, as well as by present-day examples of savages in previously remote areas of the earth.[18] Ever since man emerged to distinguish himself, however feebly, from the other anthropoids, there had been a perceptive march of progress of the intellect.[19] This larger assumption enabled Morgan to lay out a neat schema for human development, one which included three phases of savagery and three of barbarism before man arrived at a civilized state.[20] It was Leslie A White who concluded that, when Morgan observed that the American Indian possessed an inferior mental capacity, one cannot be certain whether he referred to the raw material itself, the brain, or the concepts and knowledge stored within it, or both.[21] What is clear is that Morgan felt civilization was solely owed to two races, the Semitic and the Aryan but, between the two, he chose the latter. It not only produced the finest specimens of humanity but, in addition, proved its superiority by reducing the entire earth to its mastery.[22] The other early contributor to knowledge about the American Indian, E. B. Tylor, affords us an even better example. He formulated a law of progress which might well have come straight out of J. B. Bury's *The Idea of Progress*. This was that the savage state in general represented an early stage in development of mankind and from this there gradually developed a higher culture. While the march toward civilization had not always been in a straight line, progress on the whole had far surpassed relapses.[23] It should not surprise us, therefore, that Tylor's estimation of the American Indian was a low one. It rested on the general assumption that, while the savage had moral standards, they were operationally much less reliable or effective than ours. Even his generosity was faulted. Indeed, his friendship could not be relied upon for in a moment his gentleness could pass, through a flash of anger, to frenzy. Although brave, he was also both treacherous and cruel. Finally, Tylor's contempt for the native was unmasked when he summarily dismissed his religious beliefs as absurd and his ceremonies as futile.[24] Such was the pride and arrogance of the nineteenth century anthropologist, or the act of hubris against the gods.

Modern scholars, both in the field of physical and cultural anthropology, concluded that nineteenth century representatives came by racist prejudices quite naturally. This was because anthropologists were exported to the colonies, and to its subject and "inferior" peoples, at precisely the same time as were other emissaries of imperialism. These were military and civilian administrators, merchants and missionaries. A couple of quotes suffice to reveal the general climate of opinion. Johannes Fabian concluded: "Among the historical conditions under which our discipline emerged and which affected its growth and differentiation were the rise of capitalism and its colonist- imperialist expansion into the very societies which became the target of our inquiries."[25] As a consequence, anthropology "contributed above all to the intellectual justification of the colonial enterprise."[26] Such a racist attitude, confessed Roger Lewin, persisted into the twentieth century. Physical anthropologists, even in the decade of the Thirties, were racist. They generally perceived the "putative lower races" as "living fossils."[27] According to Fabian, that was the great sin of anthropologists. They regarded living representatives of primitives as something out of the distant past and utterly unrelated to the West and present-day culture. He called it the denial of "coevalness," while asserting that ethnographers "have always acknowledged coevalness as a condition without which hardly anything could ever be learned about another culture."[28] An almost identical point was made by Jacob Pandian when putting the question: Were present day survivors of those cultures to be regarded as anomalous relics or "living fossils," out of tune with the changing world conditions?[29]

Perhaps the most convincing explanation for behavior of this sort was that advanced by Karl Mannheim; he argued that ideas themselves were not pure or divorced from reality, but that instead they could be traced or attributed to such things as social forces and interest groups. These racist anthropological ideas were merely part of the movement of Western imperialism to engulf the world and reduce colored races to servitude in the name of Christianity and progress.[30] The greatest dynamic in such a movement may have been the idea of service which the conqueror carried. It involved sterling efforts to make the colonials over in the image of the white conqueror,[31] much as God made man in His image. It was a Dutch account of late nineteenth century voluntary widow-burning in Indonesia which turned "an outcry against the oppression of women, into an argument for imperialism. It is in extirpating such foul plagues ... as this that the West earns its credentials to conquer and transform the East." Therefore, they "are right and justified in replacing ancient civilizations with their own, for they are on the side of mercy and emancipation, against deception and cruelty."[32]

An entirely different critique of perhaps the best of the nineteenth century anthropologists, Sir James George Frazer, was advanced by Charles Wagley. Because of his very erudition, Frazer settled on a methodology which modern scholars have called shreds, pieces and patches because it presented too many examples from different regions of the world on too many levels of complexity.[33]

As an avowed psychiatrically oriented anthropologist, both by predilection and training,[34] Weston La Barre felt such criticisms were a natural consequence of the low regard social anthropologists had for any other mode of learning than that derived from the field itself. Although Frazer was a learned classical scholar, and possessed a great book knowledge about primitives,[35] the limits of this were not calculated to impress those modern social anthropologists who thought they could functionally explain the present without reference to the past.[36]

An equally strong defense of Frazer was made by others who declared that the disrepute he is held in today is far from justified. Few scholars labored so diligently or set forth with such clarity useful ideas such as the one that primitives understood that the surrogate victim could assume the guilt and suffering of the entire community and expiate it.[37]

At any rate, it was this narrow-minded approach by nineteenth century anthropologists (not Frazer's)[38] which impeded progress toward a science of man. If primitives were indeed different from us, then we could learn nothing from them and any scholarly work on the subject would have nothing more than an antiquarian interest.[39]

It was no doubt early prejudices of this sort which futilely prompted Melville J. Herskovits to substitute what he believed to be a nonpejorative term, nonhistoric or nonliterate, for primitive.[40] While some scholars professed satisfaction with this terminology,[41] Sol Tax did not. He believed the term primitive could only truly be applied to men extinct since the late Pleistocene era. He preferred the term native to distinguish between unalphabetical or prescript people and ourselves.[42] Neither was Catherine H. Berndt entirely satisfied with the term nonliterate.[43] At any rate, the controversy rolled merrily along. After examining thirty anthropological works written since 1950, Francis L. K. Hsü was surprisingly forced to conclude that there was a reasonable facsimile of chaos hovering about the concept of the term primitive.[44] His dismay was shared.[45] Nor has the controversy abated with time. Only recently Jamake Highwater redefined the mission, coming up with the term primal instead of primitive. He claimed the latter was an offensive one.[46]

Meanwhile, twentieth century anthropology featured a consistent attempt at scientific detachment and reporting through the agency of university-trained specialists known as participant observers. They were required to maintain a "balance between emphatic involvement and disciplined detachment" from the human group studied. This meant both an attempt to eliminate themselves and their prejudices from the report while at the same time aiming at more factual objectivity.[47] This clear effort at divorcing the profession from other workers in the same field - all of whom wanted to influence and change the behavior of the natives - became known as cultural relativism.[48] The main presupposition was that it was possible to get at the essential truth of the tribe's existence and rationale without spending a decade or more among them mastering their language and customs. All that was required was a professional use of the language, sharp powers of observation, and an ability to identify crucial customs, or selected data. These, if properly studied and categorized, would yield up the mystery of the whole cultural complex. In short, the idea was to get at the whole through its significant parts, like the kinship system or marriage practices. Happily, this could be done in a relatively short time.[49]

With minor exceptions,[50] so heartily was this method endorsed that not only were anthropologists exclusively field workers, but that activity became the crucial distinction for the craft itself.[51] Along with paleontology,[52] therefore, anthropology became the only other social science which demeaned purely intellectual and historical activity. It was monopolized by the sensate, by the present, by the pragmatic.[53]

However, in recent times anthropologists confessed these objective aims were perhaps unattainable. As a graduate student at two anthropological departments in the Thirties and Forties, Albert C. Spaulding had no doubt his subject matter was scientific. On the contrary, his long-term experience clearly suggested that human social behavior "is indeterminate in a fundamental sense and that in consequence the search for universal laws is doomed to failure; perhaps statistical generalizations are all that can be achieved."[54]

The chief stumbling block was that, as always, anthropological writing could not be divorced from the author's background and history.[55] Therefore, it was also autobiographical, determined not only by cultural background but by age, sex, family status, class position and the like.[56] To claim that, on the contrary, one's opinions were value free was to express a discredited ideology of empirical positivism.[57] How could the researcher explain that, while there was no difference between French chemistry and physics and that of German or American, there existed perceptible differences between and among them in cultural anthropology?[58] Why have there been no cultural anthropological counterparts of Newton, Darwin or Einstein?[59]

A persuasive case against the likelihood of scientific reporting and analysis by the participant observer came from Jacob Pandian. He argued that this ritual can only occur in the context of dominant and subordinate relationships between societies "and that only members of the dominant society can perform that ritual." That fact erects almost insurmountable barriers between the outsider and "truth."[60] Other anthropologists agreed, particularly those from the Third World. Contrary to what many Western observers thought, natives themselves made no distinction between the anthropologist as researcher and the exploiting group or society he represented. This was true no matter what the personal viewpoint of the scholar.[61] Therefore, the principal aspect of white vulnerability lay in the unconscious assumption of truth-telling by local informants.[62] It proved a dangerous practice. For example, East Asian Indians, resenting their status as "rustics," took the "heroic" Western anthropologist for a ride through conscious and even gleeful deception.[63]

Much of the problem of communication was due to the fact that primitives who emphasize the primacy of the group have to deal with what may be termed the narcissism of the white observer. This is the white man's preoccupation with self. If he is well motivated, he is preoccupied with how successful he is currently, or, if less idealistic, how he is being treated by those whom he is observing. In any event, he may fail to achieve rapport with the tribe and thus truth eludes him.[64]

Nor is it difficult to document the professional limitations of the giants of the trade during that same era. The *Diary* of Bronislaw Malinowski revealed that he was anything but objective toward his informants.[65] While Ruth Benedict realized that the pursuit of national identity might be connected with a power complex, she at the same time did not hesitate to declare herself "American to the hilt." This indicated that so-called cultural relativists could easily be put to work for non-scientific purposes, such as national defense, political propaganda and manipulation of other societies and cultures.[66] It was when Claude Lévi-Strauss was a guest of the Nambikwara, the most miserable tribe in the Mato Groso region of Brazil, that a typical incident occurred. Each person there had a proper name and also a nickname, both Portuguese, which everyone knew about. But each also had a secret name, a native one, which sheltered his personality from the threats of the outside world. It might be said that this was the tribe's last possession. Unfortunately, however, Lévi-Strauss took advantage of a quarrel between children to obtain all their secret names. Worse, he even wormed out of them the secret names of their parents.[67] There was, of course, no malicious intent here. Rather it was just a disregard of the rights of privacy, like we habitually do with regard to our own poor who are either trying to get on welfare or stay there. On the contrary, he would never have taken advantage of the children of an aristocratic hostess in Paris in order to discover her secret age.

Also slow to die was the assumption, held consciously or unconsciously, that there was not only a great cultural difference between ourselves and the world of the savage, but it was also a qualitative one, one greatly in our favor. The idea of progress died hard. While one might lament the natives being forced to adopt Western culture, if, on the contrary, they voluntarily sought it out, that was an occasion for rejoicing. A classic illustration of this sort was recorded by no less an authority than Margaret Mead in 1946 at Manus in the Admiralty Islands off New Guinea. She observed with obvious satisfaction that the natives suddenly decided to discard "every evil custom of the past and set up our own form of life." Naturally, all such customs constituted the entire baggage of their ancestors and the newly-preferred style of living was but an attempted emulation of the European model, taught them by the missionaries. But Mead hailed the new freedom of the individual as "rather a sort of collective assertion of the dignity of man."[68] The inference was that, prior to the coming of the white man, the natives themselves had no conceptualization of human dignity. To the historian, the entire episode seemed one torn out of a diary of a naive eighteenth century liberal.

An even closer look at the classic literature of this epoch merely reinforces a common theory as to the subjectivity of cultural anthropology. The recent quarrel between Margaret Mead and Derek Freeman as to the true nature of Samoans is not only typical of such disputations[69] but suggests that the field researcher's mental set determines what he will find before he or she finds it. Armed with different assumptions and interests, the interpreters are apt to ask different questions and thus derive different answers.[70] Of Margaret Mead's work in New Guinea, one of her former colleagues observed that whatever tribe she happened to be studying enabled her to make the point she desired to make.[71] For example, the purpose of Mead's *Coming of Age in Samoa* was to show American parents that adolescence need not be a time of stress and rebellion on the part of the young. In short, the book was meant as a lesson in child rearing.[72]

A similar happy thing happened to another protégé of Boas at Columbia. This occurred in 1934 when Ruth Benedict "found" existing examples of three different ideal types of cultures: Apollonian, Dionysian, and a third in the middle *(Patterns of Culture)*.[73] This schema has often been employed by anthropologists and by us as well. But, in this instance a caveat was entered by John Leo. Anthropology itself was a subjective enterprise with order often imposed upon chaos via arbitrary patterns carried into the field by the researcher.[74]

Also alluded to by such critics was the almost identical quarrel over human nature, this time in Tepoztlan, Mexico, between Robert Redfield and Oscar Lewis.[75]

The third such illustration is the most dramatic of all. It involved the work of four anthropologists among the same people within a time span of only twelve years and not that of several decades apart as in the Mead-Freeman situation. Two researchers found the Pueblos to be a peaceful and well-adjusted folk while the others concluded that they were neurotic and full of social repressions.[76] Not surprisingly, social anthropologists, like the rest of humanity, tend to find what they expected or wanted to find.[77]

Unfortunately, few recent anthropologists have had the humor, the imagination and the daring to portray their own kind as if it were some exotic tribe whose behavior was calculated to arouse the customary emotions of amusement, pity, horror, and fear. It came as a source of relief, therefore, to read Horace Miner's amusing article on "Body Ritual among the Nacirema" the way other social anthropologists describe strange and exotic customs among primitive tribes.[78] In a more serious vein, Jamake Highwater, American Indian, showed us how actors in our society might be protrayed if described by anthropologists from an entirely different culture. While what these secular artists of the "make believe" do seem perfectly natural and normal to us, the same roles in primitive societies would have to be performed by shamans or priests.[79] And it was Thorstein Veblen who, with the greatest sobriety, dared to analyze our leisure classes as if they belonged to much earlier predatory cultures: they were distinguished not by their idleness per se but by studious avoidance of any useful or productive labor, particularly of a manual variety. One thinks especially of the gentry in Victorian England and its cultural impact upon the pseudo-aristocracy of America. Its male population was extremely well-versed in war, sports, gambling, hunting, pedigree dogs and race horses and its females experts on Paris fashions, syntax, drawing room music and art objects. Meanwhile, such classes were overproductive of high clergymen and sinecured scholars, historically derivative from the clergy, who were masters of dead languages and other things of equal utility. Such a conspicuous waste of time was calculated to impress all observers with the fact that this person or persons had the pecuniary ability to support himself and his family without recourse to useful labor which lacked dignity and respect. It was allegiance to high fashion instead.[80] Altogether it made for a continuation of the aristocratic ideal, one long in vogue before the Industrial Revolution and one at odds with the latter's bourgeois masters. Indeed, it was an affirmation that the finer things in life did not change despite the fact that for the masses tremendous economic and social dislocations were a consequence of that revolution.

It was Karl Mannheim who concluded that every social science analysis is closely tied with the unconscious orientation of the observer.[81] Every epoch has a distinctive point of view and thus perceives the same outside world from an entirely different perspective.[82] "Thus the concept of truth has not remained constant through all time, but has been involved in the process of historical change."[83] Mannheim's logic is the quintessence of liberal opinion and is at perpetual odds with both the primitive and Platonic views of the world which are either non-historical or anti-historical with regard for truth-seeking. But, it is precisely because of this that he provides us with as good a point of departure as is available when citing recent works or studies designed to render obsolete earlier ones. These discovered the "noble savage" in both the elementary Tasaday culture of the Philippine rain forest and in perhaps the most advanced of all "primitive" cultures, the Maya of the Classic Period, 250-700 A.D. Let us take the simplest case first.

Since 1960, the ability to read the Maya hieroglyphs destroyed the illusion of the Thirties that the Maya of the Classic Period, unlike the Aztecs, were a peaceful and scholarly people.[84] Scholars like Sylvanus G. Morley, specialist in Romance languages,[85] and J. Eric Thompson, archaeologist and ethnologist[86] (comparative cultures or folkways), first established this stereotype which was maintained until the code was cracked. Beyond the uncontested calendrical data, scholars could lay down nothing more than elaborate but false hypotheses about the glyphs and their possible historical, civic, and philosophical significance.[87] Morley's treatment of such glyphs was startling. He simply ignored them. Linda Schele and Mary E. Miller, authors of *The Blood of Kings,* assumed this meant Morley theorized that, if he could not read the glyphs, then no one else could either.[88] Thus, the false myth rested upon a base of sheer speculation, if not ignorance.[89] In Chapter V, Masculine Puberty Rites, we have explained the social needs of the investigators which "induced" them to discover just such a primitive peoples as the Mayas at that particular time.

The recent donnybrook relating to the Tasaday culture is much more confusing. Serious charges were made that the Philippine government of President Marcos, for reasons of its own, perpetrated the hoax on Western and native anthropologists that these isolated stone age people lived in caves and were remarkably unaggressive.[90]

While some of the original investigators have died, the Philippino scholarly survivors dismissed the charges, declaring that the tribe was merely in the process of rapid and drastic change as a consequence of its "discovery."[91] Fred Eggan, anthropologist of the University of Chicago, joined ranks with those defending the bona fides of the authors who originally investigated and reported on this "lost tribe."[92] Such scholarly opinion affirmed that the Marcos government, and its Minister of Interior who engineered the official discovery, would not have had enough know-how to deceive trained anthropologists.[93] John Nance, Associate Press reporter who wrote *The Gentle Tasaday* in 1975,[94] had a most interesting explanation which gives rise to more questions that it solves. Due to their tribal contacts with Defal, lone hunter, they "were already in transition when we first met them." Thus, "scientists worked to reconstruct what their life had been before and people took the reconstruction as current reality." The situation was then ripe for the charges of a hoax.[95]

Let us, first of all, exonerate the anthropologists of any intent to deceive. But, if they tried to discover what tribal life had been before they encountered it, they were certainly maximizing the opportunity for error. Even trained observers may, when encountering an exotic people, misinterpret or misunderstand what they see and hear and experience. But to reconstruct a past which has physically, and maybe even psychologically, ceased to exist is the most dangerous exercise of all. First, men and women informants are quite apt to have different versions of the past. Then again, they may try to "please" the investigator by giving him the sort of information they guess he wants. All in all, it is probably a temptation to be avoided, certainly by newcomers.

Here the explanation of Roger Lewin, physical anthropologist, is compelling: "These [recent] peaceable theories of human origins, like the beast-in-man idea, became 'a mirror which reflected back only those aspects of human experience which its authors wanted to see.... This is precisely what we would expect of a scientific myth."[96] Thus, contrary to earlier assumptions, actual field work, as opposed to that in libraries and museums, was no guarantee that objective truth could be established with regard to subject matter and/or peoples.[97] In other words, the scientific aspirations of all cultural and physical anthropologists - as well as that of other social scientists - may be foiled precisely because of the expect theory, or assumptions, as to what they expect or want to find in the field before they get there.[98]

Nor has the Eighties proved less divisive among anthropologists concerning the crucial matter of distilling meaningful generalizations. Take, for example, the question of a significant correlation between societies believing in a high god and a low status for women as opposed to societies without such gods and a higher status for them. Or that of a possible correlation between kinds of subsistence economies - say that of a hunter-gathering type versus simple horticultural, intensive agricultural and the pastoral variety - and the matter of female status. Put the two together and ask whether it is possible for anthropologists to conclude that in a simple hunting and gathering economy without high gods women are apt to enjoy a higher status than those in an intensive agricultural economy with them. Not so if we have properly interpreted the dispute between J. Patrick Gray on the one hand and Christine A. Hope and Ronald G. Stover on the other. The two parties - both from their own research and in their own understanding of current literature on the subject - disagree as to whether any meaningful generalizations may be made in the matter.[99] A much wider controversy in the same general area was this: were there "any substantial differences between societies classified as 'hunter-gatherer' and other small-scale societies." Although the question was raised openly at the Quebec conference in 1980, little or no progress has since been achieved in obtaining scholarly agreement.[100]

As important as these questions appear with regard to the scientific aspirations of the discipline, they must yield primacy to one posed by Alain Testart: "... what purpose does it serve to retain a category of hunter-gatherers, defined as they are by a similarity in way of life or in elementary economic behavior, if this category remains powerless to resolve the major problems of social anthropology?" He then proceeds to break a single category into several. For example, he excludes the American Plains Indians because they were as much stock-breeders as hunters; he does the same for so-called hunter-gatherers in Asia and Africa who maintained a food-swapping arrangement between themselves and agro-pastoral peoples nearby.[101] In addition, important distinctions can and ought to be made between hunter-gatherers who collect and store food for emergencies - or those in gathering and fishing economies-and those in meat economies which lack the same ability because the technological challenge is much greater. Once again, he makes basic distinctions between hunter-gatherers on the basis of game-sharing techniques. Where hunters monopolize the prestige of the hunt and distribute the game themselves, incentives are greater to innovate in hunting techniques, and weapons like the bow and arrow result. Where, on the contrary, those who do not participate in the hunt distribute the game - as in Australia - and where there are no material nor moral advantages obtaining to the hunters themselves, these incentives do not follow. There is, as a consequence, not only no bow and arrow but these societies lack an understanding of the kinetic principle of energy stored in a curved piece of wood.[102]

Finally, he asks: "If one cannot say of these societies that they are always egalitarian, what can one say about them in general?"[103]

Neither do the motives of the most recent anti-ethnocentric among Western anthropologists go unquestioned. They began, however, with useful assumptions: "concepts are culture bound, that analytical terms are themselves buried in premises and assumptions." Therefore, they sought to dissect the Western concept of superiority, as well as to undermine its corollary that primitive peoples were always miserable and ill-nourished. If, unfortunately, that were true, it would ethically justify the reduction, and/or disappearance of those cultures, and the substitution of another in our own image. But some anthropologists went too far. For example, in 1964, one declared that the task of field workers is to show their readers that the apparently "benighted, irrational, archaic primitives" instead "live an ordered, reasonable, perhaps even admirable social life."[104] In a scientific sense, that sort of assumption was dangerous enough to the pursuit of both fact and truth. Its exponents, however, failed to convince their colleagues of the merits of their case.[105]

Beyond methodological or ideological disputations within the craft, there were outside and much greater dangers to Western anthropology; the first was the twentieth century imperialistic threat to eliminate its traditional subject matter - primitive peoples - or those previously isolated from Western contact. For example, while there were several hundred hunting and gathering tribes in Australia when the white man arrived late in the eighteenth century, none were living in a state of nature by 1930. All had been contaminated by European contact.[106] The same fears concerning the disappearance of the uncontaminated native haunted the trained field worker in anthropology in the United States during the Thirties. Prevalent was the feeling that theirs was to be the last generation to work with pure cultures.[107] The death- knell of the primitive was finally sounded in the Fifties. "For the economist, the thing to do with the [primitive] past was to abandon it; for the anthropologist, to study it before it was abandoned, and then perhaps to mourn it." This was because of a recognition of the fact that tradition, family, religion, prestige and deference patterns were all standing in the way of the adoption of rational attitudes towards work, efficient organization and an acceptance of technological change.[108]

The physical disappearance of "pure" native cultures inevitably took its toll in the spiritual realm. Years later, Lee Drummond complained that myth, as the traditional wisdom of an isolated, indigenous group "is disappearing, if not already gone." As a continued result of Western imperialism and, still later, pressures by the newly-liberated states, few primitive myths clearly lacked outside influence.[109]

After that time the problem for the trained anthropologist for the most part[110] was how, when working with a society which was in the state of transition between "barbarism' and civilization, to reconstruct accurately the primitive past. Was this to be done by carefully reading the works of one's predecessors? By observation of present practices and then deducing what had been done in the past? Or was it to be accomplished by the interrogation of those who had lived in the pristine past, trusting to the accuracy of their reporting? Allan R. Holmberg discussed such tricky procedures when reporting on the Siriono Indians of the rain forests of East Bolivia.[111] The difficulty was further compounded by the fact that so much of the early anthropological literature was unreliable.[112] Such dilemmas may account for the fact that even today specialists cannot agree as to the basic size of the demographic unit among simple human populations in Australia or its structure in an ecological framework.[113]

One reasonable, or compromise, solution was to do what Clifford Geertz did in the Fifties. He began his field work in Bali and Java, both of which shared a common fifteenth century Eastern culture. These were anything but "pure" cultures. Bali, for example, contained a mix of Hindu, Buddhist, and Polynesian influence.[114]

An even more telling blow to the hopes of Western anthropology came in the post World War II years when it could "no longer present itself as the unique purveyor of anthropological knowledge about others." This was the direct result of the breakup of imperialistic empires and the emergence of a great many independent Third World countries.[115] Almost immediately this gave rise to a host of problems for the Western observer, now an interloper. One which would never go away was the preference for anthropologists of a local stripe rather than a Western import. "The crucial point is that insiders and outsiders may be able to ... interpret the same date differently according to their different points of view."[116] Once independent, and with growing literacy, the tendency for local inhabitants was to regard knowledge as power which ought not to be given away to outsiders who might misuse it. Meanwhile, the local scholar was presumed to have an intuitive advantage over the foreigner.[117]

Much of the prejudice against the Western anthropologist apparently lay in the surprising rise of ethnic minorities to challenge the predicted dominance of both nationalism and modernization.[118] This was because, although naturally sought-out and even cherished by the Western anthropologist, these ethnic minorities were often locally regarded as a potential menace to both nationalism and independence.[119] Certainly differences between ethnic groups in the same nation state at times produced armed conflicts. These either discouraged the Western scholar from entering the disputed arena or militated against objective and prolonged investigation while there.[120] Nor is it fair to overlook the argument that Third World governments may postulate a greater measure of control over what their own "experts" wrote about than the outsider. In India, for example, it was not merely a matter of xenophobia, but also one of a rejection of "free-ranging disinterested empirical inquiry carried out in the pursuit of knowledge for its own sake." And that is precisely what the traditional participant observer did. Native anthropologists may be more willing to undertake projects that the government seeks and is willing to subsidize.[121]

Nevertheless, this trend was strongly reinforced by a local desire to terminate Western scholarly influence; its alleged past distortions had caused a loss of self-confidence and a mistaken willingness to accept Western man as a model for human conduct.[122]

That is but another way of putting the charge that Western anthropology was a white man's version of the human drama.[123] Or, as Tom Urban summarized the ideology of anthropology during the colonial period up to World War II, it was not only imperialistic and ethnocentric, but sexist (masculine domination) as well.

All of these adverse trends may have led to the ultimate charge of virtual bankruptcy against cultural anthropology: "Because of the rapidity of change, the classical anthropological description of the people of the Third World countries are out of date, of little use in planning current action, and too recent to be regarded as hallowed historical records. The anthropologists therefore, cannot justify their profession by reference to its historic accomplishments, especially when these are seen as linked to the colonial past."[124]

Such a conclusion certainly goes far beyond our position. Forget about "hallowed historical records," whatever these are, and present-day utility for social planning. We are not resorting to either one. However flawed by prejudice, we believe these anthropological accounts are indispensable in any scholarly attempt to reconstruct a reasonable portrayal of what primitive life meant, especially in contrast to the Western concept. The argument itself is developed in the following chapter.

More to our immediate purpose, the closing of anthropology's traditional and customary frontiers had two effects. The first was a perceptible decline of student interest. All over the United States undergraduate enrollments fell off and the number of teaching-research positions in universities radically decreased. It naturally followed that graduate school numbers in anthropology declined rapidly. A couple of perceptive observers reluctantly summarized a negative situation: "There has indeed already been a painful loss of a generation of highly trained anthropological Ph.D.s to other occupations."[125]

The second effect was more or less a defensive mechanism. If the traditional base of field investigation - a study of distant, exotic and preliterate cultures - was now curtailed or denied to cultural anthropologists, then they would have to apply their knowledge and methodologies to their local scene. In the most dramatic form, this led to the study of large-scale industrialization.[126] This necessary and abrupt transition in subject matter was not without its hazards. One prominent authority concluded that, the more anthropologists analyzed their own culture, the less disposed he was to believe anything they wrote about others.[127] One welcomed change may be the appearance of intellectual and theoretical works about anthropology and anthropologists by members of that discipline.[128]

Meanwhile, post World War II developments, such as the rise of a great many Third World nations, and the almost simultaneous disappearance of "pure" primitive cultures, affected the very terminology of cultural anthropology itself. No longer was the word primitive used to convey the notion of Western superiority.[129]

Nevertheless, Third World scholars resented its historical implications, preferring what they regarded as a neutral word, or indigenous.[130] Furthermore, as its original subject matter disappeared, Western anthropology, so often identified "with the study of primitive cultures,"[131] was induced to seek other terms for what young anthropologists like Clifford Geertz did in the mixed cultures of Indonesia. Jacob Pandian, for example, settled for the use of the term, the human other.[132]

However, Jean-Paul Dumont exposed the weakness of those anthropologists who insist upon the use of the term, the other or the human other, as a sign of the elimination of prejudice. In his own experience, no matter how he tried to be accepted by the villagers he studied, and no matter the visible sign of his acceptance by the headman, there was always a tribal discrimination against him for being the other, or the different one, or the outsider.[133] Muriel Diemen-Schen had an almost identical experience in rural Greece.[134]

Finally, any facile assumption that the use of the term primitive or "primitive" was no longer used by anthropologists in the late Seventies and Eighties was undermined by an investigation of four of the most prominent anthropological journals in the last decade. There, the researcher can easily cite several usages of both primitive[135] and "primitive."[136] The same is true for books.[137] On the contrary, it is not easy to find usage of the term, the other, or the human other.

In effect, born and raised in the era of colonial expansion and Western imperialism, it was natural that anthropology would emerge as a white man's discipline. Despite rigorous attempts in the present century, largely through the adoption of the principle that every social organism is unique and worthy in its own right, unconscious prejudices remained to mar the product. These had their roots in history, race, and especially in the idea of progress and Christianity. The end result was that when Third World nations emerged following World War II, native reaction manifested itself against the Western scholar, regardless of his or her personal beliefs. The violent clash of ethnic minorities against the forces of nationalism and modernization, and the wars these produced, also militated against old freedoms of research in the one-time colonial areas. While the most recent of anthropologists divested themselves of old and traditional prejudices, their own presuppositions were equally suspect in the eyes of methodologists. Nor has the last decade produced anything like scholarly agreement concerning elementary generalizations with regard to what would appear to be the oldest type of social organization, the hunter-gatherer, or comparisons between this and other small-scale societies. Thus, in the minds of many anthropologists themselves, objectivity seemed elusive. Finally, although the core of the discipline itself was always identified with the primitive, or "primitive" i.e., small, distant, exotic, nonliterate and technologically "backward" peoples, anthropologists found themselves increasingly embarrassed by the usage of these terms. Unfortunately, they found nothing better. For the general public in the West, nothing had the clarity of the old terms. As a result of all these difficulties, especially the closing of the traditional frontiers in the non-West, the discipline suffered a sharp decline of economic opportunity and, consequently, student interest and participation.

Footnotes

1   George E. Marcus and Michael M. J. Fischer, *Anthropology as a Cultural Critique. An Experimental Moment in the Human Sciences* (Chicago, University of Chicago Press, 1986), 17. See also Elizabeth Colson, "Anthropological Dilemmas in the Late Twentieth Century," 253-262 in *Indigenous Anthropology in Non- Western Countries*. Proceedings of a Burg Wartenstein Symposium. Edited by Hussein Fahim. (Durham, North Carolina, Carolina Academic Press, 1982), 261; Gunnar M. Sörbö, "Anthropology at Home and Abroad: A Discussion of Epistemological and Ethical Issues," 152-163 in Fahin, *Indigenous Anthropology*, 161.

2   James Clifford, *The Predicament of Culture. Twentieth Century Ethnography, Literature and Art* (Cambridge, Massachusetts, Cambridge University Press, 1988), 24.

3   Stanley Diamond, "The Search for the Primitive," 96-147 in *The Concept of the Primitive*, edited by Ashley Montagu (New York, Free Press, 1968), 99.

4   Ashley Montagu, "The Fallacy of the 'Primitive,'" 1-6 in *ibid*. 3-4; Ruth Benedict, *Patterns of Culture* (New York, the New American Library of World Literature, 1960), 30.

5   E. E. Evans-Pritchard, *The Position of Women in Primitive Societies and Other Essays in Social Anthropology* (New York, Free Press, 1965), 38-39.

6   "The Mental Traits of Primitive Man," 404-412 in *The Golden Age of American Anthropology*, edited by Margaret Mead and Ruth Bunzel (New York, George Brazillier, 1960), 406.

7   Melville J. Herskovits, *Man and His Works. The Science of Cultural Anthropology* (New York, Alfred A. Knopf, 1964), 484-485.

8   George A. Bartholomew, Jr., and Joseph B. Birdsell, "Ecology and Protohominids," 481-498 in *American Anthropologist*, vol. 55, No. 4, October, 1953, 495-496.

9   Ashley Montagu, "The Concept of 'Primitive' and Related Anthropological Terms: A Study in the Systematics of Confusion," 148-168 in *The Concept of the Primitive*, edited by Montagu, 159. It is an error still to be guarded against by researchers in the field. Farley Mowat, *People of the Deer* (New York, Pyramid Books, 1952), 114.

10   "Applied Anthropology and the Development of a Science of Man," 594-616 in *Readings in Anthropology*, 2 vols., edited by Morton H. Fried (New York, Thomas Y. Crowell, 1968), *Cultural Anthropology II*, 597-598.

11   Katherine George, "The Civilized West Looks at Primitive Africa: A Study in Ethnocentrism," 175-193 in *Concept of the Primitive*, edited by Montagu, 178-182. Opinion still prevails that contact with the white man improves the character and customs of the primitive. *Ibid.*, 186. See also the chapter entitled "The Aboriginal World and Christian History," 273-287 in Vine Deloria, Jr., *God Is Red* (New York, Delta, 1973).

24

12   Edward P. Dozier, "The Concepts of 'Primitive' and 'Native' in Anthropology," 229-256 in *Concept of the Primitive*, edited by Montagu, 232-233.

13   J. F. Driberg, *The Savage as he really is* (London, George Routledge, 1929), 3-4.

14   Richard Semon, *In the Australian Bush and on the Coast of the Coral Sea* (New York, Macmillan, 1899), 206, 217.

15   Peter Farb, *Man's Rise to Civilization as Shown by the Indians of North America from Primeval Times to the Coming of the Industrialized State* (New York, E. P. Dutton, 1968), 17.

16   Dean C. Worcestor, "Head-Hunters of Northern Luzon," 883-930 in *National Geographic*, vol. XXIII, No. 9, September, 1912, 847.

17   A similar view was advanced by Jamake Highwater, *The Primal Mind. Vision and Reality in Indian America* (New York, Harper and Row, 1981), 18. Claude Lévi-Strauss believed this evolutionist view in anthropology derived from the earlier one in biology. Western civilization is thus perceived as the most advanced phase of social evolution whereas primitive peoples represent "survivals" of earlier stages, frozen in their development. *Structural Anthropology*, translated from the French by Claire Jacobson and Brooke Grundfest Schoepf (New York, Basic Books, 1963), 3.

18   *Ancient Society*, edited by Leslie A. White (Cambridge, Massachusetts, Harvard University Press, 1964), 42.

19   White, Introduction in *ibid.*, xxi.

20   *Ancient Society*, 11-23.

21   White, Introduction, *ibid.*, xxii.

22   *Ancient Society*, 468.

23   *Primitive Cultures. Researches into the Development of Mythology, Philosophy, Religion, Language, Art and Custom, 2 vols.*, (New York, Henry Holt, 1889), I, 32. Two elements were always present in such logic: time and progress, or evolution from supposedly primitive or less complex social structures to higher or superior stages of human development. This was the concept of evolution in a straight line which characterized most of the writers on the subject at that time. Ashley Montagu, "Concept of 'Primitive,'" *loc. cit.*, 151-152, 157.

24   *Primitive Cultures*, I, 31.

25   *Time and the Other. How Anthropology Makes Its Object* (New York, Columbia University Press, 1983), 143-144.

26   *Time and the Other*, 17. See also T.N. Madan, "Indigenous Anthropology in Non-Western Countries: An Overview," 263-268 in Hussein Fahim, editor, *Indigenous Anthropology in Non-Western Countries*, 264.

27   *Bones of Contention. Controversies in the Search for Human Origins* (New York, Simon and Schuster, 1987), 307.

28   *Time and the Other*, 32-33. Anthropologists "used the term *animism* (which they invented to separate primitive mentality from modern rationality) as a means to indicate that an opponent is no longer in the contemporary arena of debate." *Ibid.*, 152. Anthropology "is a science of other men in another time." *Ibid.*, 143.

29   *Anthropology and the Western Tradition* (Prospect Heights, Illinois, Waveland Press, 1985), 56. Phrased another way, a kindred viewpoint is the following: "...the main trouble with much colonial anthropology ... has been not its ideological service in the cause of imperialism, but its ideological conception of social structure and of culture." Talal Asad, "Anthropology and the Analysis of Ideology,' 607-627 in *Man. The Journal of the Royal Anthropological Institute*, vol. 14, No. 4, December 1979, 624.

30   *Ideology and Utopia. An Introduction to the Sociology of Knowledge* (New York, Harcourt-Brace, 1940), Preface, xxiii, 242, 276.

31   Captain F. D. Lugard, "The Rise of Our East African Empire," in *The Quest of a Principle of Authority in Europe, 1715 to Present. Select Problems in Historical Interpretation*, edited by Thomas C. Mendenhall *et al* (New York, Holt, Rinehart and Winston, 1948), 291-292. See also "The White Man's Burden," 1899, in *ibid.*, 292-293.

32   Clifford Geertz, *Local Knowledge, Further Essays in Interpretative Anthropology* (New York, Basic Books, 1983), 43.

33   Charles Wagley, Gainesville, Florida to Stan Urban, Parkville, Missouri, October 13, 1981.

34   Weston La Barre, *Ghost Dance. Origins of Religion* (Garden City, New York, Doubleday, 1970), Preface, xii.

35   *Ibid.*, 35, 37.

36   *Ibid.*, 290. See also La Barre's "Materials for a History of Studies of Crisis Cults, a Bibliographical Essay," 3-44 in *Current Anthropology*, vol. 12, No. 1, February, 1971, 25. Only by a careful study of the past can present-day primitive society be understood. When one arbitrarily limits study to the present-day life of a people, he is victimized by an illusion. Everything is history, including the most recent past. Lévi-Strauss, *Structural Anthropology*, 12.

37   René Girard, *Violence and the Sacred*, translated by Patrick Gregory (Baltimore, Johns Hopkins University Press, 1977), 317.

38   Frazer's conception of primitive religion was the opposite of that of Tylor. If, he said, one could trace the whole course of religious development, one might very well discover that the whole chain which links our idea of the Trinity with the savage mind is one and unbroken. *The Golden Bough*, 12 vols. Part I. *The Magic Act and the Evolution of Kings*, (New York, Macmillian, 1935), I, 375-376.

39   Franz Boas, *Introduction to Anthropology and Modern Life* (New York, W. W. Norton, 1962), 4-5. Annemarie de Waal Malefijit ascribed the origins of anthropological investigation to the "universal concern to understand human experience and behavior." *Images of Man. A History of Anthropological Thought* (New York, Alfred A. Knopf, 1974), Introduction, vii.

40   "Before the Machine," 201-214 in *Readings in Anthropology*, 2 vols., edited by Morton H. Fried, *Cultural Anthropology*, II, 202.

41   Wagley, Gainesville, Florida, to Urban, October 13, 1981.

42   "Primitive Man vs. Homo Sapiens," 81-95 in *Concept of the Primitive*, edited by Montagu, 65, 92-93.

43   "The Concept of the Primitive," in *loc. cit.*, 25-26.

44   "Rethinking the Concept 'Primitive,'" 32-63 in *ibid.*, 60.

45   In a few hours research, Sol Tax compiled twenty-three different meanings for primitives in the recent literature of ethnology and social anthropology. See "'Primitive' Peoples," 64-80 in *ibid.*, 69-70.

46   *The Primal Mind*, "Prelude," xix.

47   Jean-Paul Dumont, *The Headman and I. Ambiguity and Ambivalence in the Fieldworking Experience* (Austin, Texas, University of Texas Press, 1978), 6-7.

48   Clifford, *Predicament of Culture*, 24, 30. The traditional message of these revisionists was as follows: Natives see things and do things differently in Alaska and other remote regions of the world. Thus, "our confidence in our own seeings and doings and our resolve to bring others around to sharing them are rather poorly based." The clear mission of research and writing was framed thus: "Looking into dragons, not domesticating or abominating them, is what anthropology is all about." Clifford Geertz, "Distinguished Lecturer: Anti-Revisionism," 263-278 in *American Anthropologist*, v. 85, No. 2, June 1984, 264, 275. Some scholars, however, felt it unfortunate that the idea of revisionism hardened into doctrine as the chief contribution to liberal thought of twentieth century anthropology. Marcus and Fischer, *Anthropology as Cultural Critique*, 167.

49   Clifford, *Predicament of Culture*, 30-32.

50   Regna Darnell was unusual in that she earned a Ph.D. in anthropology at the University of Pennsylvania by writing her dissertation on the history of anthropology. Her major advisor, Dell Hymes, told her that she could be an anthropologist without the necessity of doing field work. Pandian, *Anthropology and the Western Tradition*, 108-109. Later, one historian had the temerity to observe that anthropology was too important a discipline to be left to anthropologists themselves. See C. M. Hinsley, Jr., *Savages and Scientists: The Smithsonian Institution and the Development of American Anthropology, 1846-1910* (Washington, Smithsonian Institute Press, 1981). Quoted by Pandian, *Anthropology and the Western Tradition*, 108.

51   "More than anything else, it is ethnographic fieldwork that distinguishes

social and cultural anthropology from the other social sciences and demarcates the transition from being a student of anthropology to being an anthropologist." Philip Carl Salzman, "Is Traditional Fieldwork Outmoded?," 528-583 in *Current Anthropology*, v. 27, No. 5, December 1986, 528.

52   "In most fields of science the great names are typically people who have wrought some kind of significant intellectual advance - a new concept or theory." In the case of paleontology, however, "it is different. It is the tangible discoveries that bring fame, not the intellectual theories." Lewin, *Bones of Contention*, 25-26.

53   "If we seek to know about the past, a field of study that has never seemed dishonorable to any discipline other than social anthropology, the point of departure should be the hunter-gatherers ...." Alain Testart, "Some Major Problems in the Social Anthropology of Hunter-Gatherers," 1-13 in *Current Anthropology*, v. 29, No. 1, February 1988, 12-13. "Philosophers, historians, theologians, statesmen, economists, medical doctors ... generally recognized the intellectual relevance of the other points of view. Early twentieth-century anthropologists ... developed a strong degree of professional ethnocentrism. They tended to acknowledge the existence of other disciplines only insofar as their findings stood in the service of anthropological explanations." de Waal Malefijt, *Images of Man*, Introduction, viii. "For a long time now anthropology has ceased to constitute a coherent field of intellectual inquiry." Talal Asad, "Anthropology and the Analysis of Ideology," *loc. cit.*, 608.

54   "Distinguished Lectures: Archaeology and Anthropology," 263-271 in *American Anthropologist*, v. 90, No. 2, June 1988, 264-265.

55   Fabian, *Time and the Other*, 87-88.

56   Sörbö, "Anthropology at Home and Abroad," *loc. cit.*, 154.

57   Anthropologists on the whole "have lagged behind sister disciplines in becoming conscious of the ideological biases ...." Alice B. Kehoe, "Revisionist Anthropology: Aboriginal North America," 503-517 in *Current Anthropology*, v. 22, No. 5, October 1981, 503.

58   Dumont, *Headman and I*, 45-46. "... if we intend anthropology to be a science, the results of its research must be independent of the cultural and social background of the anthropologist." Different observers from different countries and social systems should not report differently on the economic life in the Trobriand Islands. Luiz R. B. Mott, "Indigenous Anthropology and the Brazilian Indian," 112-120 in Fahim, *Indigenous Anthropology*, 116-117.

59   Spaulding, "Archaeology and Anthropology," *loc. cit.*, 265.

60   *Anthropology and the Western Tradition*, 90.

61   Nader Afshar Naderi, "Some Considerations Regarding Anthropological Dilemmas," 242-249 in Fahim, *Indigenous Anthropology*, 243.

62   Herbert C. Kelman, "A Changing Social Science for a Changing World; a Social Psychologist's Perspective," 269-283, *ibid.*, 275.

63   T. N. Mandan, "Indigenous Anthroplogy in Non-Western Countries: An Overview," 263-268 in *ibid., 266.

64   Edward T. Hall, *Beyond Culture* (Garden City, New York, Anchor Books, Anchor Press, 1977), 64, 153-154.

65   Clifford, *Predicament of Culture,* 112. The myth of "a walking miracle of empathy, tact, patience and cosmopolitanism, was demolished by the man who had perhaps done the most to create it." Clifford Geertz, *Local Knowledge. Further Essays in Interpretive Anthropology* (New York, Basic Books, 1983), 55-56.

66   Fabian, *Time and the Other*, 47-48.

67   *Triste Tropique* (Paris, France, Plon Library, 1955), 317-318.

68   "Return to Manus, 1953," in *Letters from the Field, 1925-1975* (New York, Harper and Row, 1977), 247-248.

69   There were many crucial differences but the one on adolescent sex for girls may be singled out. Mead concluded that a situation analogous to free love existed for the girls in adolescence, and that everyone was at ease about this, whereas Freeman argued that a cult of virginity held sway, backed by authoritarian and zealous parents. John Leo, "Bursting the South Sea Bubble," 68-70 in *Time*, February 14, 1983, 68.

70   Many other examples illustrate "that anthropological inquiry is not so much an objective, naturalistic science of man as it is a Western quest for meaning of contrast and integration." Pandian, *Anthropology and the Western Tradition*, 94.

71   *Ibid.,* 70. Likewise, this is the entire thrust of an article by Albert Wendt, Samoan poet and novelist, who argued that in his native land Margaret Mead found the secular utopia she and Boas wanted the world to be, rather than the repressive and Puritanical atmosphere of their own. "Three Faces of Samoa: Mead's, Freeman's and Wendt's," 10-14, 69 in *Pacific Island Monthly*, April, 1983.

72   Marcus and Fischer, *Anthropology as Cultural Critique*, 138, 158.

73   Leo, "Bursting the South Sea Bubble," *loc cit.*, 69.

74   *Ibid.*, 70.

75   *Ibid.*, 70. See also Pandian, *Anthropology and the Western Tradition*, 93.

76   Ruth Benedict and Laura Thompson exploited the Apollonian ideal whereas Dorothy Eggan and Esther Goldfrank were concerned with maladjusted actuality. "The Controversial Pueblos," 523-529 in Harold E. Driver, *Indians of North America* (Chicago, University of Chicago Press, 1966), 528.

77   While he thought that all had made scholarly contributions, Driver seemed to be more suspicious of the philosophical and poetic treatments of Benedict and Thompson than of the less ambitious and more empirical works of Eggan and Goldfrank. *Ibid.*, 528-529. See also Highwater, *The Primal Mind*, 188.

78   "Body Ritual among the Nacirema," Reprinted from *American Anthropologist*, vol. 58 (1956), 503-507 in *Students and Society*, edited by Jerome Rabow (Pacific Palisades, California, Goodyear Publishing, 1972), 124-129.

79   *Primal Mind*, 178.

80   *The Theory of the Leisure Class* (New York, Modern Library, 1931), 38-45.

81   *Ideology and Utopia*, 41.

82   *Ibid.*, 243.

83   *Ibid.*, 262.

84   Linda Schele and Mary E. Miller, *The Blood of Kings. Dynasty and Ritual in Maya Art* (Fort Worth, Texas, Kimbell Art Museum, 1986), Prologue, 15.

85   *Directory of American Scholars. A Biographical Directory*, edited by Jaques Cattell, 3rd edition (New York, R. R. Bowker, 1957), 528.

86   *American Men of Science. A Biographical Directory. The Social and Behavioral Sciences*, vol. 3, edited by Jaques Cattell (New York, R. R. Bowker, 1956), 677.

87   Schele and Miller, *Blood of Kings*, 23-24. See, for example, footnotes 88 and 89 of Chapter IV. Ritual: Shaman, Sorcerer and Priest.

88   *Blood of Kings*, 23.

89   William Weber Johnson, "Two new exhibitions explore the dark mysteries of the Maya," *Smithsonian*, vol. 17, No. 2, May, 1986, 39-49; Erik Eckholm, "Secrets of Maya Decoded at Last: Revealing Darker Human History," *New York Times*, May 13, 1986, C-1.

90   Seth Mydans, "The Tasaday Revisited: A Hoax or a Social Change at Work," New York Times, May 13, 1986, C-3; "Back from the Stone Age? An Anthropological find may be a hoax," *Newsweek*, May 5, 1986, 69. The charges, in their bluntest form, were aired on ABC's program "20/20" in the late summer of 1986. Although I did not see the program myself, several friends independently reported the same version. On September 25, 1986, I wrote the director of the program, requesting a transcript but never heard from that source.

91   "We're seeing a textbook case of social change, compressed in time." So said Jesus Peralta, Curator of Anthropology for the National Museum of the Philippines. Carlos Fernandez added: "Before we first met them, they were purely forest gatherers." Mydans, "The Tasaday Revisited," *loc. cit.*, C-3.

92   "That the Tasaday were isolated Stone Age people is nonsense - they had iron tools acquired from trade. ...But making them out to be imposters is a pretty dirty trick." "Back from the Stone Age? An Anthropological find may be a hoax," *loc. cit.*, 69.

93   Mydans, "The Tasaday Revisited," *loc. cit.*, C-3.

94   *A Stone Age People in the Philippine Rain Forest.* Foreword by Charles A. Lindburgh (New York, Harcourt Brace and Jovanovich, 1975).

95   Mydans, "The Tasaday Revisited," *loc. cit.*, C-3.

96   Lewin, *Bones of Contention*, 318.

97   While we cite the opinion of Laura Thompson, she was merely a high-priestess of a school of scholars which worshipped field experience and the publication of a monograph. See footnote 10 of this chapter.

98   Lewin, *Bones of Contention*, 26, expressed the dilemma of social scientists when he wrote: A discoverer of bones, unless very experienced, is "prone to discover new features which are partially the creation of his own concentrated imagination." There is a psychological conflict between his desire "to find primitive, unique or anthropological features which will allow him to place his specimen nearer to the apes than any previously recorded, and his own powerful urge to demonstrate the direct and central position of his new type in the ancestry of modern man." Also, *ibid.*, 18. "And scientists, contrary to the myth that they themselves publicly promulgate, are emotional human beings who carry a generous dose of subjectivity with them into the supposedly objective search for truth."

99   Hope and Stover declared that there was virtually universal academic agreement that hunting and gathering societies were "the most sexually egalitarian of all non-industrial subsistence patterns." While sexual inequality was greater in purely hunting societies than those of hunter-gatherers, they were not nearly as great as those in pastoral and agricultural ones. "Gender Status, Monotheism, and Social Complexity: Response to Gray," 1132-1138 in *Social Forces. An International Journal of Social Research Associated with the Southern Sociological Society*, v. 65, No. 4, June 1987, 1133. On the contrary, Gray rejects two major conclusions of Hope and Stover: 1) There is a definite relationship between a society's belief in a monotheistic religion and its low regard for women and 2) The subsistance pattern has a substantive and direct effect upon both gender status and religious beliefs. "Moreover, the subsistence regime Stover and Hope predict to provide the highest status for women [hunting] is actually the one in which women are awarded the lowest status." J. Patrick Gray, "Do Women Have Higher Social Status in Hunting Societies Without High Gods?," 1121-1131 in *Social Forces*, v. 65, No. 4, June 1987, 1121-1122, 1130. Furthermore, there "is no reason to assume ... that a belief in a high god is more useful than a belief in a cosmology where high gods are absent in providing such a justification," i.e., a low regard for women. *Ibid.*, 1130.

100   Alan Barnard, "Hunting and Gathering Societies. Fourth International Conference," 234-236 in *Current Anthropology*, v. 28, April 1987, 235.

101   "Some Major Problems in the Social Anthropology of Hunter-Gatherers," 1-13 in *Current Anthropology*, v. 29, No. 1, February 1988, 7.

102   *Ibid.*, 4, 9-10. "Hunting is a production process in the same way ... that mineral extraction is, for it is an activity that requires the use of tools and produces an end product which was not there at the outset of the labor process." Alain Testart, "Game-Sharing Systems and Kinship Systems Among Hunter-Gatherers," 287-304 in *Man*, v. 22,

June 1987, 300.

103   "Some Major Problems in the Social Anthropology of Hunter-Gatherers," *loc. cit.*, 4. One generalization that anthropologists might agree upon is that hunter-gatherers represented the oldest form of human society. See *ibid.*, 1 and Martin S. Day, *The Many Meanings of Myth* (Lanham, Maryland, The University Press of America, 1984), 34.

104   Marilyn Strathern, "Out of Context: the Pervasive Fictions of Anthropology," 251-281 in *Current Anthropology* v. 28, No. 3, June 1987, 260.

105   John, Pat and Bruce Caldwell, "Anthropology and Demography," 25-43 in *Current Anthropology*, v. 28, No. 1, February 1987, 26.

106   Joseph B. Birdsell, "Local Group Composition among the Australian Aborigines: A Critique of the Evidence from Fieldwork Conducted Since 1930," *Current Anthropology*, vol. 11, No. 2, April 1970, 115, 121, 129, 135.

107   Weston La Barre, "Studies of Crisis Cults," in *ibid.*, vol. 12, No. 1, February 1971, 3.

108   Clifford Geertz, "Culture and Social Change: The Indonesian Case," 511-532 in *Man*, vol. 19, No. 4, December 1984, 511.

109   "Structure and Process in the Interpretation of South American Myth," 842-868 in *American Anthropologist*, v. 79, December 1977, 846.

110   One exception was a mountain people, the Mbotgate of the New Hebrides, who remained isolated until 1968. E. Richard Sorenson, "Mbotgate," 33-56 in *Primitive Worlds. People Lost in Time* (Washington, D.C., National Geographic, 1973), 33.

111   *Nomads of the Long Bow. The Siriono of Northern Bolivia* (Garden City, New York, The Natural History Press, 1969), 3.

112   M. J. Meggitt, *Desert People. A Study of the Walbiri Aborigines of Central Australia* (Chicago, University of Chicago Press, 1962), 47.

113   Joseph B. Birdsell *et al*, "A Basic Demographic Unit," 337-356 in *Current Anthropology*, vol. 14, No. 4, October, 1973. Birdsell's position with regard to Australia is as follows: The homeostatic demographic unit is the dialectical tribe (not to be confused with the much smaller hunting band itself). Optimum numbers approximate 500 persons. *Ibid.*, 337. Of this number there are about 150 males to every 100 females; children and adults each compose about one-half of the population. *Ibid.*, 355.

114   Geertz, *Local Knowledge*, 62.

115   Clifford, *Predicament of Culture*, 22. Michel Leiris "composed the first extended analysis of the relationship between anthropological knowledge and colonialism." He pointed out "basic imbalances. Westerners had for centuries studied and spoken for the rest of the world; the reverse had not been the case." Since 1950, however, that imbalance was corrected. Clifford, *Predicament of Culture*, 255-256.

116   Sörbö, "Anthropology at Home and Abroad," *loc. cit.*, 153. "Little more than technology and sheer economic exploitation seem to be left over for the purpose of 'explaining' Western superiority." Fabian, *Time and the Other*, 35.

117   Sörbö, "Anthropology at Home and Abroad," *loc. cit.* 154, 157. Nevertheless, Jacob Pandian's prediction seems valid. It was that the role of the participant observer occurs only in interactions between dominant and subordinate societies; the price paid for this intrusion is a barrier between the scholar and truth-telling. The dilemma is also experienced when all involved are of the same race and color, but come from different sections and classes of the same country. See Koentjaraningrat, "Anthropology in Developing Countries," 176-192 in Fahim, *Indigenous Anthropology in Non-Western Countries*, 177-179.

118   Lee Drummond, "The Cultural Continuum. A Theory of Interpretative Systems," 352-374 in *Man*, v. 15, No. 2, June 1980, 354. See also Pandian, *Anthropology and the Western Tradition*, 44.

119   Nader Afshar Naderi, "Some Considerations Regarding Anthropological Dilemmas," *loc. cit.*, 247.

120   Luise Margolies, "Problems of Anthropological Revolution in Latin America," 451-452 in *Current Anthropology*, v. 23, No. 4, August 1982, 451-452.

121   J. A. Barnes, "Social Science in India: Colonial Import, Indigenous Product or Universal Truth," 19-34 in Fahim, *Indigenous Anthropology*, 25-26.

122   Mubanga E. Kashoki, "Indigenous Scholarship in African Universities: The Human Factor," 35-51 in Fahim, *Indigenous Anthropology*, 37.

123   Sörbö, "Anthropology at Home and Abroad," *loc. cit.*, 152; Kashoki, "Indigenous Scholarship in African Universities," *loc. cit.*, 43; Pandian, *Anthropology and the Western Tradition*, 92.

124   Elizabeth Colson, "Anthropological Dilemmas in the Late Twentieth Century," *loc. cit.*, 255-256.

125   Marcus and Fischer, *Anthropology as Cultural Critique*, xi. See also Nader Afshar Naderi, "Some Considerations Regarding African Dilemmas," *loc. cit.*, 242-243.

126   Colson, "Anthropological Dilemmas in the Late Twentieth Century," *loc. cit.*, 261; Deborah Reed Danahay and Susan Carol Rogers, "Anthropological Research in France; Problems and Prospects for the Study of Complex Society, Introduction," 51-55 in *Anthropological Quarterly*, v. 60, No. 2, January-October 1987, 51. One American anthropologist studied four generations of elites in Galveston, Texas and made certain comparisons with the elites of Tallensi society in West Africa. George E. Marcus, "The Predicaments of Business Dynasties as Critical Perspectives on the American Middle-Class Family," 169-177 in *Anthropology as Cultural Critique*, 171.

127   Geertz, *Local Knowledge*, 9. An interesting caveat was expressed by Talal Asad. Those few Western anthropologists who dared investigate their own culture often

found it "very difficult to investigate ... the relationship and behavior of the very rich and powerful." "A Comment on the Idea of Non-Western Anthropology," 284-287 in Fahim, *Indigenous Anthropology in Non-Western Countries*, 286. One recalls Jacob Pandian's observation that the participant observer always represents a dominant group studying a less influential and powerful one. Therefore, dominant and powerful groups could be expected to resist such a study by an outsider. See footnote 60 of this chapter.

128   See, for example, James Lett, *The Human Enterprise. A Critical Introduction to Anthropological Theory* (Boulder, Colorado, Westview Press, 1987).

129   "The primitive form of the 'primitive thought' formulation - that is, that while we, the civilized, sort matters out analytically, relate them logically, and test them systematically ... they, the savage, wander around in a hodge-podge of ... images, mystical participations, and immediate passions, as seen by their myth, ritual, magic, or art - has, of course, been progressively undermined as more about how the other half thinks has become known...." Geertz, *Local Knowledge*, 88, 148.

130   Typical of Third World response was the following: "Papua New Guinea rejects the classification of their societies as primitive and the implied and unflattering comparisons associated with this idea." Louis Morauta, "Indigenous Anthropology in Papua New Guinea," 561-576 in *Current Anthropology*, v. 20, No. 3, September 1979, 563.

131   Marcus and Fischer, *Anthropology as Cultural Critique*, 131, 134.

132   *Anthropology and the Western Tradition*, 101, 112.

133   When among the Panare, he was the embodiment of the outside world. This was not only because of his physical presence, which he had forced upon them, but also because of the possessions he carried. Both were signs of this otherness. "Even though I was different from the missionaries and civil servants who wanted to enforce cultural change, I was part of the same equation...." Dumont, *Headman and I*, 190. Thus, the "more I was integrated into the settlement, the more the hostility manifested itself." *Ibid.*, 120. "I was treated, as I deserved, as an inexhaustible provider. People approached me constantly...." When he tried to restrict his largesse, he was cursed. *Ibid.*, 49, 51-52.

134   Both she and her husband were never completely accepted by the villagers, especially the womenfolk, in a peasant society. The couple was ultimately forced to leave after Muriel fell ill and there were unsuccessful attempts by two women in the household to exorcise her demons. "At one level," she observed, "we were the evil being exorcised from their lives." *The Anthropological Imagination* (New York, McGraw-Hill, 1977), 154-155.

135   Typical of scholars using the word primitive throughout their books without quotation marks were Roger Lewin, *Bones of Contention*, 26, 191, 305, 310, 317, de Waal Malefijt, *Images of Man*, 157, 240, 316, and Martin S. Day, *The Many Meanings of Myth* (Landham, Maryland, the University Press of America, 1984), 13, 34, 73, 76, 107, 147, 208, 333, 337. A few of the many other examples are the following: Alan Barnard, "Hunting and Gathering Societies. Fourth International Conference," *loc. cit.*, 234-235; Aletta Biersack, "Nature of the Primitive Mind," 811-829 in *American Anthropologist*, v. 84, No. 4, December 1982; John, Pat and Bruce Caldwell, "Anthropology and Demography,"

loc. cit., 26; Marilyn Strathern, "Out of Context: The Pervasive Fictions of Anthropology," *loc. cit.,* 260. Sometimes qualifiers were used, as in the following example: " ... hunter-gatherers appear to be the most ancient of the so-called primitive societies..." Alain Testart, "Some Major Problems in the Social Anthropology of Hunter-Gatherer," *loc. cit.,* 1.

136   Lee Drummond, "Structure and Process in the Interpretation of South American Myth," *loc. cit.,* 846.

137   Mark Nathan Cohen, *Health and the Rise of Civilization* (New Haven, Yale University Press, 1989), 1, 130. See C. R. Hallpike, *The Foundations of Primitive Thought* (Oxford, Clarendon, 1979).

Chapter II

THE MISSION DEFINED AND EXPLAINED

Those Americans who both listened and read were seduced by the glamour of anthropology in its Golden Age. We think this largely a twentieth century phenomenon, beginning shortly before 1900 and terminating with World War II.[1] Since action is always followed by reaction, this work must be considered as a part of revisionism. For during this period, anthropologists defined their craft as actual field work, refusing recognition to any who did not serve an apprenticeship there. As a consequence, the discipline had a thousand points of light, but conspicuously lacked an Arnold Toynbee to attempt the formulation of a universal meaning out of a plethora of fascinating detail. Besides the ever-present influence of race and color on anthropologists in exotic places, psychological pressures of Christianity and progress militated against fair and accurate judgment. But, whatever prejudices displayed, they were but a mere reflection of those of our own society. Finally, since these experts were the last to see "pure" native cultures and analyze them, they must be resorted to by all succeeding generations who seek answers to elusive questions about the primitive.

Since the craft was defined as constituting only those who successfully worked in the field, it is not surprising that modern social anthropologists have been preoccupied with the publication of monographs. Thus, it seemed that a useful service might be performed if one were to attempt a synoptic view. If successful, it could lead the non-specialist to an understanding of the previously esoteric primitive. However, with such a universal canvas, independent of space and time, there can be no pretence of an in-depth study. Further, the choice exposes one to the charge that the reader has been offered too many examples from too many regions at too many different levels of complexity. Nor does it offer one the solace of a rigorous cross-cultural approach. In short, we concede the arguments of some anthropological devotees of the monograph: 1) despite a wealth of material, our work may add little to their knowledge of the subject and 2) to them, it is a flashback to the old-style universal anthropology of scholars like J. G. Frazer. For this, I am responsible. I worked alone for three years before seeking Tom's help. Meanwhile, the character of the enterprise was formed. Had I been aware of it, I certainly would have accepted A. L. Kroeber's definition of anthropology as "a science devoted to the study of man, the study of the differences and similarities of all aspects of life without limitation in time and space."[2] A suspicion of anthropological subjectivity in reporting came later, probably as a result of Tom's prodding. Nevertheless, despite the inherent limitations of this study, it would seem reasonable to conclude that, for every one thousand anthropological field studies of separate and disparate tribes, one attempted synthesis on a global level by outsiders is both necessary and proper.

It was only when we were well into the research and writing that it became apparent that cosmology, ritual, and art were the keys, or the proper elements to study, if one were to narrow the psychological gap between ourselves and aboriginal cultures.

Short of the most rudimentary of cultures, deprived of these elements because of adverse environmental conditions, it was cosmology, ritual and art which harmoniously held these native groups together, providing them with an élan vital. It was as fine an hour as conservatism ever enjoyed. This Trinity served the primitive in much the same sustaining fashion as ours did for us throughout the centuries. It was also the principal reason why the native everywhere did not need the introduction of Christianity to give him a good and virtuous life, capped by the promise of Salvation in the next.

Curiously, it was the amateur, Laurens Van Der Post, the Boer descendent of the very men most responsible for the virtual extermination of the Bushmen, who displayed the greatest sense of appreciation for primitive cosmology, ritual and art.[3] This occurred in the area of Slippery Hills, north of the Orange river, where Bushmen traditionally gathered to worship their gods.[4] In this instance an act of atonement was imperative because the trip into the sacred area had been contaminated by a careless killing of game. The gods had already demonstrated their powerful medicine over the modern machine; a relatively new and efficient camera repeatedly jammed when pictures of old rock paintings were sought.[5] However, the anger of the local gods was somewhat appeased when Van Der Post wrote a most humble apology to them. Included in the same message was a warning to other white travelers not to repeat the same sin. It was then carefully inserted in a bottle which was buried at the foot of a sacred painting of an eland. The entire episode would have done credit to the most learned shaman.[6]

However, cosmology, ritual and art are also universal elements and may be thought of as essential to man once he has developed an on-going social order. Since in effect all societies possess these elements, comparisons and similarities may be drawn which otherwise would have been in limbo. Once that is done the illusion of superiority may be stripped away and we may see ourselves as the anthropologist sees the exotic native.

Following an analysis of the history of our Judeo-Christian culture, one is induced to admit our spiritual affinity with the primitive. Much as modern man may pride himself upon both an empirical and rational approach to life, being suspicious of mysticism and the mystical, he finds that he must use the latter when discoursing about the foundation stones of Western culture: Genesis, the Ten Commandments, the Trinity, the Virgin Birth, the physical ascent of Jesus into Heaven, the Mass, the Rosary for the Dead, the Second Coming, the Resurrection and the end of history with the final triumph of Good over Evil. However, since all these "truths" yield only to emotion, intuition and mysticism, one who accepts them must realize that he is operating at precisely the same level as does the primitive and not a whit higher.[7]

No one has shown with greater clarity than Henry Adams that the beautiful union of cosmology, ritual and art, glorifying not the Trinity but the Virgin at Chartres cathedral in the twelfth century, was at the same time a remarkable energy source. It is possible that no primitive tribe ever enjoyed a greater supply of direction, purpose and meaning from a supernatural source.[8]

And when the Western world of the thirteenth century combined the ritual of the Seven Sacraments with the Aristotelian cosmology of Dante's *Divine Comedy*,[9] and capped it all with the artistic triumph of the Gothic cathedral,[10] it momentarily achieved, under the aegis of the Trinity, what the primitive always lived by and with. This was the certainty he could always call upon his gods who were not far removed and who deeply cared for their people.[11]

But the picture takes shape and form with the admission that modern science has no more respect for Mariology, or Aristotelian cosmology, than it does for primitive mythology.[12]

And, whether one shifts attention eastward to the Byzantine tie between Church and State under the Romanoffs or westward to that between the Anglican Church and Protestant monarchs in England, one finds no more sophisticated an explanation of reality in their cosmology, ritual and art than that the Middle Ages had already provided. For example, despite the political and economic break with Rome, the Six Articles of Henry VIII in 1539 displayed nothing so much as doctrinal continuity between Catholicism and the newly-established national Church.[13]

Nor is the situational dilemma remedied by an appeal to the dissenting sects in England, including the Puritans and others emigrating to America. In religious and social matters, the Puritans shared the same opinions as orthodox Anglicans for they believed in theocracy, demonology and argument as the way to truth. Dissent was not over church doctrine but rather ecclesiastical forms and government.[14] Protestantism denigrated both art and ritual because they were thought to seduce the senses and thus damage man's capacity for rationality.[15] In the late seventeenth century Protestants discovered that this was grounded upon the theory of John Locke as to the primacy and responsibility of the individual. This in turn was rooted in Newtonian physics and its theory of the atom as an indivisible particle. And when Newtonian physics was discredited in the twentieth century, the preaching of Protestantism became more verbal and divorced from the content of what it was supposedly based upon, modern philosophy and science.[16]

The conclusion, therefore, is that no Christian cosmology has any better standing and acceptance in terms of modern science than has the primitive variety.[17]

While social anthropologists did a splendid job explaining how modern technology immediately disrupted and destroyed primitive edifices everywhere,[18] they did not make us aware of the possibility that this very technology may slowly be undermining the pinnings of their own society.

Historically, the difficulty arose from a cultural acceptance of the arrogant notion nature existed only to be used by man and he would not be held accountable for anything he elected to do.[19] This paralleled the Old Testament notion that man, separately created, had been given dominion over all the animals because he was their superior and natural master.[20] It is not surprising then the present behavior of Western man resembles an over-successful parasite which is dooming itself because it is killing its host.[21]

One of the most compelling reasons for this alarming view is that, because of the aceleration of scientific discoveries and their utilization via technology, man is fast losing control of his environment. He introduces new forces so rapidly and on such a wide scale with the result that the sensitive environment is constantly being exposed to new hazards. For example, radioactive isotopes were only discovered in the human body long after nuclear testing had begun.[22] Smog was recognized as a health hazard only after the California economy made it inevitable because of an exclusive dependence upon the automobile and new industry.[23] The resistence of synthetic detergents to bacterial decomposition became evident only after a universal use by housewives of polluted water.[24] Despite many historical precedents dating back to twelfth century Iraq, we accelerated the process of silting and salination in our river valleys because of the construction of irrigation projects and the channeling of rivers.[25] We poisoned our soil and made community living in certain areas impossible by the spread of lethal chemicals like dioxin.[26] We created sulphuric acid in the sky from burning sulphur-bearing fossil fuels, thus producing a deadly acid rain in Canada and New England and points east.[27] Ironically, in the steel industry an emphasis on increased production of a lighter and better product will actually produce more of some kinds of pollution than did the older and inferior one.[28] These are just a few of the many examples of how modern man fouled his own nest in the name of a better living through chemistry.[29] This exposes *our* Wizard of Oz or the presupposition that Western man was and is rational. This always afforded us a great solace because, so the supposition ran, man was always in control of both self and environment. And now, unfortunately, we may no longer rely on such nursery tales.

Kurt Vonnegut gave us a clue as to when this all began when he described his revulsion at the dropping of the A-bomb on Hiroshima. It was not the mass killing alone which did it, or the physical devastation wrought, because he had already seen a like amount at Dresden following American bombings. It was because he understood the technology via conventional bombing which produced the fire storm at Dresden. The very technology which accomplished this destruction could be relied upon to rebuild a new and better world. But he lost his innocence at Hiroshima at precisely the same time he lost his capacity to understand technology and to identify with it. What he had left was a sickness of industrial soul, a pervasive fear of the new physics which had given birth to such a monstrosity and, finally, a whiff of disaster around the fact that ignorant politicians were going to be given the care and custody of the not so little stranger.[30]

Once this ominous process was publicly under way there was no stopping it, certainly not in the name of wisdom and rationality. Perhaps the classic example was that of Robert Oppenheimer, the father of the A-bomb, when he professed serious doubts about the advisability of putting on the Seven League boots of the H-bomb. For the open and frank sharing of his views in scientific and governmental circles, he was rewarded by the official stigma of being a national security risk and immediately separated from the service. Of course the issue was clouded by Oppenheimer's past close association with communists. However, this would never have arisen had he not lost his enthusiasm for the newest super weapon.[31]

Coupled with the foolish notion that national security could simply and immediately be obtained through the manufacture of H-bombs was the equally questionable one that atomic energy could safely be harnessed to reduce the cost of electric power. Armed with little more than such pious hopes, the Atomic Energy Commission turned over the development of such domestic power to private enterprise which, not surprisingly, largely consisted of oil companies.[32] How low the factor of public safety figured in these transactions was indicated when the Pacific Gas & Electric Company twice tried to build atomic reactors on or near the San Andreas fault in California.[33] By 1975 so many tens of billions of dollars had been invested in nuclear power plants that it caused authorities in governmental regulatory agencies to relax their vigilance nation-wide with regard to safety procedures.[34] Such a mood was indirectly responsible for the disastrous accident and near melt-down at Three Mile Island in Pennsylvania in late March, 1979. Despite the attempt the next day by the NRC Chairman Joseph Hendrie to minimize the damage, as late as the spring of 1985 it was generally conceded by government and industry experts that Unit 2 will never again be able to resume nuclear operations.[35] In 1984 the company either pled guilty or no contest in seven of eleven charges concerning falsification of pre-accident leaks at Unit 2, thereby becoming the only nuclear utility in the nation to be convicted of a criminal offense.[36] However, in spite of massive public opposition in Pennsylvania, the NRC and the Federal courts allowed Unit 1 to start up again in September,

1985.[37] Most distressing is the serious charge that the accident of 1979 has left millions of gallons of contaminated water and produced a sludge which must be safeguarded for hundreds of years - or more -because of radio-active waste.[38] Finally, despite this catastrophe, concerns in the nuclear trade for safety standards were so low that the then Chairman of the NRC, Nunzio Paladino, publicly castigated the industry for its disregard for quality controls at Diablo Canyon and nine other power plants under construction.[39]

Ever since we fell in love with science and technology, especially that involving the production of nuclear power, the list of our offenses against both nature and man is a grievously long one. By this time it is so well known to the informed person that we may instead settle for a few dramatic instances which cast the greatest doubt upon our collective rationality.

Pervading our fool's paradise was the assumption that, whatever else might be dicey, we could always safely depend upon the use of the oceans of the world as a vast garbage dump. Now, and only because of the terrible devastations wrought among all forms of sea life by the constant inroads of the cesspools of man, we must soon make a choice between using the ocean as a garbage dump or as a food source.[40]

The monumental problems of the future are likewise being ignored. Despite the fact that industries will in a few decades exhaust energy and the natural resources upon which energy depends, America meanwhile has abandoned energy-efficient sources of transportation like waterways and railroads, and adopted energy-consuming modes like trucks, autos and airplanes. Blissfully ignoring the patent problem, our society is naturally unaware of the terrible choice it must eventually, if not soon, make: either we must discover new and adequate energy sources or prepare to leap into an entirely new kind of social order.[41]

Finally, the great argument as to whether America will have enough common sense to shift from our dependence upon foreign oil to a domestic reliance upon coal is a specious one because it ignores a far greater menace. All combustion of fossil fuels produce carbon dioxide which has naturally been building up in the earth's atmosphere since the inception of the

Industrial Revolution. And this has steadily reinforced the ability of the natural atmosphere to absorb and re-radiate more of the infrared radiation given off by the earth itself. Consider an additional factor. The National Academy of Science predicted that the next two hundred years will witness an increase of four to eight times the amount of carbon dioxide produced if heavy reliance upon coal continues. And this presents us with the greatest riddle of all. The intensive burning of fossil fuels over a long time could alter the delicate heat balance of the earth itself. If there is a great deal less energy dispersed, one might legitimately expect a new ice age but, as is more probable, if there is too much heat produced by carbon dioxide, it might cause the polar ice caps to melt. This in turn would dramatically raise ocean levels which would then flood vast tracts of land and coastal cities.[42]

Perhaps enough has been said to establish the feasability of the proposition that technology itself may pose the crucial problem or threat for the Westerner today. Few, however, would suspect this were we dependent upon the social anthropologist for our information. Likewise, their past reluctance to apply demonstrative analytical skills to the magical and mystical aspects of their own society is puzzling to the historian concerned with whatever happens to man anywhere and at any time.

But these artificial restraints are apt to be self-defeating. Few would quarrel with the contention of Lévi-Strauss that the best work in anthropology has been done by those who staked out a single area or tribe and remained there for long periods of time. But the price paid for this specialization is a general ignorance about primitives in general.[43] A far more serious point was made by Sol Tax who declared that, if we define anthropologists as specialists working with primitives, we have virtually effaced the craft. Few of these societies are left and all are in terra incognito.[44]

After World War II, academicians increasingly realized that the research situation for the Western anthropologist drastically altered. His traditional market - the primitive in colonial areas - dried up or disappeared. In addition, emergent Third World nations often discouraged the "invasion" of foreign scholars. Finally, local turbulence often made research hazardous or impossible.

As a consequence, one may logically anticipate a necessary shift of emphasis and a corresponding anthropological preoccupation with both technology and the magical and mystical in Western society. Naturally, this does not mean any decline of academic interest in the primitive. Rather, it implies a concern for both him and ourselves as constituting social orders, superficially quite different, but much less so upon extended examination.

But even with this transition, we think two things are necessary. First, one must admit the kinship between primitive magic and religion and that of Christian cosmology and ritual. Second, technology, far from being a new god to worship, must ever be regarded as potentially destructive to life forces. Let us put the matter bluntly. If the field researcher believes, consciously or unconsciously, in the superiority of either Christianity or technology, he has seriously handicapped himself as a student of the primitive. And, if he believes in both, we suggest it is time to take the work less seriously.

Perhaps our inability thus far to appreciate native culture is because it eludes mere observation, analysis and reporting. For example, the Hopi let the white man in on his holy ceremonies many times without giving away his secrets. This happened because the observer was conditioned to see and hear but not to understand and appreciate the native mystical element or component.[45] A similar error, dramatically compounded, occurred in 1920 when the white man outlawed the use of the clown in the native ritual of the Southwest. This was because, failing once again to capture the spiritual aspect of the pageant, he saw only the obscenities on the empirical level.[46] The sharp limitations of the white man's ability to comprehend native cultures was demonstrated to the Curator at Musée de L'Homme of Paris. This was as a consequence of a long chat with a grandson of one of the Indians who accompanied Buffalo Bill. He described the meaning of this lock of hair, that design, why this particular color was used, and the meaning of that feather. "This garment (a painted skin tunic), formerly beautiful and interesting, but passive and indifferent ... became meaningful, active testimony to a living moment through the mediation of someone who did not observe and analyze but who lived the object for whom the object lived."[47] Victor Turner finally comprehended the truth when investigating the Ndemba culture of Africa. It would defy understanding unless and until one could overcome his prejudice against native ritual. It, and it alone, was the key to understanding tribal values and the essential constitution of human societies.[48]

The present study of the cosmology, ritual and art of the primitive, therefore, may be regarded as a mirror in which we see ourselves and, hopefully, better understand the human or existential predicament. Man can only stand alone and unaided when he is without an emotional crisis. When the latter occurs, and he for any reason cannot solve it with all the means at his disposal, he will call for supernatural help within a well-defined conceptual sphere. This is given shape and direction by the Trinity of cosmology, ritual and art.

While it is true, as Bronislaw Malinowski wrote, that magic permeated the economic life of the primitive, giving great power to its possessor,[49] the same is equally true of modern man. The great temple of our economic shamans has for generations been Wall Street and no individual has outstripped the power and charisma of J.P. Morgan. He did as much as anyone to give economic speculation, or gambling, not only a respectable position but one of veneration by the American public. His Merlin magic wand had to be waved over stock manipulations, mergers, reorganizations and such before they could legitimately be consummated. No one better realized the magical implications of this than did Lincoln Steffens. After closely observing Morgan's practices for a considerable period, he confessed to his friends that, when he ceased to be interested in journalism and became interested in money, he would do it on Wall Street: "I would quit working and make money."[50] This has since been expanded into a general principle. This occurred when one compared shells, dog's teeth and feather bands of nonliterate tribes with modern-day money and interest in the use thereof, placing both in the realm of the magical, mystical and religious.[51] These changes remind the historian of the attack by the intellectual spokesman for the Jeffersonian Democrats, John Taylor of Carolina, upon the "money-ocracy" at the time of the establishment of the First National Bank in 1790-1792. He saw this as a far greater menace than landed aristocracy which had been legislated out of existence by the Constitution. While the aristocracy, indirectly of course, was responsible for the production of agricultural commodities, the "money-ocracy" produced not wealth, but paper money instead, which acted as a tax upon all honest labor. It thus created overnight a new and more dangerous power to prey upon the body politic. To its possessors, or rather inventors, it was a mine, yielding gold without work.[52] In brief, it was a form of modern magic.

Nor is modern man's utilization of the irrational and magical limited to the creation and use of paper wealth; Julius A. Roth explained how it has invaded that temple of science, the modern hospital. While it is known, for example, that tuberculosis is a contagious disease, not much is understood as to how and when it spreads and what should be done to prevent this from occurring. As a tuberculosis patient, Roth made a careful and extended study of the behavior of a particular hospital staff at all levels. He concluded that man behaves only rationally and systematically when he understands causality. When he enters the gray areas of uncertainty, or when he does not understand nature's laws, his rules and regulations are apt to be irrationally structured and adherence to them dictated by tradition and status roles rather than by a scientific outlook. Human behavior, even at the highest levels, has more to do with magic in such an instance than prudence or sanity.[53]

While the present work focuses on the non-empirical aspects of primitive life - cosmology, ritual and art - these have a remarkable unity or cohesion about them. The work itself is heavily impregnated with philosophy and technology, poetic symbolism and abstract meanings and, at first blush, one is tempted to think of it as involving non-economic aspects. However, that is not the case because everything employed in a cosmological and/or ritualistic sense, save for witchcraft, was done in order that the tribe survive and prosper.

Just as the primitive is apt to sing a song or do a dance in honor of the game he has just slain, so it is possible that the authors' re-assessment of primitive life shares some of these same emotional qualities because it was written after a general loss of confidence in the idea of progress, the quality of civilization itself or the modern and Western style of life. However, the lack of a conviction of the superiority of all facets of our way of life enhances the probability that one will be a fairer judge of the apparently exotic primitive.

Our position is that, while man's nature is essentially the same, primitive or civilized, when man surrounds himself with the machine it becomes increasingly difficult to discover or disentangle his real or essential nature. Paradoxically, in such a circumstance it would not be surprising, but logical instead, to find a computer whose single mission was to discover the nature of man. However, if this is to be done, man himself must do the job. And so one has come full circle and we are back with Stanley Diamond's assertion: the search for the primitive is motivated by our desire to discover or rediscover the nature of human nature, or man himself.[54] Despite his hostility toward the purely deductive processes of European armchair authorities,[55] Franz Boas utilized the same technique when he concluded that we are concerned with primitive man for the same reasons we are preoccupied with the science of man.[56] But, if we are to have a science of man, it must come as a consequence of a skillful blending of the empirical and the deductive. "In short, scientific theory always asserts more than observation gives, and is not verified directly ... by mere observation; instead, it is a hypothesis proposed *a priori,* verified in part at least indirectly through its experimentally checked deductive consequences."[57] It is a manifestation of the eternal spirit of humanism. Sophocles had the chorus in *Antigone* pay tribute to it in fifth century B.C. Athens: the world is full of many wonders but none is as wondrous as man himself.[58] Modern man rediscovered this essential truth. Seventeenth century astronomy, nineteenth century biology, twentieth century psychology and anthropology "mark the path of a prodigous transfer of the focal point of human wonder. Not the animal world, not the plant world, not the miracle of spheres, but man himself is now the crucial mystery."[59]

Finally, any outsider to the field of social anthropology is eventually bound to inherit anxieties over the use of the term primitive. As for myself, I was naively hung up, early in the research, trying to construct a meaningful model of the primitive, the sort of thing suggested by Lévi-Strauss in the early Fifties.[60] Eventually, I was rescued from this futile exercise by both Tom Urban and Charles Wagley. No single model of say a dozen characteristics can fit both hunter-gatherers and the advanced civilizations of primitive America, notably the Incas, Mayas and Aztecs.

Retreating from this position, perhaps it could be maintained that at least three elements unite the most "simple" and the most sophisticated among so-called primitive cultures: 1) they were all darker skinned than their conquerors, a matter of color 2) they were inferior vis-à-vis the invader in armaments and fire power, or in technology and science and 3) they were heathen and not Christian. In effect, therefore, one always had a sort of White Man's Burden with arguments invariably involving both Christianity and the idea of progress. Even here, however, there is some difficulty. Nineteenth century China and Japan conform to all three points but few today suggest that these cultures might be thought of as primitive. Yet, it is true that the white interloper generally held them in no higher regard than he did primitive cultures. The self-assurance with which we thrust our own culture upon them would appear to validate this.

Not swayed by such logic, Tom Urban defined the primitive as the other, meaning that he can never be considered one of us. The simplest of primitive peoples may have a culture so complex and exotic in certain aspects as to baffle Western understanding. It was the first time I had heard of this term. Much later, Tom caught the spirit of the battle of nomenclature very well: those were primitives whom Western anthropologists so labeled. He thinks it is their justification for Western imperialism.

With the collapse of any valid dichotomy, whether implicit or explicit, between all so-called primitive peoples and ourselves, the effort may be seen as but another attempt to impose order upon chaos. The order is in the scholar's mind and the chaos exists out there in nature or reality. Yet, after failure in this endeavor, the human mind continues to probe the chaos, trying of necessity to reduce large segments of it to some understandable or meaningful pattern of behavior or events. The problem, however, always remains the same: not to settle for the desired or needed "comprehension" at the expense of "truth" or reality.[61] Thus one explains the constantly shifting Western views or definitions of primitive. It is a natural and continuing difficulty in the interpretation of the manifold possibilities of social structure or human order outside one's own "tribe" or people.

However, it appears to us that no other or more recent terminology is any better. Take, for example, Jamake Highwater's substitution of primal for it. This term in itself suggests an evolutionary process. Presumably, a so-called civilized society would be a secondary culture, derived from a primal source. However, consistent use of the term primitive in no way impedes one from arriving at either similar or identical points of view as those who, like Highwater, scorn its use. It would appear that terminology is less important than the clarity and consistency of one's position. So-called primitive and so-called civilized man boils down to one thing and one thing only: man himself.

Therefore, just as Third World anthropologists scorn the use of the term primitive because of its hated imperialistic connotations, so we finally elected to use it because, unlike all others, it is immediately understood by Western readers. And we are clearly writing for a limited readership, as are Third World anthropologists. Take the selection of a book title, for example. No other term seems as useful or as meaningful, whether it be any of the following: native, aboriginal, early, primal, primary, indigenous, micro, the other, or the human other. For clarity's sake, let us compare the following book titles: 1) *The Primitive and the Supernatural or 2) The Human Other and the Supernatural*. Only to the anthropologist would the latter title be clear. All that is presumably necessary, therefore, is to attempt to school the reader in its new and neutral context. This cannot come as a surprise to a learned and cognizant person. Whereas the same terms may linger on for many generations, they mean different things to different ones. But, instead of always enclosing the term primitive in quotation marks to indicate a changed meaning, we ask our readers to see it that way for themselves. We believe this will expedite reading, rather than slowing it up. At the same time, logic forces an admission that the term, the human other, best technically defines the total content of this study.

In the following chapters we concentrate on cosmology, ritual and art as the basic elements and social cement which held primitive society together and gave it its peculiar order and harmony within nature; in the chapter on Culture Clash we try to analyse the sudden death impact which Western technology had upon aboriginal cultures. Naturally, the reporting is based upon those scholars of the so-called Golden Age of Anthropology whose objectivity was seriously questioned by their anthropological successors of more recent times. While our own viewpoint of the so-called primitive is psychologically akin to that of the younger anthropologists of today, we must recognize that the error of subjectivity is not limited to earlier scholars. That liability is shared by all, including this generation and subsequent ones. Therefore, we reject the pursuit of nihilism, or that doctrine which denies the existence of any basis for knowledge or truth. We must rely on these flawed, or human, sources in the belief that, if judiciously used, they can yield a better and clearer picture of past reality than one could obtain by any other possible means. Our instinct to reconstruct the primitive past seems just as urgent as our desire to come to grips with our own. We think this a result of a preoccupation with the question of the nature of man himself. Neither an exclusive concern with either so-called primitive or so-called civilized man can satisfy that scholarly aspiration. That is the reason we deal with both.

Footnotes

1   Some scholars believe the period got under way about 1880 and ended in 1920 "before the post-World War I reorganization of university departments of anthropology." See Editor's note in *The Golden Age of American Anthropology*, selected and edited with introduction and notes by Margaret Mead and Ruth L. Bunzel (New York, George Braziller, 1960, 1963). "The first volume of the *American Anthropologist* (1888) contained articles dealing with linguistics, archaeology, physical anthropology, and ethnology." de Waal Malefijt, *Images of Man*, 225.

2   Eugene Garfield, "Anthropological Journals: What They Cite and Who Cites Them," 514-528 in *Current Anthropology*, v. 25, No. 4, August-October 1984, 514.

3   As a boy, his grandfather had found an ancient frieze of forty feet in length and twelve feet high of a female giraffe with an elegant neck which reminded one of a Modigliani painting. Its colors had not faded. The artist signed the work with the imprint of his hand on the high walls. The original conception of the work and its splendid execution produced a state of excitement in the beholder. *The Lost World of the Kalahari* (New York, William Morrow, 1958), 204-207.

4   *Ibid.*, 195.

5   *Ibid.*, 213.

6   *Ibid.*, 215.

7   The idea of the Mass and the transformation of the bread and wine into the body and blood of Christ is the "supreme instance of the development of the magic-mystery element in the Christian Church." Henry Osborn Taylor, *The Classical Heritage of the Middle Ages* (New York, Harper Torchback, Harper and Row, 1958), 96.

8   Chartres represents not the Trinity but the identity of Mother and Son. *Mont-Saint-Michel and Chartres* (Boston, Houghton Mifflin, 1904), 92, 95, 96, 100, 106.

9   F. S. C. Northrop, *The Meeting of East and West, An Inquiry Concerning World Understanding* (New York, Macmillan, 1946), 287-288.

10   Taylor, *Classical Heritage of the Middle Ages*, 316.

11   From an Aristotelian mold, as modified by Thomas Aquinas, the Christ takes on a unifying power and richness of divinity, all of which rests on claims by Jesus that he represents his Divine Father. This complicated message is reduced to meaning for the unlettered masses by means of art and ritual. Northrop, *Meeting of East and West*, 284-285, 287.

12   Since the findings of Galileo and Newton discredit the concepts of Aristotle concerning nature and man, we reject Aristotle, not because of religious or moral considerations, but scientific ones. If Aristotle were correct, then projectiles should move in a different way. Northrop, *Meeting of East and West*, 281-282.

13   These included the crucial doctrines of the real presence of Christ at the mass and

transubstantiation or the miracle of the mass. Frederick George Marcham, *A History of England* (New York, Macmillan, 1950), 263; Goldwin Smith, *A History of England* (New York, Charles Scribner's Sons, 1949), 224-225.

14   Northrop, *Meeting of East and West,* 67.

15   It was not an accident early Protestants took the color out of Church windows and attacked the theatre as the center of immorality. The Quaker Meetin' House, its congregation, without a preacher, sitting in silence in a plain church afforded a beautiful example of a modern Cartesian and Lockean man. Northrup, *Meeting of East and West,* 91-92.

16   *Ibid.,* 289.

17   Primitive religions are no less respectable than others because all respond to similar needs, play the same role and depend upon identical causes. Durkheim, *Selections from his work,* 86-87.

18   See Chapter IX, "Culture Clash."

19   "Summary and Prospect," 695-700 in *Man's Impact on Environment,* edited by Thomas R. Detwyler (New York, McGraw-Hill, 1971), 697. By contrast the primitive relationship with nature is one of intimacy and courtesy. A Wintu Indian, for example, only kills his quarry because he must survive. Having killed it, he feels obliged to utilize every possible part so that the deer or other animal will not have died in vain. Highwater, *Primal Mind,* 74.

20   Gerhard Von Rad, *Genesis. A Commentary.* The Old Testament Library. (Philadelphia, Pennsylvania, The Westminster Press, 1972), 47. As a consequence, the white man justified the destruction of both nature and man as an inevitable outcome of Christian history. The primitive, on the contrary, saw himself as a blood brother of all the animals. Vine Deloria, Jr., "An Open Letter to the Heads of Christian Churches in America," 400-407 in *Literature of the American Indian,* edited by Thomas E. Sanders and Walter W. Peek (Beverly Hills, California, Glencoe Press, 1973), 406. See also Thomas Rhuys Williams, *The Dusan: A North Borneo Society* (New York, Holt, 1965), 14.

21   C. L. Boyle, quoted from William A. Albrecht, "Physical, Chemical and Biochemical Changes in the Soil Community," 395-418 in *Man's Impact on Environment,* edited by Detwyler, 396.

22   René Dubos, "Man and His Environment: Scope, Impact and Nature," 684-694 in *Man's Impact on Environment,* edited by Detwyler, 690. We now know, partly as a consequence of tracing radioactive products of above-ground nuclear tests, that a nuclear war would disseminate radioactive isotopes around the world. At first concentrating in the latitudes where the bomb exploded, they would gradually drift toward both poles. Some of the isotopes could remain in the earth's atmosphere for thousands of years. Virginia Brodine, *Air Pollution,* (Harcourt Brace, 1973), 103.

23   Dubos, "Man and His Environment," *loc. cit.,* 690. This phenomena is common to many cities of the United States and Western Europe. When the hydrocarbons of trucks, busses, cars, and smoke stacks combine with the natural hydrogen in the air, they produce

nitrogen oxide, the deadly agent. Brodine, *Air Pollution*, 14-18.

24   Dubos, "Man and His Environment," *loc. cit.*, 690. In 1968, industrial sources were responsible for more pollution than any other source. They supplied thirty-four percent of the total amount. Municipal waste ran a close second. *Water Pollution*, edited by Julian McCaull, (New York, Harcourt Brace and Javanovich, 1974), 90.

25   Thorkild Jacobsen and Robert M. Adams, "Salt and Silt in Ancient Mesopotamian Agriculture," 383-394 in *Man's Impact on Environment*, edited by Detwyler, 383.

26   Love Canal in Niagara Falls, New York, and Times Beach, Missouri, simply afford the most notorious cases of land poisoning by dioxin, one of the most toxic chemicals made by man. It is known to have caused cancer in animals. Times Beach is one of fifteen confirmed contamination sites in Missouri and there are as many as eighty other suspected sites in the same state. The waste products of a defunct chemical company at Verona, Missouri, were ultimately disposed of in 1971 by spraying oil on dirt roads to hold down the dust. They were also used as landfill, improperly stored on farms and the like. "Dioxin in Missouri: Troubled Times," 60-62 in *Science News*, vol. 123, No. 4, January 22, 1983; *Time*, January 10, 1983, 21; March 7, 1983, 39; *Newsweek*, January 10, 1983, 24.

27   Lester R. Brown, *The Twenty-Ninth Day. Accommodating Human Needs and Numbers to the Earth's Resources* (New York, W.W. Norton, 1978), 43.

28   *Water Pollution*, edited by McCaull, 93.

29   Some scientists believe that the danger to the environment was sharply aggravated because of a departure from the utilization of natural chemicals. Brown, *The Twenty-Ninth Day*, 38.

30   *Palm Sunday. An Autobiographical Collage* (New York, Delacourte Press, 1981), 69-70.

31   The Oppenheimer affair occurred when the nation was obsessed with questions of national security as a consequence of McCarthyism. Philip M. Stern, *The Oppenheimer Case: Security on Trial* (New York, Harper and Row, 1969), Preface xi. The Gray Board, chief investigative agency, found that Oppenheimer did not openly oppose the bomb as did Albert Einstein and others. His fault lay in the fact that he did not openly recant his prior opposition to the manufacture of the bomb. This, however was enough to deny him security clearance. *Ibid.*, 371.

32   *Radioactive Contamination*, Virginia Brodine, Consulting Editor in Environmental Issue Series. Scientists' Institute for Public Information, edited by Barry Commoner (New York, Harcourt Brace and Javanovich, 1975), 123.

33   *Ibid.*, 114.

34   Jan Beyea and Frank von Hippel, "Containment of a Reactor Meltdown," 52-61 in *Bulletin of the Atomic Scientist*, August/ September, 1982, 54.

35   Industry spokesmen estimate the cost of cleaning up Unit 2 will be a billion dollars but half that amount has already been spent and only one-third of the necessary work has

been done. The task of removing the badly damaged core is the biggest remaining challenge. Susan Q. Stranahan, "Three Mile Island. It's Worse than You Think," 54-57 plus in *Science Digest*, June, 1985, vol. 93, No. 6, 56.

36   Edward J. Walsh, "Three Mile Island: the Battle of Unit 1," 30-31 in *Bulletin of Atomic Scientists*, vol. 41, No. 5, May, 1985, 30; "TMI Tests Trashed," *Science News*, Vol. 128, No. 12, September 12, 1985, 186.

37   "The Battle of Unit 1," *loc cit.*, 31; "A fresh start at Three Mile Island?," *Science News*, vol. 127, No. 23, June 8, 1985, 359; "TMI Restart Underway," *Science News*, vol. 128, No. 15, October 12, 1985, 229. As late as 1982, more than 15,000 leaking steam tubes were discovered in the Unit 1 reactor. Walsh, "The Battle of Unit 1," *loc. cit.*, 30.

38   Jim Harding, "Three Mile Island. Three Years After," 20-23 in *Sierra*, March-April, 1982.

39   *Ibid.*, 21-22. Other sources are more optimistic. Despite the human error which was responsible for the very heavy damage at Three Mile Island, and analagous episodes in at least five other plants, F.R. Mynatt was optimistic about the future of atomic power. He felt that both the NRC and the industry itself had behaved quite responsibly with regard to safety standards since the TMI affair in 1979. Future research should be sufficient by the first quarter of the next century so that a new generation of nuclear reactors could combine both simplicity and safety. "Nuclear Reactor Safety Research Since Three Mile Island," 131-135 in *Science*, vol. 216, Number 4542, April 9, 1982.

40   Brown, *The Twenty-Ninth Day*, 51-53. See also *Water Pollution*, edited by McCaull, 82, and *Man's Impact on the Global Environment. Assessment and Recommendations for Action. Report of the Study of Critical Environmental Problems* (SCEPO). Sponsored by the Massachusetts Institute of Technology (Cambridge, Massachusetts, MIT Press, 1970), 127-128. Man has also seriously threatened his marine food chain by oil pollution of the ocean. While the immediate and disastrous effects upon fish and bird life in coastal spills is well-known, it appears from recent scientific explorations from Woods Hole and elsewhere that the oceans are polluted as well. Three times as much tar as Sargossa weed came to the surface from tests in the Sargossa Sea. Crude oil ingested by sea life is productive of carcinogenic compounds which are passed along to other predators, ultimately to reach man himself as the final consumer. Max Blumer, "Oil Pollution in the Ocean," 295-301 in *Man's Impact on the Environment*, edited by Detwyler, 297, 299.

41   W. Jackson Davis, *The Seventh Year. Industrial Civilization in Transition* (New York, W.W. Norton, 1979), 148, 151.

42   Brown, *The Twenty-Ninth Day*, 61-62. See also Brodine, *Air Pollution*, 62-63 and *Man's Impact on Global Environment*, MIT Study, 11.

43   *Structural Anthropology*, translated from the French by Claire Jacobson and Brooks Grondfest Schoepf (New York, Basic Books, 1963).

44   "'Primitive' Peoples," 64-80 in *The Concept of the Primitive*, edited by Ashley Montagu (New York, Free Press, 1968, 65.

45   Frank Waters, *Book of the Hopi* (New York, Viking Press, 1963), xii-xiii. The same book with the same title was also published in New York by Ballantine books, 1963. The element of time, as it is known in the West, disappears in Hopi culture and their concept of space is unrelated to that of Newtonian classical physics. Highwater, *Primal Mind*, 105.

46   Hightower, *Primal Mind*, 177-180.

47   Clifford, *Predicament of Culture*, 246.

48   *The Ritual Process: Structure and Anti-Structure* (Chicago, Aldine, 1969), 6-7.

49   *The Sexual Life of Savages in North-Western Melanesia....*
2 vols., (London, George Routledge, 1929), I, 40, 42.

50   *The Autobiography of Lincoln Steffens* (New York, Literary Guild, 1931), 188-191.

51   Norman O. Brown, *Life Against Death. The Psychoanalytical Meaning of History* (Middletown, Connecticut, Wesleyan University Press, 1959), 245, 268, 279, 281.

52   Charles A. Beard, *Economic Origins of Jeffersonian Democracy* (New York, MacMillan, 1915), 207-209.

53   "Ritual and Magic in the Control of Contagion," 310-314 in *American Sociological Review*, vol. 22 (1957).

54   See footnote 3 of Chapter I.

55   Weston La Barre, *Culture in Context. Selected Writings* (Durham, North Carolina, Duke University Press, 1980), 166-167.

56   See footnote 39 of Chapter I.

57   Northrop, *Meeting of East and West*, 294.

58   *The Tragedies of Sophocles*, translated by E.H. Plumptree (New York, George Routledge, no date), 141.

59   Joseph Campbell, *The Hero with a Thousand Faces* (New York, Pantheon Books, Bollingen Series XVII, 1961), 391.

60   "Social Structure," 524-553 in *Anthropology Today. An Encyclopedic Inventory.* Prepared under the chairmanship of A. L. Kroeber (Chicago, University of Chicago Press, 1953).

61   "All order ... is theoretical, unreal - a harmless, sensible, smiling mask men slide between the two great dark realities, the self and the world." John Gardner, *Grendel*, in Lett, *The Human Enterprise*, 1.

Chapter III

COSMOLOGY

A tribal cosmology was imperative in order to allay the fears and anxieties of a naive people living in a frightening world and the educational vehicle for this was mythology, combined with ritual. Although distinct entities, magic and religion were used to ease man's fears and give the necessary courage to carry on.

The Western and Christian world received its cosmology from the ancient Hebrew in the Book of Genesis which began thus: "In the beginning God created the heavens and the earth .... And God said, 'Let there be light'; and there was light." Finally, after all else had made its appearance, God elected to make man in his own image. After resting on the seventh day, He decided it was fitting and proper that man have a mate who was made out of his rib. The Social Contract between God and man followed but that was broken when Eve ate the apple and persuaded Adam to do likewise. God's curse and man's exile may be said to have launched Hebrew "history."

For the most part the cosmology of the primitive followed a similar pattern and served a like purpose. Above all, it established the fact that the tribe's origin was a supernatural one. Their ancestors were the first men and they formed a Social Contract with their Creator. Primitives would easily have comprehended the story about Abram building an altar to Jehovah in return for His promise to give the Hebrews the land of Canaan. This was a reasonable *quid pro quo,* or something for something.

In this chapter we raise and attempt to answer a half-dozen crucial questions: 1) Was cosmology natural to man, or did it develop as an evolutionary process, a reflection of tribal sophistication? 2) What were the well-springs of its origin and what purpose did cosmology serve the tribe? 3) Why and how account for the fascinating similarity between primitive and Christian mythologies? 4) What was the relationship between a heavenly cosmology and reality, or nature, as primitives knew it? 5) Was the primitive solely interested in nature as a pragmatist, i.e., a time to plant and a time to reap, or was he capable of abstract thought? and 6) What was the intimate relationship between myth and ritual and between magic and religion? Let us make clear, however, that, like Emilé Durkheim, when we speak of religious or cosmological origins, we do not mean the "absolute beginning" but rather, the simplest condition which is known or beyond which at present we have no evidence.[1]

With regard to cosmology, the natural questions to emerge would be when, where and under what conditions is it apt to arise? Does it come first to individuals or to the group itself? If to individuals, one would presuppose they were unusually gifted or perceptive; but if to groups, what sorts of groups and under what general conditions? For example, if tribe A is forced continually to quest for food on the daily level, is it as apt to develop a cosmology as a group which has more leisure due to an ample food supply? Does it also somehow relate to the very size of the group, let us say, one large enough to allow for a division of labor between the secular and the sacred?

We are aware of the fact that Durkheim and Malinowski are clearly at loggerheads over these same questions: the former stressed the necessity of collective efforts in this regard[2] and the latter individual contributions, as in solitude and meditation.[3] We have tried not to let either argument prejudice our own inquiry.

One assumes that there were bands and tribes before the existence of cosmology, theology or religion; there is, however, evidence that in the most elementary of cultures, it - cosmology -was at the very least without readily identifiable form and substance. Of the Fuegan Indians, Darwin confessed he could see no evidence of religious worship. Nor could Captain Fitz Roy determine whether or not the Fuegans believed in an after life. Neither did they have any identifiable political structure. Nor did they appear to have a strong social or tribal one or even a close family life. The central fact of life was an inhospitable and miserly nature which forced both the individual and group continually to grub for a living. The Fuegians were, as a consequence, said Darwin, the lowest order of creatures he had ever seen.[4]

The modern counterpart of that experience was that of Allan R. Holmberg in his contact with the Siriono of the Amazon river basin. There, once again, the central fact of human existence was the necessity of unrelenting struggle for enough food to be able efficiently to search for more. First of all, there were no shamans. There was neither an identifiable religious apparatus nor worship ceremonies. The absence of all these was, of course, explained when the author observed that there was no dogma about a god or gods who controlled man's destiny. As a logical extension of this, there was an equally vague and unstructured concept of mythology or the origin of things. It was never articulated voluntarily. When asked about it, the young men referred their questioners to old men, and the old ones shook their heads. Although Moon was credited with being the creator, there were no stories of how this happened. Holmberg could not obtain any buttressing myths about the origin of the world, man or fire, even though all the informants proclaimed that Moon created them. One of the reasons for the lack of a religious edifice was the tribe's preoccupation with obtaining its daily food supply.[5] When in the early eighteen nineties, a German naturalist visited the dry bush country of New South Wales and Queensland, he was baffled in his attempt to detect any religious belief or edifice. Although the inhabitants believed in the existence of ghosts, they apparently did not subscribe to the belief in the existence of a higher supernatural being.[6] Because both Baldwin Spencer and F. J. Gillen had been accepted as fully initiated males into the Arunta tribe, resulting from the latter's intimate contact of two decades, their remarks on religious matters carry more weight than those of an outsider. The natives of Central Australia had no idea whatsoever of a Deity who both created the world and rewarded virtue, while punishing vice.[7]

A somewhat different case was that of the Negritos of the East Coast of Luzon who had both a conspicuously low level of material development and an absence of shamanism and religious ritual; however, their physical environment seemed not to be responsible for the lack of cultural development, at least in the sense that it provided ample food. Although the Negritos practiced some agriculture, they were quite inconsistent, sometimes not planting, and at others, not staying to harvest what was planted. Perhaps it was the very ease with which nature provided food that made them indifferent agriculturalists.[8]

Their cousins, the Semangs or Negritos of the Malay jungle forests, appeared to have had both a very low level of material civilization and a conspicuous lack of religious apparatus and ritual. Likewise, their cosmology appeared to be vague. This may have been due to the reluctance of the natives to share information with the white man.[9]

Irving Goldman's experience among the Cubeo Indians, living on the Northwest Amazon river system, offered a problem; this was because currently, and without economic stress, they are, strangely enough, without any gods and, therefore, no worship practices. But he himself supplied the clue when observing that, before they learned farming and the techniques of hunting and fishing, they always lived on the verge of starvation. Traditionally, this area has been dominated by a complex of many small and scattered communities of no more than thirty to thirty-five people who were perhaps an hour's steady paddling away from most of their neighbors.[10] Therefore, one might surmise that their failure to develop a cosmology was the result of both perennial economic stress as well as low population clusters.

This was the sort of experience which led Betty J. Meggers to conclude that, among hunter-gatherers, supernaturalism was vaguely defined. There were few shamans and no tribal religious purposes, only individual ones.[11] Tribes at the hunting-gathering level usually acknowledge the existence of a Supreme Being but know little about him. They have few myths and these are quite simple.[12] It is only rarely that a primitive people can conceive of the creation of the universe out of nothing material, i.e., out of the mind of God.[13]

The available data would tend to suggest a cosmology is not apt to be developed unless the group possesses both an ample food supply and a sufficient tribal population which is organized and coordinated to produce that same food. Without such, the band is doomed to use all its human resources to obtain food in order to search for the same on the morrow. Allan Holmberg drew such a conclusion about the nomadic Siriono in the tropical forests of the Upper Amazon region.[14] My own guess was that, until adequate human numbers are available, the tribe will never be able to release enough men from hunting in order that they might search for sacred stones or bones or feathers or whatever so that the tribe might collect its equivalent to the sacred ark of the Covenant. However, Tom Urban, my son and co-author, argued that tribal numbers were not a necessary condition. These merely reflected both the natural environment and the degree of social organization. It was precisely at this juncture that Jeff, my younger son, injected an observation which appeared plausible. He argued that, since both a cosmology and a ritual are devised by man to posit both a god or gods who can be appealed to by man to change his fate or destiny, this is not apt to happen when the tribe is confronted by a nature which "never" changes. If environmental conditions are always miserable, man eventually learns that he cannot change this, whether by work, by prayer, or a combination thereof. If, on the contrary, nature is always bountiful, then there is no tribal "cost" to pay for individual "sin," no matter what predictions are made by holy men or prophets. Man appears essentially pragmatic and, if something doesn't work, it is eventually abandoned. Or the cosmological structure was not erected in the first instance because it did not appear promising enough. Regardless of our theoretical differences on the origins of cosmology, all conceded that a division of masculine labor will give rise to a leisure class. It consumes material goods produced by others while at the same time producing a heavenly return by its mediation with the gods. At this level it would appear that cosmology is dependent upon the collective tribal efforts. Individual endeavor seems not to suffice. It is more apt to result in anarchy than in order.[15]

But, regardless of the anthropological reaction, it is clear to us that, among the peoples we have discussed thus far, it is not a matter of intelligence, racial inferiority or other traditional arguments, but rather one of the interaction between a physical environment and social organization, or the tribal reaction to it.

Once, however, beyond that extremely limited or primitive level - and one can never be sure that these tribes were not being secretive and/or deceptive for purposes of ensuring their own security - few anthropologists, apparently, would deny that a tribal cosmology was imperative in order to allay fears and anxieties of a naive people living in a frightening world.

The next logical series of questions involves the why of cosmology and its origins; what were the unique and indispensable goods and services which it conveyed or supplied to the band or tribe?

It appears that, as a consequence of cosmology, the primitive lived in an ordered world, subject to law and controlled by unseen forces; this law was not physical but moral. The primitive discovered or, more accurately, was given this moral law and conformed by declaring right action was conformity with the law and wrong or anti-social action was contrary to it.[16] This helps explain why the characteristics found among the Southeastern Indians of the United States were but a reflection of a universal attitude among preliterate societies. If there were a single word to summarize the Indian belief system, it was "order." And they zealously protected that "order" both from Socratic challenge and outside erosion.[17]

This cosmology answered all primitive queries as to the origins, nature and destiny of man.[18] As was universally the case in Africa, it anticipated basic Christian beliefs, postulating both the existence of a Supreme Being who created the world and the survival of man's soul following his death.[19] Of course this might mean more of a continuity of the soul than immortality, for there was no positive notion of eternity as such. Nevertheless, the lowest "savages" believed in the continued existence of the departed soul.[20] The good life was universally defined as the faithful observance of custom and tradition because these were founded upon the will of the Creator, or something like the Ten Commandments.

However, the need of the West to be both different and superior to the primitive was afforded by the fact that there were basic differences in the cosmologies. Primitives did not appeal to another life to redress the injustices found in this one. There were no rewards and punishments, no sin and salvation, no Heaven and Hell, no need for a Saviour.[21] Any such reward or punishment followed as a natural consequence here and now and was not one meted out by some Deity following one's demise.[22] For example, among the Nuer in the Sudan it was believed that incest with one's mother would be followed by immediate death.[23] The Siriono had an almost identical belief.[24] It is clear, therefore, that the outcome of such a primitive cosmology was a behavioral and not an ideological one. The American Indian, for example, was far less concerned about a person's profession of belief, let us say in Christ, than he was with regard to that individual's ethical behavior. An idea of a future existence might be no more imaginative, but no more misleading than the empirical experiences in this one.[25]

With regard to probable cause, Bronislaw Malinowski believed that religion, or cosmology or theology, arose as a direct result of the human personality refusing to accept the prospect of annihilation by death. Primitives, like us, found this fate repellent and unacceptable. "And he who is faced by death turns to the promise of life. Death and its denial - Immortality - have always formed, as they form today, the most poignant of man's forebodings."[26]

Deprive the Christian religion, for example, of the myth of the Resurrection and it becomes devoid of all meaning to the man seeking Immortality and Heaven for himself. True, a laudable ethic remains, but the West would never have separated it from the notion of the triumph over the cross and death. And Christians can always give ethics lip service - because it relates to others - while clutching that lust of everlasting life to their own bosoms.

Other scholars offered more pragmatic reasons for the origin of religion. According to Ruth Benedict, religion stemmed from the mind of the man who conceived that behind the facade of nature and sensory perception lay a tremendous power, an energy with which the universe was charged. The act of man's attempted manipulation of this mysterious force represented the origin of religion. First man's piety, then God's material blessings.[27] Because of the fear of the primitive, and his sense of helplessness in a harsh and unresponsive environment, he felt that somewhere there must exist a transcendent power who could manipulate or avoid the dangers confronting man and that if man could put himself in harmony with that power, all would be well.[28] The less scientific knowledge a people have about nature, the more they know, or think they know, about supernaturalism.[29] This yielded practical outcomes. The basic function of religion everywhere was to give a sense of security to people living in a frightening world which, according to the naturalistic point of view, was full of the unpredictable, capricious and tragic. Nervous but assertive, people built their cultures next door to the Unknown. In the face of chance, want, and death, all mortals were apprehensive. Therefore, they tried to restore order by bringing in the supernatural, which was then used to affirm there was an order after all. They invested the future with the appearance of safety by affirming that Someone-up-there had been looking after them in the past.[30]

From a cosmological point of view, it is difficult to conceive of a more comforting idea than the Second Coming, an idea shared by many separate and disparate peoples. Perhaps it may come as a bit of a shock to some to realize that the most dramatic idea in Christendom - Christ coming to earth again "to save" - is old hat to the primitive mind. Here the story line focuses on a hero-god who loved, protected and instructed his people in the basic arts, working miracles meanwhile, but who for some reason beyond his immediate control had to leave abruptly. However, before he left, he promised to return to bail the tribe out of a supreme difficulty. Then he vanished. But the inspiration remains. What he did before, he will do again. His people are in effect in the palm of his hand. It has been called the Frederick Barbarossa motif of history, after the medieval German hero and emperor who died on the Third Crusade.[31]

Although the idea of a saviour for the community is a universal one, it is not dependent upon the spread of Christianity. Everywhere it was a hero like Jesus who was gifted with extra-ordinary powers from the moment of conception and later birth.[32] He enjoyed supernatural assistance throughout life[33] and, following a tragic death, was resurrected in order to restore the world and bring joy.[34] Likewise, so many episodes we thought peculiar to the life of Jesus were but part of the universal apparatus belonging to the hero, i.e., a threatened adult male (King Herod) tries to kill the hero infant whose miraculous powers frighten him;[35] genuine heroes always have a "moment of truth" before their death[36] (as did Jesus when he told Peter he would betray him three times before the cock crowed); heroes descend into the bowels of the earth and the realm of the dead[37] (as did Jesus just after death and before reappearing to his disciples), and, of course, the vision of the tragic hero of his own death and resurrection in paradise.[38] A genuine hero can never afford to die in bed.[39] Like the misfortune of being born as a rich man's son in a mansion, that would spoil the narrative for romantics, unless, of course, the hero later renounced his wealth. The universal story line, we conclude, is pretty well fixed and few departures from it can be tolerated.

It is in the three comparatively advanced primitive cultures of Latin America that one may see the story line in its clearest form. In the Aztec culture, the earliest hero-god was Quetzacoatl, a kind of Prometheus-like protector and teacher of mankind with regard to the arts and sciences. When this white god was forced to leave his people, because of the jealousy of the other gods, he promised to return to them as he sailed away to the east on the Gulf of Mexico. However, the promise turned into disaster. Since Spaniard invader, Cortes, was mistaken for Quetzacoatl, Montezuma immediately knew he was doomed because he could not fight the god who kept his promise to return.[40] Inca mythology was similar. First Viracocha created the world and then set forth across the Pacific, walking on the waters. His people believed that he would reappear in a crisis to save them. When Pizarro first appeared in Peru, he interrupted a civil war between two brothers and claimants to the throne, Huascar and Atahuallpa, and the losers at Cuzco at first thought the the Spanish had been dispatched by their god to save them from the usurper, Atahuallpa.[41] This was obviously based on the same myth as reported by Piedro de Cieza de Leon, soldier and explorer in Peru in the early days of the Spanish conquest. There are, of course, certain differences in detail. In de Leon's account, the god's name was Ticiviracoacha and he was white. He not only gave birth to men and animals but could work miracles, like changing plains into mountains and great hills into valleys and making water flow out of stones. Finally, he appeared, a Christ-like figure, telling men that they should be loving and charitable to all. A long time later, another white man appeared who resembled the first and who healed the sick and the blind and worked great miracles when his enemies treacherously sought to kill him. It was this man who disappeared into the sea and who, as a consequence, was given the name Viracocha, which means "the foam of the sea." When Huascar's followers realized the Spaniards had imprisoned Atahuallpa, they hailed them as emissaries of the great god Ticiviracoacha, sent to aid his loyal Peruvian sons. At the same time, they called the Spaniards Viracoacha.[42]

This myth was so prevalent throughout pre-Columbian societies, and so commonly hailed by local prophets, that it may be understood as part of the unconscious. The Hopis, for example, had a quite similar myth about a long lost white brother, Pahana, which caused them to mistake the first Spaniard they met for him.[43]

The idea of the magic reappearance of the tragic hero also characterized the earliest civilizations of the Western world. Throughout the history of the Mediterranean-Mesopotamian world, man's sufferings were tied with those of a god who suffered, died and was resurrected. This theme struck countless times throughout the Paleo-Oriental world. Just as the blameless and virtuous god survived the torments of pain and humiliation to be revived or resurrected, so men learn through this lesson that suffering and death are but temporary. Resurrection follows after. All defeats are effaced and only victory remains.[44]

It is also essential to note that this heroic saviour of mankind was universally portrayed as a product of a Virgin Birth. Let two examples illustrate. Mayan cosmology had its great culture-hero in Zamnan, a co-founder of that civilization along with Quetzacoatl, the virgin-born deity. One temple at Merida was dedicated to Zamnan who had miraculous powers of curing the sick, the halt, the blind and even that of raising the dead.[45] In the sixteenth century this recurring theme of the culture-hero, born of a virgin mother, made its appearance among the Iroquois. He was the prophet Deganawidah, who acted as the prince of peace for the contending Six Nations.[46]

Once again, we see that what we were taught to believe was a story unique to Chrisianity turns out to be but a part of a universal myth. The story of the virgin birth was recounted everywhere "and with such striking uniformity of the main contours, that the early Christian missionaries were forced to think that the devil himself must be throwing up mockeries of their teaching...."[47] For the best explanation of this phenomenon, one turns to Lee Drummond. When confronted with the essential question of the origin of matter, the primitive had to choose between the idea of spontaneous generation (inanimate matter produces life, or something, out of nothing). "The spirituality of virgin birth is the polar opposite of spontaneous generation." In primitive myth the latter idea was always associated with rottenness and worms. Thus, it was always rejected for the purely spiritual explanation of the virgin birth.[48]

On the basis of the available evidence, therefore, it would appear that cosmology gave the requisite structure, form and spiritual inspiration to primitive peoples which supplied not only the courage for the struggle for life but the very reason to do so. In short, it was the élan vital or the life force of the tribe which came to it directly from supernatural sources and which they were as bound to observe forever as the Hebrews were the Ten Commandments. There could be neither nine nor eleven. To summarize, it was conservatism at its best, because it acted as a force to conserve and preserve a way of life and not as a dissipating or disoriented one. Change, development and progress on the contrary were but paths into the void.

The religiously-minded man, both primitive and modern, recognized the fact that ultimately he was without power in a world he did not comprehend and therefore sought in a mystical sense a union with the unseen and unknown. Curiously enough, the individual's confession of inadequacy, and that of the power and majesty of God, enabled him to shed his own fears and exchange them for certainty and security. The very act released one from the fear and humility induced by the overwhelming presence of an indifferent universe which remained callous to human thought and action. This process could not be understood by the application of rationality nor by that of common sense and experience. Nor could it be successfully conveyed to others by any form of communication system. It had to be experienced to be known. Therefore, it was both irrational and mystical. And yet, and this is the paradox that one cannot ignore, the process had pragmatic outcomes. It equipped the believer to live confidently and effectively.[49]

This tribal cosmology or theology universally took the form of myth which rested upon the same assumption made by the Hebrew authors of the Book of Job: "... the universe and all in it are governed by conscious supernatural agency, by willful and capricious power...."[50] Thus it was always a narration of sacred history, the fabled time of creation or beginnings, or how reality came into being or existence.[51] Such stories invariably taught that the world, man and life itself have a supernatural origin and history and this history is significant, precious and exemplary.[52] Take, for example, the myths of the Bemba in Africa: "Myth relates the actions of the heroic founders of the cosmos. ... The sacred time and place of these mythic origins lie, not so much in the past, as at the very center. Indeed, they are the constructive substratum of present reality."[53] William Prescott anticipated logic of this sort when he spoke of myth as religion's flower, or poetry in action, a poetic unfolding in primitive times of religious principles.[54] One modern authority, however, reduced the affair to a simple but meaningful generalization "In a bewildering cosmos man must construct the mythical views that offer order and meaning."[55] Like Christianity, the universal myth of mankind always postulates "a paradise at the start of things and a paradise at the end."[56]

It was Mircea Eliade who exposed perhaps the unconscious assumption of the Judeo-Christian world that it alone was privy to the sacred knowledge of the "fall of man" from a state of grace. Primitives were equally aware of this mythology, accepting it, as in our culture, as historical fact. It happened something like this. All peoples were convinced, like the ancient Hebrews of Jerusalem, that they lived at the vital center of all things, or that their temple and palace were the core of the world and the navel of the universe.[57] Originally, man lived at peace with the animals and, most important, had easy access to Heaven for direct and inspiring encounters with the Creator. In this Garden of Eden man was innocent of suffering, work or death. But, then came the "fall" and the estrangement of the group from God.[58] It was, of course, precisely because of this fact that shamans and priests came into existence. It was only through these dedicated and holy men that the sought-for intercourse between man and God could be resumed.

It is scarcely surprising, therefore, that one is frequently struck by the similarity between primitive myths of the origins of creation and those of the Hebrew and Christian as contained in the Book of Genesis. The Desana tribe of the Tukano people of the Amazon river basin believed that their Sun God was preexistant - or outside of space and time - and that He was omnipotent, omniscient and omnipresent.[59] Quite similar to this was the belief of several Indian tribes of the Americas that the Supreme Being alone existed, originally that is, in the midst of a void, and that He, therefore, was the universe at that time. From this solitary Mind came the decision to build or construct the world, the sun, moon and universe.[60] According to the Ojibway account, God first created two men and two women, gave them reasoning power, paired them, told them to multiply, and from the Heavenly edict, came Indians.[61] From the Dinka tribe in the South Sudan came a myth of lost innocence and woman's sin, severing close ties between the people and its god.[62] The Tentehara Indians of the Brazilian rain forest captured the idea of original sin with their folk-tale that it was woman who first tempted man to sexual congress after the Creator forbade it.[63] One such African myth, affirming the separate creation of man and the fashioning of woman from his ribs, apparently was of foreign origin, although not Christian. It clearly related to the account in Genesis, and had probably reached the Nandi in Kenya through some remote Islamic culture.[64]

It was at this point that Tom Urban raised a most interesting query. Isn't it amazing that the same anthropologists who admitted the primitive anticipated the crucial cosmological aspects of Judeo-Christianity also relegated him to an inferior status? By their writings, intentionally or not, they justified subjugation in the name of Christianity, an obviously superior religion. That was hubris with a vengeance. However unorthodox the query, it cannot be glossed over. It is difficult to refute.

Another impression, both immediate and lasting, was the virtual universal prevalence of such myths. To take Africa as but one example, authorities were agreed that all peoples there possessed and utilized mythology. Once those myths originated, always very early in tribal history, they remained much the same because the culture itself had no idea of change.[65] Mythology, therefore, was the quintessence of conservatism. It yielded everything one could expect of an ideal system—a cosmology, a history and a moral system.[66]

Radcliffe-Brown, who seemed to make no distinction between myth and legend, or who meant by legend the same as others meant by myth, nevertheless identified its four great contributions: 1) it gave an account of how order came into the world; 2) it placed a simple and crude value on human actions, right and wrong; 3) it gave expression to the social value of the past or that derived from tradition; and, 4) it set forth the value of natural phenomena, or that of sense perception.[67]

Another pertinent question concerns the nature of a god or gods who figured in this cosmology. African religions were uniform in conceding supreme creative powers to a single Deity.[68] However, tribes on the Northwest Coast of North America felt that many spirits pervading earth, water and sky could grant to human beings some of their power to succeed at enterprises which had the social sanction of the tribe.[69] The moral distinction here is crucial. Whether one supreme god or many, the supernatural world responded only to those prayers which sought help for legitimate or "good" purposes. This sharply contrasted with sorcery or witchcraft, as discussed in the following chapter. It has evil for its motivation and purpose. Wherever a Supreme Being was worshipped, he eluded precise definition and identity. As pure spirit, he was ineffable, unobservable and indefinable at the empirical level. This merely meant that god was seen as a disembodied spirit.[70] The height of sophisticated cosmology among primitives may have been attained among the Peruvians when Pachacutec, Inca Emperor of the late fifteenth century, lectured an assembly of priests at Cuzco. To those who already taught the immortality of the soul and the existence of a Creator God, Pachacutec introduced the revolutionary idea that, because the Sun behaves so predictably, it too must have a Master and that was the Supreme Being.[71] But, in the final analysis Marshall D. Sahlins aptly summarized: if one finds a people, one also finds its god there likewise. He stays with the tribe and he moves with it. He is with it in a universal sense, like God was with the Hebrews in their Egyptian captivity.[72]

Perhaps it required an agricultural society with its hierarchy of small groups and loyalties to eventuate in a monotheistic belief system, or one in a Supreme Being who as the First Cause not only created a Heavenly hierarchy but the universe, the world and man. For example, the Iroquois were caught up in a mass of allegiances due to nuclear families, households, residents of long houses, clans, moieties, and, finally a League. The sole way to reduce such complexities to meaning was to assume that everything was related in an orderly way and this arrangement was the will of a caring god.[73]

This ties in with the assumption of Paul Radin that the primary and immediate function of cosmology and/or mythology was for the purpose of reconciling the primitive with nature. The fundamental characteristic about him was his assumption that the highest satisfaction must be found here on earth and that the gods themselves reject those who spurn life or who have no understanding and respect for the things of this world.[74] The chief virtue of Radin's argument is that it seems in complete harmony and accord with everything else one knows about the primitive, i.e., his complete adaptation and accommodation to nature or the things of this world.[75]

However, Radcliff-Brown inserted an interesting but questionable caveat at this point. Since the primitive showed no capacity for abstract thought, he had no desire to understand the processes of nature for the mere sake of knowledge. Thus, his interest in nature was purely pragmatic, dominated by the principle of immediacy. He was interested in natural phenomena only so far as it impinged upon his social order, say the progressions of the seasons as related to planting, growing and harvesting of crops.[76]

While one must admit the pragmatic character of the primitive with regard to nature, it certainly does not include an admission that he was not capable of abstract thought. The assumption itself is probably rooted in our cultural prejudices and particular thought modes. Such assertions concerning the incapacity of primitive man might be no more meaningful than to say that, because he could not comprehend quantum mechanics, he was incompetent with regard to abstract thought. It would be fairer to say that he was uninterested in such questions because to him they were meaningless and unrelated to his universe as he experienced it.

But, even the defenders of the primitive in this matter are not above criticism. After a prolonged study of the Bantus, Father Placide Tempels concluded that they have a system of thought, metaphysics and ethics. Their ontology, or that system connected with being and reality, he thought comparable to a Western one, despite its being tinctured with magic. Their conception of a vital force at the center of things, or a universal energy system and one at the same time omnipotent, is the same as we mean by the term God.[77] But the Bantus, in the mind of Father Tempels, were accepted as an intelligent people because their thought processes were very much like that of ours. Had they thought and reasoned differently, he might easily have concluded they were inferior in an intellectual sense. And it is precisely this error - cultural and intellectual differences are immediately suspect - which has been the cultural heritage of the West.

There is a kindred and even more compelling argument that primitive man had the capacity for abstract thought. He had a very high capacity indeed for this intellectual operation but he chose largely to display it on the organizations of kins within the social group itself. Anthropologists find this intricate system - differing in all groups - must be mastered before one can describe and analyze the social structure of any tribe.[78]

While Western arrogance was probably responsible for the contention of Radcliffe-Brown that the primitive was incapable of abstract reasoning, his argument that he was only interested in the consequences of nature, and not its earthly causal factors, is persuasive. Left alone in such a mood, the primitive would never have mastered the comparative simplicity of Newtonian physics.

Although acceding to the advice of my co-author to spare the reader the details of the anthropological controversy, I found the preoccupation of prominent scholars a fruitful one as to whether myth or ritual was more important. And this for one reason only: it showed that myth and ritual were mutually dependent. Ritual gave the necessary present-day form or procedure to myth, something indispensable.[79] Myth then invested that form with both antiquity and divinity and this with the purpose of rendering it immune from vulgar change and/or innovation.[80] Durkheim's thoughts have a special appeal. If myth were withdrawn from religion, it would be necessary to withdraw the rite also because frequently rite is nothing more than myth put into action. The Christian communion we have today is inseparable from the myth of the Last Supper.[81]

However, and as a result of the research of Gregory Bateson in Bali, it was apparent that, despite the unquestioned antiquity of both, myth and ritual could historically be manipulated out of considerations for public need or social welfare. The then-current desire, at least by the priesthood, for the forging of a socio-political unity among three communities gave rise and acceptance to a current myth coupling all the local gods in a single family relationship. The hierarchy of mother-son, mother-daughter, and older and younger brothers immediately made crystal clear all otherwise complicated relationships between the gods and their worshippers. Public acceptance of the priestly innovation was earmarked by community participation in ceremonial song and dance and in the renovation of an old sacred temple site. The latter was done out of a feeling that, if a temple had been deemed appropriate by past generations, it ought to be equally appropriate to this one. One did not search the past for causal relationships to the present but rather it served as a model for proper and correct conduct. It symbolized a period when the world was peaceful and at rest, before the Europeans introduced confusion and disorder masked as progress. This move by the priestly hierarchy might have been an effort to strengthen native conservatism against the winds of change as were represented by the Christian Church.[82]

Apparently, however, such a view had been anticipated by Franz Boas who hit upon it while studying the Ghost Dance of the North American Indians. While doctrines of the prophets were new, they were based upon the old ideas the tribe already possessed: its image of itself, other Indian tribes and, finally, even that of white missionaries. Thus, he concluded, both myth and belief have been shifted about or transmitted and have in the process undergone significant changes themselves.[83]

Finally, most authorities, with the exception of Lévi-Strauss,[84] believe that primitive magic and religion, although performing kindred functions, are separate and distinct. Man, recognizing his own helplessness and/or unworthiness, uses religious rites and prayers to appeal for supernatural help in this world and the next. Religion teaches man of the immortality of the soul and of the existence of the spiritual world, sanctifies tradition and gives emotional security. Power here is heaven-based.[85] On the contrary, magic is earthly based. It depends on the ability of man, via the manipulation of objects and ritual, to compel or coerce impersonal forces of a supernatural character.[86] It wards off accidents which otherwise would be beyond the control of man. With the Nandi in Kenya, for example, magic is that body of beliefs and practices which combines to give man the necessary confidence to cope with the unknown. Significantly, this is in addition to the assurances already received from religious practices. In that agricultural society, magic is intimately associated with crop insurance.[87] The Maori of New Zealand also used magic for the success of all economic ventures connected with land or sea.[88] Thus, it would appear that, while magic is restricted to worldly affairs and religion deals with the next as well, the two are designed to ease man's fears and give him the necessary courage to carry on.

Because it gave order, security and assurance to tribes living in an otherwise bewildering and incomprehensible world, cosmology appeared inevitable in all but the most primitive of societies. Its form was myth, wrapped in ritual, and it likewise employed both religion and magic to effect its sought-for outcomes.

Regardless of the tribe's supernatural and heroic past, however, once easy access to their gods had been interrupted or terminated, "the reality of now" was that only the shaman for the hunter-gatherer, or the priest for the sedentary and densely populated centers, could act as the indispensable intermediary between God and man. Their contrasting roles will be examined in the following chapter. To make them more understandable we try to establish certain parallels between the functions of the shaman and priest in primitive societies and between the prophet and the priest in Old Testament days and in the time of Jesus.

Before abandoning cosmology, however, one must call attention to a caveat by Talal Asad which has been ignored throughout this chapter. It deals with the question of how physical power or powers creates spirituality or religion itself. We make a mistake, he declared, if we approach religion only with questions about sociological meaning of doctrine and practice, or even about the psychological effects of symbols used in rituals. Instead, we ought to ask what are the historic conditions, i.e., movements, classes, institutions and ideologies which are necessary or pre-conditions for the existence of particular religious practices and discoveries. But, whatever the merits of his contention, it is safe to assert that it was something completely outside the ken of the primitive.[89] It denied the basic assumption of all his myths. This was the idea of the supernatural origins of the universe, the earth and, above all, of the tribe itself.

Footnotes

1   *Selections from his work,* with an introduction and commentaries by George Simpson (New York, 1969), ft. p. 88.

2   *The Elementary Forms of Religious Life,* translated from the French by Joseph Ward Swain (London, George Allen and Unwin, 1968), 206-207, 214, 219, 417, 446. The 1915 edition of this same book was also used in a minority of instances but, when cited, will be referred to in the footnotes as the earlier work.

3   *Magic, Science and Religion and Other Essays.* Selected and with an Introduction by Robert Redfield (Glencoe, Illinois, Free Press, 1948), 37-41.

4   *Journal of Researches into the Geology & Natural History of the Various Countries Visited during the Voyage of H.M.S. Beagle Round the World* (New York, E.P. Dutton, 1912), 204-205. In modern times René Girard expressed the same sentiment more graphically when declaring that no society was without religion because it depended upon the latter for its existence. *Violence and the Sacred,* 221.

5   *Nomads of the Long Bow,* 116-118, 238-239.

6   Richard Semon, *Australian Bush,* 222.

7   *The Northern Tribes of Central Australia* (New York, Macmillan, 1904), 491-492.

8   Herbert W. Krieger, *Peoples of the Philippines. War Background Studies, No. 4,* November, 1912 (Washington, D.C., Smithsonian Institute, 1912), 39-42, 45. Some observers of the Negritos thought their intelligence was very low. See Dean C. Worcester, "Head-Hunters of Northern Luzon," 833-930 in *National Geographic,* vol. XIII, No. 9, September, 1912, 841-847.

9   W.W. Skeat, "Wild Tribes of the Malay Peninsula," 463-478 in *Smithsonian Institute Annual Reports, 1902* (Washington, D.C., Smithsonian Institute, 1902), 477.

10   *The Cubeo Indians of the Northwest Amazon. Illinois Studies in Anthropology, No. 2* (Urbana, University of Illinois Press, 1963), 25, 51, 253.

11   "Environmental Limitation to the Development of Culture," 19-45 in *Environments of Man,* edited by Jack B. Bresler (Menlo Park, California, Addison-Wesley Publishing Company, 1968), 25.

12   Eliade, *Myth and Reality.* Translated from the French by Willard R. Trask. Planned and edited by Ruth Nanda Anshen (New York, Harper and Row, 1963), 93-94.

13   Huxley, *Affable Savages* (New York, Viking Press, 1957), 215.

14   *Nomads of the Long Bow,* 38, 90, 98.

15   It is the clan which acquaints the mind of man with the idea of gods who both dominate and care for him. Only society has that power. It is to its members what god is to the group. However, to attribute religion to societal origins is in no way to imply that it lacks veracity. The unanimous sentiment of the believers of all times cannot be entirely illusory. Durkheim, *The Elementary Forms of Religious Life*, 206-207, 214, 219, 417, 446.

16   Radcliffe-Brown, *Andaman Islanders, A Study in Social Anthropology* (London, Cambridge University Press, 1922), 384. This book was also published as a single volume in Glencoe, Illinois, by the Free Press in 1948. A typical example would be those primitive tribes like the Pirá-piraná who perceived themselves as living in an ordered cosmos, one created in the ancestral past. To this cosmos, and with it the mythical deeds performed by the ancestors, was attributed the vital control of present-day social life and one which also supplied an indispensable moral code. Christine Hugh-Jones, *From the Milk River: Spatial and Temporal Processes in Northwest Amazonia* (London, Cambridge University Press, 1979), 1.

17   Charles Hudson, *The Southeastern Indians* (Knoxville, University of Tennessee Press, 1976), 121, 147. The argument appears a tautological one. All sacred things must have their specific place and being in their place is what makes them sacred. Objects make their contribution to order merely by occupying the place assigned them by the supernatural. Claude Lévi-Strauss, *Savage Mind*, 10.

18   Emilé Durkheim and Marcel Mauss, *Primitive Classification* (Chicago, University of Chicago Press, 1963), 86-87. A specific observation, identical to that of Durkheim, was made by a team of anthropologists after visits with Australian aborigines at Cape Arnheim and Echo Island in 1946. Catherine H. and Ronald M. Berndt, "Australian Aborigines: Blending Past and Present," 114-131 in *Vanishing Peoples of the Earth* (Washington, D.C., National Geographic, 1971), 119.

19   The missionary-explorer, David Livingston, was perhaps the first white man to observe this truth. Armand de Quatrefages, *The Pygmies*, translated by Frederick Starr, (New York, Negro Universities Press, 1969), 200. See also Robin Horton, "Ritual Man in Africa," 651-673 in *Readings in Anthropology*, 2 vols., edited by Fried, *Cultural Anthropology*, II, 663; George M. Theal, *The Yellow and Dark-Skinned People of Africa South of the Zambeisi* (New York, Negro Universities Press, 1910), 185.

20   Rafael Karsten, *The Civilization of the South American Indian. With Special Reference to Magic and Religion* (New York, Alfred A. Knopf, 1926), 35.

21   Firth, *Tikopia, Ritual and Belief* (Boston, Beacon Press, 1965), 331, 336.

22   James Montgomery Cooper, "The Relation Between Religion and Morality in Primitive Cultures," 560-572 in *Golden Age of American Anthropology*, edited by Mead and Bunzel, 567.

23   E.E. Evans-Pritchard, "Nuer Rules of Exogamy and Incest," 85-103 in *Social Structure. Studies Presented to A.R. Radcliffe-Brown*, edited by Meyer Fortes (New York, Russell & Russell, 1963), 94.

24   Holmberg, *Nomads of the Long Bow*, 64.

78

25   Robert H. Lowie, *Indians of the Plains*. American Museum Science Books (Garden City, New York. The Natural History Press, 1963), 180-181.

26   *Magic, Science and Religion and Other Essays* (Garden City, New York, Doubleday, 1948), 29.

27   "Religion," 627-665 in *General Anthropology*, edited by Franz Boas (New York, D.C. Heath, 1938), 630. Yet, primitives did not attribute omnipotence to any of the gods. Ideologically, this was a comparatively late development. *Ibid.*, 641. R.H. Codrington popularized the use of the term *mana*, one from Melanesia and Polynesia. Currently, it is out of favor with anthropologists. It has some validity, however, if defined as power or magic possessed by a living being, or images of gods. This quality may be transferred to others. Martin S. Day, *The Many Meanings of Myth* (Lanham, Maryland, University Press of America, 1984), 145.

28   Clark Wissler, "The Conflict and Survival of Cultures," 592-601 in *Golden Age of American Anthropology*, edited by Mead and Bunzel, 596-597.

29   Elman R. Service, *The Hunters. Foundations of Modern Anthropology Series*. (Englewood Cliffs, New Jersey, Prentice-Hall, 1966), 65. "Religion, as [Clifford] Geertz sees it, is an anxiety-reducing institution. It explains events for which neither common sense nor science can account. ... Religion provides a method of reading everyday experience that ... protects us from having to confront the dreadful possibility of meaningless." Stephen Karathedoris, "From Social to Cultural Systems and Beyond: Twenty Years after 'Religion as a Cultural System,'" 53-94 in *Soundings. An Interdisciplinary Journal*, vol. LXXI, No. 1, 1988, 86.

30   Clyde Kluckholn and Dorothy Leighton, *The Navajo*. American Museum of Natural History. The Natural History Library (Garden City, New York, Doubleday, 1962), 233. However, this theory that religion came into being because of primitive man's fear of his hostile environment has been rejected by Emilé Durkheim. The primitive did not regard his gods as foreigners or as enemies or malevolent beings whose favors must be obtained at all costs. On the contrary, his gods were both friendly and kindred to him. They were very near to him and were his natural protector. The terrible, jealous and angry gods appear later in the historic evolution of gods. *Elementary Forms of Religious Life*. 223-224.

31   *Ghost Dance*, 270.

32   Day, *Many Meanings of Myth*, 380; Campbell, *Hero with a Thousand Faces*, 319.

33   Campbell, *Hero with a Thousand Faces*, 97.

34   *Ibid.*, 245-246. The hero is not really dead, but asleep. Day, *Many Meanings of Myth*, 390.

35   Day, *Many Meanings of Myth*, 380.

36   *Ibid.*, 391.

37   *Ibid.*, 386.

38   *Ibid.,* 391.

39   *Ibid.,* 389.

40   William Prescott, *History of the Conquest of Mexico* in 3 vols., (New York, Harper and Brothers, 1849), I, 59-60; Ignacio Bernal, *Mexico Before Cortez: Art, History, Legend* (Garden City, New York, Doubleday, 1963), 123.

41   Loren McIntyre, "The Lost Empire of the Incas," 729-787 in *National Geographic,* vol. 144, No. 6, December, 1973, 779.

42   *Chronicle of Peru,* edited by Clements R. Markham. (Originally published by the Hakluyt Society and reprinted by Burt Franklin, New York, 1883), No. 33 and 68, Second Part, 5-9.

43   Waters, *Book of the Hopi,* 251-252. A similar phenomena was reported from the other side of the world. When the Kumans, a headhunting tribe in the mountainous interior of New Guinea, first encountered whites in 1933 they were confounded. Since all their gods were white, they quite naturally mistook the visitors for supernatural beings. Jens Bjerre, *The Last Cannibals,* translated from the Danish by Estrid Bannister (New York, William Morrow, 1957), 123.

44   Mircea Eliade, *The Myth of the Eternal Return.* Translated from the French by Willard R. Trask. Bollingen Series XLVI (New York, Pantheon Books, 1954), 100-101.

45   Desiré Charney, *The Ancient Cities of the New World, Being Voyages and Explorations in Mexico and Central America from 1857-1882* (New York, Harper, 1887), 308.

46   Farb, *Indians of North America,* 97.

47   Campbell, *Hero with a Thousand Faces,* 309.

48   "Structure and Process in the Interpretation of South American Myth: The Arawak Dog Spirit People," 842-868 in *American Anthropologist,* v. 79. December 1977, 849.

49   Edward Sapir, *Selected Writings in Language, Culture and Personality* (Berkeley, California, University of California Press, 1949), 347. A believer who is convinced he has communicated with his god is not merely one who perceives new truths denied to his neighbor who has not communicated, but he is stronger than before. He senses more force within him, either to endure what he must endure or conquer what he does not have to endure. He feels him-self raised beyond the station of mere man for he has been saved from evil. Durkheim, *Elementary Forms of Religious Life,* 416.

50   Day, *Many Meanings of Myth,* 393. Universally, mythology teaches that "all things and beings are the effects of a ubiquitous power out of which they rise, which supports them ... during their period of manifestation, and back into which they must ultimately dissolve." Campbell, *Hero with a Thousand Faces,* 257.

51   Mircea Eliade, *The Sacred and the Profane. The Nature of Religion.* Translated from the French by Willard R. Trask (New York, Harper and Row, 1959), 95.

52   *Ibid.*, 95; Eliade, *Myths and Reality,* 5-6. See also Robin Clarke and Geoffrey Hindley, *Challenge of the Primitives* (New York, McGraw-Hill, 1975), 210. An excellent example is the Aymara Indians of lake Titicaca who have two myths of this kind. The first is the belief that the original settlers emerged from the lake itself which is, therefore, worshipped as a mother. The second is the belief that the first Inca and his sister-wife came from an island in Lake Titicaca, equipped with a golden wedge which would sink into the earth at a point designated by the Sun, their father. It so sank at Cuzco which was appropriately named for being the navel of the world. Weston La Barre, *Aymara Indians of the Lake Titicaca Plateau of Bolivia, 1-250 in American Anthropologist*, vol. 50, No. 1, Part 2, January, 1948.

53   Kevin B. Maxwell, *Bemba Myth and Ritual. The Impact of Literacy on an Oral Culture* (New York, Peter Lang, 1983), 48-49. "... to ask the Bemba for a time when Mumbi Mukasa came down from heaven is a senseless question. The mythical action is outside real time. It did not occur on a date in the past. It occurs continuously in the depths of the present community, where it maintains the link between the divine and the human world of the Bemba." *Ibid.*, 92.

54   *Conquest of Mexico*, I, 54. Also see Huxley, *Affable Savages*, 215.

55   Day, *Many Meanings of Myth*, 9.

56   *Ibid.*, 330.

57   *The Sacred and the Profane*, 36, 43. God's grace, or food and sustenance flows from an invisible point or source to "the point of entry being the center of the symbolic circle of the universe, the Immovable Spot .... around which the world may be said to revolve." Campbell, *Hero with a Thousand Faces*, 40-41. "The World Navel, then, is ubiquitous." *Ibid.*, 44.

58   Mircea Eliade, *Myths, Dreams and Mysteries. The Encounter between Contemporary Faiths and Archaic Realities.* Translated by Philip Mairet (New York, Harper & Brothers, 1960), 41, 43, 97.

59   Gerardo Reichel-Dolmatoff, *Amazonian Cosmos. The Sexual and Religious Symbolism of the Tukano Indians* (Chicago, University of Chicago Press, 1971), 41.

60   This belief was shared by the Cheyenne, the Winnebago, the Yakima and the Luiseno, a Shoshoean tribe in California. It was also quite similar to the religious beliefs of the Uitoto of Columbia in South America. *Literature of the American Indian*, edited by Sanders and Peek, 22, 36-37, 46-47, 60-62.

61   *Ibid.*, 27-29.

62   Clarke and Hindley, *Challenge of the Primitives*, 180-181.

63   Charles Wagley, *The Tentehara Indians of Brazil* (New York, AMS Press, 1969), 131.

64   G. W. B. Huntington, *Nandi of Kenya: Tribal Control in Pastoral Society* (London, Routledge and Kegan Paul, 1953), 124.

65   Elman R. Service, *A Profile of Primitive Culture* (New York, Harper, 1958), 61.

66   Firth, *Tikopia, Ritual and Belief*, 284.

67   *Andaman Islanders*, 193, 385, 398.

68   Paul Bohannan, *Africa and Africans*. Published for the American Museum of Natural History (Garden City, New York, Natural History Press, 1964), 222.

69   Erna Gunther, "Northwest Coast Art," 18-40 in *Anthropology and Art. Readings in Cross-Cultural Aesthetics*, edited by Charlotte M. Otten. Published for The American Museum of Natural History (Garden City, New York, Natural History Press, 1971), 324.

70   M. F. Ashley Montagu, *Anthropology and Human Nature* (Boston, Porter Sargent, 1957), 297; Marshall Sahlins, *Tribesman* (Prentice Hall, 1968), 103.

71   Philip H. Means, "The Incas: Empire Builders of the Andes," 225-264 in *National Geographic*, vol. LXXIII, No. 1, January, 1938, 251. See also *Travels of Piedro de Cieza de Leon*, First Part, 152.

72   *Tribesmen*, 18, 103.

73   Farb, *Indians of North America*, 107-108.

74   *The World of Primitive Man* (New York, Henry Schuman, 1953), 358.

75   The following is an excellent illustration of this generalization: "The Bemba are tenaciously terrestrial, and their vision of themselves — their life, their world and divinity — is determined by their earthly fixation. ... Satisfaction is not postponed to any other-worldly, future dimension. There is finality in this world now." Maxwell, *Bemba Myth and Ritual*, 22.

76   *Andaman Islanders*, 379, 385, 393.

77   Elsy Leuzinger, *Africa. The Art of the Negro Peoples* (New York, McGraw-Hill, 1960), 21. See also Lévi-Strauss, *Savage Mind*, 251.

78   Clarke and Hindley, *Challenge of the Primitives*, 205.

79   David Bidney, *Theoretical Anthropology* (New York, Columbia University Press, 1953), 292; Robert Lowie, *Selected Papers in Anthropology* (Berkeley, University of California Press, 1960), 342, 345.

80   Malinowski, *Magic, Science and Religion*, 146, Radcliffe-Brown, *Structure and Function in Primitive Society* (New York, Free Press, 1952), 144-145. See Malinowski's *Argonauts of the Western Pacific. An Account of Native Enterprise and Adventure in the Archipelagoes of Melanesia and New Guinea* (London, Routledge & Kegan, 1966), 303-304.

81   *Elementary Forms of Religious Life* (1915), 101.

82   "An Old Temple and a New Myth," 291-307 in *Djawa* (Weltevreden, Java), vol. XVII, 1937, 305-307.

83   Franz Boas, "The Mental Traits of Primitive Man," 404-412 in *Golden Age of American Anthropology*, edited by Mead and Bunzel, 411.

84   *Savage Mind*, 221.

85   W. H. R. Rivers, *Medicine, Magic and Religion* (New York, Harcourt-Brace, 1927), 4. Sir James George Frazer believed this accounted for the hostility of priests to magicians. To the former, the magician seems an impious man usurping the powers of God or, rather, one who pretends to do so. *The Golden Bough; a Study in Magic and Religion*, 12 vols. (New York, Macmillan, 1935), I, 226.

86   Driberg, *Savage as he really is*, 45-47; Cooper, "The Relations Between Religion and Morality in Primitive Cultures," *loc. cit.*, 561.

87   Huntingford, *Nandi*, 123, 130, 154.

88   Firth, *Primitive Economics of the New Zealand Maori* (New York, E.P. Dutton, 1929), 234, 242, 253, 266.

89   "Anthropological conceptions of religion: reflections on Geertz," 237-259 in *Man*, v. 18, No. 2, June 1983, 252.

Chapter IV

RITUAL:
Shaman, Sorcerer and Priest

*Everywhere elaborate rituals were
necessary: first, for the honest religious purpose
of placating and influencing the gods who were
responsible for the happenings or events in
nature; second, for the honest and public use of
magic, consisting of man's sacred objects, secret
formulas and incantations, for the purpose of
providing the community full insurance coverage
to ward off disaster, and, third, for the private
and dishonest purpose of black magic or sorcery.*

For the primitive the relationship between the shaman and the priest
was for the most part comparable to that between the prophet in the time of
Jesus and the priest, or members of a cult,[1] like the Pharisees[2] or the
Saducees.[3] After hearing of his performance of miracles, a *sine qua non* for
prophets of that age,[4] the priesthood demanded of Jesus that he show them
a sign of his favor from Heaven. In other words, they demanded a miracle
in their presence and not in that of the multitudes who came prepared to

believe. Jesus declined. However, as soon as he removed himself from the presence of unbelievers, his miracles began again.[5] This, along with the gift of prophecy, was known as the ecstatic factor. It made for the closest intimacy between God and man in the person of the prophet, or the messiah.

Of course, the generation of Jesus inherited this peculiarity from Old Testament prophets. One thinks of Isaiah who anticipated Jesus on several counts: that from the lineage of Jesse and David there shall come a messiah who in the spirit of the Lord shall usher in the Day of Judgment and, following that, Paradise, at least for the innocent. Wolves "shall dwell with the lamb and the leopard shall lie down with the kid... and a little child shall lead them."[6] For the Old Testament prophet, ecstasy appeared to be a combination of factors: first, the prophet suffered a physical seizure by Yahweh,[7] during which he uttered prophecies either in some strange tongue or in his own voice which had been wrenched out of him;[8] finally, there were a series of miracles, real or alleged, worked by these prophets. In Kings, Elisha raised a dead boy to life; Elijah had an inexhaustible cruze of holy oil, made a return from the land of the dead and a journey to Heaven; finally, when Elijah was carried off bodily to Heaven, the sons of fifty prophets stood at some distance and witnesssed the event.[9]

Such ecstatic feats, however, were virtually identical to those claimed by the primitive shaman, as will later become apparent. As one might expect, Hebrew prophets disparaged the magic worked by religious leaders of the East, contrasting this with the miracles they performed by the grace of Yahweh.[10] Yet, Max Weber tended to put all such seers in the category of charismatic magicians.[11] Religion could not attain a certain level of intensity without achieving a psychological state which was a near cousin of delirium. That was why prophets, founders of religion and saints -men whose religious consciousness can be regarded as exceptionally sensitive - betray signs of nervousness which border on the pathological.[12] Whether a particular shaman could achieve this exulted state himself or not, he knew that ecstasy was possible. It was that brief period when God and man were virtually one or where their spirits comingled. It was a state almost equivalent to a trance, where the "victim" was impervious to messages from without, even feeling no pain.[13] A state of true ecstasy followed the purposive annihilation of self by the mystic.[14]

Although this was certainly a common occurence among shaman, some authorities believed it not to be true of the Old Testament prophet. They concluded he had to be understandable to both the Hebrew king and the people. He was essentially an activist and not a passive receptacle as was the mystic. Further, the classical prophets did not seek ecstasy through either fasting or intoxication. It simply came to them.[15] Finally, the most obvious difference between the Old Testament prophet and the shaman was that the former's character had been institutionalized long before the time of Jesus. From the time of Amos, the prophet belonged to or issued from a society in which he had been taught the prophetic experience as an art form. From the time of Samuel, the prophet, like the priest, belonged in the sactuary and Samuel himself officiated at offerings. Jeremiah complained that both prophet and priest desecrated the house of Yahweh. Although, when inspired, prophets might appear singly in temples, they were more likely to appear in a body because they constituted a stable staff at each.[16] On the contrary, in the world of the primitive the shaman and the priest customarily - although not always - performed different kinds of roles in separate and distinctive societies.

With regard to the ritual of the primitive, we are concerned with five aspects: 1) the reasons for its origin and maintenance, 2) the process itself or the drama involved, 3) the contrast between the symbolic manipulators of ritual, the shaman and the priest, i.e., their source of authority, difference of function, why it was and is the shaman who must be the mystic, 4) how the chief hazard of the shaman's craft was the real or suspected danger that he could veer into the art of black magic, or witchcraft, the serpent in the Garden of Eden and 5) why agriculture was Janus-faced, i.e., while spiritually deeply wedded to the past through the practice of an elaborate and precise ritual by an organized priesthood, there was always the possibility that this leisure and learned class might discover new production techniques which rendered those precious rituals unnecessary and obsolete.

To understand the primacy of ritual for the primitive, one must first devote attention to the reasons for its origin, its usage and extent or range, including both magic and religion, to all aspects of tribal life.

Perhaps the best starting point for the origin of ritual was its usage among the Nandi in Kenya. They regarded nature primarily in terms of its utility, or non-utility, to man. Whatever was useful or necessary to his survival or comfort was recognized as having a practical or social value. It was because of this ritual value arose. The reason was simple enough. It was recognized that, apart from a sense of immediate well-being which was a direct consequence of its observance, ritual had to be repeated periodically in order not to break the invisible chain of prosperity which existed between this and the supernatural world.[17] A somewhat more philosophical explanation was that man celebrates rites not only to remain faithful to his past but as a way for the social group to reaffirm itself periodically.[18] Through the medium of poetry, it bathes itself in the sacred pool.[19] More than any other thing, it shows the interdependence of the gods and man. Gods cannot dispense with worshippers any more than the latter can with the gods themselves.[20]

Consider the primitive's cultural plight in the absence of ritual, like the Yucatan Indians, caught between the culture of two worlds. People no longer believe because they no longer understand. This occurs because they no longer do the things, like a rain dance, which shows one understands and believes. Rituals which involve prayers, both heard and recited, perform the same function. When one no longer performs such rituals, they become meaningless. One is left only with the fear of misfortune because the old and sacred ways have been abandoned.[21]

There was, unexpectedly, an element about the ritual of the primitive which reminds one of classical Greek philosophy and drama. By 1915, as Tom Urban pointed out, Durkheim had sounded the correct theme. Because ritual focuses upon common beliefs, traditions, ancestral memories and the collective idea of which they are the incarnation, the individual soul is regenerated by being immersed into this life source. He experiences the thrill of renewal, of spiritual regeneration, or a sense of being born again. It is in no way imaginary for he feels and acts stronger and more confidently.[22] But even more graphic was the analysis of Robin Horton. When attempting to define African ritual man, he might have been talking about Platonic thought. Ritual man was one who had a dependency upon pure existence or pure-act-of-being and who used ritual to try to overcome the inherent difficulty of expressing this dependence. It, ritual, represented an attempt to explain life on the empirical level by identifying the eternal principles that lie behind the so-called event world or the random flow of sense data or experience.[23] However, to others rituals provided primitives a sort of Aristotelian order in the universe by assigning every single existing thing a position within a category or a class.[24] On a non-intellectual level, ritual and ceremony were indispensable. They allowed the ordinary individual to grasp the emotional intensity of tribal sentiments and thus to transmit them from one generation to another.[25] Man is that paradoxical creature who does not know himself. He discovers who and what he is through the employment of ritual which depicts his ancestral image.[26]

One suspects that Irving Goldman captured the essence of much primitive drama when he described the Cubeo rituals of the Amazon river basin as studies in Dionysian frenzy. The central theme of all endeavors of this sort was deliberately calculated to dramatize the whole range of human emotions. The dance progressed from the calm to the frenzied, as the music went from a slow to an exciting tempo. The dancers were themselves transformed from sobriety to intoxication, from a state of dignity to one of sexual excitation. The drinking party, for example, satisfied all of these requirements. Intoxication itself was a sacred state, providing it was carefully stage-managed. It is not hard to imagine that as a result the entire community experienced a catharsis.[27]

The relationship between this frenzied primitive drama and those of the ancient Dionysian rites is dramatized by an examination of Euripides' *The Bacchae* of the late 5th century B.C. Greece. There the god Dionysus leads his ecstatic followers to revelry and dancing while feasting on the flesh of the slaughtered goat. The god's gift of prophecy is an integral part of this drama.[28] His cult experienced a revival about the time of the Persian invasions and even then the theme of human sacrifice persisted.[29] Originally, the catharsis referred to mysterious but beneficial effects, or those which came to the community after the death of a human *katharma* or *pharmakos*. Willingly or not, the victim acted as a surrogate sacrifice for the entire community. His death effaced the collective guilt, draining away any impurities.[30] The ritual and drama of the cult merged god and man because its belief system immortalized both. Finally, its principle attribute was violence because its patron saint taught that wisdom followed after, and because of, emotional excess.[31]

Think for a moment how closely Christian drama parallels this Dionysian scene. First, God and man truly merged in the person of Jesus. He was fully God but, at the same time in an irrational sense, fully man. Consequently, as all such heroes and gods, he had the gift of prophecy. In his case, it was the ability to see his own bloody demise and the traitors within his own ranks who would betray or deny him. His lingering, painful and bloody death on the cross would be enough to satisfy the blood lust of most Dionysian social orders. And what was the significance of this great sacrifice, willingly undertaken? It was for the purpose of effacing original sin or the act of wiping out the collective guilt of the entire community. Finally, because of pagan sin and guilt, Christian wisdom followed and triumphed. Ever since, his followers have, in the greatest ceremony of them all, been partaking of his flesh and blood. This supreme act of Western community catharsis has been for the past two thousand years at the beck and call of an established priesthood through ritual.

If an anthropologist took an objective look at those three varieties of the Dionysian drama, he would be hard put to certify that, on an ideological level, any one was inherently superior to the others. Subtract the elements of blood, suffering and sacrifice from all three and one has emasculated them. Only on the refine ments of the presentation do the Christians excel. And yet, our social order has both implicitly and explicitly asserted the superiority of Christian ritual and drama. Anthropologists have taken little trouble to deny it.

Ritual man was compounded from several elements and the most important of these were discernable. First, there was his fear of life's uncertainties. Second, his belief that the fortunes of the hunt were dependent upon supernatural will or favor. As a corollary of this grand design, the animals themselves might be wooed or seduced by ritual for man's needs. Third, his conviction that God paid as much attention to his people as they did to him. Ritual and ceremony enabled the primitive to obtain a certain tranquility through apparent mastery over the unknown which everywhere surrounded and menaced him.[32] Like the early Hebrews and their Covenant with God, the primitive struck a bargain with the Almighty. In return for man's daily piety and dutiful ceremonials, the supernatural would share his bounty, or goodness, from his vast store of things.

Thus, nature did not work independently of man as it did in a natural cause and effect theory. In Tikopia it depended upon a peculiar relationship between man and spiritual beings as maintained in ritual. From this flowed *manu*, or *mana*, or the gift of the gods which included excellent weather, ample game, good crops, and tribal welfare.[33] Among the Tsembaga of New Guinea, ritual regulated such mundane matters as the distribution of land, the frequency of intergroup fighting and the parcelling out of animal protein in the form of surplus pigs.[34] Likewise, the same thing appeared to be true of certain societies. Kund Rausmussen told a pertinent story about how the success or failure of the hunt altered the theological loyalty of the Eskimo. In the fall of 1907 he found them purely pagan, but the next year he was surprised to discover they had converted to a curious form of Christianity. This was due to a partly Christianized Eskimo whose prayers appeared much more effective in bringing caribous within the hunter's range. Later, when the new prayers declined in productivity, Eskimos reverted to the old faith.[35]

Two kindred explanations of such a unique event, both plausible, can be advanced. With the Waswanipi Cree, who hunted moose, there was a god, or a master moose, whose good will must be secured if there were to be a successful hunt.[36] The North Alaskan Eskimo believed the animals themselves might be attracted within the hunter's range by proper ritual and ceremony. On the other hand, the spirits of the animal might be repulsed because of the lack of proper respect.[37] No Bushman ever bagged an eland without later formally thanking it by means of a dance.[38]

When, therefore, in the late eighteenth century a cleric observed that everything the Yumanguis (of the interior highlands of Northern Luzon) did was accompanied by ritual,[39] he unconsciously hit upon a universal truth. Perhaps no one has better captured primitive reasons for a dedication to ritual than an American GI writing about the "backward" Montagnards in the highlands of Vietnam. Through their sacrificial ceremonies and food offerings to the gods, they were merely keeping their insurance up-to-date. To avoid misfortune at the village and earthly level, they had to keep the spirits well-fed and well-disposed towards them.[40]

There is also another intriguing aspect about ritual, or the magic quality of ritual in and by itself. Economists may have been the first to understand that to an economic endeavor a secondary aspect of religious and/or magical proportions was often added.[41] No illustration served better than canoe-making in the Central and Western Pacific. In the Polynesian island of Tikopia even the essential tools were dedicated to the gods. In both Hawaii and the Trobriand islands no canoe was fabricated without ritual, ceremony and magical rite from start to finish. The reason was simple. To the natives, magic, both in the ritual itself and the words used, must be coupled with the mechanical operations if there were to be any hope of ultimate success in the fabrication and use of the object.[42] In much the same fashion the American Indian artist believed the design itself on functional weapons or tools was the cause of favorable outcomes. The supreme example of the belief in the efficacy of ritual *per se* was noted of the Hupa Indians in California when they recited a mythical formula of a traditional acorn god who controlled all vegetable food. The words themselves were judged more powerful than those of any herb. The words used in the ceremony were not prayers to some deity who had the power to assist if properly approached, but rather a description of a former cure. Magic entered because it was believed that the mere repeating of the account carried the power to heal as often as it was used. It was the exact sequence, the wearying repetition and the incredible wealth of images which were designed to overwhelm the senses or subdue the intellect. It was this intricate pattern which constituted the magic of the ritual.[43]

It is equally fascinating to realize how religion, warfare and economic activity were all bound up together. The chief stimulus of canoe-making in Eddystone Island of the Solomons originated from the impulse to go head-hunting. When the tribe wanted to ask the blessing of the gods on some special undertaking, they had in turn to propitiate the ancestral ghosts by presenting them with new heads from an enemy. This in turn demanded the fabrication of a new war canoe which might engross tribal energies for many months, if not years. Meanwhile, ceremonial feasts leading up to the great event stimulated horticulture and pig breeding.[44]

Our next consideration is the very process of ritual or the drama itself. This deals with such matters as when, under what conditions, where, how long and by whom, and how the major roles are played. Answers to these queries give insight into what might be termed the behavioral connection with cosmology. Those who controlled this facet of symbolic manipulation of the universe, were persons of power. Invariably they were the old men of the tribe. Yet the pervasive mythology among Brazilian tribes was that there had been a time when women dominated ceremonial life. Finally, the men revolted, took charge of the sacred paraphernalia and thus became the dominant sex.[45]

It would appear that, by assigning himself the sole custody of the sacred, mysterious and dangerous, or the supernatural, primitive man maintained and reinforced masculine domination. First women and children were excluded from such ceremonies on the ground that the sacred was intrinsically dangerous to them.[46] A brotherhood, purified only by abstaining from sexual relations, was in charge of ritual and ceremony.[47]

According to the interpretation of Edward Sapir, this was an affair which involved the safety and happiness of the tribe.[48] It appears more likely that, as my co-author insisted, Sapir brought with him the assumption of masculine superiority. He was thus willing to accept as fact whatever he was told by the village elders, all of whom were males.

However, if this were a charade, it was well-acted everywhere. Two examples probably suffice. Chiefly by reliance upon communal song and dance, the ceremonies were carefully orchestrated to bring great emotional tension by establishing contact with the supernatural world. Take for example the magic dances devised to protect women and children among the Piaroas on the right bank of the Orinoco. In a region where it was universally believed that a woman would die were she to see a sacred mask, both women and children were naturally exiled from the ceremonies specifically designed to excise demons from a newly-built home. The magic instrument in this case was the plummage from beautiful birds and each man had to provide as many plumes as he had women and children. The danger, of course, was greatest at the moment when the shaman had to force the demons either to enter his magical instruments, such as drums made from the skin of an enemy or flutes of human hands and thigh bones, or himself, in order to conquer them.[49]

Consider the solemn preparations for such sacred ceremonies as the rain dance among the Pueblos which was generally held in mid-July and might last from four to twelve days. Fasting and sex continence prior to the exercises were not only required of the priests but of those lay persons who opted to assist them. At the Isleta settlement the sacred rites lasted twelve days and on the last night the public, including women, might attend. However, the latter seldom came because they were afraid of the thunder and lightning which invariably appeared in the show. Sexual continence was also required of the participants for four days following the conclusion of the holy spectacle.[50] Sex and the sacred were everywhere carefully segregated. This may have been, as my co-author observed, to show that men could do without women, and thus keep them in their place.

The apex of these ceremonies, or the most spectacular and complete, occurred at the gatherings of the larger kinship or intermarriage group. These places and times were determined by nature. In Australia, the meetings, which put a great strain upon the ecology, had to take place at those spots especially favored by nature with regard to food and water. Such places were swamps, lily lagoons and rivers where fish and game were abundant. Even then, the meetings might not be held annually because they could quickly mine out the territory of its natural resources. Furthermore, they had to occur at a time when the tribe was at rest or between economically productive efforts.[51] It was the new mobility provided by the horse which made it possible for the Plains Indians to congregate in one location in order to hold a week long Sun Dance.[52] A typical example of such festivities occurred recently in New Guinea at Kuaas which was attended by, among others, those who had a thirteen hour walk from Ubaigubi. All gathered for a three-week ceremonial cluster of events which might be given only once every five or ten years. As one of the many features, marriages were performed for which the parties were previously contracted.[53] However, perhaps the classic account of such ceremonies, both for the time span involved and the wealth of detail given it, was that of Baldwin Spencer and F. J. Gillen of the Arunta tribes at Alice Springs in Central Australia in the summer of 1896. Participants came from as much as 200 miles away for the sacred rites, such as the fire ceremony, and courtship and marriage rituals. These truly spectacular events apparently lasted an incredible three months, even though the participants seemed exhausted after the first ten days.[54]

These symbolic manipulators of the world of the primitive fell into two distinct categories, shamans and priests. As a product of loosely-organized food gatherers, the shaman, called by supernatural agencies, was a maker of myth. A medium for dissociational experience, he specialized in ecstatic alteration of consciousness. The priest, a product of well-organized agriculture, was merely a steward or caretaker. He specialized in ritual or the detailed pedagogical indoctrination and theological structure he inherited from previous generations. Instead of supernatural origins, his position was often hereditary, designed by the family, or chosen as one opts for a career. "The individualistic religious experience of the shaman will constantly erupt, exposing the staid, conservative, entrenched priesthood."[55]

A study of their contrasting roles reveals how and why it was agricultural orders developed ritual in a most elaborate, yet precise form or formula, as well as its school of disciplined priests which perpetuated it without change. However, and at the same time, their earthly needs gave rise to the science of astronomy, mathematics and the calendar, the very factors which ultimately led to civilization and a displacement of the primitive. Finally, the rise of technology, dependent on science, appeared to lessen reliance on the symbolic manipulation of the universe through ritual.

Hunting and gathering tribes tended to consume almost as much food per day as they produced and thus had no surplus from which to support a priestly class. That is why their artists and shaman, or medicine men, pursued these crafts in addition to their regular tribal duties. This probably explained the fact that, although a good deal of time was spent by hunters in assuaging the gods, supernaturalism was poorly defined and their religious edifice badly structured.[56] Finally, and somewhat paradoxically, a society of hunter-gatherers generated greater tribal self-confidence and optimism about the world than obtained in purely agricultural economies. A farmer might experience the work of many months swept away in a matter of hours by adverse weather or pests, whereas what the hunter lost today he could bag tomorrow. Consequently, hunters had little fear of angry gods who had their egos bruised by man. They appeared free of the neuroses possessed by technologically more advanced societies.[57]

As a class or category nothing helps us define the shaman or medicine man better and with more clarity than by way of contrast with two rivals. First, was his inter-tribal struggle with the sorcerer, the alleged practitioner of black magic or the art of destruction. Second, his sharp role divergence when compared with that of the priest in a settled agricultural community.

Nevertheless, certain assumptions have to be made explicit at this point. The first of these was that belief in the shaman rested on a prior belief in witchcraft. This theory of behavior seemed particularly appropriate for primitive social orders. Jealousy and ambiguity were the foundation stones for the belief in witchcraft in such societies. Even kinsmen and close neighbors could, working through mystical means, effect much supernatural harm. "What did X mean by that statement? Did he mean what he said or the direct opposite of it?" In such small-scale societies a single troubled relationship could affect a great many areas of an individual's life.[58]

We have a plausible explanation for the universal belief in the powers of the shaman. Those gods who created man were believed not normally to interfere with tribal events unless some male ritualist or shaman specifically put the request to them. Of course the primary function of the shaman was to prevent or mitigate natural disasters adversely affecting the tribe.[59] The shaman had the role as supreme mediator between the present-day and the ancestral past and between secular and ritual times in contemporary society.[60] Man's specific approach of the supernatural could take two forms. In the case of the Tlingit Indians of Alaska the shaman's powers were assumed to be the result of impersonal and supernatural forces which came to him while he was in a trance.[61] With the Sioux they were thought to be the end product of a supernatural parent responding to the pleas of a solitary and earthly child for warm and personal ties.[62]

Quite naturally, the post was everywhere highly honorific, being regarded as the noblest occupation of them all. This was certainly true of the

Tapirapé society of central Brazil.[63] In the Blackfoot tribe of the Great Plains every member had attempted, at one time or another, to practice the craft.[64] Among the tribes of the Northwest Coast of American and Siberia, the purely spiritual aspect of the post was emphasized when those who scorned to become warriors and husbands were recognized as shamans.[65] Even those among them who were married abstained from sex relations when seeking supernatural inspiration because they found it interfered with their dreams of the spirit world.[66]

While the Chukchee of Northern Siberia did not exclude women as shaman, indeed the majority were, they nevertheless occupied the lower grades of that art. The highest ranks were reserved for males.[67] In South America females who were shamans were invariably old women who had already passed the period of child-bearing and thus were virtually regarded as impotent old men. Nevertheless, females had to undergo a greater trial to attain the status of shaman than did male rivals.[68] Tribes like the Igorots in the interior of Luzon also allowed women to serve as shaman or priestess as did the Bogobo of Mindanao.[69] By and large, however, the primitive shaman in the hunting and gathering tribe was of the masculine gender.

Since, unlike the priest, the shaman was never a part of a school system, often being without any instruction whatever, his religious calling and performance was most often an individual one.[70] There were shamans before priests, if not the gods themselves.[71] Nevertheless, there were certain primitive social orders where the shamans surrendered freedom for membership in an organized group which directed rites in the healing arts, like the False Face Society of the Iroquois.[72]

The great majority of anthropologists conceded that these seers were, by and large, sincere and dedicated men. If at times they doubted their own powers, they did not doubt the existence of such delegated supernatural powers.[73] Among the Northern tribes of Central Australia, for example, the function of the shaman everywhere, with only one exception, was to withdraw evil magic and not to give rise to it.[74]

The peculiar position of the primitive shaman was that these physical weaklings and social perverts, or those at the bottom of the ash heap of hunter-gatherer societies, were at the same time depended upon to save the tribe because of their monopoly of access to supernatural powers.[75]

Such knowledge may make more meaningful the contrast between the source of the powers of priest and shaman. Those of the priest rest upon his esoteric knowledge and it is because of this that he may make uncontested claims to be the keeper and demonstrator of rituals. On the contrary, the primitive conception of the shaman is one who is essentially dependent upon some supernatural power. As a consequence, it is not the priest who has to resort to trances and mystic poses but the shaman who cannot depend upon an established ritual - like the formula of the Mass - to effect the desired contact.[76]

Mystics have a contempt for sensed space and historical time. They feel that in a moment of ecstasy, or communion with the Divine, they may glimpse ultimate and permanent truths which transcend history and the empirical realm of sensed experience. Therefore, the mystic lives either in a fierce longing for the moment of ecstasy or in complete absorption in its precious recollection.[77] This shamanistic trance is spontaneous and is an organic phenomenon in which the subject is believed to have passed beyond the human condition and thus to partake of the condition of spirits. It is that aspect of mysticism which prompts the charge by some that the condition itself borders on madness.[78] Old Testament prophets elicited the same criticism.[79]

Nevertheless, one of the most fascinating aspects about the shaman was that Western experts have concluded they had what amounted to extra-sensory powers. This is a peculiar but fascinating phenomenon. Unlike Western man, the Australian aborigine made no sharp distinction between dreams and reality. This meant that to qualify as a shaman one's dreams and spiritual experiences had to possess a special visionary quality. Above all, the shaman had to demonstrate hypnotic and telepathic powers of communication. After much study, Professor A. P. Elkin, Australia's leading specialist on native cults, concluded that shamans have what amounted to a sixth sense. Many times he saw a shaman go into a trance and give minute - and later confirmed - descriptions on what his tribesman were doing on the other side of the hill. When pressed for an explanation, the shaman would merely say that his spirit left him and wandered over the hill while his body remained in a trance.[80] Recently, an ethnologist subjected the testimonials of Western explorers to the extra-sensory powers of the shaman on a global level and concluded that they were real. For example, W. Bogoras made disk records of the voices of spirits and shamans, previously written off as the product of ventriloquism. This now seems improbable because the voices obviously came from a source far removed from the apparatus in front of the shaman. The problem belongs to parapsychology.[81]

Since in primitive or archaic societies the shaman is above all a specialist in ecstasy, it is precisely this ability to pass out of his body and undertake mystical journeys through cosmic regions that underscores the fact that he is a director and healer of souls as well as a visionary and mystic. Only the shaman is able to pursue the wandering soul of a sick person, capture it, and return it intact to the human body. He also accompanies the souls of the dead to their new dwelling place, or journeys to Heaven on missions of piety and mercy. They claim the ability to fly like birds, either mounted on horses or astride their sacred drums.[82] From Central Asia it has been reported by white explorers that, relying upon supernatural powers, shaman divest themselves of flesh and blood until nothing remains but their skeleton. Then, in the sacred language of the shaman, they proceed to identify every bone in their body. This ritual is undertaken both for the purpose of sidestepping time and the contemplation of the eternal source of life.[83] Other feats of magic are harder to deny. Their exploits with fire, either by holding it in their mouths for a period or walking on heated coals without damage to human tissue, is well known.[84] But it is the experiments not with fire but ice which most fascinates us. In the Indo-Tibetan initiatory ordeal, sheets are plunged into icy water. Each candidate must wrap himself with one, drying it with the heat of his own body. As soon as the sheet is dried, it is dipped into the water again and placed on the body. Finally, the boy who has dried the most sheets is declared the winner. However, it is the ordeal for the Eskimo shaman which must puzzle all Western observers. There he must spend five days in icy water and emerge without getting his garments wet.[85]

We are left with the sobering thought that the shaman was the historic ancestor of our contemporary philosophers and poets. That bridge was afforded by his techniques for ecstatic departures from the body, soul-levitation, soul-transmigration and celestial navigation.[86] It was precisely the shaman's insistence on the mastery of the mind over the body which provided the lure to many modern men of exceptional perception and competence.

The shaman's constant preoccupation with the realm of magic and mystery naturally culminated in his most controversial role, and that was as physician and healer of the sick.[87] This task compounded the awe and fear with which he was already regarded by the little community.[88] Here, too, the shaman was in clear confrontation with both the sorcerer and the priest or medical missionary. Members of certain California tribes only needed the medical services of a shaman because another shaman, or sorcerer, had placed a curse in the first instance.[89] And the fees, both before and after the healing, as well as the onerous taboos imposed by the shaman upon the patient and his family, made him particularly vulnerable later when the Christian medical missionary dispensed these same services without immediate monetary payment.[90]

This man of unusual talent and good intentions became the center of an epic struggle between good and evil, like that of the Faustian theme in the modern West. The power of the shaman, which rests upon his ability to manipulate the supernatural, must be used exclusively for the public or community good. The failure to do so may cause him to degenerate into a sorcerer or a practitioner of black magic.[91] We know something of the origin of this perpetual struggle between good and evil, at least as far as Africa was concerned. Most native religions there rested upon the postulate that human beings would live eternally in health and happiness were it not for the presence of evil.[92] Presumably, this was manifested in the form of lust, greed, envy and jealousy. The same was thought to be true concerning the tribes of Central Australia. Further, any native, armed with the proper stick or bone, could pronounce a workable curse upon a foe, beginning with the comparatively mild wish that his heart might be split in two.[93] In the Andaman Islands the spirits of the dead were believed responsible for causing sickness and death. However, since it was possible for the shaman to be on friendly terms with these spirits, he was ultimately responsible.[94]

Evil was the serpent in the Garden of Eden of the primitive. Motives of personal envy and jealousy were attributed to those resorting to the practice of black magic in Tikopia.[95] A sorcerer's curse in New Guinea heaped as much misery and pain upon its victim as did a bishop's pronouncement of excommunication and anathema in the Middle Ages.[96] The description of Navajo sorcery reads like that of a text on voodooism in the West Indies.[97]

Almost universally, therefore, when a member of a society suddenly fell ill or died, the survivors immediately assumed that one of their neighbors had resorted to the evil eye of sorcery. It had all the dramatic aspects of Reverend Cotton Mather's struggle to drive out demons from innocent adolescent girls in the Salem witchcraft episode of the late seventeenth century.[98] At Kedah on the Malay peninsula at the beginning of the twentieth century there was an apparent impromptu but successful exorcism of demons from a woman in a dense forest.[99] And, like Salem, the center of the primitive drama was the theory that the Devil had human confederates and that these might be apprehended.[100] Of the Nigerian head-hunters, it was reported that, since they assume all deaths are due to black magic, it makes sense that, when one gets seriously ill, his family and friends immediately set out to find the guilty party.[101] In the late Sixties in New Guinea, Malcom Kirk witnessed the mysterious but incredible effect that sorcery had upon its believers. Two hours after a victim of a curse predicted his own death, when there was seemingly nothing wrong with him, the man was dead. His companions, like the victim himself, stoically accepted sorcery as the cause and were convinced that the offender would be discovered and the death of their friend avenged.[102] From Melanesia, evidence for the same phenomena was overwhelming. If a native believed that an enemy had succeeded in casting a spell upon him, he would sicken and die within a few hours or days.[103] In Southwestern United States, the Navajo Indian apparently believed that the victim died within four days of the ceremonial curse.[104] Sometimes the "guilty" person was discovered and punished. Among the Didinga, a young girl was victimized by a sorcerer. He was later detected, tried before the village council, condemned and stoned to death by the multitude.[105]

Quite naturally, as the open repository of supernatural powers, the shaman himself was often suspect number one. Among the Tapirapé of Central Brazil, ten shamans in a forty-year period were killed in revenge by relatives of the supposedly cursed victims.[106] During Charles Wagley's second visit to the Tentehara Indians in Brazil, he and his party were convinced that they had spotted a minority of Elmer Gantrys among the shamans or those who had become morally perverted by success and power.[107]

As for agriculture, dependence upon it increased the emphasis upon ritual and ceremony because the tribe was held hostage by the gods from the time of the seeding of the grain to its harvesting and storage. The proper apportionment of sun and rain was just one of the many crucial elements needed from time to time and natural or supernatural catastrophes could come in many forms. However, the foundation stone for ritual among agricultural peoples was the general belief that rain could be induced or stopped by the application of magic.[108] In addition to an elaborate ritual devised to honor earth gods, agriculture originated mathematics and astronomy necessary for an accurate calendar and the prediction of seasonal variations. This required the creation of a special class, or priesthood, exempt from ordinary toil.[109]

Because the early Mayas were farmers, they became interested in the phenomena of time, the passing of the seasons. They needed to know the proper times in which to fell the forest, to burn the leaves and wood, and to plant the corn and harvest it. These needs were so vital that in the first millenium before Christ the priests turned their attention to the measurement of time and the study of astronomy. One of the most amazing things to eventuate was their use of the abstract mathematical quality of zero, not to be found in nature.[110] Among the most admirable of achievements by Maya priests was an amazingly accurate plot of long-time movements by the planet Venus and uncanny predictions of solar eclipses. Even when the predicted eclipse could not be viewed by the Maya themselves, it could in every instance be seen somewhere in the world. This achievement was all the more remarkable because in Maya country clear observations of the heavens was a rarity. In addition to a sacred calendar of 260 days, they had a 365-day secular one. This was divided into eighteen months of twenty days each, plus a five-day unlucky spill-over. This eventuated in an amazing calendar precision with the mistake of only a minute a year, or two and a half days in almost 3,900 years.[111]

In ancient Mexico belief and ritual rested entirely upon the requirements of a primitive agriculture. Abundant rain was an imperative in an arid climate and the gods had constantly to be invoked for this happy occasion to come to pass.[112] In one of the principal temples in Mexico City there were five thousand priests with highly diversified duties. Some had the management of choirs while others arranged festivals according to the calendar. Still others superintended the education of the young or had charge of hieroglyphical paintings and oral traditions.[113] Only the highest category of priests participated in human sacrifices. They used the same calendar system as the Mayas. The discovery in 1790 of the Aztec Stone of the Fifth Sun and the 260-day divinity calendar gave typical evidence of priestly contributions with regard to the intricate relationship between and among cosmology, astronomy, mathematics and the calendar. A fixed catastrophic date re-occurred every fifty-two years, or every century, according to the Stone. Priestly sacrifices could avert disaster.[114] Unfortunately, the traditional archives of written materials were ordered destroyed by the ruler Izccatl in the mid-fifteenth century. This may have been done to preserve the monopolistic power of the priesthood.[115]

The Incas possessed as complex a priestly ritual and ceremony as existed anywhere in the world. This too was rooted in agricultural necessities.[116] From the use of instruments like sun dials and groups of properly-positioned towers they learned to measure time almost as accurately as we do. Learned men understood the sun's position at times of equinoxes and solstices.[117] Lacking the compass, and deprived of a knowledge of the North Star because they were in the Southern hemisphere, the Incas, nevertheless, amazed Hiram Bingham with their practical application of astronomy and mathematics. This was displayed in the precision of the lay-out of the town of Ilacta in Palcay, discovered in 1912.[118] With regard to the calendar they divided the year into twelve quilla or moons of thirty days each and a five-day period was added to achieve the proper 365 days. A rule for adding a day every fifth year kept the calendar correct.[119]

As a way of life agriculture proved a constant source of concern for both religion and magic. Their daily employment in its behalf is easy to comprehend. In old Hawaii the appropriate priestly ceremonials accompanied all phases of the process from the breaking of the soil to the harvesting of the crops and the subsequent thanksgiving to the gods.[120] One authority analyzed the response of the Didinga tribe on the East Sudan and Uganda border, a hill people, possessing a mixed pastoral and agricultural economy. The Didinga farmer knew when to start cultivating. He had a good knowledge of soils and climate. He also understood how to match the needed crops with appropriate soils and had the necessary tools to dig. But he was also realistic enough to know that there were mysterious forces beyond his control. In agriculture, life was dicey. Rather than expose himself to these unknown forces, the agriculturalist devised magical rites for every seasonal operation and each was intended to combat chance disaster and hold it at bay.[121] Before spring planting in Mindanao by the Bagobo, people religiously set aside sacred food before the altar of the gods in the rice fields so that they would grant a bountiful harvest.[122] The agricultural operations themselves, from planting to harvesting, and the annual revival of plant and herd life, supplied a more central and meaningful focus for religious beliefs than had heretofore existed.[123] The Navajo believed that nature, and the mysterious forces behind it, was more responsible for the production of foodstuffs than man himself. That perspective enables one to understand why their priesthood was designed to try to influence nature by virtue of song and story.[124]

On the other hand it is not surprising to find that among the Siriono, primarily hunter-gatherers who also practice some agriculture in a daily preoccupation for survival, there are no magical practices connected with tilling top soil and harvesting the crops.[125]

Contrary to the individualistic style and inspiration of the shaman found in smaller and mobile cultures like hunters and nomads, agrarian societies produced priests who were disciplined members of an authoritarian and esoteric cult. Indian North America provided some representative cases. Among the Menomini priesthood in the Great Lakes region, it was a most difficult task to memorize the highly complicated and meaningless train of syllables used in sacred song.[126] The Western Pueblo technique for influencing the gods—the movers of the world—required the priests to memorize a staggering amount of word-perfect ritual.[127] The shepherd Navajos borrowed much ceremonial content or ritual from the Pueblos without all the accompanying pomp and ceremony.[128] Their ritual poetry stressed great numbers of repetitions in unpredictable sequences.[129] Pueblo ritual has been described as a Catholic mass. The individual himself is helpless to understand this depersonalized and cosmic drama unless he surrenders his intellect and, indeed, his very being to mystical tribal traditions. One feels truth, or its pervasive qualities, rather than intellectualizing it.[130]

Finally, when and where Western man's technology, rationality and cause-effect theory have inundated or taken over a once primitive agricultural economy, tremendously enhancing man's feeling of control over events in nature, one might legitimately expect less attention by natives to magic and rite. This was true of the Maori of New Zealand.[131] As a matter of fact, there was some evidence that technology itself, non-Western that is, brought about a decline of ritual. In the wet rice culture of the Tanala of Madagascar there were no rituals to make the rice grow. Irrigation farming terminated a dependence on nature and nature's gods to make it rain at the proper time. Since man controlled the water supply, and apportioned it himself throughout the year, he had no practical need of appealing to the gods to perform that function. Man's acceptance of a natural cause and effect theory would appear to be responsible for the fact that there were no longer any rain rituals in that culture.[132]

To summarize, all three, shaman, sorcerer and priest resorted to ritual out of necessity. It was the only way to contact the spirit world whose aid and assistance were necessary if the tribe or people were to survive and prosper. Only that of the priest, however, was formalized and predictable. As a moral entrepreneur, the shaman had to resort to trances, mysticism and ecstasy, including elements of both prophecy and miracles, to achieve the sought-for union with the Divine. In that respect, he was like the prophets of the Old Testament. Oftentimes the tribal rites inspired by the shaman were reminiscent of the god-man Dionysian rites of the sixth and fifth century B.C. Greece. These exulted emotional excesses as the mother of community catharsis or as the fount of wisdom. Significantly, these rites anticipated the Christian belief that the sacrificial victim, whether willing or unwilling, could expiate the guilt of an entire community. Primitive cultures often shared the same belief in the efficacy of sacrifice, whether that of the lower animals or human beings.

Whatever the purpose, ritual was performed with community good in mind and the failure to do so was to flirt with witchcraft or sorcery. Real or alleged, there never was any shortage of this in hunter-gatherer societies because of the wide-spread assumption that there would be no disease or death unless for the intercession of Evil. "Good" shaman were resorted to in order to allay the mortal spell put upon the victim by a "bad" one. Thus, the natural vocation of the shaman was a healer of the sick and infirm. It is no wonder that his sound herbal remedies got entangled with religion and magic. He was both physician and faith healer, prone to use whatever would work in a particular situation. For his mistakes, he sometimes paid with his life. This was because his society rejected the concept of natural cause and effect. Fate had been determined in a supernatural sense and he had been in touch with those powers. More importantly, he failed. On purpose?

On the contrary, priestly classes emerged in sedentary - or agricultural - communities; these had amassed enough surplus or wealth to allow this minority exemption from common labor in order to normalize the relationship with the Divine. Once leisured, they could, under strict discipline, develop the mathematics and astronomy necessary for an accurate calendar and the prediction of seasonal variations. As custodians of the esoteric and sacred, their prayers for rain at appropriate times merely reinforced community beliefs in priestly ability to arrange for supernatural intervention for happy outcomes. Ultimately, of course, the danger was that their education and technological efficiency would result in dams or irrigation projects which would ensure the sufficiency of water the year around. This would obviate the need for rain dances. Ritual, once abandoned, corroded the culture. One no longer performed but was left with the fear of misfortune because the old and sacred ways had been neglected.

Ritual seems no less important in modern times. Even in modern, secular and hierarchial societies, i.e., mental hospitals, the universal concept of self is a fragile thing, dependent upon ritual and ceremony to restore its self-image.[133]

Whether, therefore, one discourses about characters in the Old or New Testament, those of 6th century B.C. Athens, primitive, or modern man, the one thing that unites all is ritual man. He can only be explained to us in terms of Platonic thought. Ritual man represented an attempt to explain life on the every day level - the changing world - by identifying the eternal or true principles that lie behind the so-called event world or the random flow of sense data or experience.[134] If more clarity is desired, let us say that it requires ritual man to accept as historical fact that Jesus turned water into wine and at the miracle of the Mass, wine is "really" converted into the blood of Christ.

The next two chapters are devoted to an analysis of puberty rites of both male and female because the recognition of the coming of age - sexual age or the rite of passage - was a universal primitive preoccupation. It also represented the quintessence of primitive man as a creature wholly bound up in the act of ritual.

Footnotes

1   The priesthood was characterized by cultic centers and the apparatus of learning centers. There was no priesthood without a cult. Max Weber, *The Sociology of Religion.* Translated by Ephraim Fischoff. Introduction by Talcott Parsons (Boston, Beacon Press, 1963), 28-30.

2   Stemming from the old Hassidic movement, the principle characteristic of the Pharisses was the most rigid Levitical purity, or the insistence on the separation of self from "impure" persons and objects. Philosophical speculation was dangerous and quite Hellenistic or foreign to the "good" or orthodox Jew. Everything must be tithed in accordance with the priestly law. They looked for a messiah and believed in the resurrection of the dead. Its appeal was primarily to civil servants, especially the petty bourgeoisie rooted there. Max Weber, *Ancient Judaism.* Translated and edited by Hans H. Gerth and Don Martindale (Glencoe, Illinois, The Free Press, 1952), 386-390. Modern Jewish Orthodoxy stemmed from the Pharisees. Weston La Barre, *The Ghost Dance.* 581-582.

3   Its sophisticated doctrines appealed to patrician aristocrats and other worldly men. It believed neither in the immortality of the soul nor rewards and punishments after death. It rejected the doctrines of Davidic messiah as contrary to the Torah. Resurrection was discarded for the same reason. There were neither angels nor spirits. Fate had no influence and God might not be blamed for the actions of free men. Saducees were entrenched in the Temple until 50-60 A.D. when the reactionary Pharisees wrenched power from them. They were the legitimate ancestors of reformed Jewry. La Barre, *Ghost Dance,* 580-582, 605. See also Weber, *Ancient Judaism,* 387-389.

4   Weber, *Sociology of Religion,* 47.

5   Matthew 16 in *The Holy Bible.* Revised Standard Version Containing the Old and New Testament (New York, Thomas Nelson and Sons, 1952), New Testament, 19.

6   Isaiah 11, *ibid.,* Old Testament 720.

7   The prophet Jeremiah felt raped by God, as a maiden by a man, or overpowered, as in a wrestling match. Weber, *Ancient Judaism,* 312-313. Ecstasy in the Old Testament, especially with regard to prophecy, was indicated by the use of the phrase,"and the spirit of the Lord (Yahweh) came upon him." *The New Schall-Herzog Encyclopedia of Religious Knowledge,* 12 vols., edited by Samuel Macauley Jackson (New York, Funk and Wagnal, 1909), IV, 71.

8   "In the ecstatic state it might consist of mere exclamations, a fact which shows the tense feeling had gained all mastery: all control of self had gone." Johs. Pedersen, *Israel. Its Life and Culture* (London, Oxford University Press, 1963),, 2 vols., II, 117. In the time of Hosea and Jeremiah, prophets were frequently charged with being "mad." *Ibid.,* 111.

9   Pedersen, *Israel,* vol. II, 109, 118, 119. Likewise, the prophet could see people far away and understand distant talk. He could behold far-off events and, in a more practical manner, see the coming of rain. *Ibid.,* 119.

10   Weber, *Ancient Judaism,* 222.

11 *Sociology of Religion*, 47.

12 Durkheim, *Elementary Forms of Religious Life*, 226.

13 Rudolph Otto, *The Idea of the Holy. An Inquiry into the non-rational factor in the idea of the divine and its relation to the rational*. Translated by John W. Harvey (London, Oxford University Press, 1946), 31-34.

14 *Ibid.*, 21.

15 Weber, *Ancient Judaism*, 108, 289, 291. See also Pederson, *Israel*, vol. 2, 127, 133-134, 136, 138.

16 Pedersen, *Israel*, vol. 2, 108, 115-117.

17 Huntingford, *Nandi*, 127-128. Phrased quite differently, but meaning the same, is the following observation: "God pays as much attention to people as people do to Him." Sahlins, *Tribesmen*, 105. Ritual perpetuated this sense of well-being by keeping everything in stasis or, failing that, holding any tribal change to an absolute minimum. Order, peace and fecundity were all threatened by change which was interpreted as disorder. Girard, *Violence and the Sacred*, 49, 120, 284.

18 Emilé Durkheim, *The Elementary Forms of the Religious Life*. Translated from the French by Joseph Ward Swain. (New York, Free Press, 1915. George Allen & Unwin Ltd.), 415, 432. This is an earlier edition of the same work used throughout this book. However, page numbers seem not to correspond.

19 *Ibid.*, 427.

20 *Ibid.*, 389.

21 Robert Redfield, *The Folk Culture of Yucatan* (Chicago, University of Chicago Press, 1942), 363-364. Girard thought this fear not displaced. When men abandon ritual and violate its injunctions, they invoke transcendental violence and are plunged again into a Hobbesian state of nature, or a perpetual war of man against his neighbors. *Violence and the Sacred*, 259.

22 *The Elementary Forms of Religious Life* (1915), 390. Also see Turner, *The Ritual Process, Structure and Anti-Structure*, 138, 203; Wolf, *Anthropology*, 84.

23 "Ritual Man in Africa," 651-673 in *Readings in Anthropology*, 2 vols., edited by Fried, *Cultural Anthropology*, II, 661-664. Using different images, Jamake Highwater came to the same conclusion. For the primal mind, reality or truth itself did not lie in the outward manifestations of the every-day world. Rather it resided in great cosmic forces working great events in nature, which then gave rise to myth, repeated in ritual. And it was this mystical process which actually gave meaning to tribal "history." *Primal Mind*, 65.

24 Lévi-Strauss, *Savage Mind*, 10.

25 Radcliffe-Brown, *Andaman Islanders*, 234.

26   Huxley, *Affable Savages*, 249. See also Thomas Gregor, "Secrets, Exclusion and Dramatization of Men's Roles," 260-269 in *Brazil. Anthropological Prospect. Essays in Honor of Charles Wagley*, edited by Maxine L. Margolis and William E. Carter (New York, Columbia University Press, 1979), 259; Wolf, *Anthropology*, 39; Sahlins, *Tribesmen*, 12.

27   *Cubeo*, 214-215, 247, 282. " ... ritual is felt to be an occasion for consuming food and drink in quantities over and above those normally consumed. This excessive expenditure of material and spiritual resources is paralleled by the risky relaxation of the culture's regulations. These limit symbols signal: (1) the threat of nature's chaotic intrusion into a well ordered culture, and (2) the need for occasional relief from the pressures of conforming to social standards." Maxwell, *Bemba Myth and Ritual*, 50.

28   *Medea, Hippolytus, The Bacchae*, translated by Phillip Vallocott (New York, The Heritage Press, 1963), 117-122, 172.

29   La Barre, *Ghost Dance*, 535. "Archaic societies are uniformly Dionysian, and it is doubtful that any appreciable Apollonion religion precedes Ikhanaton, the pharaoh reigning 1375 B.C." Day, *Many Meanings of Myth*, 88.

30   René Girard, *Violence and the Sacred*, translated by Patrick Gregory (Baltimore, Johns Hopkins Press, 1977), 287. See also Diamond, "Search for the Primitive," in *Concept of the Primitive*, edited by Montagu, 131.

31   Brown, *Life Against Death*, 175.

32   Paul S. Wingert, *Primitive Art. Its Traditions and Styles* (New York, Oxford Press, 1962), 30.

33   Raymond Firth, *Tikopia. Ritual and Belief* (Boston, Beacon Press, 1967), 44, 191.

34   Lett, *Human Enterprise*, 50. The authority he cited was Roy Rappaport. The Mayan agriculturalists of Southern Yucatan had an almost identical philosophy. Before a Mayan planted a crop, he built an altar to the gods and prayed. Thus, the very cornfield itself became an altar. By the agreement struck there, the gods contracted to share their bounty in return for man's daily display of devotion and piety. Clarke and Hindley, *Challenge of the Primitives*, 73.

35   George A. Pettitt, "The Vision Quest and the Guardian Spirit," 265-271 in *Readings in Anthropology*, 3rd edition, edited by Jesse E. Jennings and E. Adamson Hoebel (New York, McGraw-Hill, 1972), 287.

36   Robert Paine, "Animals as Capital: Comparisons Among Northern Nomadic Hunters and Herders," 157-170 in Philip Salzman, "Comparative Studies of Nomadism and Pastoralism," [104-210] in *Anthropological Quarterly*, Vol. 44 (1970-71), 163-164. Weston La Barre thought that the idea of God itself as a master of men may have arisen from the idea of a Master Moose or the like. *Ghost Dance*, 163-164.

37   Robert F. Spencer, *The North Alaskan Eskimo. A Study in Ecology and Society* (Washington, D.C., Bureau of American Ethnology, Smithsonian Institute, 1959), 255, 264. In Tikopia there was a belief that crabs and fishes would respond to particular ritual

songs inviting them to be captured. Firth, *Tokopia. Ritual and Belief,* 201-202.

38   Laurens Van der Post, *Lost World of Kalahari,* 259.

39   William Henry Scott, *Discovery of Igorots* (Quezon City, Philippines, New Day Publications, 1974), 193.

40   Jonathan Rubin, *The Barking Deer* (New York, George Brazillier, 1974), 38.

41   Paul Radin, *The World of Primitive Man* (New York, Henry Schuman, 1953), 135.

42   Preface by Sir James George Frazer, xi in Malinowski, *Argonauts of the Western Pacific.* See also *ibid.,* 115; Kenneth P. Emory, "Navigation," 241-249 in *Ancient Hawaiian Civilization.* A series of lectures delivered at the Kamehameha Schools, edited by E. S. C. Handy *et al* (Reprinted, Tokoyo, Japan, Charles E. Tuttle, 1965) 242; Firth, *Tikopia. Ritual and Belief,* 225.

43   Gene Weltfish, *The Origins of Art* (Indianapolis, Indiana, Bobbs-Merrill, 1953), 53, 148. Among the North American Indian the design itself on the object or weapon was believed to call for the magic result desired. Harold E. Driver, *Indians of North America* (Chicago, University of Chicago Press, 1966), 176.

44   W. H. R. Rivers, "Psychological Factor," *Essays on the Depopulation of Melanesia* (Cambridge, England, Cambridge University Press, 1922), 93, 102, 108.

45   Huxley, *Affable Savages,* 152. Christine Hugh-Jones narrated a similar myth. See *From the Milk River,* 137.

46   Meggitt, *Desert People,* 49, 287; Karsten, *South American Indians,* 216. See also W. H. R. Rivers, *History of Melanesian Society,* 2 vols. (Cambridge, England, Cambridge University Press, 1914), I, 226; Clarke and Hindley, *Challenge of the Primitives,* 97; Benedict, *Bagobo Ceremony,* 155; Firth, *Tikopia. Ritual and Belief,* 198; Charles P. Mountford, "Earth's Most Primitive People. A Journey with the Aborigines of Central Australia," 89-102 in *National Geographic,* vol LXXXIX, No. 1, 1946, 100-101.

47   L. P. Muir, *African People in the Twentieth Century* (New York, Russell and Russell, 1965), 121; Huntingford, *Nandi,* 128; Charles Wagley, *The Social and Religious Life of a Guatemalan Village,* 1-150 in *American Anthropologist,* vol. 51, No. 4 Part 2, October, 1949, 32.

48   *Selected Writings,* 354.

49   Rafael Karsten, *South American Indians,* 89-90, 209-210.

50   Elsie Clews Parson, *Isleta, New Mexico,* 193-466 in *47th Annual Report of the Bureau of American Ethnology to the Secretary of the Smithsonian Institute, 1929-1930* (Washington, D.C., Smithsonian Institute, 1932), 330-331. See also Leslie A. White, *Acoma Indians,* 23-192 in *ibid.,* 84, 132.

51   Joseph B. Birdsell, "A Basic Demographic Unit," 337-357 in *Current Anthropology,*

vol. 14, No. 4, October, 1973, 347; "Local Group Composition Among the Australian Aborigines. A Critique of the Evidence from Fieldwork Conducted Since 1930," in *ibid.*, vol. 11, No. 2, April, 1970, 128.

52   A. L. Kroeber, *Cultural and Natural Areas of Native North America* (Berkeley, California, University of California Press, 1963), 77.

53   Gillian Gillison, "Fertility Rites and Sorcery in a New Guinea Village," 124-146 in *National Geographic*, vol. 152, No. 1, July, 1977, 129-130.

54   *Northern Tribes of Central Australia*, vi, 276, 360, 381.

55   Day, *Many Meanings of Myth*, 140-141.

56   Meggers, "Environmental Limitations on Culture," in *Environments of Man*, edited by Bresler, 25. See also Service, *Hunters*, 82.

57   Colin M. Turnbull, *The Mountain People* (New York, Simon & Schuster, 1972), 21-24 and *The Forest People* (New York, Simon & Schuster, 1961), 14.

58   Charles Hudson, *The Southeastern Indians* (Knoxville, University of Tennessee Press, 1976), 174-175.

59   Williams, *Dusan*, 12.

60   Hugh-Jones, *From the Milk River*, 66.

61   Weltfish, *Origins of Art*, 150; Benedict, *Bagobo Ceremony, Magic and Myth*, 195.

62   Weltfish, *Origins of Art*, 151.

63   Charles Wagley, "Tapirapé Shamanism," 617-635 in *Readings in Anthropology* 2 vols, edited by Fried, *Cultural Anthropology*, II, 631.

64   George A Pettitt, *Primitive Education in North America*. California University Publication in *American Archaeology and Ethnology*, vol. 43 No. 1 (Berkeley, University of California Press, 1946), 142.

65   *Ibid.*, 123.

66   Wagley, "Tapirapé Shamanism," *loc. cit.*, 634.

67   Waldemar Bogoras, "The Chukchee," 320-330 in *Golden Age of American Anthropology*, edited by Mead and Bunzel, 320.

68   Karsten, *South American Indians*, 15.

69   Scott, *Discovery of Igorots*, 193-194.

70   Borgoras, "The Chukchee," *loc. cit.*, 326; La Barre, *Ghost Dance*, 573.

71   La Barre, *Ghost Dance*, 161.

72   Farb, *Indians of North America*, 108.

73   George Pettitt, *Primitive Education in North America*, 118-119. See also Farley Mowat, *People of the Deer*, (New York, Pyramid Books, 1952), 246.

74   Spencer and Gillen, *Northern Tribes of Central Australia*, 479.

75   La Barre, *Ghost Dance*, 138-139. "It is entirely reassuring that someone in the community can actually perceive what is invisible to the rest of us and can bring back direct and reliable information from supernatural realms. We are not alone and helpless, for we have a great champion and savior." Day, *Many Meanings of Myths*, 121. The shaman fights supernatural demons so that the rest of the tribe may be allowed to concentrate on its earthly problems. Campbell, *Hero with a Thousand Faces*, 101.

76   Clark Wissler, *The American Indian. An Introduction to the Anthropology of the New World* (New York, Oxford University Press, 1922), 199-201.

77   Mannheim, *Ideology and Utopia*, 81-82, 193.

78   Eliade, *Myths, Dreams and Mysteries*, 69, 79.

79   "Possession by angry spirits was culturally expected of Hebrew prophet or *nabi*, for *hitnabbe* means "to rage, to fume, to be crazy." La Barre, *Ghost Dance*, 576.

80   Jens Bjerre, *Last Cannibals*, 43-45. The frequent dream experience of leaving body, flying through the air and visiting a totally different world "suggests the shaman's familiar pattern, the quite widespread belief in soul not coterminous with the body, and the myths of paradisical and demonical realm." Day, *Many Meanings of Myths*, 83.

81   The ethnologist and philosopher was Ernesto de Martino. Eliade, *Myths, Dreams and Mysteries*, 87-88.

82   *Ibid.*, 61, 102. "The shaman himself interprets this *ekstasis* as transcendence, and certainly we may accept his flight as an emblem of escape from the routine world and the conscious to the other-worldlike unconscious." Day, *Many Meanings of Myth*, 111. "The shaman will enact his journey to the spirit world or his own death and resurrection," *Ibid.*, 117.

83   Eliade, *Myths, Dreams and Mysteries*, 83.

84   *Ibid.*, 69.

85   *Ibid.*, 76, 93.

86   Brown, *Life Against Death*, 157-158.

87   Wagley, "Tapirapé Shamanism," *loc. cit.*, 627. The influence of this duty persisted even after people had accepted Christianity. Among the Toba Indians of the Argentinian Chaco, a native Christian minister abruptly resigned, not only from his pulpit but from the

Church body itself. When pressed for his reasons for this peculiar action, he explained that he did it because he himself had gotten sick. How could he keep his flock well when he himself was in poor health? This strange logic had traditionally been that of the native shaman. *Selections from the Writings of Jacob A. Loewen. Cultural and Human Values: Christian Interpretation in Anthropological Perspective* (South Pasadena, California, William Carey Library, no date), 178.

88   Spencer, *North Alaskan Eskimo*, 303.

89   Herskovits, *The Economic Life of Primitive Peoples* (New York, Alfred A. Knopf, 1940), 402-403. See also La Barre, "The Aymara Indians", in *American Anthropologist*, vol. 50, No. 1, Part 2, January, 1948, 220. Jacob A. Loewen claimed that once a man became a shaman he was necessarily engaged in a perpetual power struggle, or one to increase his own authority and decrease that of other shamans around him. *Selections from the Writings of Jacob A. Loewen*, 182-183.

90   Spencer, *North Alaskan Eskimo*, 381. See also Judith Shapiro, "The Tapirapé during the Era of Reconstruction," 61-85 in *Brazil. Anthropological Prospect*, edited by Margolis and Carter, 68; *Selections from the Writings of Jacob A. Loewen*, 189.

91   Huxley, *Affable Savages*, 199.

92   Paul Bohannan, *Africa and Africans*. Published for the American Museum of Natural History (Garden City, New York, Natural History Press, 1964), 227. See also E. R. Sorenson, "Mbotgate," 33-56 in *Primitive Worlds. People Lost in Time*, 34.

93   Spencer and Gillen, *Northern Tribes of Central Australia*, 457, 468, 476.

94   Radcliffe-Brown, *Andaman Islanders*, 302, 304.

95   Firth, *Tikopia. Ritual and Belief*, 211.

96   Rivers, *Medicine, Magic and Religion*, 21. This was precisely the way in which Lévi-Strauss described the custom in universal terms. Not only was the victim of the curse convinced that he was a dead man but so was his community. Friends and family not only stood aloof from him but regarded him as one who menaced the community by his mere presence. *Structural Anthropology*, 167-168.

97   Clyde Kluckholn, *Navaho Witchcraft* (Boston, Beacon Press, 1944), 31-32.

98   *Diary of Cotton Mather (1681-1709)*, 2 vols. (New York, Frederick Unger, 1911), I, 160-161. "Cause and effect relationships are relevant to the Bemba conceptions of the world, but only as personally construed: if something happens, it is because somebody has done something. Some perverse or benevolent will is acting." Maxwell, *Bemba Myth and Ritual*, 77.

99   W. W. Skeet, "The Wild Tribes of the Melanesian Peninsula," in *Smithsonian Institute Annual Reports*, 1902, 476-477.

100   Bohannan, *Africa and Africans*, 232.

101   Major A. J. N. Tremearne, "Notes on the Kagora and Other Nigerian Head-hunters," 136-199 in *The Journal of the Royal Anthropological Institute*, vol. 43, 1912, 160. The Zande tribes made a like assumption. Evans-Pritchard, *Social Anthropology*, 300.

102   "Journey into Stone Age New Guinea," 568-592 in *National Geographic*, vol. 135, April, 1969, 583. This was also a common occurence in New Guinea. Gillison, "Fertility Rites in a New Guinea Village," *loc. cit.*, 141-145; Wilson Wheatcroft, "Tifalmin," 57-84 in *Primitive Worlds. People Lost in Time*, 58. Man appears to be the only animal who can be killed by the powers of suggestion. Lett, *Human Enterprise*, 50.

103   Rivers, "Psychological Factor," in *Essays on the Depopulation of Melanesia*, 95. Father Alphonse Sowada told how in one dramatic instance he successfully broke such a curse in New Guinea. "New Guinea's Fierce Asmat: a Heritage of Headhunting," 186-203 in *Vanishing Peoples of the Earth* (Washington, D.C., National Geographic, 1971) 201.

104   Kluckholn, *Navaho Witchcraft*, 32.

105   J. H. Driberg, *People of the Small Arrow* (New York, Payson & Clarke, 1930), 247-255.

106   Charles Wagley, "Tapirapé Shamanism," *loc. cit.*, 625. See also Judith Shapiro, "The Tapirapé During the Era of Reconstruction," 61-65 in *Brazil. Anthropological Prospect*, edited by Margolis and Carter, 68.

107   Charles Wagley and Eduardo Galvão, *The Tentehara Indians of Brazil. A Culture in Transition* (New York, Columbia University Press, 1949), 119. See also Waldemar Bogoras, "The Chukchee," *loc. cit.*, 326.

108   Evans-Pritchard, *Social Anthropology*, 314, 324. The application of this general principle is perhaps best seen in the instance of the Aymara Indians of Lake Titicaca. As an agricultural people in a drought-prone area, they perennially used magic as a device to overcome the hostile environment. The chief purpose was to secure enough rainfall to raise a good crop of potatoes. La Barre, *The Aymara Indians, loc. cit.*, 173, 182.

109   Julian H. Steward, "The Development of Early Civilizations," 640-657 in *Readings in Anthropology*, 2 vols., edited by Fried, *Physical Anthropology, Linguistics, and Archaeology*, I, 660.

110   Sylvanus G. Morley, "Yucatan, Home of the Gifted Maya," 591-644 in *National Geographic*, vol. LXX, No. 5, November, 1936, 593, 595.

111   Eric Thompson, *The Rise and Fall of Maya Civilization* (Norman, Oklahoma, University of Oklahoma Press, 1955), 146, 153.

112   Martí and Kurath, *Dances of the Anáhuac. The Choreography and Music of Precortesian Dances. Viking Fund Publication in Anthropology No. 38* (New York, Wenner-Gren Foundation for Anthropological Research, 1964), 192-193.

113   William Prescott, *History of the Conquest of Mexico* in 3 vols., (New York, Harper & Brothers, 1847), I, 66.

114   F. Melina Morales, "The Building of Tenochtitian," 753-766 in *National Geographic*, vol. 158, No. 6, December, 1980, 759-760. See also Miguel León-Portilla, *Aztec Thought and Culture, a Study of the Ancient Nahuatl Mind* (Norman, Oklahoma, University of Oklahoma Press, 1963), 34.

115   Martí and Kurath, *Dances of the Anáhuac*, 192.

116   William Prescott, *History of the Conquest of Peru*, 2 vols. (Boston, Phillips, Samson and Co., 1856), I, 103.

117   Philip A. Means, "The Incas: Empire Builders of the Andes," 225-264 in *National Geographic*, vol. LXXIII, No. 1, January, 1938, 258-259.

118   *In the Wonderland of Peru*, 387-573 in *National Geographic*, vol. XXIV, No. 4, April, 1913, 559.

119   Sir Clements Markham, *The Incas of Peru* (New York, E. P. Dutton, 1911), 117.

120   Juliet Rice Wichman, "Agriculture," 113-121 in *Ancient Hawaiian Civilization*, 119, edited by Handy, *et al*. Thanksgiving ceremonies for crop yields are believed to be almost universal. E. S. C. Handy, "Feasts and Holidays," 61-68 in *ibid.*, 66.

121   Driberg, *Savage As He Really Is*, 50.

122   Benedict, *Bagobo Ceremonial, Magic and Myth*, 22, ft. 153, 268. See also Fay Cooper Cole, *The Wild Tribes of Davao District, Mindanao. Anthropological Series No. 12* (Chicago, Field Museum of Natural History, 1913), 139, 185.

123   Robert M. Adams, "The Origins of Agriculture," 120-131 in *Horizons of Anthropology*, edited by Sol Tax (Chicago, Aldine, 1964), 127-128.

124   Kluckholn and Leighton, *Navaho*, 308. The other side of the same coin was marked "Man's contribution." Scholars think it possible that by about 1200 A.D. the ancestors of the Pueblos had a calendar for planting, harvesting, and ritual observances. Highwater, *Primal Mind*, 129.

125   Holmberg, *Nomads of the Long Bow*, 29.

126   Pettitt, *Primitive Education*, 110.

127   Ruth Benedict, *Patterns of Culture*, 64-65. See also Sahlins, *Tribesmen*, 44.

128   Driver, *Indians of North America*, 378.

129   Kluckholn and Leighton, *Navaho*, 304-305. Navaho religion, magic and medicine represented a curious mixture of primitive shamanism of the Mackenzie Sub-Artic with the priest-dominated religion of the Pueblos. Thus, his religious leaders possessed attributes of both shaman and priest. For example, they learned the words of long and complicated chants verbatim, along with the associated tunes, from established shamans, just as in priestly cultures. However, the shamans or medicine men of the Navaho were not members of any organized cult nor were they officials of any government unit, as priests

often were. Driver, *Indians of North America*, 493.

130   Sapir, *Selected Writings*, 350-351.

131   Raymond Firth, *Primitive Economics*, 476. The fear is that a cycle of rituals which had meaning for an agricultural population, one based on the growing season, may be essentially meaningless for a people which earns its living performing industrial chores for the white man. Arthur P. Miller, Jr., "Hopis: 'The Peaceful Ones' Confront the Twentieth Century," 170-184 in *Vanishing Peoples of the Earth* (Washington, D.C., National Geographic, 1971), 179.

132   Ralph Linton, "Analysis of Tanala Culture," 291-351 in *Individual and His Society*, edited by Abram Kardiner (New York, Columbia University Press, 1947), 298. This ties in with Malinowski's idea that man called for supernatural help only in instances of great stress and anxiety. In the Trobriand islands, for example, ritual and magic were seldom if ever used in the inner lagoon where fishing was safe and easy but, on the contrary, was always resorted to where the prospect was the open sea. There the fishing was uncertain and quite hazardous. *Science, Magic and Religion*, 30-31.

133   Erving Goffman, "The Nature of Deference and Demeanor," 473-502 in *American Anthropologist*, vol. LVIII (1956), 497-499. For example, inception of the Booger Dance provided an element of revenge for the Cherokees after their defeat by the whites. It enabled them to celebrate their cultural victory over the race which conquered them militarily. It provided a means of consolation, holding up tribal pride and keeping it intact. Highwater, *Primal Mind*, 146.

134   See footnote 23 of this chapter.

Chapter V

RITUAL:

(Continued)

Masculine Puberty Rites

Puberty rites were designed to identify and distinguish perhaps the most important metamorphosis that the individual experiences. That is the transition from childhood and play to that of an adult and responsibility. Since old men had a monopoly of the esoteric, it is probable that they utilized it both to dominate young men, who threatened them with a remarkable energy source, and to overawe women. Thus, they maintained masculine domination.

Although primitives ritualized all aspects of an integrated life from the cradle to the grave, when the question arises as to which promises to yield the most insight into the mind and life of the group, puberty rites leap to the fore.

While the masculine canvas is broad and sweeping, our brush concentrates on six strokes: 1) What was their history or antiquity? 2) Why were they of such symbolic importance? 3) What were their general aims and purposes? 4) What were some typical varieties, focusing for example on the question of penile operations in the New World? 5) Were there, despite differences, unifying threads or themes which reveal a common approach to the meaning of life and how best to accomodate to its supernatural overlords? and 6) How may one best explain the pronounced sexual anxiety and hostility toward females as manifested in the masculine puberty rites?

As for the primacy of puberty rites, the primitive never regarded himself as finished or as "given," i.e., the natural man. To become a man in the "real" sense, he must first die in this natural condition in order to be reborn to a higher life. This was at once religious and ethical. Symbolic of the mystical rebirth was the fact that candidates were given new names. These were their "true" names henceforth.[1] On the pragmatic level, of course, one could justify the selection of puberty rites over its chief rival, death rites, as the epitome of a life force. With the Desana tribe of the Tukano in the Amazon river basin their principal rites dealt with life and death. One represented the beginning of sexual energy and the other its demise. Without the former, tribal continuity would grind to a halt and the saga of God's Chosen People terminated.[2]

Many of these male puberty rites in many parts of the globe featured a symbolic wound which marked the social transition from boyhood to that of manhood. Concerning the actual varieties of operations on the penis itself, we follow Clark Wissler's lead. He made a distinction between circumcision, or cutting around the tip of the penis, or foreskin, and incision, or operations upon its base or trunk. Although not necessarily originated by them, the Hebrews practiced the former. Mohammedians later borrowed the practice of circumcision from them. According to this authority, circumcision was largely practiced in the Middle East and Africa while incision occurred in Polynesia, Melanesia, and the New World. While Australia had both forms, each developed independently. Throughout his discourse, however, he failed to mention subincision which was the most radical operation of all and this upon the trunk. By Wissler's limited definitions, therefore, we are throughout this chapter speaking of penile operations at puberty or thereabouts.[3]

There were, of course, conspicuous exceptions to the sort of operations we describe in this and the following chapter. The Trobrian islanders of Melanesia had no initiation rites at puberty for either sex.[4] Nor were there any among the Aymara Indians of Lake Titicaca in Bolivia.[5] While the Siriono of the Bolivian rain forest had a puberty ceremony for girls, there was none for the boys.[6] At the other extreme were the Nigerian head-hunters who did not circumcise women because that was a supernatural event. Due to their inferiority, women could not enter such a holy rite.[7]

Since we are dealing with preliterate tribes, no one really knows the history of the institution or its antiquity, but every tribe assumed that it began with the "first man." Circumcision in Africa, for example, was far older than Islam. Herodotus spoke of it as existing among the Egyptians.[8] Both the Egytians and Hebrews used stone knives for circumcision long after becoming knowledgeable about metals. This made sense because stone knives were the sacred instruments given by the gods.[9] However, in the Australian aboriginal traditions, the ancient fire stick preceded even the stone knife as the cutting instrument.[10] The rites were certainly among the oldest known to man. Writing about the Bushmen, one authority thought it a ceremony of great antiquity, one arising very early in the history of man. The Bantus probably borrowed the custom from the Bushmen.[11] However, this was the arena of the gods and it was inconsequential what man himself knew. Unlike Job, they did not need to be reminded of the fact. This was also true among the Masai. According to myth, one day a god called to Marumi, one of their ancestors who established traditions. From now on, the god intoned, the Masai shall circumcise with this small double-edged knife and girls with this piece of sheet metal.[12] Tribes accepted this "gift" with great solemnity. Among the Nigerian head-hunters, for example, only old men and, therefore, the most important in the tribe, performed the operation. They were specifically appointed for the mission and did it only with a particular and sacred instrument.[13]

The rites themselves insured the continuity of miracle, mystery and authority. On an earthly level, they ensured the domination of old men, keepers of esoteric and sacred knowledge. On a supernatural one, the ritual itself was adhered to even when knowledge of the meaning had been lost. It was sufficient to know that the ancestors understood the meaning of the god-given ritual. The gods themselves were pleased at the unchanging ceremony. Thus, it was the greatest possible support for tribal conservatism and the perpetuation of institutions. It not only subjected the present to the past but the future as well.[14]

In New Guinea, Gillian Gillison was privileged to watch a rare spectacle, a symbolic umbilical cord ritual between a mother and her son just prior to his big break with her. And that was precisely what the rite of passage involved for the male.[15] When a boy attained the age of puberty, moving out of his mother's house into that of his father, he must be ritually purified. He must be rid of woman's contamination, produced by many years of close association. Without this cleansing process, he could never be strong enough to play the masculine role.[16] This was due to the fact that females and mothers did not produce enough of a harsh and stern atmosphere to enable a boy to become a man in a man's world. On the contrary, fathers represented a boy's first appearance with the reality principle. Thus, without a father, and the father's world, a boy never learned who he was with respect both to the application of power as well as its limitations.[17]

As for the rites themselves, Arnold van Gennep divided them into three phases: 1) The separation of the young male from the world of women and children 2) The period of transition in the bush, highlighted by the act of bodily mutilation, during which period he was considered dead and 3) The rites of incorporation as a man, signifying his resurrection and the completely new sex role which he was to play for the rest of his life.[18] Lévi-Strauss[19] and Eliade wrote similar accounts.[20] The reports elsewhere are as uniform. The Wiko tribes of the Upper Zambeisi dramatized the tradition when they called the spot where the circumcisions took place the dying place.[21] When children left home to be initiated in Melanesia, they were mourned by their families as if they were dead.[22] At the time pygmy boys were prepared for initiations by specialists from nearby agricultural tribes, they were smeared with white clay from head to toe as a sign of their death as children.[23]

Where the operation was painful these societies thought highly of pain. Manhood was the ability to surmount pain and thus increase spiritual strength.[24] The pygmies of the Congo forest represented one conspicuous exception. Their sympathetic attitude toward boys undergoing this rite was probably due to the fact the institution was not their own. The knife wielders all belonged to nearby agricultural villages. Superficially, such circumstances would normally indicate a cultural dependence upon the part of the pygmies. When isolated in their own company, however, old and young behaved as if all the sacred taboos of circumcision were not only without meaning but belonged to a suspect and alien world.[25] Much more frequent was the belief that to endure pain demanded discipline and fortitude which were the keys to tribal survival. The pain inflicted upon the initiate was also devised to make him remember all the sacred lore to which he had been exposed for the first time.[26]

On the sub-continent of Australia, tribes which inflicted the greatest pain upon initiates prided themselves upon that fact. They were contemptuous of neighboring ones which had less stressful exercises. Thus, the rites were particularly brutal and got more so as one progressed into the interior. Many tribes accompanied circumcision by the removal of an upper incisor tooth in order to add to the rigor of the ceremony.[27] Within a month or two after the boy recovered from the effects of such an operation, he was sometimes subjected to another and much more painful one. This was sub-incision, the origins of which are unknown.[28] Here the penile uretha was laid open from the meatus to the injunction with the scrotum.[29] Natives subjected to the gruesome ordeal believed that it heightened sexual pleasure.[30] However, it made the penis look like the vulva and those so operated on had to squat to urinate.[31] Although the natives had no idea of the meaning of either operation, they insisted upon both before the boy could be regarded as a man. Only the Warramunga tribe of Central Australia permitted women within close enough range to watch the subincision ceremonies. This was probably a surviving relic of the past when women had a greater share in ceremonies now regarded as sacred and restricted to man. Finally, as but another example of primitive fascination with blood, the parents of the boy later drank the blood which dripped from his penis during the operation.[32]

René Wassing may have best narrated the monumental changes that the African puberty rites effected in the subsequent lives of the boys. After their symbolic death as children, they were guided through the supernatural world by their mentors who taught them the meaning of manhood by exposing them to privation, humiliation, pain and fear. It was an experience presumed to harden and prepare them for life's burdens and pain. The more courageous the candidate's attitude the more useful he was presumed to be for the greater community. In addition to the circumcision itself, the candidates had to graduate from the tough bush school. There, isolated for weeks, they learned not only survival and endurance skills but secret tribal lore, sacred dances and songs, as well as their future rights and responsibilities.[33] Wherever secret societies prevailed with their mask techniques, a symbolic ceremony always followed the successful completion of the training process. The entire endeavor had taken place because the young men had to be made independent of their mothers, shown their adult tasks and responsibilities, prepared for marriage and parenthood in order to ensure the continued existence of the tribe. Acts of such monumental importance had to culminate in a ceremonial form which was celebrated with impressive masked dances and song. Sometimes these culminated in sexual orgies.[34]

The unfortunate boys who failed this supreme test were everywhere discriminated against. In Walbiri society they were branded as non-persons. Thus, they were unable to enter their father's lodge, or to participate in religious ceremonies or legitimately acquire a wife.[35] Among the Nandi in Kenya, a boy who uttered a single cry during the proceedings was branded as a coward for life.[36] The most compelling reasons for penalties of this sort was that hunting and gathering tribes had no use for bachelors and spinsters. Everything else rested on the postulate that survival depended upon the cooperation of husband and wife.[37] First, however, the husband had to pass the test for manhood itself.

However, since the circumcision rite was accompanied by general festivities, and might come only once every five to seven years,[38] everyone in the tribe, including the initiates themselves, was conditioned to welcome the challenge.[39] The circumcision ceremonies of the Northern Rhodesian Wiko tribes showed how the cooperation of all was necessary if the common enterprise were to be successful. Sexual abstention was required of all.

Quarreling was taboo. The contribution of women in the village in song, dance and drama was constantly required from the time the boys were spirited away until they returned with their wounds healed two months afterwards. The very fact that much of the meaning of the song, dance and drama had long since been forgotten by the tribe merely enhanced everyone's feeling of excitation at the renewed contact with the supernatural.[40] From the other side of the world came a similar report. Despite the rigor of the rites among the Tifalmin of New Guinea, the natives remembered the event as the most meaningful one of the entire lives.[41]

A single observation by Victor Turner makes meaningful everything considered thus far about male puberty rites. Widespread evidence indicates that a great many societies melt the various personalities or individuals down into a kind of "prima materia," devoid of differences. They are reduced to a condition in the bush that, while social, is lower than that they occupied as pre-adolescents. The implication is clear: for an individual to climb the status ladder, he must first undergo a lower one.[42] A little reflection convinces one that, as a so-called civilized society, we have not lost that urge. Military elites, such as West Point and the Marines, habitually utilize it. Marine training is dedicated to the principle that every man's individuality must be effaced before he can be resurrected as a member of the corps. Plebe training at the academy has always had the same goal. Anyone who has willingly endured the tyranny of being a fraternity pledge - and the stupid and often dangerous hazing which occurs in that event for the purpose of ultimately becoming a "brother" to his tormentors - is apt to admit the truth of Turner's principle.

It is also profitable to reflect upon an interesting postulate by René Girard, who based it upon what he thought were obvious contrasts between Apollonian and Dionysian models of tribal behavior. The former represents a rather serene and confident society, one valuing harmony and moderation. The Pueblos are one such people. The latter believes that wisdom comes only after exhausting the range of emotions from the calm to the frenzied or the frenetic. Physical violence results in catharsis as does intimacy with angry or vengeful gods. Wisdom likewise follows. With Girard, one might logically expect either no puberty ceremonies, or comparatively mild ones, in Apollonian societies, and both brutal and spectacular ones on those based upon the Dionysian model. In the latter there is never any hint of a deviation from the norm. A single careless word or act could immediately cause the downfall and destruction of the entire tribe. Compared with the much milder model, it can be characterized as anxiety-prone. But what the gods gave, they may take away. What they erected, they may destroy. And this without any delay or explanation. They have all the power and lack of responsibility as the god of the ancient Hebrews.[43]

Beyond this general analysis lay the intriguing proposition that the rites of passage for adolecent males revealed sexual antagonism and a conspiracy to maintain masculine domination. The case may be said to have begun with the accusation that Brazilian men were jealous of their wives for their child-bearing capacity. They preferred to believe, as their mythology taught them, that creation was a masculine business in which women were conspicuously absent. Man made the children and women merely acted as the incubator.[44]

From this flowed a revolutionary idea: the blood of the circumcision rites, both actual and symbolic, was designed to show that men too had the ability to give birth. This was demonstrated at the climax of the ceremonies when the boys were symbolically reborn.[45] Among the Tifalmin tribe, in New Guinea, the initiates had to crawl between the legs of the men from front to back of the ancestral hut where the shrine was located. Meanwhile, they were severely whipped. Since this was a symbolic birth to manhood itself, it was designed to be both slow and painful.[46] But many tribes, including those who circumcised and those who did not, had puberty rites which can be most readily explained as male efforts to exact childbirth.[47]

The use of flutes, trumpets, bull-roarers and other devices to summon up the spirits of the dead at these ceremonies were kept hidden and secret from females in order to overawe them in the role of the masculine guardian of the sacred and mysterious.[48] Masks in New Guinea were utilized by men's societies for that purpose, as were those of the Arunta tribe of Australia.[49] The nightmarish masks of the Congo were for the purpose of scaring off intruders, particularly women, from the masculine rites.[50] The circumcision ceremony, carrying as it did the death penalty for revealing its secrets to women and children, was consistent with the philosophy of tribes which were inundated with the lore of culture-heroes but had no such heroines.[51] Among the Tifalmin of New Guinea, they were designed to emphasize both the ritual separation of the sexes and the superiority, as well as the purity, of the male, symbolically and actually. Tribal existence was impossible without such formal and periodic reaffirmations.[52] The ambivalent male attitude toward the female was well illustrated by the Wiko rites in Rhodesia. These were full of joyful references to copulation but at the same time contained repeated insults hurled at women.[53]

All this symbolic and/or ritualistic behavior on the part of the masculine community was made meaningful by a recent observation concerning the Mae Enga of the Papua New Guinea Highlands: "Male fear of female sexuality appears to be a central organizing principle of daily life."[54]

The other side of the same coin - masculine sexual aggression and hostility - was captured by Clifford Geertz when discussing the obsession of the Balinese male with cock fighting: " ... the deep psychological identification of Balinese men with their cocks is unmistakable. The double entendre here is deliberate. It works in exactly the same way in Balinese as in English...."[55] Demanding a blood sacrifice, the drama illustrates "the creative power of aroused masculinity and the destructive power of loosened animality which fuse in a bloody drama of hatred, cruelty, violence and death."[56]

Parenthetically, this primitive concept that creation, or procreation, was an essentially masculine affair in which women either had no part, or merely a passive one, had significant parallels in Christianity. Mary Daly summed up the Christian version as well as anyone when she called it a deliberate reversal of sex roles. First, there was the unique event when the Father recreated or reproduced himself in his only begotten Son without the aid of a heavenly mother. This, she felt, legitimized male mating.[57] Second, Adam may be said to have created Eve with his own body, sacrificing a rib instead of semen.[58] Third, Mary was completely passive throughout the course of events culminating in the birth of Jesus. Incredibly, she remained a virgin with her hyman intact. Skipping the whole biological process involving conception and childbirth, Mary merely provided the hollow shell wherein the infant could remain for the customary period in incubation. Finally, when the priest used the chalice, a female symbol, to change the wine into the blood of Christ, this was a Christian version of male menstruation.[59]

As always, unanimity is difficult to achieve among anthropologists concerning generalizations about primitive behavior patterns. Following Tom's suggestion, we mention but two significant deviations in the matter of sexual hostility observed in masculine puberty rites. The most conspicuous, of course, is that of Raymond Firth. In fifty pages concerning these rites among the Polynesian culture of Tikopia, he was silent with regard to matters of sexual rivalry and hostility. Instead, a close reading would prompt the conclusion that the operation on the boy's penis was less a puberty than a maturity rite. The ceremonial scar, inflicted within a matter of minutes, was meant as a badge of distinction in a society lacking the ability to confer diplomas upon graduates. At times this bar mitzvah-like affair had to be deferred because the boy's family could not afford the economic outlay demanded of it.[60] Anthropological work among the Masai of South Africa prompted similar conclusions. While initiation rites occurred between the ages of twelve and sixteen, they happened earlier if the parents were wealthy and later if poor. Widespread variation in ceremony among different peoples led to the conviction by some that circumcision itself was a social act, one unrelated to physical puberty.[61]

With regard to South America, we accept the contention of Charles Wagley that circumcision did not exist there. He also extended that generalization to include the entire Western hemisphere.[62] When, for example, he gave a graphic account of male puberty rites of the Tapirapé tribes of Brazil, it proved to be a combination of three factors: 1) Veblen's conspicuous consumption (an elaborate and costly livery), 2) artistry (dancing), and 3) a test of strength and endurance (a twenty-four hour dance marathon).[63]

Nevertheless, there were very often other painful ways to set up and maintain puberty rites in South American and that fact becomes central to our later arguments. Often it involved the bloodletting of a foe. Among the

Urubus, manhood could not be achieved until one participated in a raid upon the enemy and killed an enemy prisoner in a public ritual.[64] With the Tupinamba no man could marry until he had killed a foe.[65] With the Indians of Western Ecuador, participants had to pass through a painful nose-piercing ceremony which had to be endured silently.[66] Whipping and mock battles, designed to make the candidates strong and fierce, were an integral part of the puberty ceremonies of the Pirá-piraná Indians at the Colombian border with Brazil.[67] Young boys among the Cubeo of the Amazon river basin were periodically whipped from ages eight to fifteen in order to supply them with vigor and growth of stature through the intercession of their ancestors. When past fifteen, and admitted to adulthood, boys had to demonstrate courage and endurance by placing their hands in a calabash of red ants. Unlike the whipping ceremonies, this had no supernatural overtones.[68]

Perhaps the best explanation for the rigors of initiations for adolescent boys in South America was that of Thomas Gregor. Because of prolonged nursing by the mothers, and the fact that the child slept with her until his fourth year when another sibling arrived, the lad developed an unusually strong identification with her. It was this relationship of dependence by the male upon the female that the initiation ceremonies were purposely devised to obliterate.

Some psychologists believed that this sudden reversal of values created its own social problems. Ambivalence toward the opposite sex, and insecurity in the male role, was also suggested by later masculine fears of excessive contact with women and the numerous rituals which incorporated elements of sexual antagonism. Derisive comments with regard to the structure of a woman's sex organ were judged but another facet of masculine insecurity.[69]

While Robert F. Murphy did not discuss puberty rites for males among the Mundurcu of Brazil, he left little doubt that tribal ritual and ceremony were both devised to stress the segregation of the sexes and masculine superiority. First, all the sacred instruments appeared as phallic symbols. Further, men enforced female submission, or sexual conformity, by constant threats of a gang bang with their "bananas." Such punishments, or social justice as they termed it, was always the subject of merriment in the men's house. It was often accompanied by derisive comments about the external appearance of the female sex organ. The authors' conclusion, however, was much the same as that of Gregor. All these facets of male sexual behavior, while serving as ego props, merely reflected a deep sense of insecurity and an ambivalence towards the opposite sex. Those whom they pretended to scorn, they actually feared as possible usurpers.[70] Murphy also reminded us of a conclusion reached long ago by many anthropologists. That was of a remarkable similarity of social attitudes and behavior in men's houses in such scattered areas as Africa, Melanesia, Australia and South American.[71]

While evidence suggests that individual displays of prowess or bravery were acceptable norms of conduct for the rites of passage in South America, there is none to link these with the practice of circumcision. Since the Orinoco and Amazon river basins are in reality one common lowland,[72] it is difficult to conceive how, if the practice of circumcision once existed in the Orinoco,[73] it would not have spread among the tribes of the Amazon. Now, as well as in the past, tribes on the Northwest Amazon have a vastly complex trading practice, acting as the middle men for the products of both Colombia and Brazil.[74] It is, of course, virtually impossible to swap commodities for a long time without a subsequent impact upon ideas and institutions. We need to be reminded that it was Alexander von Humboldt who, in a seventy-five day passage on five great rivers in 1800, was the first to establish the fact that the Orinoco and Amazon river systems were in reality but one.[75]

Neither is there evidence of past or present circumcision practices by any tribe in the continental United States. The only puberty ceremony concerning the Indians of Southeastern United States was one of the menstrual hut.[76] Despite initiations into ceremonial organizations, the Plains Indians had nothing comparable to the puberty customs of Africa and Australia.[77] While the Navahos held initiation ceremonies for both sexes, ranging in age from seven to thirteen, they had a solely religious purpose. They lacked any intent to subject the boys to a physical ordeal.[78] There were basically three ways of meeting the problem of puberty among American

Indians. The first was to have no puberty rites or ceremony. Typical examples were afforded by the Piegan of Montana, the Haida of British Columbia and the Yokuts of the Sacramento area of California.[79] The second method was to send the boy into mountainous regions, or deserted areas, at night in search of a religious experience. This system was predicated upon the supposition that man, via purification, fasting and vigils, could communicate with the spirit world. It would give a vision or a message which would stand him in good stead for the remainder of his life. Ultimately, his secret was revealed by song in the winter ceremonies. With the Achomawi of the Upper Pitt river and Goose Lake Valley, this event marked his manhood. The Salishan tribe of the Northwest coast of Washington and Canada was also an excellent example of such a procedure.[80] The third mode was to induct the candidate into fraternal lodges, such as was done among the Dieguenos and Hopis of the Southwest desert country. This, no doubt, was quite similar to the puberty ceremonies of the Plains Indians.[81]

It is, however, when we come to the question of penile operations in Central America that Mannheim's thesis is dramatized, i.e., every epoch has a distinctive point of view and thus sees the same outside world from a different perspective. One may recall that in our first chapter scholars like S.G. Morley and J. Eric Thompson presented the lost civilization of the Mayas of the Classic Period as if the Yucatan jungle had yielded up the remnants and artifacts of something "almost like a glorious Camelot."[82]

Thompson, for example, concluded that this scholarly, philosophical, religious and mathematically-minded people lived at peace with both the universe and man. Order, harmony and moderation were the characteristics of this typically Apollonian society. Its art of the Classic Period reflected the serenity and beauty of the religious component of this society.[83] While some phallic sculpture made its appearance late in the period, this was a foreign importation and one distasteful to the Mayas.[84] While Thomas Gann and Thompson had a chapter entitled "Religious Ceremonies and Traditions" in their *History of the Maya,* it did not, although dealing with blood sacrifices, mention penile operations.[85]

When Kenneth Burke observed that a way of seeing always involves at the same time a way of not seeing, he gave us a key to understanding.[86]

Scholars like Ruth Benedict and others had found the concepts of Apollonian and Dionysian a useful tool in their dissection of primitive cultures. Nevertheless, the model was in their head and not in the world itself and certainly not in that of the primitive. Here the diffculty was that, once identifying the Mayas as Apollonian, it was extremely difficult to accept as fact manners and customs which sharply deviated from the notion of a peaceful, moderate and harmonious society. All Morley could see, for example, was a ball court "where a game something like our modern basketball was played."[87] A generation later, scholars discovered that the ball might be a human head or a skull and that the victorious players might decapitate the losers.[88]

In the absence of an ability to decipher the glyph writing of the Mayas, both scholars and public saw what they wanted to see. Thompson, himself a pious High Anglican, thought the Mayas were wonderful because of their great faith and piety.[89] The public perceived them as the Greeks of the New World, i.e., as pure, original and beautiful. They served as a foil to the Romans of that same world, the Aztecs, who were slavish, cold and imitative in their art forms.[90] Even Roger Fry, artist and critic, accepted the dichotomy for the entire world of art.[91]

It is also possible that the events of the early and middle Thirties themselves had something to do with the acceptance of the false image of Camelot. The brutalities of the Stalin regime in Soviet Russia, and the international revulsion caused by Hitler's Third Reich in Germany, may have made the average American and anthropologist eager to salvage the notion of the "goodness of man." This the Maya excavations afforded. And our own deep depression may have eroded faith in a materialistic culture and substituted a willingness to accept the Maya devotion to matters of the mind and heart. With the recent publication of *The Blood of Kings* by Linda Schele and Mary E. Miller, the serenity and beauty of the Maya religious experience is superceded by its worship of blood and the voluntary and involuntary endurance of physical torture. This was highlighted by public demonstrations of self-incision on the penis of kings. To say that blood "was the mortar of ancient Maya life" would have "been unthinkable 25 years ago."[92]

This peculiar practice, indulged in by Maya aristocrats, and even male dancers,[93] had distinct religious origins. The Maya myth was that both the earth and its first men were created by the gods through their sacrificial gift. As part of the Social Contract, human beings in turn were required to give blood sacrifices to the gods so that they might be nourished and the universe they created maintained. Neither man nor the gods could separately exist.[94] This would, of course, explain why certain artifacts display gods squatting over bowls of blood which dripped from their penises.[95] As far as mankind was concerned, the blood of kings was the crucial element in working the miracle. As the bearer of the most potent blood among humankind the king was the focus of great power. "Through this gift of blood, the king brought the gods to life and drew the power of the supernatural into the daily lives of the people." This concept was an "awe-inspiring " one.[96] However, we in the West have a kindred miracle. The Catholic priest, through prescribed ritual, summons up the physical presence of God (the Christ) and then distributes his body to his parishioners, while reserving the Lord's blood for himself.

Scientists now know the body, after a trauma or a considerable loss of blood, releases chemicals which are related to opiates. They might be capable of inducing hallucinations. Coupled with physical deprivation beforehand, and amid public hysteria, the Mayas knew that severe blood letting could produce the religious visions. These were the *raison d'être* of such spectacles. The blood from the king's penis and the queen's tongue dripped on blue papers which, along with a gummy substance, were thrown into braziers which produced columns of black smoke. This provided a perfect field for the monarch to catch a glimpse of the Vision Serpent, his contact with both his ancestors and the supernatural world. The chosen instrument for this affair might be a stingray spine or a lancet of flint or obsidian, a sacred object known as the Perforator God.[97]

Thus far these practices as described were bloody but voluntary, or those undertaken by the ruling powers as personal obligations. But they, and other highly imaginative tortures, were also characteristically imposed upon war captives. Their agonies in stone are still quite apparent and shocking.[98]

The use of the term, the Perforator God, for the obsidian knife slicing the trunk of the penis, clearly indicates the practice of incision which Clark Wissler declared was prevalent in Central America. However, Wissler clearly differentiated between this and circumcision, an operation performed upon the foreskin. Therefore, Wagley's insistence that there were no circumcision rites in the New World would appear to stand. However, he would have to modify that statement significantly with regard to penile operations there.

At the same time one would have to concede that the masculine initiation rites among Brazilian Indians bore a remarkable similiarity to painful circumcision and/or incision ceremonies in Africa, Australia and New Guinea. This is particularly true of their social and sexual overtones and consequences. The latter provides the common thread for male adolescent rites. In South America, as elsewhere, the primitive was occupied with the spectacular, the violent, the dramatic. Men there, as elsewhere, deliberately exposed to women a part, but only that, of their secret ritual and the effort was clearly designed to overawe them.[99] Man, as the predecessor of woman, was the chosen instrument of the gods and thus essentially at home in the sacred sphere.[100] Woman was merely the laity and in charge of the mundane or profane aspects of life.[101] It was precisely against this sharp division of labor and privilege that Christine Hugh-Jones protested. Being forced to eat after the men did, and excluded from most formal occasions, she was depressed by the feeling she was not learning anything of consequence about the Pirá-piraná. This all took place in the exclusive men's world.[102] This is no doubt what primitive women everywhere were supposed to feel. Their universal exclusion from male puberty rites was calculated to reinforce this feeling of awe and dependency.

An amusing but fair assessment of reasons for such masculine intent to dominate the opposite sex came from the Kumans of the Central Highlands in New Guinea. There men kept the magic flute a secret from females because it performed the useful purpose of striking terror into them. Meanwhile, men told their womenfolk that if they ever caught sight of the magic flute they would be struck blind, their bodies would rot and their pigs would die. When asked by their white guest why such lies prevailed, native men replied that, if they showed the flutes to women and explained how, through the use of this instrument, they controlled the spirits, women would laugh at them. All authority would be lost.[103]

Meanwhile, the protests of Christine Hugh-Jones reminds one of the widespread myth that, when the world was very young, women monopolized the sacred instruments which summoned up the gods for tribal purposes. They may have done this either by theft or trickery. It required a revolution by the men to restore the so-called "natural order." This has faithfully been adhered to since. Other authorities also note the presence of similar myths among Brazilian tribes.[104] A somewhat kindred myth from New Guinea, was that women originally possessed the sacred flutes which summoned up the gods until men stole them. They retained them until the present day.[105]

One would be forced to conclude, therefore, that Wagley's correct insistence upon the absence of circumcision in the masculine puberty rites of South America, and therefore the stress upon the particular, must be countered by anthropologists who emphasized factors in the puberty rites on that continent which closely paralleled that of peoples practicing circumcision or incision in Africa, Australia, New Guinea and elsewhere.

Let us conclude by singling out some perceptive observations. Primitive or archaic man was not content until he altered his body by a penile operation which paved the way for his rebirth as a spiritual and moral being. By the perpetuation of such ceremonies, old men not only subjected the present to the past but the future as well. It was the most conservative of all institutions. Many societies first attempt to melt individual personalities into "prima materia," a lower status position than they occupied beforehand, as the price of elevating them to a higher and more privileged one. While some scholars found the concepts of Apollonian and Dionysian useful in predicting or explaining the degree of the brutal, the violent and the spectacular in masculine puberty rites, we stressed the danger of their too ready application, i.e., Apollonian for the Mayas. A great many tribes had puberty ceremonies best explained as masculine efforts to exact childbirth. Masculine efforts to denigrate females reflected sexual insecurity and ambivalence. Regardless of variety, - circumcision, incision, subincision, or none at all - it was the spectacular, the violent and the dramatic which provided common world-wide themes at masculine puberty ceremonies.

Footnotes

1   Eliade, *The Sacred and the Profane*, 187.

2   Reichel-Domatoff, *Amazonian Cosmos*, 139.

3   *The Relation of Nature to Man in Aboriginal America* (New York, Oxford University Press, 1926, reprinted AMS Press), 107-108.

4   Bronislaw Malinowski, *Sex and Repression in Savage Society* (New York, Harcourt Brace, 1927), 59.

5   Weston La Barre, *The Aymara Indians in American Anthropologist*, vol. 50, No. 1, Part 2, January, 1948, 128-129.

6   Holmberg, *Nomads of the Long Bow*, 80.

7   A.J.N. Tremearne, "Notes on the Kagora and Other Nigerian Head-hunters," in *Journal of the Royal Anthropological Institute*, vol. 43 (1912), 161-162, 169.

8   Galbraith Welch, *Africa. Before They Came* (Norman, Oklahoma, University of Oklahoma Press, 1963), 225.

9   R.U. Sayce, *Primitive Arts and Crafts. An Introduction to the Study of Material Culture* (New York, Biblio and Tannen, 1963), 139.

10   Spencer and Gillen, *Northern Tribes of Central Australia*, 223-224, 394.

11   S.S. Dornan, *Pygmies and Bushmen of the Kalahari* (London, Seeley, Service, 1925), 158-160.

12   Bruno Bettelheim, *Symbolic Wounds. Puberty Rites and the Envious Male* (Glencoe, Illinois, Free Press, 1954), 220.

13   Tremearne, "Nigerian Headhunters," in *loc. cit.*, 161.

14   Girard, *Violence and the Sacred*, 284-285.

15   "Fertility Rites and Sorcery in a New Guinea Village," 124-146 in *National Geographic*, vol. 152, No. 1, July, 1957, 137. This merely dramatized a situation which was the norm among primitive tribes. E. E. Evans-Pritchard, *The Position of Women in Primitive Societies and Other Essays* (New York, Free Press, 1965), 38. For example, after the circumcision ceremony in Wiko society, a boy might no longer sleep in his mother's hut, allow her to see his penis, or even buddy around with her. Max Gluckman, "The Role of the Sexes in Wiko Circumcision Ceremonies," 145-167 in *Social Structure, Studies presented to Radcliffe Brown*, edited by Meyer Fortes (New York, Russell and Russell, 1963), 151.

16   Philip Newman, "Sorcery, Religion and Man," 21-29 in *Natural History*, vol. 71,

February, 1962, 22. At masculine puberty ceremonies among the Morombo tribes of the interior mountains of New Guinea, each boy had to have the gristle of his nose pierced by a sharp bone. He then held his head over a river so that it would carry away his mother's blood which had been stored up in him ever since he was in her womb. Bjerre, *Last Cannibals*, 17. Men maintained separate houses in order to avoid a renewal of such contamination. E. Richard Sorenson, "Mbotgate," 33-56 in *Primitive Worlds, People Lost in Time* (Washington, D.C., National Geographic, 1973), 35.

17   La Barre, *Ghost Dance*, 103.

18   *The Rites of Passage*, translated by M.B. Vizedom and G.L. Caffee. Introduction by Solon T. Kimball (Chicago, University of Chicago Press, 1960), 74-75.

19   *Savage Mind*, 264.

20   *Myths, Dreams and Mysteries*, 192-193.

21   Gluckman, "Role of the Sexes in Wiko Circumcision Ceremonies," *loc. cit.*, 148.

22   Rivers, *Social Organization* (New York, A.A. Knopf, 1924), 125.

23   Colin M. Turnbull, *The Forest People. A Study of the Pygmies of the Congo.* Clarion Book (New York, Simon and Schuster, 1961), 223.

24   Huxley, *Affable Savages*, 147.

25   Turnbull, *Forest People*, 224.

26   Bjerre, *Last Cannibals*, 97.

27   Joseph B. Birdsell, "Basic Demographic Unit," *Current Anthropology*, vol. 14, October, 1973, 342, 347-348.

28   Elman R. Service, *A Profile of Primitive Culture* (New York, Harper, 1958), 21; Spencer and Gillen, *Northern Tribes of Central Australia*, 263.

29   Spencer and Gillen, *Northern Tribes of Central Australia*, 263. See also Rivers, *Magic, Medicine and Religion*, 104, who asserted that there were similar operations in Fija and Tonga.

30   Meggitt, *Desert People*, 313.

31   Bettelheim, *Symbolic Wounds*, 112. Such a opening was called a "penis womb." It was meant to be a symbolic male vagina. "The hero has become, by virtue of the ceremony, more than man." Campbell, *Hero with a Thousand Faces*, 154.

32   Spencer and Gillen, *Northern Tribes of Central Australia*, 329-330, 354-357.

33   *African Art. Its Background and Traditions* (New York, Henry N. Abrams, 1968), 66, 70. Since menstruation related to a girl's physical growth, the purpose of the male puberty rites was growth by analogy. Growth had to be engineered by one's male elders.

Per Hage, "On Male Initiation and Dual Organization in New Guinea," 268-285 in *Man*, vol. 16, No. 2, 1981, 269.

34   Elsy Leuzinger, *Africa. The Art of the Negro Peoples* (New York, McGraw-Hill, 1960), 3.

35   Meggitt, *Desert People*, 309, 314.

36   Huntingford, *Nandi*, 88.

37   Holmberg, *Nomads of the Long Bow*, 219.

38   Huntingford, *Nandi*, 55.

39   Dorothy D. Lee, *Freedom and Culture* (New York, A Spectrum Book, Prentice-Hall, 1958), 38.

40   Gluckman, "Wiko Circumcision Ceremonies," *loc. cit.*, 147, 156, 164. It was not the current meaning of the ritual which caused its performance from year to year but merely the fact that one's ancestors always did it. Vilma Chiara Schultz, "Indians of Central Brazil: A Struggle to Survive," 152-169 in *Vanishing Peoples of the Earth*, 160.

41   Wheatcroft, "Tifalmin," in *Primitive Worlds, People Lost in Time*, 67.

42   *The Ritual Process. Structure and Anti-Structure* (Chicago, Aldine, 1969), 169-170.

43   *Violence and the Sacred*, 282. Following the lead of W. Robertson Smith, Durkheim concluded that "the gods are terrible blind forces; they are tied to no moral commitment; following the circumstances, or simply caprice, they can be beneficient or awful." Thus, they are not approachable, save with the greatest precaution. Durkheim, *Incest. The Nature and Origin of the Incest Taboo*, 96. The people who wrote the Book of Job would understand such a theology.

44   Huxley, *Affable Savages*, 148.

45   Gillison, "Fertility Rites in a New Guinea Village," *loc. cit.*, 146.

46   Wheatcroft, "Tifalmin," *loc. cit.*, 67.

47   Bettelheim, *Symbolic Wounds*, 207, 214. "Woman creates *naturally from within her own being* whereas man is free to, or forced to, create artificially." J.S. La Fontaine, "The Domestication of the Savage Male," 333-349 in *Man*, vol. 16, No. 3, September 1981, 334.

48   Bjerre, *Last Cannibals*, 94. See also Raymond Firth, *Art and Life in New Guinea* (New York, AMS Press, 1976), 23-25.

49   Paul Wingart, *Primitive Art. Its Transition and Styles* (New York, Oxford University Press, 1962), 212; Spencer and Gillen *Northern Tribes of Central Australia*, 130.

50   Margaret Trowell, *African and Oceanic Art* (New York, Henry Abrams, 1968), 23.

51   Huxley, *Affable Savages*, 149, 152.

52   Wheatcroft, "Tifalmin," *loc. cit.*, 67.

53   Gluckman, "Wiko Circumcision Ceremonies," *loc. cit.*, 156.

54   Marc Howard Ross, "The Limits to Social Structure: Social Structural and Psychocultural Explanations for Political Conflict and Violence," 171-176 in *Anthropological Quarterly*, vol. 59, No. 4, October 1986, 173.

55   *The Interpretation of Cultures. Selected Essays* (New York, Basic Books, 1973), 417.

56   *Ibid.*, 420-421.

57   *Gyn/Ecology. The Metaphysics of Radical Feminism* (Boston, Beacon, 1978), 37-38, 74.

58   *Ibid.*, 8.

59   *Ibid.*, 82-83.

60   *We, the Tikopia. Kinship in Primitive Polynesia* (Boston, Beacon Press, 1965), 380-430, *passim*.

61   *Rites of Passage*, 70-72, 85.

62   Wagley, Gainsville, Florida, to Stan Urban, Parkville, Missouri, October 13, 1981.

63   *Welcome of Tears. The Tapirapé Indians of Central Brazil* (New York, Oxford University Press, 1977), 153-156.

64   Huxley, *Affable Savages*, 153.

65   *Ibid.*, 95.

66   Von Hagen, *Tsatchela Indians of Western Ecuador*, 42-43.

67   Hugh-Jones, *From the Milk River*, 143-147. Ceremonial whipping of young boys at puberty was widespread throughout the Americas. La Barre, *Ghost Dance*, 136.

68   Goldman, *Cubeo*, 179, 194, 199, 201. A similar ceremony among the Mauhes in Brazil was described by Karsten, *South American Indians*, 98.

69   "Secret, Exclusion and Dramatization of Men's Roles," in *Brazil. Anthropological Prospect*, edited by Margolis and Carter, 266-267. The same phenomena was reported from Africa. See Gluckman, "Wiko Circumcision Ceremonies." *loc. cit.*, 156.

70   "Social Structure and Sexual Antagonism," 89-98 in *Southwestern Journal of Anthropology*, vol. 15 (1959), 93-95. See also Huxley, *Affable Savages*, 152.

71   "Social Structure and Sexual Antagonism," *loc. cit.*, 90.

72   Goldman, *Cubeo*, 1-2.

73   See Karsten, *South American Indians*, 176.

74   Goldman, *Cubeo*, 68.

75   *The Life Travels and Books of Alexander von Humboldt* with an Introduction by Bayard Taylor (New York, Rudd and Charleton, 1959), 187.

76   Hudson, *Southeastern Indians*, 320.

77   Robert Lowie, *Indians of the Plains*. American Museum Science Books (New York, Natural History Press, 1963), 90.

78   Kluckholn and Leighton, *The Navaho*. The Natural History Library (New York, Doubleday, 1962) 207-209.

79   Edward S. Curtis, *The North American Indian*, 20 vols. (New York, Edward S. Curtis, 1924), VI, 155; XI, 126; XIV, 160.

80   *Ibid.*, VII, 10; VIII, 175; IX, 158; XIII, 149, 179.

81   *Ibid.*, XII, 37; XV, 166.

82   Schele and Miller, *Blood of Kings*, 18.

83   *Rise and Fall of Maya Civilization* (Norman, Oklahoma, University of Oklahoma Press, 1954), 264-265. "It was the highest civilization, judged both by its intellectual and esthetic achievements, ever produced by the American Indian." Sylvanus G. Morley, "Yucatan, Home of the Gifted Maya," 591-644 in *National Geographic Magazine*, vol. LXX, no. 5, November, 1936, 598.

84   Thompson, *Maya Civilization*, 93.

85   *The History of the Maya. From the Earliest Times to the Present Day* (New York, Scribners, 1934), 143.

86   *Permanence and Change* (New York, New Republic and Co., 1935), 70.

87   "Yucatan. Home of the Gifted Maya," *loc. cit.*, 597.

88   *Blood of Kings*, 245.

89   Michael Cole in Preface, in *Blood of Kings*, 2.

90   *Blood of Kings*, 19-21.

91   *Ibid.*, 23.

92   Michael Cole, Preface, 1, to Schele and Miller, *Blood of Kings*. See also Johnson, "Dark Mysteries of the Maya," *loc. cit.*, 46.

93   Schele and Miller, *Blood of Kings*, 180-181.

94   *Ibid.*, 176.

95   *Ibid.*, 181.

96   *Ibid.*, 184. To be king was the equivalent of being a living sacrifice for one's people. Eric Eckholm, "Secrets of Mayas Decoded," New York *Times*, May 13, 1986, C 1.

97   Schele and Miller, *Blood of Kings*, 177-178.

98   "In rituals that paralleled the auto-sacrifice of the reigning royal family, captives were bled and mutilated - their blood and flesh offered to the gods and ancestors - and eventually killed. ...almost every Maya site has monuments that display captives." Schele and Miller, *Blood of Kings*, 210.

99   Gregor, "Secrets, Exclusion and Dramatization of Men's Roles," *loc. cit.*, 260-261.

100   Reichell-Dolmatoff, *Amazonian Cosmos*, 30.

101   Goldman, *Cubeo*, 285; Bjerre, *Last Cannibals*, 94. Men and women were different spiritual beings. Wilson Wheatcroft, "Tifalmin," 54-84 in *Primitive Worlds, Peoples Lost in Time* (Washington, D.C., National Geographic, 1973), 61. Among the Bushmen of the Kalahari, women were prohibited both from hunting and lighting fires, both of which functions dealt with the supernatural. Elizabeth Marshall Thomas, "The Bushmen: Gentle Nomads of Africa's Harsh Kalahari," 58-75 in *Vanishing Peoples of the Earth*, 65. The same idea, expressed in another form, came from Lévi-Strauss with regard to Australian tribes. Whereas natural fertility, they said, belonged to women, social power belonged to men. *Savage Mind*, 94.

102   *Milk River*, Preface. At the same time it might be true that native women were much more eager informants for the white woman than native males were for the white man. Sorenson, "Mbotgate," in *Primitive Worlds, Peoples Lost in Time*, 36.

103   Bjerre, *Last Cannibals*, 129-130. Their men may be foolish, as women assert "but they remain in control: their ideology is imposed upon the group; they retain political control over women; they can manipulate the ideology, while the female group has to be content with merely being aware of it." Dumont, *The Headman and I*, 137.

104   Gregor, "Secrets, Exclusion and Dramatization of Men's Roles," *loc. cit.*, 251, 257; Murphy, "Social Structure and Sexual Antogonism," *loc. cit.*, 92-93; Reichel-Dolmatoff, *Amazonian Cosmos*, 169-171.

105   Gillison, "Fertility Rites in a New Guinea Village" *loc. cit.*, 146. A quite similar

myth was prevalent in Australia. Catherine H. and Ronald M. Berndt, "Australian Aborigine: Blending Past and Present," 114-131 in *Vanishing Peoples of the Earth*, 121. See also Day, *Many Meanings of Myths*, 221.

Chapter VI

RITUAL:

(Continued)

Female Puberty Rites

Consider the almost universal preoccupation of the primitive with human blood. Add to that the association of blood with death or serious injury in battle, or as that of a sacrificial victim. Now, since the sole and steady exception to this in peace time was menstrual blood, it is of little wonder that Dionysian societies regarded it as a supernatural thing of horror and danger. They took elaborate precautions to protect the positively charged, but unwary male, from the negatively charged menstruating female who cancelled it out.

With regard to puberty rites for females, we found ourselves absorbed with five questions: 1) The antiquity of circumcision   2) Kinds or varieties 3) Male attitudes toward menstruation   4) The girl's consequent seclusion during her first period and   5) The magical properties of menstrual blood.

While female circumcision was, like that of the male, a religious ceremony of great antiquity, it appeared to differ. It marked the subordination of the individual woman not only to the social customs of the tribe but to the convenience of the future husband or owner. According to legend, the practice was initiated by the wife of Abraham who, jealous of a favorite Negro concubine, sought to eliminate her as a sex rival. Sex operations on females in African history were not only more common than male circumcision but more ancient. They largely stemmed from the custom of trying to safeguard virginity. This was done in East Africa by sewing up the girl's private parts when she was very young. Elsewhere the practice was called infibulation where rings or clasps were used and withdrawn at will.[1]

Altogether, there were three kinds of female circumcision. First, there was the sunna or the mere removal of the tip of the clitoris. Since this operation deadened female sensitivity, it was supposed to result in female fidelity to the husband.[2] This kind of operation was not as painful as male circumcision. The Bantu tribe probably borrowed this custom from the Kalahari Bushmen. They always used a stone knife to perforate the clitoris. Second, there was excision or removal of the entire clitoris with *labia minor* and some or most of the external gentilia. Among the Loder tribes near the French Ivory coast, a girl of five or six had her clitoris cut out in order to make sexual relations later possible with a male.[3] Third, there was excision and infibulation which involved removal of the entire clitoris, *labia minor* and part of the *labia major*. Two sides of the vulva were then sewed together with catgut or thorns with the object of making a hole just large enough for urine and menstrual blood to pass through. Among the Somalis, for example, the smaller the hole, the larger the girl's value. The object was to offer the male master a "tight" vagina or one which rivaled a sex experience by a male with another through the anus.[4]

At root, like all other actions of the primitive, it was a symbolic act, as Arnold van Gennep explained. Circumcision rites cut the girl adrift from an asexual world, marking her entrance into a sexual one.[5] My co-author thought this expression ironic in as much as the operation performs just the opposite effect, i.e., a transition from a sexual world to an asexual one. It snuffs out the joy of sex for the female. Other scholars spoke of the act as one of cutting off the girl from her childhood past.[6]

However varied the operations in many parts of the globe, the crucial difference between the ceremonies for the circumcision of the sexes was that women specialists never had to pretend by ritual, as did the man, that they had the power to give birth.[7]

Closely associated with this unquestioned fact are those female puberty rites in agricultural societies, such as the Bemba. There the symbols associate "human sexuality with agricultural prosperity ... identifying the earth's fertility with that of woman."[8]

While the primitive seemed fascinated by human blood, and therefore obsessed by the periodic but mysterious bleeding of the menstrual cycle, Ruth Benedict has given us an interesting clue to this phenomena. She did it when discussing the actions of the Pueblos who were the only tribe in their region to ignore the menses. She was, confessedly, following the lead of Nietzsche when discussing ancient Greek attitudes toward tragedy.[9] As what she termed an Apollonian society, the Pueblos found no need to develop themes of terror and danger, fear and contamination. Thus, not only did they not have menstrual huts but no special precautions at all for the female or the tribe at this time.[10] The Navaho followed the same basic pattern. On the girl's first menses, she was honored by a four-night public ceremony. To become a woman in this society was something to be proud of, rather than something of which to be ashamed.[11]

On the contrary, a Dionysian society valued frenzy, generally achieved through intoxication, believing that it ultimately resulted in wisdom. It sought the supernatural not only because it was deemed to be powerful but because the process itself was dangerous. Every life crisis situation was wrapped in a veil of terror. In such societies one would naturally expect the menses to be received in a much more dramatic fashion and one quite negative in tone or shrouded in dread and even disgust.[12] In the island of Bali, for example, east of Java, a menstruating woman was forbidden to enter a temple.[13] The same stricture prevailed in Hebrew Biblical tradition.[14] Among the Nandi in Kenya, menstrating women were regarded as unclean, like those who had broken some sacred taboo.[15] It was for reasons such as this which caused the Azande in the North Sudan to forbid a man to have sexual intercourse with his wife while she was having her period.[16]

Parenthetically, this primitive preoccupation with the uncleanliness of the menstruating woman has carried over into our own times on a global basis. The Buddhist, Catholic and Muslim religions are all impregnated with negative views of menstruation. All are concerned with the restoration of ritual cleanliness.[17]

A somewhat different, and thoroughly Freudian, explanation has been advanced. The fact that the sexual organ of women bleeds periodically has always made a big impression on men, particularly the primitive. Since blood was rare in peace time, it was always associated with violence and disorder. In view of the fact that the elders considered any blood impure - unless associated with a sacrificial act presided over by males - it was only natural that menstrual blood should invoke virtual universal fear. It was thought of as the greatest of impurities, possibly for a sexual reason. It seemed to confirm an affinity between sexuality and the various forms of violence which terminated in bloodshed.[18]

Thus, there was a widespread primitive notion that, since menstrual blood was highly polluted, it was imperative to protect the adult male from its hazardous effects. Brazilian men thought menstruation the most menacing of all bodily processes and that the moon was its source.[19] Upon the Northwest Coast of America menstrual blood was regarded as a polluting agent almost without parallel.[20] When investigators asked the Indians of Northwestern California what polluted the world, and why their annual World Renewal ceremonies were necessary, they immediately identified menstrual blood.[21] This obsession was shared by Indians of the Great Plains.[22] Among the Southeastern Indians of the United States a menstruating woman was forbidden to bathe upstream from a man or even to stand upwind from him.[23] A Bemba myth dramatizes the danger to an unwary male: "Metaphorically she is like a 'smelting furnace' *Mutanda*, a womb-like structure full of fire, which pours out its molten metal like a 'child' *Mwana*."[24]

The most interesting explanation encountered for this pronounced male fear of female menstruation was proferred by Jacob Loewen. It came after prolonged contact with the Toba Indians of the Argentine Chaco. The female in question not only lacked all positive power at the time but, on the contrary, was charged with a negative power. This neutralized all the positive power it encountered (adult males). The result was that the victim was deprived of all strength and fell ill.[25] Weston La Barre added a Freudian explanation for this idea of negative power. As a child, the young girl has already suffered from a sense of deprivation of the penis which her brother and other young males possess. Then at puberty, the menses offers further proof of her deprived and mutilated state, a sort of castration complex. When in this state, women are unclean and thus the primitive male fears them.[26]

From the Desana tribe of the Tukano people of the Amazon river basin we can isolate a myth which perhaps best explains primitive feelings of shame and anxiety concerning the act of menstruation. It rested in original sin. The Lord of Creation, the Sun God, violated his daughter by committing incest with her at Wainambi rapids. This caused her to bleed. Since then, women must bleed every month in remembrance of this deed of violence and shame. It was a criminal act which weighs heavily upon the conscience of mankind.[27] Many scattered societies isolated the first-time menstruating female because of the persistence of the myth that the Sun God had and has "a particular taste for mortal young girls." Thanks to her isolation by her parents, the maiden escaped as the object of such dangerous attention.[28]

The uniform isolation of the first-time menstruating female is attributable to the fact that the primitive felt in harmony with sacred history through mythology. He was condemned to re-enact the first primordial murder of a divine maiden. It was this earliest of tragedies which threw man, as an exile, out into the world, inaugurating basic needs of food and sex and the doom of death. Since man's true sin constituted the act of forgetting his divine origin, the girl at the onset of menstruation spends three days in a dark hut without speaking to anyone. She does this because the murdered maiden became the moon and remained invisible for three days.[29]

Throughout the primitive world, therefore, the girl, as a matter of "logic," was secluded during her coming of age or her first menstruation. Whether there was a special lodge for this ceremony, as with the Tifalmin of New Guinea, or mere isolation and seclusion, as among the North American Eskimo, it was a wide-spread practice to isolate the first-timer. Reasons for this seem clear enough. First of all, this was a supernatural process. Incorrect or careless behavior could result in much harm to the girl herself.[30] Furthermore, she was regarded as temporarily unclean. Thus she could do no work nor prepare food for others, particularly for grown men to eat, because she would contaminate it.[31] In her seclusion she was cared for by women and recognized as undergoing the mysterious process of being converted from a child into a woman or one who had the remarkable powers of reproduction.[32]

While Sigmund Freud condemned such practices as a result of learned behavior, or organic repression,[33] the best defense for isolation in menstural huts came from one authority writing about the Southeastern Indians. He thought it based on sound social and psychological principles. These reinforce what folk knowledge has already told us, i.e., women do experience mood changes during menstruation. They may become anxiety-prone, despondent or even socially combative just before or during menstruation when hormone levels are at the lowest. This would have been devastating to a close-knit society such as these Indians enjoyed.[34] As for the disagreeable odor accompanying menstruation, the primitive made a connection between the mysterious substances secreted by the menstruating woman and their deleterious effects upon living things. This form of magic - bad magic - could be alleviated by the isolation of menstruating women.[35]

As a consequence all sorts of incredible powers were associated with menstruation. In the Arapesh society of New Guinea it was believed that physical contact with a menstruating woman could ward off the black arts of the sorcerer.[36] Likewise, on the northwest coast of America it was believed to render impotent the shaman's craft.[37]

It was, however, Lévi-Strauss who wrote about the remarkable fact that in eagle hunting, engaged in by tribes all over the continent of North America, a menstruating woman was thought to have had a beneficial effect. In all other cases the opposite was true among hunting tribes. His explanation was couched in almost purely sexual terms. It reminds one of Freud's hypothesis that the reason for the unique odor of menstruation was to enable the sexes to find each other in a state of nature or for the female to excite the male;[38] the menses, or the blood, was the bait to attract the male to the female. Likewise in eagle hunting, the primary problem for the hunter was to reduce the vast distance between himself and the quarry so that he might close with it and force a surrender. Menstrual blood was a principal part of the bait, a blood-stained carcass, and nearby there was a hunter who was prepared to capture the eagle when he descended upon the bait. The same term was used for this act, that of the bird grasping the bait, as that for the embrace of human lovers.[39]

We have a good explanation for much of this superstitious behavior with regard to menstruation. The primitive had two choices before him: 1) woman was a dangerous magician or 2) she was a born priestess. The inferior position that she occupied throughout that society precluded the acceptance of the priestess role. Therefore, woman was perceived as a dangerous magician.[40]

Reflecting upon the universality of the puberty rites, and the air of supernaturalism and mystery which surrounded them, as well as the importance to the contestants of attaining the privileged status of an adult, it is small wonder that puberty rites were everywhere the most important. They were both basic and fundamental to the primitive's entire culture.[41]

My co-author remarked that the comparative length of our chapter on male, as opposed to female, puberty rites, probably reflected the prejudices of male anthropologists who themselves shared the same phobia about menstruation as did primitives. They could scarcely have gained the confidence of their female informants and, obviously, would not have had access to the menstrual hut. Had more women anthropologists been involved we might have received a quite different picture of female puberty rites. Margaret Mead and Ruth Benedict could have done much to right our perspective. Unfortunately, their mentors were male, they worked in a predominantly male craft and they ended up asking the same sort of questions that a male interrogator would have asked. And they were among the last, he lamented, to have had access to primitive tribes before their culture was hopelessly corroded by contact with the white man. It is, of course, hard to refute logic of this sort.

The situation was a bit different, however, when he asked: "Why had I not utilized an article, one by Gloria Steinem, which exposed the male phobia to menstruation in our own society?" Why had I ignored it? The only useful thing perceived about the article was that it was based upon an apparently sound generalization: "Whatever a 'superior' group has will be used to justify its superiority, and whatever an 'inferior' group has will be used to justify its plight." But, past that, I am uncertain as to whether she was serious or just having fun by the display of undisputed wit. If, however, she were serious, she wanted us males to believe that, if *we* menstruated, we would regard it as but another sign of the Good Lord's favor and openly brag about it.[42]

Three factors prevent a ready acceptance of such logic: 1) Menstruation is certainly a nuisance, one accompanied by physical discomfort 2) menstrual blood does have a disagreeable odor and 3) it is not accepted at blood banks as "normal" blood.

Nevertheless, with regard to male menstruation, certain concessions have to be made to Steinem's reasoning. Because men have always monopolized the priesthood, and because priests have always been preoccupied with physical and ritual cleanliness, it probably would have been necessary long ago to have offered some new and unusual rationalizations for menstruation. The only other option - admittedly much easier to formulate and explain - would be to herald it, or dismiss it, as The Will of God.

However, thanks to Clifford Geertz, we may end on a happier note. He offers us an excellent example of "womb envy" and female power, the illustration of which appeared to elude Steinem. He himself was dependent upon the reporting by Anthony Forge of the four-color flat painting by the Abelam people of New Guinea. Everywhere the one constant feature of it was a pointed oval, representing the belly of a woman. The Abelam perceived woman's creativity as a precultural one, a product of their physical being. Man's creativity was cultural, derived from his ability to manipulate the gods through ritual. Women not only were the first agriculturalists but at one time the lovers of the gods until men revolted and acquired a monopoly of the supernatural. Finally, man appeared only from the swell of a woman's belly. Thus, male power was always at some hazard, because it might be stolen or appropriated, whereas female power, dependent only upon biology, was a natural monopoly. From this one might postulate the normal condition of each sex: insecurity for males and security for females.[43]

Thus, it would appear that female circumcision rites were older than that of the male, motivated by desires to insure virginity, fidelity to a future husband, or to present a more attractive sexual aspect. While both ceremonies were designed to insure tribal benefits from the blessings of the supernatural, it would seem that, while girls themselves were treated as "an object," boys, on the other hand, were lionized as "the subject" of the exercise.

Regardless of the strategy and tactics employed throughout the globe, Bruno Bettelheim reminded us of a central truth: unlike male specialists, women never had to pretend by ritual that they had the power to give birth. Ruth Benedict found that Apollonian societies, like that of the Pueblos and Navahos, took menstruation purely on the natural event level. On the contrary, Dionysian social orders, of whom the ancient Hebrews were one, regarded it as a violent and supernatural event from which the unwary male had to be isolated. Menstruation was shrouded in silence, dread and even disgust. It was frequently regarded as a polluting agent without parallel and could only be excised by annual rituals. While Sigmund Freud condemned the seclusion of the first-timer in the menstrual hut, others thought it sound social practice. Violent and sudden physical changes in the organism of a young girl often produced mood changes of equal strength and import. These, if unchecked, could be devastating to small, intimate and cohesive social orders. Invariably accompanying the postulate that menstruation was a supernatural event was the corollary that the blood itself had all sorts of magical properties.

Before leaving the subject of ritual, it is imperative that warfare among primitive peoples be analyzed as an extremely important aspect. In the process three crucial questions were formulated which will be explored in the following chapter.

Footnotes

1   Galbraith Welch, *Before They Came*, 225-226.

2   Daly, *Gyn/Ecology*, 159.

3   Captain R.S. Rattray, *The Tribes of the Ashanti Hinterlands* (Oxford, England, Clarendon Press, 1969), 439.

4   Daly, *Gyn/Ecology*, 156, 160, 165.

5   *Rites of Passage*, 67.

6   Mead, "Mountain-Dwelling Arapesh," *loc. cit.*, 93.

7   Bettelheim, *Symbolic Wounds*, 123.

8   Maxwell, *Bemba*, 54.

9   *Patterns of Culture*, 79-80.

10   *Ibid.*, 112.

11   Dorothea Leighton and Clyde Kluckholn, *Children of the People* (Cambridge, Massachusetts, Harvard University Press, 1947), 76-77. The Apaches of the Southwest, as well as the Indians of Northern California, had similar customs. Driver, *Indians of North America*, 371.

12   Benedict, *Patterns of Culture*, 111-112.

13   Gregory Bateson, "Bali: The Value System of a Steady State," 35-53 in *Social Structure. Studies presented to A. R. Radcliffe-Brown*, edited by Meyer Fortes, 46.

14   Daly, *Gyn/Ecology*, ft. 82.

15   Huntingford, *Nandi*, 103.

16   E. E. Evans-Pritchard, *Social Anthropology and Other Essays* (New York, Free Press, 1962), 249.

17   Deborah Winslow, "Rituals of First Menstruation in Sri Lanka," 603-625 in *Man*, v. 15, No. 4, December 1980, 621.

18   Girard, *Violence and the Sacred*, 34-35.

19   Huxley, *Affable Savages*, 145-146, 164. While the Cubeo of Brazil believed that menstrual blood was not human blood, but that of the moon, they had no dread of menstruation and their taboos in that regard were relatively minor. Goldman, *Cubeo*, 181. From the other side of the world, however, came a myth less offensive. It derived from the

Wawilak in Australia. Their folklore declared that the moon regulates the menstrual flow so that it will not continue indefinitely, but will reappear each moon, unless the woman herself is pregnant. Chris Knight, "Lévi-Strauss and the dragon: Mythologies reconsidered in the light of an Australian Aboriginal Myth," 21-50 in *Man*, v. 18, No. 1, March 1983, 47.

20   Benedict, *Patterns of Culture*, 162.

21   Driver, *Indians of North America*, 371.

22   Robert H. Lowie, *Indians of the Plains*. American Museum Science Books (Garden City, New York, The Natural History Press, 1963), 90.

23   Hudson, *Southeastern Indians*, 319-320.

24   Maxwell, *Bemba*, 29.

25   *Culture & Human Values: Christian Intervention in Anthro- pological Perspective*, 186.

26   *Ghost Dance*, 103-105.

27   Reichel-Dolmatoff, *Amazonian Cosmos*, 28, 60.

28   Emilé Durkheim, *Incest. The Nature and Origin of the Taboo*. Translated by Edward Sagarin (New York, Lyle Stuart, Inc., 1963), 72-74.

29   Eliade, *The Sacred and the Profane*, 100-102.

30   Driver, *Indians of North America*, 371; Spencer, *North Alaskan Eskimo*, 243; Wheatcroft, "Tifalmin," *loc. cit.*, 61.

31   George Bird Grinnel, "The Cheyenne Indians," 139-148 in *Golden Age of Anthropology*, edited by Mead and Bunzel, 145. See also Bjerre, *Last Cannibals*, 138. In Arapesh society it was quite convenient for a man to have two wives because, when one was menstruating, the other could cook for him. Mead, *Sex and Temperament in Three Primitive Societies, loc. cit.*, 109.

32   Huxley, *Affable Savages*, 164. Primitive woman herself had ambivalent feelings about menstruation. Among the Dusan of Borneo, for example, a woman would feel ashamed if it were generally known that she was menstruating. At the same time she was proud of her ability to do so. It meant that she was capable of conceiving and bearing children. Williams, *Dusan*, 84.

33   *Civilization and Its Discontents* (London, Hogarth Press, 1957), ft. to page 66.

34   Hudson, *Southeastern Indians*, 320.

35   Ashley Montagu, *Anthropology and Human Nature* (Boston, Porter Sergent, 1957), 201.

36   Mead, *Sex and Temperament in Three Primitive Societies, loc. cit.*, 103.

37   Benedict, *Patterns of Culture*, 162.

38   *Civilization and Its Discontents*, ft. to page 66.

39   *Savage Mind*, 51-52.

40   Durkheim, *Incest. Nature and Origin of the Taboo*, 92. He cited Ernest Crawley.

41   Paul Radin, *The World of Primitive Man* (New York, Henry Schumann, 1953), 152.

42   From *Outrageous Acts and Everyday Rebellions* (New York, Holt, Rinehart and Winston, 1983), 337-340.

43   Anthony Forge was the reporter, *Local Knowledge*, 100-101.

Chapter VII

RITUAL:

(continued)

War

Although war was neither instinctive nor universal, it did occur for many reasons. These stemmed from judicial impulses, a desire for play, acquisitive motivations, Malthusian pressures or as a means of promoting internal unity and the like. Whatever its cause and/or purpose, war was inevitably ritualized at every phase of its operation, and even beyond. This meant that the gods were invoked to protect both the individual warrior and the sacred society.

The content of this chapter is confined to an attempted response to three basic questions: 1) From evidence derived from examinations of the most primitive societies can it be deduced that warfare was innate and instinctive to man, or on the contrary, a form of learned behavior? 2) When and where war occurred, what were the various types and for what varied reasons? and 3) Why was ritual and magic indispensable for warfare at every stage from beginning to end of hostilities and past that point?

While Robert Ardrey was on sound ground arguing that the history of man was largely influenced by technologically superior weapons, evidence simply does not support him when he maintained this was caused by man's innately predatory character.[1] Indeed, an analysis of the behavior of hunting societies - and perhaps one cannot get closer to man's real nature than through this avenue -casts doubt on the idea that war is instinctive to man.

A most interesting explanation accounting for the complete absence of institutionalized warfare among hunting societies was the one with regard to the tribes of Australia. First of all, since they possessed no property, there was nothing to steal and loot from one another. The only thing they possessed were boundaries, within which they had a tribal monopoly of hunting and fishing, and these boundaries were mutually respected by neighboring tribes. Finally, any contests or quarrels over women were regarded purely as personal and not tribal affairs. So here no face of Helen could launch a military enterprise of any size and none of an official capacity.[2]

There was a remarkably similar explanation for the lack of warfare among the Shoshone Indians prior to their obtaining the horse. They had no territory to defend because a territory was only valuable when producing food. As for aggression against one's neighbors, they lacked a society sufficiently organized to wage a concerted and successful effort.[3]

With regard to societies which primarily depended upon hunting, one observer saw man not as a natural predator of his own kind but as one who was quite likely to establish a gentle social order. He cited, for example, the Arapesh of New Guinea, the Lepchas of Sikkim in the Himalayas, and the pygmies of the Ituri rain forest in Africa.[4] With regard to the Arapesh, warfare was also virtually unknown.[5]

There were many other such societies. The Bushmen of South Africa were so peaceful they did not even have a name for war and they attached no honor to aggression. The Mission Indians of Southern California found war an impossible concept to grasp. The Alaskan Arctic Eskimo was innocent of warfare. There was no organized warfare of any kind among the Yahgan Indians of South America. Contrary to the popular notion, the

Siriono of Eastern Bolivia were not warlike. The most dramatic - and in light of subsequent history the most suspect - was with regard to the Tasadays, stone age men inhabiting the caves of the dense forests of Mindanao. They had no word for war. They did not regard their tools as weapons. This made sense because they did not even hunt the deer which abounded. Their behavior, gentle and affectionate, was supportive of the noble savage theory of Jean Jacques Rousseau.[6] With evidence such as this, it is difficult to support the contention of scholars who argued that man was innately and instinctively a killer of his own kind.[7]

The origin and kind of conflict most often experienced among hunting bands and tribes was aptly explained by one authority when referring to the island of Borneo. First of all, no political machinery existed for the settlement of disputes between members of two separate tribes. Therefore, a solution was often sought by resort to armed force. This generally took the form of a raid by a small number of men who sought to correct an offense which could not be dealt with within the structure of traditional law and justice.[8] Another anthropologist had an almost identical explanation when speaking of African practices.[9] The same situation resulted among the Arunta and Walbiri of Australia where there was no institutionalized warfare and conflict was restricted to private individuals. These were in reality engaged in a form of judicial procedure rather than war.[10]

No one has given us a better description of how such a system worked than did M. Fortes when speaking of the Tallensi of the northern territory of the Gold Coast. War came into being solely as an act of reprisal for a specific criminal act. It did not exist on a permanent basis as state policy. Since punishment, and not conquest, was the aim, territorial annexation was forbidden and neither slaves nor booty could be carried home. There was, as a matter of fact, the strictest injunctions against retaining any food or even livestock of him who had been attacked. Presumably, all such material gain would contaminate the purity of the original purpose of the venture which was to punish a stipulated offender. Finally, since war only occurred between neighbors, and one had many kinsmen in such a tribe, the warrior had to be extremely careful whom he slayed. It was an onerous sin to kill a relative.[11]

When such conflicts occurred in and among hunting societies, they could not be long sustained because of food shortages which could only be resolved when the tribe was at peace.[12] Tribal war also caused sexual abstinence, another compelling reason to terminate it.[13] Such forays were usually dependent upon the element of surprise, as in the Andaman Islands; if this were foiled, the venture was abandoned. At any rate, the casualties were uniformly light. Conflict among the Southeastern Indians of the United States was much the same. Warfare in the modern sense did not exist. However, the principle of clan retaliation prevailed. That is to say, an injury or death suffered by one of its members was interpreted as an injury to all. The object became, therefore, one of surprising and terrorizing the offender and his tribe. Since the element of surprise was considered essential, a war party often returned home without striking a blow because its cover was blown. Finally, no group discipline existed. Each man fought as he thought best.[14]

The fact that man possessed sufficient rationality to rise above a devotion to the practice of war was indicated with regard to the Tinguian in the Northern Philippines. It had been a long time since war had successfully been outlawed by treaties which were buttressed by marriages between neighboring villages and maintained by tribal headmen. As a result trade and travel were made possible over an extended area.[15]

Despite this, we must ponder the puzzling fact that many primitive peoples seemed to be continually in a state of hostility with tribes of their own race and culture.[16] Philip Newman specifically focused on the question with regard to the twelve thousand people occupying a wide valley in the mountainous interior of New Guinea. While the natives were culturally and linguistically alike, they did not form a single political unit. Instead, they engaged in almost constant tribal wars with each other.[17] The same chaotic situation was observed in many other scattered areas throughout the world: Northern Luzon, Hawaii, the Marguesas, New Zealand (Maori), Southeastern Nigeria (Ibo), the African Sudan (Zande), the Orinoco in Northern South America (Yanomamö), the Southeastern Indians and those of the Great Plains of the United States (Blackfoot, Crow and others). Certainly the most dramatic account of the adverse effect of this Hobbesian-like behavior came from A. L. Kroeber when writing about the American Indian east of the Mississippi. He believed it was this essentially meaningless and incessant warfare, and not poor soil or agricultural methods, which caused the thin population. It was, he lamented, a kind of insane warfare and one without end, causing high casualities. Yet it was a practice so integrated into the Eastern culture pattern as to make it almost impossible to eradicate.[18] In a similar fashion, the causal factor of war in South America prior to the arrival of the white man was the instilled belief that the only way to obtain spirit power was to slay the foe.[19] Of the Yanomamö on the Venezuelan-Brazilian border, such aggressive behavior was motivated by the desire to demonstrate sovereignty or the capacity to initiate and sustain fighting in such a spirit as to prove tribal capacity or superiority to others.[20]

Warfare as an institution may have begun with agricultural societies and their constant need for more arable land to support an ever-burgeoning population. Although the early Danubian hunters were a peaceful folk, later inhabitants found war to be a natural state once unoccupied fertile land became scarce or exhausted.[21] The competitive situation was compounded by the fact that Pleistocene man spread rapidly over much of the globe. As a consequence, no suitable and accessible areas were unoccupied. What followed was that the expanding societies with technological skills took land away from those who previously possesssed it but were without means to defend it.[22] For the first time, agriculture made it possible to have continuous warfare. Agriculture itself could be carried on by women in the absence of their warrior husbands.[23] Save for exceptional instances, the depiction of warfare in art forms also began with agrarian social orders.[24]

However, this entire train of logic was rejected by those scholars who thought of agriculture as the first civilizing influence. As long as man had not progressed beyond the hunting and fishing stage, he was doomed to a perpetual food shortage and, therefore, hostility to strangers. Until man learned to work and plan wisely to effect surpluses, as was done under agriculture, he often preferred to raid the harvests of others. Agriculture, as it did for the Incas, released man from these predatory instincts.[25] A similar argument was made for the cultivators of the land in Africa.[26]

Aggression sometimes developed as a consequence of sharp and abrupt changes in the physical environment of a people. It was the introduction of the horse to the Great Plains which greatly increased tribal mobility. It resulted in almost constant attacks against one's neighbors.[27] Likewise, progressive technology generally produced like results.[28]

In a great many instances the persistence of war as a social institution could be attributed to a kind of game adult males played. The warfare of the primitive was so subordinated to rules and ceremony as to place it in the same category as European chivalry of the Middle Ages.[29] In Hawaii the system was like feudalism. It possessed strict rules and regulations and was accompanied by prayers, ritual and ceremony.[30] To many Africans war was a kind of sport because it lent excitement to an otherwise drab life. This was behind the other reasons given for war.[31] Peter Matthiessen dramatically pointed out this fact with regard to the primitive tribes in the Baliem Valley of Netherland New Guinea. Occurring several times a month, their wars might be likened to formalized sporting events. There was no other plausible explanation. There was not only a striking cultural similarity among the several tribes, but there were no economic pressures. Both land and food were plentiful.[32] Likewise in New Guinea in the frequent wars between the Tsembaga and Maring tribes, the victor was content merely to drive the vanquished from the battle zone and then destroy his houses and crops. He sought neither to annihilate the foe nor to occupy his country which was under the protection of gods foreign to him. Limited warfare with restricted casualities appeared as an integral part of this game. Thus play could be resumed the following year.[33] Play, rather than the serious purpose of destroying the foe or dispossessing him of his homeland, seemed to account for both the dramatics and the low casualty rates of warfare in the Marquesas.[34] Finally, there was a distinct chivalry about it all as noted of the Ifuago of Luzon. The young men were admonished to fight to avenge the life of a kinsman and to show bravery when in battle. But when it was won, they were instructed not to seize the land of the foe because this would deprive him of his food source.[35]

The same kind of ground rules prevailed in the warfare among the Plains Indians of America.[36] It was a sort of play or game. First of all, there was a respect for the sturdy foe, rather than hatred. No one sought to destroy an adversary, nor drive him from his country nor to reduce him to servitude.[37] A display of individual talent, or a lust for fame seemed to be the name of the game in the almost perpetual raids of small magnitude with low casualty rates.[38] Both scalps and horses were perceived of as evidence of prowess with the former often being a prerequisite for marriage. Highest honors were paid to the warrior who executed a coup or to one able to touch a foe without harming him, while in danger of losing his own life.[39] Indian wars were ideal because of their small-scale nature. They were both particularized and personalized. The fact that acts of heroism were seen by all simply encouraged more of it. Among the Plains Indians, no warrior thought of marriage until bringing back the scalp of a foe.[40]

In other areas of the primitive world, warfare also gave the youth an opportunity to display prowess, or masculinity, and this often involved bloody prizes. Among the Tupinamba of the jungle forests of Brazil a young warrior could not marry until he had killed a foe.[41] In the fierce Asmat tribe of New Guinea a young man could marry without having taken the head of a foe, but the subsequent ridicule by his wife generally forced him to the deed.[42] Among the head-hunters of Northern Luzon, marriage was easy for the youth once he had taken a head. Indeed, the support tribal women gave to this practice made it quite difficult for whites to stamp it out.[43]

The exotic element in war games, at least as far as civilized man is concerned, was the high level of personal pain apt to be involved. The primitive seemingly thought highly of pain and especially of its conquest by man.[44] Torture, whether inflicted on self, as an act of atonement for the taking of life, or upon others, involved elements of both masochism and sadism. The endurance of great pain was a test of manhood and displayed a capacity for spirituality.[45] Part of the physical fitness programs among primitive man were designed to enable a warrior to endure torture when captured. If the Dakota were guilty of perpetrating horrible cruelties upon the Ute, it was no more than they expected in turn if captured. This pain they endured with great fortitude.[46] The same insistence on using warfare as a masculine test to rise above and master pain was manifested among the Brazilian Indians of the tropical rain forest. Certain tribes, like those in the Telefolmin area in the interior of New Guinea, were ingenious enough to devise tests which put both the giver and taker of pain in anguish. Here candidates for the puberty rites were required to commit ritual murder and, if necessary, elders guided their spear into the victim, the bound captive.[47] With regard to the Iroquois, some psychologists believed public torture of the foe provided a necessary emotional release for people who lived in crowded quarters and were ordinarily subjected to a strict behavior pattern.[48]

The acquisitive society theme, or the desire to aggrandize oneself materialistically at the expense of one's neighbor, has consistently and universally been a cause for war. Thorstein Veblen argued man has habitually prized the spoils of war as a badge of distinction, valuing aggression over labor as a means of acquiring property. In the lower barbarian stage, women were valued as trophies of war, or as public evidence of the helplessness of the foe.[49] For example, in the northern part of Central Australia, tribes raided each other not merely for food but to combine the sport of hunting with the luxury of wife-napping.[50] In South America among warlike tribes the capture of an alien wife was regarded as evidence of bravery.[51] Because of their monopoly of childbirth, women might also be seized from the enemy in order to replenish or revitalize the stock of the victor. This was especially important in small tribes, such as the Yanomamö on the Venezuelan-Brazilian border, where there was always a chronic shortage of women. Even if the sex ratio were favorable, pregnant or nursing women were denied sexual privileges, which meant that they were not available to any of the tribal men for a period of three years. So constant was the threat of woman stealing here that, if a woman left a village, she always took her youngest with her so that they would not be left motherless in the event she was spirited away by strangers.[52] In the interior Xingu region of Brazil wars occurred over child stealing and for much the same reasons.[53] It is probably fair to say that the Ute Indians were working on this problem from two different directions when they warred for the purpose of acquiring women and horses.[54] The Cheyenne warred not because they loved aggression but to deny it to their foe. They appeared more eager to acquire horses than to fight.[55] It always seemed to be the young buck who constantly threatened the peace on the Plains because of his desire to acquire property and status by horse stealing. Indeed, the horse quickly became the first cause behind the continual raids which tribes sprang on each other. In the nineteenth century the most honored war deed was to pluck and lead away a captured horse from within an armed enemy camp.[56]

For many aggressive pastoral tribes in Africa, war, sport and plunder formed an integral part of the life pattern. This was true not only for tribes in East Africa, like the Karimojong and the Nandi, but for the Nuer and others in the Sudan as well as the tribes in the Sahara. Cattle stealing was a legitimate, even laudable activity, for it gave young men an opportunity to distinguish themselves as warriors while at the same time enriching them.[57] Further, cattle stealing provided great motivation for the African pastoralist: the cattle he inherited were entailed for his heirs. They could not be disposed of as he chose. However, the cattle that he stole were unconditionally his in the free enterprise sense. Absolute, as opposed to conditional, property rights had a universal appeal.[58] As one old man of the Baganda tribe on the western shores of Lake Victoria explained, drought did not bother the tribe in the old days because it simply took what it needed from its neighbors.[59] Of course it was done by the rules. In East Africa the raiding season began in October when the crops were harvested so there would be plenty to eat before the foray and while on it. Finally, the raids did not entail mass destruction upon the foe nor did he lose land. They merely left him temporarily with less cattle than before.[60] The Masai in East Africa afforded a classic example of this technique. Since the land of their neighbors was not ideal grazing country, the Masai did not conduct bona fide invasions for the purpose of acquiring lands on a permanent basis. Instead, they struck silently and quickly and as quickly retreated with their booty, usually consisting of cattle.[61] Yet, with regard to camel stealing among the Bedouins in Northern Arabia, the victor emerged in a stronger and more strategic position to exercise political and regional dominance.[62]

Perhaps no one has done a better job at analyzing the conflicting aims and aspirations of cattle pilferers in East Africa than did Günter Wagner when analyzing the behavior of the Bantu of Kavirondo with regard to other Bantu tribes. With non-Bantus their war aims were very simple, i.e., to exterminate or at least drive them away and acquire their land and possessions. But with other Bantu tribes matters were more complicated.

There remained the old desire to settle matters by driving neighbors away. But, if one did that, then how was one to continue to steal cattle from him? Owing to the imperative of balancing the advantages of these two conflicting aims, war tended to settle into a chivalrous pattern. Both groups conceded the right of existence to one another. The rights of women and children were carefully safeguarded as was the treatment of the honored war dead. Likewise, the periods of hostilities themselves were controlled. What eventuated, therefore, was the fact that war between and among Bantu tribes acted as a kind of balance wheel, making for a rough but even distribution of property among the tribes.[63] Yet even within a system of this sort there were occasional casualties. Among the Logoli, for example, continual and successful raids upon their neighbors sometimes produced an eventual retreat on the latter's part so that the victor began grazing his stock in what was previously a no-man's zone and even cultivating gardens there.[64]

In many instances Malthusian pressures in Africa terminated war as sport, substituting a more pragmatic basis but one which was at the same time more grim and bloody. In East Africa, for example, purposive overpopulation of animals and man on arid tracts ultimately caused massive aggression against one's pastoral neighbor with the intent of driving him off his homeland. The Karimojong were ruthless exploiters of the land. As they exhausted it, they simply took adjoining lands away from the tribes who were unfortunate enough to be in their way.[65] In Somali society land titles were no firmer than one's ability to defend them with military might.[66] Perhaps a classic illustration of Malthusian pressures causing tribal aggression was that of the Turkana following the decline of the Masai as a result of famine and disease toward the end of the nineteenth century.[67] To the south, the Bemba in Northern Rhodesia found the land empty upon arrival. Apparently, their peaceful tactics were later abandoned when population pressures caused them to aggress against their neighbors, pushing them back.[68] Much of the same thing apparently happened to the Zulus who came into South Africa in the mid-fifteenth century as cattle raiders. However, by the late eighteenth century there were wars of conquest, possibly because of population pressures.[69] Aridity was likewise the cause of tribal aggressions and conquest to the north in the Sahara.[70]

In the Pacific similar pressures were in operation. Twice in the history of Tikopia, Malthusian pressures resulted in a segment of the people having been driven off the island.[71] In New Zealand the Maori frequently fought for the possession of fertile tracts.[72] In Hawaii the practice of redistributing land as a consequence of the coming to power of a new king insured the fact that land would be a perpetual source of conflict.[73] The cause for continual strife in the highlands of New Guinea was probably the lack of enough land in relation to the population. However, the conflicts themselves were basically a maneuver for strategic position to control the land, rather than simple possession of it. This would have entailed massive invasion and considerable casualties.[74]

For these acts of theft and deprivation there appeared a two-pronged justification. First of all, there was the invariable theme of this particular society being the sacred one, the chosen people of God placed at the center or the navel of the earth. Indeed, there was nothing outside of this area which merited any serious consideration. In that sense the universe was confined to the space occupied by the tribe. That is why some primitive tribes, such as the Yanomamö of the Venezuelan-Brazilian border, had the same word for the tribe as for mankind itself. This sentiment is what Emilé Durkheim called sociocentrism.[75] Second, this heroic self-image was frequently accompanied by the mythology of The Terrible People Next Door. This is why anthropologists often encountered tribes which were unwilling to accord their neighbors the status of human beings, despite the fact the two tribes were of the same race and culture. An excellent example of this kind of paranoid behavior was the Urubus of the Brazilian rain forest. Suspicious of all outsiders whom they shot on sight, they remained in a state of perpetual hostility with all their neighbors.[76] Add the fact that a sub-human foe might possess much desirable land which could not be shared because of conflicting lifestyles, for example, hunters versus agriculturalists or pastorals.[77] The result is a sound explanation for the persistent attempts of the invading Hottentots and Bantus to exterminate the Bushmen. The Hottentots, for example, did not regard Bushmen as human beings with all the rights customarily given to that species but merely as odious and to be terminated as quickly as possible.[78] Later, the Boer farmer cheerfully accepted the same philosophy of exclusivism as he sought to exterminate the breed.[79]

There is evidence, however, that sometimes tribes could circumvent Malthusian pressures on the land by the simple practice of blood-letting through the practice of war. The Tsembaga of New Guinea was a classic example of this technique. There were few casualties in this ritualistic warfare. War itself was stopped by common agreement when enough deaths had occurred to ease the economic competition. Computer research at the Massachusetts Institute of Technology indicated this spilling of blood every two decades could keep the economy stabilized for five hundred or more years.[80] Not only do such practices solve the overpopulation problems in societies which prefer males, and thus raise more boy babies than girls, but it has an additional social value. It directs hostility towards the enemy rather than to the tribal fathers who dictated the sexual imbalance in the first instance.[81]

Finally, Peter Farb gave an explanation for war origins which appears convincing to the modern-day scholar. Writing about the Iroquois, who existed in a state of perpetual readiness for war with all their neighbors, he concluded that tribes often resort to war in order to promote internal unity. This is otherwise lacking because they are without those institutions which ordinarily provide it. For the tribe to survive, it must have that unity war alone can bring. On the contrary, although an agricultural people, the Iroquois had no interest in driving their neighbors off and acquiring their lands. They lacked both the political machinery and the manpower to exploit such gains. War's object in such an event, was to obtain both prisoners and booty.[82]

No matter the cause or course of war for the primitive, it was invariably ritualized from start to finish, and even beyond.[83] This meant that every phase of war had either a supernatural, magical aspect or both. Among the Crow Indians every single venture, no matter how small and for what materialistic or psychological purpose, was clothed in the sanction of the supernatural.[84] In Hawaii no warfare was begun until after the priests in the temple asserted the will of the gods was favorable.[85] With the Bagobo of Mindanao, Mandaragan was the god of war for whom men died in battle, but who could be depended upon to place heroes under his special protection.[86] Crashing Thunder, an American Plains Indian, insisted that fasting and prayer to all the gods must be the first two stages of any war.[87] Anthropologists discovered an answered prayer of a Zuni war party[88] and the Social Contract between a Kansa war captain and the Sun God, Wakanda. The former promised specific and stipulated goods in return for services rendered, i.e., assistance in killing a Pawnee and a successful return with enemy horses.[89]

Prayer finished and the contract signed between man and his gods, the ritual proceeded in a prescribed way. If desirous of making war, one must sing and dance, paint and sign in the traditional way.[90] The more horrible and frightening the body painting the greater the strength it was believed to impart, insuring the safety of its wearer.[91] When a Central Australian aborigine rubbed an arrow against a certain stone, he thereby charged it with a magical power, ensuring that it would find its mark and slay the foe.[92] In South America the feathers on an arrow not only had the function of guiding the weapon but were believed to have the power to ward off evil spirits and bring good luck.[93] Before the Nandi in Africa began a raid, the head and chest of every warrior was touched with a club doused with war medicine and the sacred club was then carried by the section commander on the expedition itself.[94] The Southeastern Indians had similar practices. There a medicine bundle of holy objects was carried by the Great Warrior on a raid. It must never touch the ground, was always placed on a pedestal when the party halted, and was only handled by the Great Warrior and his waiter.[95] Black Elk's recollection of a battle, mystical to modern man, probably made sense to the primitive everywhere. Lacking a gun, he just held the sacred bow in his right hand and caused all the bullets to miss their target.[96] An even more fantastic version of the powers of the magical medicines of war came from the Bagobo. If a shield were properly prepared, its holder could cause his foe to drop dead merely by pointing his spear at him.[97]

Certain rituals inevitably followed the termination of battle. These were apparently caused by a recognition of the fact that violence uprooted the natural order of things and had to be atoned for by confession and sacrifice. Here one is not thinking of the mourning for the domestic dead and the honors invariably paid them in the death ritual,[98] but rather of those performed by the victor as a form of compensation in the name of the vanquished. After victory over the foe, the Didinga quickly expunged their sins. They were in haste to enact the ritual of purification which was demanded of those who shed blood. Without this who knew what price would be exacted by the ghosts of their foes for the dishonor done them by an arrogant or careless victor.[99] The Zuni Indians had post-war rituals for identical purposes, that is, purification of the victor and pacification of the vanquished.[100] Following the return of the victor among the Southeastern Indians the medicine bundle was placed before the door of the winter house of the Great Warrior. Three times he circled the house before he and his party entered for purposes of purification or to efface the pollution caused by the shedding of blood. There the party fasted for three days.[101] The behavior of the Nandi probably carried universal application. True, they made a sharp distinction between the offense of killing a kinsman and that of an outsider which was no offense at all. Nevertheless, because human blood had been shed, the killer was contaminated by the crime itself and must be purified by a ritualistic act of atonement. Until then he was unclean and, like one excommunicated by the eleventh century Catholic Church, could pass this curse on to his associates.[102] Likewise, in the Brazilian rain forest, the warrior who killed a foe voluntarily underwent ritualistic self-punishment. With the Jaboro in Southeastern Ecuador the period of penance, including sexual abstinence, might last from several months to two years.[103] Among the Acoma Indians in Southwestern United States an enemy could be scalped only in rigorously defined ceremonial ways.[104] The victor then had to remain outside his native village for twelve days. After his return, his women folk had to "feed" the scalps regularly in order to keep them quiet, especially at night.[105]

There were other, and diametrically different, rituals following battle, or those which forced the loser to make a public sacrifice of himself in the home of his conqueror. Such a genre may be seen in all phases of Maya art in the Classic period. Religious monuments, depicting the fruits of warfare or the humiliated captives of royal blood, were designed to be witnessed and sanctioned by the public in ceremonies.[106] These were devised to assuage the anger or wrath of supernatural forces which might otherwise feel neglected and vengeful.[107] Blood and sacrifice were the themes dominating this culture and they gave a world which "was filled with sanctity, power and beauty."[108] Blood spilled abroad without ritual was acceptable. The *sine qua non* was blood be spilled in a ritualized fashion at home. It was better still if that were royal blood of foreigners. The bigger the hit list of royal captives, the greater the king's prestige.[109] They sometimes were dragged through bloody ceremonies - their blood - many times before being dispatched following torture in a manner which suggested the quick death under an Aztec knife was merciful by comparison.[110] Three benefits were clearly obtained and these may be listed in rank order. The gods who originally gave blood for the creation of man, and who now needed it returned, were satisfied. The vanity of the king was assuaged, at least for the time being. Finally, the populace witnessed a stirring event and one which yielded up the desired-for public catharsis. War was the institution which provided this three-fold blessing and that appeared to be its chief purpose.

Cannibalism, sometimes called the first sacrament, followed a similar pattern. It could not occur in the free enterprise zone of the forest but had to be played out according to an elaborately prescribed ritual in the village itself, the religious navel of the universe. Thus, religious cannibalism is man's observance of an act which he believes was the mystery instituted by the gods in mythic times. The neophyte, accordingly, must kill and eat a man in honor of that deed and, doing so, he particpates in the eating of a divine body.[111] But what this primitive did in actuality the Catholic worshipper has done symbolically in his Mass for almost two thousand years, for he has eagerly partaken of the body of his Saviour.

But, like the warrior who slew the foe in battle, those who took the life of a captive amid solemn village ceremonies recognized they had committed an act of hubris against world order. This accounted for ritualistic self-punishment following the act of cannibalism.[112]

What then were the secular reasons for cannibalism? While in general one ate a dead relative to ensure his continuity among the living,[113] one might eat a foe in order to absorb his heroic qualities.[114] The Bagobo practice of eating an enemy's liver was precisely that reason.[115] In South America one drank from his foe's skull for the same purpose.[116] A significant variation upon this theme occurred during the puberty rites for young boys from the Asmat tribe in New Guinea. There the initiate sat with the skull of an enemy taken by a close relative and after such a period, presumably allowed him to soak up the sterling qualities of the dead.[117] Such practices might also be done with a desire to humiliate an enemy[118] or to gain vengeance in the name of a previous member of the tribe.[119] Although hunger and pleasure were also motives,[120] the greatest insult one could give to a foe was not to eat his flesh after being cooked. The excuse was that it was not fit for human consumption.[121] Finally, there is a Freudian note: "Apparently man has practiced cannibalism not from any natural proclivity but from psychological urgings toward the forbidden and the exceptional."[122]

In South America, hunter-gatherers who engaged in cannibalism were more likely to eat friends and relatives to ensure their continuity. Almost all agricultural people who were cannibals ate their foes.[123] In a book published in the mid-Eighties, one author argued that the custom "is [now] known only among agrarian peoples, not in food-gathering or hunting societies."[124]

However, it was from my co-author that I first learned about a current debate among anthropologists as to the extent and institutional significance of cannibalism. Later, I understood that current authorities raise the possiblity that cannibalism may be a Western creation. Documented evidence may consist of nothing but heresay.[125] A book by William Arens is one often quoted. His conclusion is easy to identify: " ... although the theoretical possibility of customary cannibalism cannot be dismissed, the available evidence does not permit the facile assumption that the act was or ever has been a prevalent cultural feature. It is more reasonable to conclude that the idea of the cannibalistic nature of others is a myth.... ... this means that the idea precedes whatever evidence has been offered to support it and that in some instances the position is maintained in spite of evidence to the contrary." It is clear that Arens regards this as The Terrible People Next Door argument. As for modern anthropologists perpetuating the myth, this reporting represents "little more than nineteenth century reinterpretations in contemporary scientific jargon." It is yet another way of establishing Western spiritual and moral superiority between "we" and "they."[126]

Finally, one must confess the presence throughout the game of war of the wild card, the element of chance, the unpredictable, or primitive anarchy, i.e., that which made war possible at all times. It was the free enterprise system of individual warfare which fell outside all the rules and logic as well.[127] It was the antithesis of the spirit of Voltaire who made a separate peace with England when his sovereign was at war with that power. Here the primitive might say to himself and others that, while his tribe was at peace with its neighbors, he was at war. For example, with the Winnebago Indians of North America any person was free to go on the warpath contrary to the wishes of the chief. If he were killed, it was regarded as suicide, unfair and wrong because of pain inflicted upon kinsmen. But, if the leader persuaded others to accompany him and they were killed, when the chief did not sanction the expedition, the charge was that of murder.[128] Community sanctions, therefore, were the best defense against the maverick, the war lover.

Thus, while warfare appeared the result of learned experiences by mankind, it might take either fairly innocuous forms, such as vigilante action and sport or play, or, on the contrary, possess much more serious and grim objectives. When the latter occurred, it was probably the result of Malthusian pressures on both pastoral and agricultural economies. Sometimes it seemed easier to achieve such ends by the extermination of the foe. When this happened any primitive people were always as self-righteous as the Old Testament Hebrew who, as God's Chosen People, found it easy to extirpate the enemy because he offended God. Naturally, ritual was indispensable because war had supernatural origins. Since blood could not be shed without just cause, this meant that permission of the gods had to be invoked and their special protection sought for that particular venture. When, despite this, enemy blood had been spilled, the victor immediately knew he had to expiate his sin in order to appease both the dead enemy and the gods themselves. The primitive was always quick to avoid the grievous offenses of pride and arrogance.

Elaborately staged rituals at the home of the victor, or those which demanded the blood of the captive as a sort of High Mass at the sacred center of the universe, were epitomized by the Maya of the Classic period. Some authorities argued that cannibalism in agricultural societies simply went one step further by utilizing the body of the victim for the physical and spiritual benefit of the conqueror. In hunting and gathering communities the practice was generally designed to insure that a relative would not have to part company with his or her survivors. Cannibalism, therefore, was sometimes called the first sacrament, being a thoroughly ritualized activity.

In most recent times, however, anthropologists entered a caveat. They charged that such "practices" were nothing more than romanticized distillations of reality. They stem from nineteenth century convictions that the white man's customs and morality justified the imposition of his way of life.

This anthropological disputation aside, one is inclined to conclude that warfare and religiosity are one and inseparable. Every society appears to have its own version of the emotional slogan: "For God, King and St. George!"

Footnotes

1   Robert Ardrey, *African Genesis. A Personal Investigation into the Animal Origins and Nature of Man* (New York, Athenum, 1961), 316.

2   Semon, *In the Australian Bush*, 225.

3   Farb, *Indians of North America*, 31.

4   Geoffrey Gorer, "Man Has no 'Killer' Instinct," 27-36 in *Man and Aggression*, edited by Ashley Montagu (New York, Oxford Press, 1968), 34.

5   Margaret Mead, "Sex and Temperament in Three Primitive Societies", in *From the South Seas*, 23.

6   Kenneth MacLeish, "Stone Age Cavemen of Mindanao," in *National Geographic*, vol. 142, No. 2, August, 1972, 226.

7   Farb, *Indians of North America*, 125. On the contrary, the Conrad Lorenz theory, if popularly accepted, is apt to make war inevitable. This need not be so. Sally Carrighar, "War is Not in Our Genes," 37-50 in *Man and Aggression*, edited by Montagu, 40, 50. "It is much more likely that warfare is a cultural invention rather than the inevitable consequence of man's so-called animal nature." de Waal Malefijt, *Images of Man*, 345.

8   Williams, *Dunsun*, 66.

9   Huntingford, *Nandi*, 76.

10   Service, *Profile of Primitive Culture*, 18.

11   "The Political System of the Tallensi of the Northern Territory of the Gold Coast," 239-271 in *African Political Systems*, edited by M. Fortes and E. E. Evans-Pritchard, (New York, Oxford University Press, 1966), 242. Like the Eskimo, the Bushmen were astonished that the white man purposely went out to kill people they did not know. Van Der Post, *Lost World of the Kalahari*, 244.

12   Service, *Hunters*, 59.

13   Linton, *Marquesan Culture*, in *Individual and His Society*, edited by Kardiner, 178.

14   Hudson, *Southeastern Indians*, 239, 249.

15   Fred Eggan, "Some Aspects of Culture Change in the Northern Philippines," 11-18 in *American Anthropologist*, vol. 43, 1941, 17.

16   Benedict apparently approached this problem somewhat differently in the 1959 and 1960 paperback editions of her *Patterns of Culture*. In the former she observed that, because certain tribes classify all outsiders as subhuman, even though some may be of the

172

same race and culture, they find the idea of peace with these groups repugnant. If they did not, they would have to admit them to the status of human beings. This is something the culture itself will not allow. Therefore, the normal state is one of war. (Boston, Houghton-Mifflin, 1959), 31. In the 1960 edition - used exclusively throughout this monograph - the emphasis on internecine war among kindred peoples dropped out. Emphasis on the uniqueness felt by each tribe did not. They alone were human beings and all outsiders, even those of the same race and culture, were not. Obviously, from such a state of rejection and hostility, perpetual alertness for war must result. (New York, Mentor book, New American Library of World Literature, 1960), 21-22. It was, no doubt, for reasons like this that René Girard believed the concept of permanent war was known to the primitive. *Violence and the Sacred*, 280.

17   "Sorcery, Religion and the Man," in *Natural History*, vol. 71, February, 1962, 21.

18   *Cultural and Natural Areas of Native North America* (Berkeley, University of California Press, 1963), Foreword, viii, 148. Not contested was the fact that the Southeastern Indians loved warfare, undisciplined as it was. Hudson, *Southeastern Indians*, 240-241.

19   *Selections from the Writings of Jacob A. Loewen, Cultural and Human Values*, Preface, xi-xii.

20   Napoleon A. Chagnon, "Yanomamö-the Fierce People," 22-31 in *Natural History*, vol. 76, No. 1, January, 1967, 26.

21   Childe, *What Happened in History*, 67.

22   George A. Bartholomew and Joseph B. Birdsell, "Ecology and Protohominids," in *American Anthropologist*, vol. 55, No. 4, October, 1953, 495.

23   Kroeber, *Cultural and Natural Areas*, 149. Kenneth Boulding attributed the origins of warfare as an institution to civilized societies because precivilized societies lacked the technical capacity for it. "Where Are We Going If Anywhere? A look at Post-Civilization," 368-374 in *Readings in Anthropology*, edited by Jessee D. Jennings and E. Adamson Hoebel, 3rd edition (New York, McGraw-Hill, 1972), 372.

24   Leakey and Lewin, *People of the Lake*, 276.

25   O. F. Cook, "Staircase Farms of the Ancients. Astounding Farming Skill of Ancient Peruvians ....," 474-534 in *National Geographic*, vol. 29, No. 6, June, 1916, 519.

26   I. M. Lewis, *A Pastoral Democracy, a Study of Pastoralism and Politics Among the Northern Somali of the Horn of Africa* (New York, International African Institute, Oxford University Press, 1961), 237.

27   Farb, *Indians of North America*, 31, 115.

28   Sahlins, *Tribesmen*, 7-8. After the following situation, as depicted by J. F. Driberg, it is not hard to imagine which party became more aggressive. The vast army of the Topotha, all spear throwers, were routed by the bow and arrow of the Nyangiya because they had never seen this weapon before. They were killed and wounded by arrows

at too great a distance to retaliate with spears. Their shields afforded no protection from arrows fired both high and low. *People of the Small Arrow* (New York, Payson and Clarke, 1930), 62.

29   Service, *Primitive Culture*, 121.

30   Emory, "Warfare," 233-240 in *Ancient Hawaiian Civilization*, 234.

31   Huntingford, *Nandi*, 77.

32   "The Death of Weake," 53-60 in *Harpers*, vol. 225, October, 1962, 53.

33   Roy A. Rappaport, "Ritual Regulation of Environmental Relations Among a New Guinea People," 181-201 in *Environmental and Cultural Behavior. Ecological Studies in Cultural Anthropology*, edited by A. P. Vayada (Garden City, New York, Natural History Press, 1969), 190-191.

34   Linton, *Marquesan Culture, loc. cit.*, 180.

35   James Montgomery Cooper, "The Relation between Religion and Morality in Primitive Culture," 560-572 in *Golden Age of American Anthropology*, edited by Mead and Bunzel, 564.

36   Farb, *Indians of North America*, 122.

37   Stanley Diamond, "Search for the Primitive," in *Concept of the Primitive*, edited by Montagu, 135.

38   Robert H. Lowie, "The Crow Indians," 362-376 in *Golden Age of American Anthropology*, edited by Mead and Bunzel, 366.

39   Driver, *Indians of North America*, 323-324; John Beatty, "Taking Issue with Lorenz on the Ute," 111-115 in *Man and Aggression*, edited by Montagu, 114.

40   Driver, *Indians of North America*, 320.

41   Huxley, *Affable Savages*, 95.

42   Father Alphonse Sowada, "New Guinea's Fierce Asmat: a Heritage of Headhunting," 186-203 in *The Vanishing Primitive*, (Washington, D.C., National Geographic, 1971), 193.

43   Worcester, "Head-Hunters of Northern Luzon," in *National Geographic*, vol. 13, No. 9, September, 1912, 911.

44   Huxley, *Affable Savages*, 147.

45   Diamond, "Search for the Primitive," *loc. cit.*, 134.

46   Dorothy D. Lee, *Freedom and Culture* (New York, A Spectrum Book, Prentice-Hall, 1959), 60.

47   E.T. Gilliard, "In the Land of the Headhunters," 437-486 in *National Geographic,* vol. 108, October, 1955, 461.

48   Farb, *Indians of North America,* 106.

49   *Theory of the Leisure Class,* (New York, The Modern Library, Random House, 1934), 17-27. In a North Borneo society, theft covered all forms of coercive acquisitions of property save that acquired during raids on an enemy. Williams, *Dusun,* 59.

50   Meggitt, *Desert People,* 38.

51   Karsten, *South American Indians,* 168. Wife raiding, however, was restructed to interaction between two semi-distant communities and was incompatible with friendly relations between close and related groups which had an amicable exchange of women. Christine Hugh-Jones, *From the Milk River,* 97.

52   Napoleon A. Chagnon, "Yanomamö-The Fierce People," 22-31 in *Natural History,* vol. 76, No. 1, January, 1967, 25, 27-28. Raids on enemy villages for women often came as an alternative to adultery and intra-tribal frictions. Marvin Harris, "The Yanomamo and the Cause for War in Band and Village Societies," 121-132 in *Brazil. Anthropological Prospect,* edited by Margolis and Carter, 132.

53   Harald Schultz, "The Waura. Brazilian Indians of the Hidden Xingu," 130-152 in *National Geographic,* vol. 129, No. 1, January, 1966, 151.

54   Beatty, "Taking Issue with Lorenz on the Ute," in *Man and Aggression,* edited by Montagu, 114.

55   Service, *Primitive Culture,* 121.

56   Driver, *Indians of North America,* 215. See also Melville J. Herskovits, *The Economic Life of Primitive Peoples* (New York, Alfred A. Knopf, 1940), 234.

57   Huntingford, *Nandi,* 77; Rada and Neville Dyson-Hudson, "Subsistence Herding in Uganda," 76-89 in *Scientific American,* vol. 220, February, 1969, 87; Schneider, "Pakot Resistance to Change," in *Continuity and Change in African Culture,* edited by Bascom and Herskovits, 167; Evans-Pritchard, *Nuer,* 49; Briggs, *Tribes of the Sahara,* 227.

58   Driberg, *Savage as he really is,* 36.

59   L.P. Muir, *An African People in the Twentieth Century* (New York, Russell & Russell, 1965), 191-192.

60   Huntingford, *Nandi,* 77. Dry weather was the usual season for fighting and the season for raiding commenced in October after the harvest had been gathered. This insured food before and during the raids. *Ibid.,* 83.

61   K. Oberg, "The Kingdom of Ankele in Uganda," 121-162 in *African Political Systems,* edited by Fortes and Pritchard, 127.

62   Louise Sweet, "Camel Pastoralism in North Arabia," 157-180 in *Environmental*

and Cultural Behavior, edited by Vayada, 169.

63   "The Political Organization of the Bantu of Kavirondo," 197-236 in *African Political Systems*, edited by Fortes and Evans-Pritchard, 228.

64   *Ibid.*, 227.

65   Rada and Neville Dyson-Hudson, "Subsistence Herding in Uganda," in *Scientific American*, vol. 220, February, 1969, 79.Likewise, in Brazil, one authority accounted for the growth of warfare on grounds of population pressures on land and the natural desire to maintain standards of living at the expense of weaker and neighboring tribes. Harris, "Causes of War in Band Societies," *loc. cit.*, 127.

66   Lewis, *Pastoral Democracy*, 3, 49, 89.

67   William Allan, *The African Husbandman* (New York, Barnes and Noble, 1967), 317. Also published at Edinburgh, Scotland by Oliver & Lloyd, 1967. P.R. Gulliver, *The Family Herds. Two Pastoral Tribes of East Africa* (London, Routledge and Kegan Paul, 1955), 7.

68   Audrey L. Richards, "The Political System of the Bemba Tribe -Northeastern Rhodesia," 83-120 in *African Political Systems*, edited by Fortes and Evans-Pritchard, 86.

69   Gluckman, "Kingdom of the Zulu of South Africa," 25-55 in *ibid.*, 25.

70   Briggs, *Tribes of the Sahara*, 120, 122.

71   Firth, *We, the Tikopia*, 374.

72   Raymond Firth, *Primitive Economics of the New Zealand Maori* (New York, E. P. Dutton, 1929), 40.

73   E. S. C. Handy, "Government and Society," 35-46 in *Ancient Hawaiian Civilization, A Series of Lectures* delivered at the Kamehameha Schools, 37.

74   Sahlins, *Tribesmen*, 52, 62.

75   Durkheim and Mauss, *Primitive Classification*, 86-87. See also Rubin, *Barking Deer*, 39.

76   Huxley, *Affable Savages*, 90.

77   Theal, *South of the Zambeisi*, 168-169; Frank B. Livingston, "Human Populations," 60-70 in *Horizons of Anthropology*, edited by Sol Tax, 69.

78   Theal, *South of the Zambeisi*, 63.

79   Van Der Post, *Lost World of the Kalahari*, 35-37, 55.

80   Clarke and Hindley, *Challenge of the Primitives*, 187, 190, 192.

81   Harris, "The Causes for War in Band Societies," *loc. cit.*, 126-127.

82   *Indians of North America*, 106.

83   Diamond, "Search for the Primitive," *loc. cit.*, 135.

84   Lowie, "Crow Indians," *loc. cit.*, 363, 365.

85   Kenneth Emory, "Warfare," in *Ancient Hawaiian Civilization*, 236.

86   Benedict, *Bagobo Ceremonial, Magic and Myth*, 25.

87   Crashing Thunder, "The Teachings of My Father," 229-235 in *Readings in Anthropology*, 3rd edition, edited by Jessee D. Jennings and E. Adamson Hoebel (New York, McGraw-Hill, 1972), 230.

88   Ruth Bunzel, *Zuni Ritual Poetry*, 611-835 in *Forty-Seventh Annual Report of the Bureau of American Ethnology to the Secretary of the Smithsonian Institute, 1929-1930* (Washington, D.C., Government Printing Office, 1932), 669-674.

89   Lowie, *Indians of the Plains*, 185.

90   Huxley, *Affable Savages*, 244.

91   Karsten, *South American Indians*, 30, 39.

92   Clarke and Hindley, *Challenge of the Primitives*, 171.

93   Karsten, *South American Indians*, 93.

94   Huntingford, *Nandi*, 79.

95   Hudson, *Southeastern Indians*, 247.

96   *Black Elk Speaks. Being the Life Story of a Holy Man of the Oglala Sioux, as told through John G. Neihardt* (Lincoln, University of Nebraska Press, 1961), 262.

97   Benedict, *Bagobo Ceremonial, Magic and Myth*. 220.

98   See, for example, Matthiessen, "The Death of Weake," in *Harpers*, vol. 225, October, 1962, 53-60.

99   Driberg, *People of the Small Arrow*, 80-81.

100   Bunzel, *Zuni Ritual Poetry, loc. cit.*, 674.

101   Hudson, *Southeastern Indians*, 252.

102   Huntingford, *Nandi*, 103, 111.

103   Karsten, *South American Indians*, 63.

104   White, *Acomo Indians*, in *47th Annual Report of the Bureau of American Ethnology to the Secretary of the Smithsonian*, 96.

105   Parsons, *Isleta, New Mexico, ibid.*, 260.

106   Schele and Miller, *Blood of Kings*, 210.

107   *Ibid.*, 113.

108   *Ibid.*, 305.

109   Michael Coe in "Preface" to *ibid.*, 3.

110   Schele and Miller, *Blood of Kings*, 212-213.

111   Eliade, *Myths, Dreams and Mysteries*, 200 and the *Sacred and Profane*, 102-103.

112   Huxley, *Affable Savages*, 148, 234, 252. Once outside the community, there was no place for ritual. An enemy killed in battle was eaten on the spot without grace being said. The ritualistic form of cannibalism was reserved for those captured and brought to the village itself. Girard, *Violence and the Sacred*, 274-275. Among the Bagobo, a Malay cultural group on the island of Mindanao in the Philippines, the sacrificial victim was taken away from the village into the jungle where he was stabbed and hacked to pieces. Apparently the act itself was supposed to provide health and prosperity for those dispatching the victim. Benedict, *Bagobo Ceremonial, Magic and Myth*, 167-169.

113   Huxley, *Affable Savages*, 263.

114   *Ibid.*, 262. Cannibalism was one of the three ways of incorporating *mana*, or the power of the supernatural, into oneself. Amazonia was the *locus classicus* of American cannibalism. La Barre, *Ghost Dance*, 133-135. In ancient times in the Andes, it was customary during warfare to drink the blood of a fallen foe, probably with the intent to gain his strength and power. La Barre, *Aymara Indian*, in *American Anthropologist*, vol. 50, No. 1, Part 2, January, 1948, 162.

115   Benedict, *Bagobo Ceremonial, Magic and Myth*, 215. See also Bjerre, *Last Cannibals*, 81.

116   Karsten, *South American Indians*, 68. See also Steward and Faron, "Nomadic Hunters and Gatherers," in *Cultural and Social Anthropology*, edited by Hammond (1965), 52.

117   Father Alphonse Sowada, "New Guinea's Fierce Asmat," 186-203 in *Vanishing Peoples of the Earth*, 193. See also Malcolm Kirk, "Headhunters in Today's World: The Asmat of New Guinea," 382-408 in *National Geographic*, vol. 141, No. 3, March, 1972, footnote, pg. 391.

118   Diamond, "Search for the Primitive," *loc. cit.*, 134.

119   Linton, *Marquesan Culture, loc. cit.*, 178.

120   Linton, *Marquesan Culture, loc. cit.,* 142; Evans-Pritchard, *Women in Primitive Society,* 159; Ralph Linton, "Analysis of Marquesan Culture," 197-250 in *Individual and His Society,* edited by Kardiner, 222-223.

121   Ralph Linton and Paul S. Wingert, "Introduction, New Zealand, Sepik River and New Ireland." From "Arts of the South Seas," 383-404 in *Anthropology and Art,* edited by Otten, 390.

122   Day, *Many Meanings of Myth,* 296.

123   Leakey and Lewin, *People of the Lake,* 274-275.

124   Day, *Many Meanings of Myth,* 296.

125   Pandian, *Anthropology and the Western Tradition,* 92.

126   William Arens, *The Man-Eating Myth. Anthropology and Anthropophagy* (New York, Oxford Press, 1979), 182-183.

127   Sahlins thought anarchy the unconscious element in the primitive system. *Tribesmen,* 5, 7.

128   Radin, *World of Primitive Man,* 346.

Chapter VIII

ART

*Art originated and was maintained as a
conservative art because it was in itself a ritual
designed to invoke and maintain the protection
and favor of the gods. At the same time all the
art forms combined in public ceremony to keep
the tribe constantly in touch with its sacred
origins or mythology. This provided a common
or community education, like Athenian drama.
The two functions combined for the preservation
of social order, harmony and confidence.*

As laymen, it was not easy for us to determine areas of primary
artistic concern and thereby risk shunting the remainder to those of lesser
importance. All we have done, therefore, is to indicate questions which
attracted us. These promised to reduce complexity and to give the non-
specialist an opportunity to understand and appreciate primitive art.

Within these parameters, therefore, we are absorbed in the following:
1) Art as magic 2) Artistic utilization of emotion, intuition and mysticism
3) The contrast between individual creativity and freedom, or as an act of
joy or a seizure by the gods, versus village tradition and conformity 4) The

role of tribal conservatism in cultural and artistic borrowing 5) The contrasting art of Dionysian social orders (frenzy, fear and violence must be experienced when approaching the dangerous supernatural in order to obtain wisdom and security) versus those of the Apollonian type (order, harmony, moderation in all things) 6) Art as a vehicle of the primitive Passion Play and, finally, 7) The cultural and artistic impact of the white intruder.

If we ask what characteristics art possessed from its origin with early man, and that of the primitive, the common element was the belief in magic. Our first task is to attempt an explanation of how and why that process was believed to be effective as a life force.

The above generalization is not meant to invalidate or deny certain scholarly propositions, such as the art of the hunter's society of the Paleolithic era reflected the aesthetic component, or the beauty of the composition and man's enjoyment of it.[1] Nor is it meant to cause one to ignore the wide variations in the European art of that age, ranging from what we call naturalism and impressionism to that of abstract art.[2] Candor also compels the admission that some anthropologists remain quite skeptical of the theories that Paleolithic man used cave art for its magical properties.[3]

Nevertheless, to the great majority of the experts in the field, cave art, as well as other contemporary artistic facets, had its origin in a mixed bag of magic and religion and thus appeared both functional and conservative in nature. Art was so highly ritualized because it began as an attempt on the part of man, through the use of the supernatural, to control both the social order and nature itself.[4]

It was Paleolithic art related to the hunt, relying on the principle of sympathetic magic, which most clearly revealed its conservative and ritualistic character. Before the hunt it was imperative that drawings be made of the game animal and that it be pierced by the requisite wounds, fatal in nature. Powerless as he was as a physical animal in the face of both nature itself, and the wild beasts which it supported, man necessarily resorted to his faith in magic and his ability to draw in order to inspire faith in the future. Thus, magic and art always preceded the great hunt. A classic example is of the bear depicted in the cave at Montespan, whose body revealed thirty man-induced wounds.[5] These depictions were not intended for public viewing for they were generally done in the darkest, most remote and inaccessible places, as opposed to the reliefs on the walls of shallow half-caves.[6] The product was meant for the gods and not the tribe and the art itself was meant as prophecy or divination. The artistic representation was interpreted as the thing or the act in nature itself. Since a bison magically made its appearance upon the wall of a cave, so a real bison would appear in nature for the hunters to prey upon.[7] With regard to the bison in the great cave at Miaux, France, some authorities believed it possible that the creature itself was already dead and that the art product was designed as a ritualistic way of restoring life by way of compensation for having killed it.[8] It was quite possibly a ritualistic act of atonement or an apology for having violated nature. Since a great animal had been killed, his animal essence had been returned to nature by the mere fact that his image reappeared on the sacred spot.[9]

The same facets of ritual and magic applied to the hunter's societies of recent times and oftentimes the vehicle for this was an art form. Primitives believed that magic, worked in connection with the fabrication of something useful, like that of a war canoe, was just as necessary for the efficiency of the instrument as the mechanical operations.[10] Among the North American Indians the artistic design itself was thought to work the magic, i.e., to bring down the game or to slay the foe. In the early days of the white man's imperialism, the !Kung Bushmen drew in the sand an outline of the game to be hunted. Then, amid elaborate ceremonies, they shot an arrow at the drawing, careful to hit it in the precise spot calculated most readily to bring down the live game. This was divination or an attempt to foretell events in the future.[11] Similar practices were carried on by the natives in the rain forests of the Congo-Kasai. When, in 1961, Australian bush artists denied that their pictorial of the hunt was meant to have any qualities of sympathetic magic, it is significant that they admitted they resorted to a magical song to capture the emu.[12] While this custom may have been fairly universal, nowhere was it practiced so rigorously as in North Alaska, whether the game was the whale off the coast or the caribou in the interior.[13] It, therefore, does not appear plausible to attempt to separate magic and the hunt, either in the case of early or primitive man. Finally, one suspects that the reluctance of the Australian natives to discuss the relationship between their artistry, and its magical aspects, with regard to the hunt may fall into the same category as the hesitancy of the African Bushmen to discuss the fertility concept as it related to their art. Speaking candidly about these affairs was to live dangerously as a consequence of having offended the spirits.[14]

Both Paleolithic and primitive man perceived an intelligence behind nature and one which could be negotiated with or propitiated. If man subtracted something from nature, big game for example, he must make a restitution or give something in return, say a likeness of that animal. Otherwise the continued source of food supply was jeopardized. The fact that in the rock paintings in Arnhem Land, Australia, one was superimposed on others suggests the aim was not primarily the enjoyment of viewing. Rather, it was ritualistic in character. Man made the necessary obeisance to nature. Supporting this primitive theology were certain convictions. First of all an image is what it purports to be. Second, restitution of life can and must be made to the gods who preside over nature and its animal life. Third, this was required since the very act of killing could offend not only the spirit of the victim but of the gods who planned and effected the animal's existence. Lastly, the failure to perform these required art rituals would jeopardize tomorrow's food supply.[15]

Despite the truth of the admonition primitive societies widely differed from each other in the arts,[16] there must be an attempt to reduce the subject to order. We have to understand the essentially conservative environment in which the artist lived, worked and had his being. First, let us ponder the influence of the greater community upon him.

It was universally true that primitive societies postulated an order in the universe, refusing to submit to the idea of pure chance or chaos.[17] This order, imposed upon the world by the supernatural, could not be perceived and rendered meaningful simply by observation and experiment, but could only succumb to emotion, intuition, and mysticism.[18] This accounted for the virtual universal prevalence of Platonic Idealism in primitive art. It conveyed the idea that the summit of aesthetic perfection, or beauty, transcended human experience and was unchanging and unchangeable. This meant it was alien to human values and unaffected by both history and cultural evolution.[19] This philosophy helped explain how, despite the widespread prevalence of what we call naturalistic art, the primitive almost invariably moved into the geometric and abstract varieties to express his idea of the sacred. Central Polynesia represented a classic instance of this religious tendency. The same principle apparently permeated African art. It searched for a basic principle which lay behind both the kinship system and tribal religion. Once it stripped the individual of a personality through the art form, one was left with the awe-inspiring presence of ancestorhood of humanity itself.[20] On the individual level it was personified by the Indian artist of the Northwest Coast who declared that he saw the spirit of the animal[21] he was painting. The spirit was the animal. In brief, instead of saying that primitive art was permeated by Platonic Idealism, it might be more accurate to conclude that primitive man either originated or gave form and substance to the movement which later bore the name of Platonic Idealism.

Our dilemma was aptly summed up by Margaret Trowell when she used the term expressionistic to describe a dance mask of the Congo. She understood it was somewhat hazardous to use Western terminology for an African mentality so mysterious to us. Yet that term seemed the closest we could get in our own vocabulary.[22] An even sterner warning was issued by Philip J.C. Dark when writing about misleading Western interpretations of the use of primitive symbolism, such as a snake, bird or portion of the human anatomy, or those involving varying degrees of what might be termed naturalism.[23]

As soon as attention was focused on the question of the freedom of the individual artist, as opposed to community pressures for conformity, consciously or unconsciously applied, scholarly opinions differed. One suspects that the disagreements originated not so much because of subjective interpretations by anthropologists but rather because of differences in primitive tribal structures. While this matter will be touched upon with regard to North American societies, the data was too scanty to support dogma or anything other than an intriguing hypothesis for further study.

However, all we are concerned with at the moment is a few crucial areas to make it clear that authorities themselves were in basic disagreement.

With regard to the freedom of individual African dancers, differences of opinion were soon evident. True, Stanley Diamond was convinced that individual styles clearly emerged[24] and Paul Bohannan agreed they allowed dancers considerable freedom to express themselves.[25] However, E.E. Evans-Pritchard subtracted considerably from this sort of generalization. While the dances of some African tribes were both high-spirited and relatively free with regard to form, the Zande beer dance, which was characterized by its discipline and order, seemed to be closer to that of the average African one. In general tribal dances required a rigid form, a set performance, appointed leaders, and, in short, the most rigorous kind of organization and supervision throughout. In Zande dances, for example, the movements of the individuals might differ but all were made to the same rhythm. Furthermore, there were stereotype routines for the movement of the feet.[26]

As far as the freedom of the sculptor in Black Africa was concerned, René S. Wassing began with basic differences between the sacred and profane. In the former, art forms were rigidly circumscribed, being entirely governed by traditional models, whereas in the latter field the artist was much more free to innovate. Yet, despite this, the fact most manifest to the impartial observer was the overriding influence of tradition in both areas, the ceremonial and ritualistic on one hand and the commonplace and mundane on the other.[27]

This conclusion appears valid when applied to a single artistic area such as Dahomey on the West Coast. If one were to try to explain the artistry of that area from an individual point of view, this would be to ignore the much more important fact that his art was dominated by the peculiarities of his particular village or environment.[28]

To us, the best defense of artistic independence with regard to the African sculptor came from a work by Frank Willett. Until recently, and under the dominance of European museum art, authorities were uninterested in the name of the individual African artist. In the identification process, it was presumed that the only necessary thing was to obtain the tribal affiliation.

The supposition was that any artist, whatever his merit, merely followed the dictates of the established tradition. Field work, however, not only revealed the names of individual artists but brought a new appreciation of their individual vision or design, their excellent tools and motor skills.[29]

Perhaps the best summary of the contrasting role of artist and community in Black Africa was given by Elsy Leuzinger. First of all, the author had a tremendous respect for the artist's plan of execution, his sure grasp of style, his appreciation for the aesthetic and capacity for understanding the essentials of his craft. Nevertheless, the artist's environment was limited by the range of his idea system; tribal myths were shared by everyone within the charmed circle. Once a structural form was developed and accepted by that community as one of supernatural power - which was its purpose all along - it could maintain that essential form for centuries. Minor changes would not alter its symbolic style which was regarded as infallible by the native as long as his political and social system was secure.[30]

There is no better single illustration of why conservatism, or the perpetuation of form, style and function, and/or the absence of innovation, generally persisted in primitive art forms than one concerning the Northern tribes of Central Australia. There observers discovered an absence of any representation on weapons or implements of any objects found in nature. The conventional signs, however, of wavy circles, lines and spirals no longer had any earthly meaning for those who continued to duplicate them.[31] That was precisely the point. Something which was completely unrelated to this world might and could be fully related to the next, the world of the supernatural. And no native artist was apt to damn the judgment and wishes of dead spirits by flouting that which was no doubt meaningful to them.

Even in the artistically diversified and culturally-rich area of Northern New Guinea, particularly in the Sepik river area, artistic freedom was restrained in crucial areas. In mask-making the artist was not free to innovate. He had to adhere either to the design practiced by the dead man before his demise or to the traditional masks of the demons. The same rigid limitations were imposed by secret men's societies when dramatically depicting the heroic and supernatural past of the tribe.[32] Old forms were given utter devotion and only gradually and accidentally were errors or deviations allowed to creep into the conservative arts. Likewise, there was the dominance of traditional art in New Guinea.[33]

Yet in the same area there existed many creative and dynamic art forms, like shield and drum designs and sculpted dance figures. These and many other art objects manifested original composition and vigor. Its many creative forms may have been due to artistic isolation produced by almost continual warfare. It was a peasant and insular culture, contrary to the seafaring spread of the Polynesian type, but it achieved quality because its tools were well-made and well-shaped and of native proficiency in handling them. Likewise in the Melanesian area of the East Solomons the ceremonial bowls were not only artistically beautiful but unique.[34]

Much more sophisticated, because of navigation and trade, was Polynesian art. It was culturally determined by the high gods and tribal chiefs who allegedly descended from them. Therefore, it was aristocratic and perhaps because of this it resisted tendencies toward regional conformity. Reflecting the characteristics of a progressive people, Polynesia's art and culture were abruptly terminated by the invasion of Angle-Saxons.[35]

Admittedly deficient in religious art, which lacked aesthetic appeal, the Bush African secular art of Surinam in South America profited by outside contacts to the point where it evolved a unique style and one possessing considerable vitality. Even more important was the fact that the secular art, especially that involving sexual themes, varied considerably from artist to artist.[36]

As soon as one considers the question of the freedom of the artist in North America, a startling query must be cited. It concerned a unique aspect of twelfth century Mimbres art, one featuring a reproduction of organic forms in deep food bowls. Painting of this type was creative and its artistic excellence consistently high. Yet, at the same time its life-span was so brief it caused the authors to wonder if the entire school were not the product of a single genius. Its disappearance left geometric art, arranged in complex patterns, in a monopolistic position throughout the Southwest.[37]

In more modern times it was the contrasting situation in North

America which caused the authors to suspect that, among the thinly-populated and nomadic Indians on the Great Plains, artists tended to enjoy more freedom than they did among the thickly-populated and agrarian communities to the Southwest. However, such freedom was reserved for male artists whose naturalistic reproductions alone bore the stamp of the individual whereas the geometric art for females was rigidly traditional.[38] This masculine art was often connected with magic and religion. The designs on the shields of the warriors of the Plains were believed to contain such magical powers that they, and not the shield itself, protected its bearer from harm. The artistic designs had been received from the gods while the artist was in a trance.[39] The only sculpture on the Plains was that done for pipes in red or black "pipestone" converted into a plain L or T-shaped bowl. Occasionally, however, artistic freedom and imagination could effect something entirely different, such as a horse's head.

With regard to individual artistic freedom, the greatest scholarly attention appeared to be focused on the dances in the Plains and here again the art form was intimately associated with magic and religion. In the Ghost Dance, for instance, because of the belief that the individual dancer merely reflected the will of some higher power, there was no attempt to interfere with his unique performance.[40] The very purposes responsible for the Sun Dance were of an individual order because the dancers hoped, if successful, to obtain a vision or a communication from the sun.[41] Success hinged upon the ability to dance the dance to its completion which occurred whenever the individual dancers succeeded in tearing the sticks from their body which bound them by thongs to a central pole.[42] However, torture was only obligatory among the Dakota and Ponca and was completely lacking among the Ute, Shoshone and Kiowa. Moreover, for the mass participant the dance was stereotyped. What most individuals were asked to do was very easy to comply with since it merely involved blowing whistles while rising on their toes.[43] Among the Sioux on one occasion, Sitting Bull had charge of the Horse Dance which featured the trance of Black Elk in which he saw visions and bedazzled his people. After the dance was over, and the dog had been sacrificed, everyone, apparently even the horses, felt better, being rejuvenated by the experience.[44]

Reflection on the Black Elk episode naturally led to the puzzling question as to the relationship of primitive ritual and ceremony to mysticism. This is that facet of human experience which is incapable of being explained to others but has to be experienced first-hand to be known. It was no doubt a study of such practices which caused scholars like Edward Sapir and Clark Wissler to dissent from the generalizations of Dorothy D. Lee. The last named scholar argued that mysticism could only occur in those societies which had already separated man from nature. Mysticism was the pious attempt to reunite the two.[45] Yet, the Plains Indians were clearly not guilty of having severed man from nature. Sapir was convinced of the individual mystical experience derived from the Sun Dance.[46] Wissler maintained that, at one time or another, virtually every adult male attempted, under the tutelage of a shaman, to achieve a mystical experience. Any art which rested upon mysticism was bound to reflect an erratic pattern and undisciplined character.[47]

However, any such individual and artistic freedom enjoyed by the shamanistic societies of the Great Plains was at sharp variance from established patterns in the more rigorous and stylized world of the priest of the Southwest. Among the Navaho no one was allowed to tamper with the Night Way chant, designed to promote well-being. The one time it was tried with many innovations, unfortunately, it was followed by general disaster. Today no one tampers with tradition.[48] Save for minor aspects, the Navaho painter was not free to improvise at will. He could design and color the kilts of the gods as he chose, but tradition dictated everything else. The grand design of both the sand painting itself and the healing chant was handed down from one singer and his assistants to their successors.[49] Among Zuni artists the situation is much the same. Despite differences in detail, the masks displayed a pronounced uniformity with regard to style.[50] Rigidity dominated the ceremonial use of both music and the dance among the Aztecs. The slightest deviation was detected and the culprit punished.[51]

When Ruth Bunzel was studying the art of the female Pueblo potters, she hit upon a fundamental truth concerning most, if not all, primitive art. While the artist might think of herself as an individual deviant concerning such matters as style and design, the ethnologist understood that the product of each village displayed a pronounced tendency for likeness with regard to both technical and aesthetic aspects.[52] On the empirical level this observation was verified by an analysis of the works of the Mimbres artist of an older culture in the same region. While no two designs of 741 extant pottery artifacts were alike, nevertheless there were no basic changes in the village style itself for over 250 years.[53] And while there were four basic changes in the art of the Basket Makers of the American Southwest during a one-thousand-year period, the physical progression was far less important to the people than the notion of no change in the art form. There were no historical records and no museums in which to display the evolutionary process of basket-making as it occurred within the tribe itself.[54]

Authorities were in substantial agreement that the individual of the Northwest Coast was subordinated to both tribal and regional influences. Here too, as in the Plains, the shaman, and not the priest, dominated. Unlike the Plains, the seacoast yielded so much food so readily an entire culture practiced what Veblen would have termed the conspicuous consumption of wealth.[55] While wood-carving in the area was unquestionably one of the finest primitive accomplishments, mask-making was so remarkably consistent that one would be forced to conclude a single tradition dominated. The same was true of totem-pole art.[56] This uncompromising position was supported by others.[57]

Anthropologists offer several convincing reasons why authoritarianism of this type appeared acceptable to the artist. If true isolation has been imposed upon the primitive artist, he is probably unconscious of the fact that he works within the parameters of a community style or pattern and finds it congenial. It is no harder to utilize, really, than one's native language which one uses correctly and without great internal stresses for mastery.[58] On the other hand, the conscious conformity of the primitive artist to the *Weltanschauung* of his people was stressed by Raymond Firth. Ever since ritual became inextricably interwoven with art and craft, which happened very early in the history of man, certain art forms have become sacred. To innovate merely as a result of artistic whim would certainly invoke punishment from the dead ancestors who were the guardians of that art. Even in those instances where the designs were not sacred, their identification with magic was sufficient to perpetuate the same kind of thing. Finally, there is always present the element of inertia. It is always easier to let oneself be guided by a familiar design than to innovate another.[59] It makes for a situation in which isolation begot the archaic.[60] Community concert as to art values might even help explain why several neighbors of the Pomo Indians in California, none of whom had more than one basket-weaving technique, bothered to borrow from the innovating Pomos who had six.[61] Fear and repugnance for anything new, and therefore the exotic, insured the continuance and dominance of the old and familiar. Another possibility, although one less plausible to me than to my co-author, is that, if the function of primitive art were faithfully to reproduce traditional patterns, projecting them into the future, then it was not so much that change was feared but simply not pursued, and therefore, not likely to occur.

It would, therefore, appear reasonable to conclude that, concerning ceremonial and ritual art, the primitive artist worked within strictly defined limits. These were imposed by the greater community which believed in their religious sanction and, because of this, their immutability. Few artists indeed would have had the courage to challenge the artistic order established by the gods and supported by the disciplined priesthood and/or the secret societies. Change in that quarter occurred by accident or human fallibility and not by design. In areas of profane art, however, the artist apparently enjoyed wider latitudes of freedom, both from the sense of vision, or mental projection of the piece, and its execution or fabrication. But even here, traditional restraints were still in evidence. Innovation as such - at least that in North America - was more apt to arise in those shamanistic societies which believed it was not the individual who introduced deviations into his craft but rather the gods with whom he effected a liaison while in a trance or prayer. Nevertheless, however authoritarian the social context, the individual primitive artist seemed unaware of its drag upon creativity or at least, so far as we know, did not kick against the pricks of fortune. In a curious sense, conservatism prevailed in the arts at the same time the artist felt his individualism was manifested in his craft. Harmony was the theme. Everybody belonged, everybody had his place and few, if any, felt frustrated.

Even in the instances of cultural borrowing, which represented a tendency toward tolerance and liberalism, there were strong conservative forces still at work and these generally prevailed. Dominated by the fear of the new, the very changes that conservatism accepts are part of its strategy to secure the persistence of the established order. Magic was in the form and, without the familiar form, there was no magic.[62] For example, the Kadiak Eskimos borrowed Indian designs with which they ornamented their implements, but the implements themselves remained of Eskimo origin. The Israelites and the Egyptians used stone knives for circumcision and embalming long after they became knowledgeable about metal. When the Indians on the Northwest Coast obtained ivory from the Eskimos, it was never used in its original shape, as was the Eskimo habit, but cut into small pieces to work up, as the local craftsmen were accustomed into charms and amulets. In the Sepik river region of New Guinea, where objects were constantly being traded, an artifact which originally had been sacred might become, in the course of its travels, one of amusement to a people not hesitating to adapt it to tribal needs.[63] The continent of Africa was especially noted for changing the character of a borrowed idea or institution. In the nineteenth century a crucifix was customarily carried around in the native village of Wari but was otherwise devoid of any Christian significance.[64] The shepherd Navahos had such a talent at effecting a transformation in these cultural borrowings that at last they became virtually indistinguishable from native products.[65]

There were common anthropological explanations for this phenomena. First, people borrowed without really understanding what they were borrowing. An excellent example of this was Australia where tribes held dance festivals at night and in rote fashion sang long and complicated foreign passages, not a word of which either the singers or the audience comprehended.[66] Second, people borrowed only that which could quickly and easily be assimilated into their own culture. Or, to put it another way, they borrowed only that to which they were already predisposed.[67] The Sun Dance of the Plains Indians must have been diffused from a common source because on an empirical level it was so alike in many different tribes. Despite this, the alleged aims of the ceremony differed widely. This was not only due to the local religious needs but also to tribal notions of aesthetic enjoyment and public entertainment.[68] Third, and as a consequence, what they borrowed was frequently transformed into something entirely different. It might, of course, bear its original name.[69] One key to this phenomena has been passed to us and this involves the meaning of symbols. While the design may remain the same between two tribes, the symbolic meaning may be quite different. Indeed, within the same tribe male and female may assign two different symbolic meanings to the same design.[70]

In an attempt to understand the conservative motivations, characteristics and limitations of primitive art, we are at last free to examine the artist and his craft and here certain basic facts must be clarified. First of all there existed a kind of a "careers open to talent" sort of thing. In most societies, particularly in simply structured ones, every man might become an artist and in others, like the Indian cultures in the American Southwest, women could, using geometric designs, become folk artists in basket-making, pottery, textiles and the like.[71] But it must immediately be understood that one was an artist in addition to his regular community duties. A sculptor of a West African mask remained a farmer. Thus there was no conscious separation between the artist and his public. No one regarded art as an essential mystery or one beyond his sphere of competence. Art was a tribal heritage and in virtual stateless societies everyone might act as an art critic.[72] In West Africa, and in Surinam in South America, where most Negro carvings had a symbolic association with sex and were created by males, females were quite discriminating judges of that craft.[73] However democratic its many features, an elite could still emerge. An individual artist might gain special recognition among his own people who could perceive unique distinctions in the craft where to the outsider there were none. An especially gifted artist might, in trading areas such as Nigeria and New Guinea, be honored beyond his own village and be remembered for generations.[74]

The materials with which the artist worked were determined by nature and not artistic choice. The center of a culture area coincides with and is largely explained by climate and ecology.[75] It was no accident that, using the colors of red, blue, yellow and white, the artists of the Western Plains had to work their designs (naturalistic for the males and geometric for females) into tanned buffalo skins. Or that later they found it relatively easy to adopt from the village tribes of the Upper Missouri the practice of fabricating from eagle feathers a great headdress, often with a long tail.[76] Likewise, it is not surprising that wood was exclusively used for sculpture on the Northwest Coast, or conversely, that pottery never made its appearance in Polynesia because of an absence of clay. When a people were pressured to migrate, frequently they were forced to abandon old vehicles or instruments of artistic expression for new ones. While the natives of Central Australia are today still free to draw with bits of bark upon cave walls the abstract figure of a kangaroo-man ancestor,[77] the Bushmen of the Kalahari have virtually lost this art because they were driven from cave regions into the desert.[78] Whalebone net, characteristic of Eskimo art elsewhere, was absent from the Eskimo culture of Hudson Bay because of a lack of raw material. When the Maori emigrated from the Polynesian islands to New Zealand, they found the climate too cool for mulberry trees to grow so they were forced to substitute a new material, flax, for the traditional cloth from bark fibre.[79] And, finally, the very shape of that natural object, which furnished the representational background, almost invariably limited what the artist himself might attempt.[80] An excellent illustration of this generalization was with regard to the carved totem pole of Northwest Coast art. With few exceptions the poles are only half or three-quarters round, the back of the pole having been cut off as a flat surface. The basic shape, therefore, is of a vertical column, solid or hollow as the case may be, and a rounded surface which provides the native "canvas." This means that the curvature of the surface of the wooden block provides the opportunity for the artist and at the same time limits what he may elect to do.[81]

As a producer the primitive artist was a craftsman in the Veblen sense or one who, creatively, joyfully and pridefully, produced a product or fabrication which bore his particular stamp of creation.[82] Secondly, and again in the Veblen sense, he produced things meant for a functional end or one which stressed the utility of an object. Regardless of the wide variations or functions of the end product it was always designed for use by someone.[83] Both of those principles were enunciated when the Semangs of the Malay peninsula, a Negritos people of a very low material level, displayed beautiful artisanship of design and execution in the decorations on their blowpipes and quivers.[84] An almost identical conclusion was reached concerning the Mareas tribe on the St. Joseph river, not far from the southern tip of New Guinea. The superb artistic workmanship on their weapons, when contrasted with their low technological culture, compelled European admiration.[85] Like Oceania, the arts of Africa and the Americas were mainly functional. As far as the Eskimo was concerned, however, Franz Boas disagreed. He produced an art for art's sake or one without practical ends.[86]

However, there was no single economic activity not at some stage accompanied by magic and ritual. In a secular sense, like that of Veblen, this acted as a pronounced flaw in the productive process and usage.[87] In the Hervey Island of Polynesia useful adzes were so deeply cut with religious or geometric designs that the original purpose of the instrument was forgotten. As a consequence, these ritualistic endeavors changed the original and utilitarian form of an object until it became an abstract and religious one.[88] Or, again, in the usage of a functionally-designed instrument, tradition and ritual often impeded the most effective operations. Thus it might be said to be anti-utilitarian to its user.[89]

Primitive art had its finest hour when devoted to supernatural ends. Here it was truly functional. It enabled the tribe to speak with ancestors, ghosts and gods who controlled an energy force which might do the tribe either infinite good or harm. One splendid example of this was mask-making. The African mask was not intended to influence the earthly beholder but the spiritual world.[90] The African mask was recognized as the most likely and efficacious means of communication with and influencing the ancestral dead. As a consequence, when a man decided to make a mask, he must purify himself. He abstained from sex relations, offered a sacrifice and kept his tools hidden from the sight of women and uninitiated persons.[91] Finally, the mask itself represented or became a kind of supernatural being. The process worked this way in the culturally-rich Sepik river area of New Guinea. When a man donned a mask of a demon or the ancestral dead he was more than simply a man in costume. He actually became what the mask represented. In effect he was possessed by the demon or spirit it portrayed.[92] An almost identical spiritual reaction was evident among the sedentary

Indians of the Southwest. When a man put on a mask, he immediately assumed the identity of the god that the mask itself represented. The Zunis explained this as a process transforming a god into a living person.[93] The Iroquois had the same practice.[94] The mask always shared the personality and power of the god represented. In South America, the possession of a bit of a man's hair or the discards of his nails meant in magic the possession of his soul and bodily movements. Likewise, so did the possession of an image of the god control the god. The mask was made with the intent to resemble the demon in question. The dancer in dressing and acting like the demon identified himself with him. Thus, the mysterious powers of the supernatural were transferred to the dancer through the agency or instrumentality of the mask itself. The wearer transcended worldly limitations and became capable of appeasing or exiling other demons.[95] In Black Africa, the entire affair was carefully stage managed. The horrifying mask was always worn at night and in conjunction with sacrificial blood and drum beats. Mesmerized by a combination of his belief system, the rhythmic beating of the drums and the impressionistic images by the flickering firelight, the wearer of the masks fell into a trance and took on the manner and voice of the god or demon. He now spoke with a different voice on esoteric matters and performed with queer steps the movements which successfully exorcised the demon. It was at that very moment he had, in the opinion of the tribe, become a supernatural being. Man become god and god man.[96]

This may indeed be what Ruth Benedict stressed when analyzing the dances of Dionysian societies. They were fond of treating each life crisis - birth, puberty, marriage and death - as terror situations. Also they pursued the supernatural not only because it was a very powerful agency but because the pursuit itself was regarded as highly dangerous. Such societies placed a premium upon passion, violence, and frenzy. It was believed such strong emotions enabled the individual and the tribe to break through the level of sensory experience to a higher and nobler extra-sensory one. Intoxication was often the vehicle used to achieve the desired outcome.[97] These societies offer the most fruitful source for the investigator who is intrigued by the process of how primitives sought to find the supernatural order through the mechanisms of emotion, intuition and mysticism. Their postulate was that truth and beauty transcended and was independent of what we call the empirical level of events. Such analysis of Dionysian art can be subsumed under the term Platonic Idealism. This was the way it was used at the outset of this chapter.[98]

One may perceive the fruits of such a philosophy in the dances of the Kwakiutl Indians of Vancouver Island, and other tribes of the Northwest Coast, dances honoring gods of Fear and Unreason. Dancers not only sought ecstasy but meant to convey it to the audience as well. As the tempo increased, and emotional pressures mounted, there was a precise moment when it should become apparent the chief dancer had lost control of himself. Terrible supernatural forces had taken over both his mind and body. Meanwhile death was honored as the price the dancer must pay for making a mistake, particularly an important one. In the dances given by the highly honored Cannibal Society even the spectators were occasionally expected to yield up their pound of flesh, torn from their arms by the teeth of the frenzied dancer. The entire sequence seemed to be calculated to make the individual feel as if he had been seized and shaken to the core of his being by angry and vengeful gods who could have destroyed him unfeelingly. Yet, they left him to survive in order to contemplate the awful mystery and power which invariably accompanied them.[99]

When discussing the dances of the Cubeo Indians of the Northwest Amazon, a different facet of Dionysian society - sexual attitudes - was analyzed by Irving Goldman. The main themes remained the same. It could be summed up with his conclusion that the central theme of all Cubeo ceremonials was the dramatization of emotion.[100] In both the Drinking party and Mourning ceremony the structure of events was basically the same, each going from the calm to the frenzied. Vehicles for the passage were the large consumption of both alcohol and tobacco, together with music and the dance. The prolonged situation progressed to that point where, before the entire audience, frenzied sex was symbolically portrayed. This was later followed by frequent sexual copulation among the dancers who would steal away in the bush for a few moments and then return to seek new sexual partners. While events were chaotic at this point, no open sex acts occurred. At the same time it must be emphasized that the Cubeo frowned upon individual and secular acts of intoxication. That state was meant as both a public and a sacred one.[101] The entire event, wrapped up in drunkenness, mystic self-abnegation and sexual excess amid music glorifying awe and horror, was reminiscent of the Dionysian orgies as described by Frederick Nietsche in *The Birth of Tragedy*.[102]

There is a third and quite different facet of religious experience among Dionysian societies. The fundamental basis of the religion of the Desana tribe of the Northwest Amazon was the calculated use of hallucinogenic drugs for the purpose of producing and interpreting visions. The drug itself was reserved for sacred use by mature males. They must both smoke and drink and then share their visions with the Kumú, a master teacher and possessor of esoteric knowledge. The latter spoke and sang continually, explaining to the group the meaning of the individual's experience while he had been in a trance. What was taught and understood here was that the individual had left one plane of human experience or transcended it to another level where he established the sought-for contact with the Divine. Necessarily emanating from the Kumú himself was the art and drama of the situation.[103] As for the participants they underwent the mystic self-abnegation theme seen as an integral feature of Dionysian societies.[104] Naturally, one is reminded of similar experiences today in the large number of peyote cults among the Dionysian Indian tribes from Mexico to the Canadian border.[105] Not so generally understood perhaps is the fact that historically the Dionysian Indians on the Great Plains underwent terrible self-deprivations and torture in order to try and achieve such visions. Without such a spiritual experience, the future life held up scant prospects of reward. With it the gods promised success and fame.[106]

On the contrary, the dances of the Pueblos, an Apollonian model, offer a most interesting contrast, as one might expect from a society which placed value on order, harmony and tradition and, above all, the validity of sensory experience. The Pueblos would not tolerate public displays which were wild and frenzied or individual efforts to achieve self-oblivion as the result of torture or drug-inducing ecstasy. No one better described the philosophy and purpose of Pueblo dances than D.H. Lawrence. He concluded it was contained in the precise movements of a forty-man chorus line, the monotonous beatings of the drums and the incredible patience of all dance participants. The process itself reflected their faith that these natural and human powers could eventually act in the same manner as a natural force upon storm clouds and thus bring rain.[107]

It was Ruth Bunzel who best described the way primitive man combined art with religion as a form of compelling magic to make the gods come with all their attributes, including rain. She found it in the Zuni music and the dance. For them it functioned in much the same way as a Catholic priest summoning up the Christ at mass. For the Zunis this involved a group dance which, subordinated to music, was restricted to straight lines. There were no elaborate dance figures nor interweaving of dancers nor grouping of aesthetic figures. Bodily movement was quite restricted, being limited to the feet and slight gestures of the arms. The dance precision, the rhythm's regularity, the simplicity and uniformity of line and form, combined with the haunting music, produced the desired religious atmosphere. The viewer was ultimately put in a state of hypnosis as a result of the depersonalized and monotonous tone and style and the utter absorption it demanded from the audience.[108]

Even a consideration of the fascinating Snake Dance does nothing to change this interpretation of the Pueblo as an Apollonian society. The perceptive reader, who has pondered the beautiful description of the Hopi Snake Dance by D.H. Lawrence,[109] is not apt to quarrel with Ruth Benedict when she declared that such dances were not Dionysian either in a secular or supernatural context. There was indeed no frenzy to it nor any freedom of latitude allowed the individual dancers, no more so, said Benedict, than to the dancers of the Virginia Reel.[110] Indeed the whole sequence of events lies upon the Hopi philosohy of life which affirms that both men and snake have their proper roles in a common desert environment. During the carefully-structured ceremony no violence was intended for either species.[111] Once divesting ourselves of our own cultural abhorrence for snakes, we may conclude the episode beautifully depicts the Hopi view of the natural and unfolding order in the universe and man's determination to fulfill his destiny - to conquer what he can and submit to what he must. He knows the Golden Age lies far ahead and, like Moses, he personally will never see the

Promised Land. At the same time, unlike Christianity, the Hopi is not burdened with the Paradise Lost myth and, therefore, is under no theological curse.[112] As a consequence, he is a man of moderation, avoiding extremes, a man of tradition. He views himself somewhat in the Edward Burkeian sense, i.e., indebted to the past and responsible to the future.[113]

It was, however, Martí and Kurath who most closely approximated the authors' own concept of the trinity of primitive man: cosmology, ritual and art. Ritual, they argued, was the spiritual mother of all the arts and myth (cosmology) was the sister of ritual. Although dance emanated from ritual, they were all three in reality but one. Dancing was always used to obtain supernatural power in order that earthly affairs could be altered to one's heart's desire. The fact that music was believed to be of divine origin was indicated by the practice of depicting the god Quetzalcoatl with a flute. Musicians and artists who created and played such remarkable instruments as triple and quadruple flutes had expert knowledge of acoustics and of harmonic series and were probably cognizant of more than a five-tone scale.[114]

All primitive art might be said to have culminated with the building of the temple and the altar. It was certainly true with regard to Mexico. The most impressive Aztec architecture found religious expression and their temples reflected the majesty of the spiritual world. The remains of the Toltec idols found in the valley of Teluca in Morales represent the finest modeling ever achieved in Mexico.[115] The animals represented on the door of the temple at Malinalco in the Teluca valley were the most beautiful examples of Aztec art.[116] For observers like Piedro de Cieza de Leon and Clements R. Markham, the splendid Temple of the Sun at Cuzco represented in its beauty and its symmetry the apogee of Inca architecture.[117] Lacking the ornateness of Aztec and Maya structures, this temple, like other Inca buildings, had to depend for its striking effect upon balance and proportion.

Among the Navaho there was a peculiar custom called sandpainting or, more properly, drypainting which combined in an intricate fashion elements of art, magic supernaturalism and medicine. Basic materials were the four principal colors of white, blue, yellow and black; designs compounded from vegetable substances like pollen, meal and crushed flowers; a buckskin to spread the stuff out on, and fine sand which served as a background for the artistic endeavor. The ceremony itself, which might be as prolonged as four separate paintings on successive days, was invariably designed to heal the sick and afflicted. Like the sacred works in medieval glass, the paintings were designed to make Holy persons and doctrines tangible and experiential to the masses.[118] However, once the patient had been subjected to the magic, or the treatment, while sitting in the midst of the painting, these works of art were destroyed in the very order in which they had been constructed that same day. Otherwise, the supernatural aspect would have been reduced to the commonplace.[119] According to legend, these same paintings, painted on skins, had been bequeathed to the Navahos by the gods themselves. However, the shamans of old became fearful that the sacred objects might fall into the hands of enemies and, having memorized the designs, destroyed the originals.[120]

Among the rug-makers of the Yörük and Turkmen shamanistic cosmology influenced the design and pattern of the product. It was no doubt true that the number seven, used in so many of the designs, was derived from the theological belief that seven levels of the universe existed.[121] It was also true that so much of this native art was donated to the mosques that in effect today they serve as art museums for the expert. Indeed, it was these rugs hanging on the walls of the mosques which diffused the art forms throughout the region. The artistic product on display both influenced, and was influenced by, that from other tribes. It became difficult to distinguish anything other than regional characteristics of the art form itself.[122]

It was Paul Bohannan who best expressed the crucial role that art had in bringing the old mythology concerning cosmology and tribal "history" to light before the eyes of the tribe itself. This included elements of body painting or scarifying, masks, ornaments, music, song, dance and drama or all the conservative arts of primitive man. They were all expertly woven together in a kind of Passion Play whose end and purpose was to reinforce tribal beliefs in its own divine creation and mission. When drama and art were used to make the myth come alive, the combination proved the most effective way possible to make individuals recognize their emotional dependence both upon the myth and the larger community which lived by it.

The perpetual resurrection of this "historical" drama meant that every generation in turn could experience for itself the thrill of tribal creation by the gods, as well as the forging of the Social Contract between the supernatural world and its heroic ancestors, the first settlers.[123]

Erna Gunther made precisely the same point with regard to the Indians of the Northwest Coast. Nowhere was the theatre, during the leisure months of winter, used with more emotional impact for religious reasons than among the Cannibal Society of the Kwakiutl Indians.[124] Diverse accounts of the genius of these Indians to fabricate and utilize mechanical contrivances for unusual stage effects reminds one of the achievements of Hellenistic Greece. They had contraptions, controlled by weights, pulleys and strings, so fantastic-looking birds could snap their beaks and open and close their eyes. Mouths of masks were removable and noses could be telescoped. Using, for example, a wooden mask with real hair and a gruesome expression, the stage managers could persuade an audience that a man had been beheaded. Objects flew through the air by means of suspended ropes. There were trap doors for disappearing acts. Finally, there were magnificent sound effects throughout, as, for example, speaking tubes for underground voices below fireplaces where no human being apparently could have survived.[125] Had the Wizard of Oz possessed all this paraphernalia, and operated it as well, he might never have been unmasked.

In this social process all the primitive arts combined to educate or indoctrinate the entire tribe with a single morality and purpose. Instead of a Thomistic use of Aristotelian logic to teach morality, the Hako Indians of California used all the visual arts. "Thus by the use of symbols and significant rites and songs, the Hako taught principles and attitudes rather than a detailed code of conventional morality." It was "poetic symbolism."[126] Much the same thing was said with regard to the origins of Indian art in Mexico.[127]

Despite this imposition by the community of a cultural pattern upon the individual artist, particularly in the sacred sphere so central to his craft, such subordination has not appeared to be an inhibiting factor as judged by the quality of the art itself. For the artist it was as if, freed from demands of constantly coming up with something new in order to titillate the consumer, he could perfect his technique. At the same time he was exercising creativity in improvising artistic variations within the larger traditional framework.[128] Concerning the folk-art of the carpet-maker of the Middle East, their woven goods were more interesting to the expert than any others in the entire region.[129] Furthermore, within this same context there occurred artistic change and development. On the North Pacific Coast, for example, decorative art originally was composed almost exclusively of animals realistically portrayed. With the passage of time, however, they were depicted instead in geometric form. Despite this, parts of animal bodies were still perceptible.[130]

This argument appears even more compelling in view of the fact that, generally speaking, the white man's intrusion and dominance of native cultures in Asia, Africa and the Americas has not, despite the introduction of better artistic tools, improved the quality of native art as a result of its liberation from old restrictions. On the contrary it has perceptively deteriorated or even become obliterated. For example, in the native culture of Nigeria the chief mask of Igala, endowed with spiritual authority, was traditionally appealed to in the event of murder and operated as an effective sanction. With European political dominance, however, came the imposition of the white man's law which swept aside traditional procedures. Devoid of political and social reality, mask-making virtually disappeared.[131] This phenomena can perhaps best be explained on the grounds that native art is but a reflection of tribal life and ideology. The artist understands nothing else and when these go, as inevitably they do under white hegemony, the artist may be free, so to speak, for the first time in his life. But, he no longer has any subject matter or anything to say.[132]

The white man's commercial impulses dried up the well-springs of Veblen's instinct of workmanship among the primitive. For example, in Pueblo country the tourist now dominated the new market and the native female artist had to fabricate what the Indian trader thought would sell fast and profitably. These false values resulted in the production of things the white woman wanted to clutter up her home in the form of cups, candlesticks, baskets, vases and such. All which proved barren ground for the traditional Navaho style of decoration. It was a travesty on art, pure and simple. Second, and because of recent archaeological discoveries, the native artist was asked by the trader to duplicate this much older art, one exotic to her. Meanwhile the art forms with which she was familiar carried no market demand and, therefore, no respect from the whites. Thus the Indian was forced to emulate but imperfectly the ancient but revived art and, as with the Zunis, genuine art forms died.[133]

Commercial instincts, which supplanted the influence of the mosque by the late nineteenth or early twentieth century, resulted in the wide-spread deterioration of the artistic quality of rugs woven by the women of nomadic tribes of the Middle East. The demands of the urban Western market for mass production had obliterated creativity among artist of the wandering Yörüks, among the Qashqā'i federation of South Persia or Iran. While their rugs were still hand-made, they were now mechanically produced by designs on graph paper.[134] The same lamentable decline in artistry was detected whenever and wherever the West penetrated the consciousness of a heretofore primitive tribe. For example, when first contacted by Europeans shortly after the beginning of the nineteenth century, the native product of the Baluchi tribes featured truly magnificent colors of red and black. But, by the end of the century, there was a distinct decline in artistic judgment and execution. Beginning with an abysmal choice of dyes, continuing through a deterioration of proportion and balance, it naturally culminated in poor craftsmanship.[135] The new Baluchi productions offered nothing more than a simpler design which lacked the artistic detail and color variations of the older product.[136] To compound misfortune, the new product had a garish look. Equally lamentable was the fact that young native women no longer cared to learn the old craft of weaving, flouting history and tradition by buying sweaters for their youngsters from town shops.[137]

While the native pottery of the Southwest invariably deteriorated when the white man's commercial instincts dominated, it could be revived in a creative fashion. This occurred when the same interloper encouraged the native artist to resurrect and improve upon the aboriginal arts themselves.[138] An identical point was made with regard to the actions of the Indian Art and Craft Board in 1938 when it rescued the superior Navaho jewelry from being swept from the market place as a result of competition from cheap and shoddy "Indian jewelry."[139]

Art, therefore, may be perceived as the indispensable vehicle. Through ritual and prayer, the tribe was made perpetually aware of its cosmology and mythology, involving the creation of the universe, the First Man - its direct ancestors - and the original Social Contract between him and the gods. If we think of Cosmology and Ritual as the arms of the Cross or the laterals, the vertical pole uniting the two is undoubtedly Art. These three elements together provided the navel of the universe, that point where the tribe lived, dramatic interation between man and his gods and, finally, purpose, which was to live up to the terms of the Social Contract between man and the supernatural. The net effect was that every tribe has progressed that far armed with the same comfortable assurances about past, present and future as were the ancient Hebrews with the concept of Jehovah.

How effective this trinity was in fortifying and protecting these native tribes against the arrogance and power of white Christianity will be explored in the next chapter.

Footnotes

1   Raymond S. Stites, *The Arts and Man* (New York, McGraw-Hill, 1940), 49-50.

2   Paul S. Wingert, *Primitive Art. Its Traditions and Styles* (New York, Oxford Press, 1962), 31-32; *Prehistoric Art of the Western Mediterranean and the Sahara*, edited by L.P. Garcia and E.R. Perello. *Viking Fund Publications in Anthropology No. 39* (New York, Wenner-Gren Foundation for Anthropological Research, Inc., 1954) 45-46; T.G.E. Powell, *Prehistoric Art* (New York, Frederick A. Praeger, 1966), 13; Stites, *The Arts and Man*, 44.

3   Peter J. Ucko and Andrée Rosenfeld, "Critical Analysis of Interpretations and Conclusions from Paleolithic Cave Art," 247-281 in *Anthropologoy and Art*, edited by Charlotte M. Otten, 265.

4   *Service, Hunters*, 83. This is not to deny the fact that these painters approached their subject matter, often involving a sexuality theme, reverently as the central mystery of life. La Barre, *Ghost Dance*, 396-398.

5   Maringer and Bandi, *Art in the Ice Age. Spanish Levant Art. Arctic Art* (New York, Frederick A. Praeger, 1953), 112. See also Josef Poulik, *Prehistoric Art ... Up to Roman Times*, translated by R.F. Samsour (London, Spring Books, no publication date), 14; Montagu "Fallacy of the Primitive," in *Concept of the Primitive*, edited by Montagu, 5.

6   Maringer and Bandi, *Art in the Ice Age*, 49; John Derek Mulvaney, *The Prehistory of Australia* (New York, Praeger Press, 1969), 176-177.

7   Childe, *What Happened in History*, 40.

8   Powell, *Prehistoric Art*, 42.

9   Morton R. Levine, "Prehistoric Art and Ideology," 708-724 in *Readings in Anthropology*, 2 vols., edited by Fried, *Cultural Anthropology*, II, 721.

10   Preface, xi in Malinowski, *Argonauts of the Western Pacific*.

11   Burchard Brentjes, *African Rock Art* (New York, Clarkson N. Potter, 1965), 7-8.

12   Ucko and Rosenfeld, "Paleolithic Cave Art," *loc. cit.*, 248-249.

13   Spencer, *North Alaskan Eskimo*, 445.

14   Dark, *Bush Negro Art*, 39.

15   Levine, "Prehistoric Art and Ideology," *loc. cit.*, 712, 720-721.

16   Robert Goldwater, Introduction to the *Art of Oceania, Africa and the Americas*, from the Museum of Primitive Art (Greenwich, Connecticut, The Metropolitan Museum of Art, distributed by the New York Graphic Society, 1969), pages unnumbered.

17   Redfield, "Art and Icon," 39-65 in *Anthropology and Art*, edited by Otten, 52.

18   Wissler, *The Relation of Nature to Man in Aboriginal America*, 90-91; Edmund Carpenter, "The Eskimo Artist," 163-171 in *Anthropology and Art*, edited by Otten, 169.

19   Sieber, "The Arts and Their Changing Function," 203-211 in *ibid.*, 205.

20   Bohannon, *Africa and the Africans*, 152-153.

21   Erna Gunther, "Northwest Coast Art," 318-340 in *Anthropology and Art*, edited by Otten, 333.

22   *African and Oceanic Art* (New York, Harry N. Abrams, no date), 47.

23   *Bush Negro Art*, 40.

24   "Search for the Primitive," in *Concept of the Primitive*, edited by Montagu, 139.

25   *Africa and the Africans*, 142-143.

26   *Women in Primitive Societies*, 165, 170, 172.

27   *African Art. Its Backgrounds and Traditions*, 46.

28   F. C. Bartlett, *Psychology and Primitive Culture* (Westport, Connecticut, Greenwood Press, reprint of 1923 edition, 1970), 12.

29   *African Art. An Introduction* (New York, Frederick A. Praeger, 1971), 153, 156.

30   *Africa. The Art of the Negro Peoples* (New York, McGraw-Hill, 1960), 52-53.

31   Spencer and Gillen, *Northern Tribes of Central Australia*, 696-697. Lévi-Strauss offered a wider and more general explanation for this sort of thing. Primitives tried to deny change and to make their present states as permanent as possible. *Savage Mind*, 234.

32   Neverman, *African and Oceanic Art*, 206, 215.

33   Raymond Firth, *Art and Life in New Guinea* (London, the Studio, Ltd., 1936, reprint New York, AMS, 1976), 30-31.

34   Wingert, *Primitive Art*, 196-197, 207-208, 220, 247.

35   Trowell and Neverman, *African and Oceanic Art*, 205, 207-208. However, scientific evidence makes it clear that all important and basic aspects of Pacific island culture came from the West - or Asiatic mainland - either directly or by way of island archapelagoes. Wingert, *Primitive Art*, 188.

36   Dark, *Negro Bush Art*, 21, 34, 39, 43.

37   Frederick H. Douglas and René D'Harnoncourt *Indian Art of the United States* (New York, Museum of Modern Art, 1941), 104.

38   *Ibid.*, 146; Miguel Covarrubias, *The Eagle, the Jaguar, and the Serpent. Indian Art of the Americas* ... (New York, Alfred A. Knopf, 1954), 289.

39   Douglas and D'Harnoncourt, *Indian Art of the United States*, 149. Jamake Highwater thought that the basis for the difference between the very conservative and tradition-ridden Southwest, where individualism was of very little value, and the Great Plains, where it was highly regarded, was a religious one. The vision quests of the Plains were recognized as highly individualistic. *Primal Mind*, 179.

40   James Mooney, "The Ghost Dance Religion," 257-274 in *Golden Age of American Anthropology*, edited by Mead and Bunzel, 267.

41   J.R. Walker, "The Sun Dance of the Oglala," 377-391 in *ibid.*, 377. The Crow Sun Dance differed from all others in having a single desire for revenge on the enemy for the death of a relative. Leslie Spier, "The Sun Dance of the Plains Indians, Comparison with the Tribal Ceremonial System," 392-397 in *ibid.*, 393.

42   Walker, "The Sun Dance of the Oglala," *loc. cit.*, 390; Farb, *Indians of North America*, 128.

43   Lowie, *Indians of the Plains*, 199.

44   *Black Elk Speaks*, 179, 197, 247.

45   Robert Redfield agreed with Dorothy Lee. *The Primitive World and Its Transformation* (Ithaca, Cornell University Press, 1953), 105.

46   *Selected Writings*, 350-351.

47   *American Indian*, 204. This ties in with Ruth Benedict's insistence that the terms of self-reliance and personal initiative characterized the Indians of the Great Plains. *Patterns of Culture*, 94.

48   Melville J. Herskovits, *Man and His Works. The Science of Cultural Anthropology* (New York, Alfred A. Knopf, 1964), 486. The words to this chant have been given to us by Washington Matthews, "The Night Chant: A Navaho Ceremony," 220-226 in *The Golden Age of American Anthropology*, edited by Mead and Bunzel.

49   Kluckholn and Leighton, *Navaho*, 215.

50   Ruth Bunzel, *Zuni Ritual Poetry*, in *47th Annual Report of the Bureau of American Ethnology to the Smithsonian*, 857.

51   Martí and Kurath, *Dances of Anáhuac*, 15.

52   *The Pueblo Potter. A Study of Creative Imagination in Primitive Art* (New York, AMS Press, 1969), 52-53, 86-87.

53   Gene Weltfish, *Origins of Art* (Indianapolis, Indiana, Bobbs-Merrill, 1953), 85.

54   *Ibid.*, 153.

208

55   The very act of consumption itself, in this instance, is *the* evidence of wealth and prowess. These in turn convey honor and dignity. *Theory of the Leisure Class*, 68-69.

56   Paul Wingert, *The Tsimshian Indians and Their Arts. The Tsimshian and Their Neighbors*, by Viola E. Garfield, and Tsimshian Sculpture by Paul S. Wingert (Seattle, University of Washington Press, no date), 80, 85.

57   Douglas and D'Harnoncourt, *Indian Art of the United States*, 173; Covarrubias, *Eagle, Jaguar and Serpent*, 109, 168.

58   Redfield, "Art and Icon," in *Anthropology and Art*, edited by Otten, 48.

59   *Art in New Guinea*, 31.

60   R. U. Sayce, *Primitive Arts and Crafts. An Introduction to the Study of Material Culture* (New York, Biblio and Tannen, 1963), 138.

61   Weltfish, *Origins of Art*, 240.

62   Bartlett, *Psychology and Primitive Culture*, 115, 151-152.

63   Linton and Wingert, "Arts of the South Seas," in *Anthropology and Art*, edited by Otten, 396; Sayce, *Primitive Art*, 173-174.

64   Sayce, *Primitive Art*, 190.

65   Douglas and D'Harnoncourt, *Indian Art of the United States*, 134.

66   Bartlett, *Psychology and Primitive Culture*, 143.

67   *Ibid.*, 216.

68   *Indians of the Plains*, 199.

69   Turnbull, *Forest People*, 184-185.

70   Lowie, quoting Clark Wissler in *Indians of the Plains*, 158-159.

71   Driver, *Indians of North America* 176, 181; Weltfish, *Origins of Art*, 94.

72   Adrian A. Gerbrands, "Art as an Element of Culture in Africa," 366-382 in *Anthropology and Art*, edited by Otten, 367. Firth, *Art in New Guinea*, 31; Paul Bohannan, "An Artist and Critic in an African Society," 738-745 in *Readings in Anthropology*, 2 vols., edited by Fried, *Cultural Anthropology*, II, 741.

73   Dark, *Bush Negro Art*, 39.

74   Ucko and Rosenfeld, "Paleolithic Cave Art," in *Anthropology and Art*, edited by Otten, 251; Robert Goldwater, Introduction to the *Art of Oceania, Africa and the Americas*, from the Museum of Primitive Art, pages unnumbered.

75   Sayce, *Primitive Art,* 39-41.

76   Wissler, *Relation of Nature to Man,* 59-60; Weltfish, *Origins of Art,* 130.

77   Charles P. Montford, "Earth's Most Primitive People, A Journey with the Aborigines of Central Australia," 89-112 in *National Geographic,* vol. 89, No. 1 (1946), 105. See also Erna Gunther, "Northwest Indian Coast Art," in *Anthropology and Art,* edited by Otten, 327.

78   Sayce, *Primitive Arts and Crafts,* 133. Natives cried in pain when shown paintings by the Bushmen of old but they had forgotten how to duplicate the process. Van Der Post, *Lost World of the Kalahari,* 241-242.

79   Sayce, *Primitive Arts and Crafts,* 79, 125.

80   Franz Boas, "Decorative Art of the North Pacific Coast," 305-317 in *Golden Age of American Anthropology,* edited by Mead and Bunzel, 307.

81   Wingert, *Tsimshian Indians and Their Arts,* 81.

82   Raymond Firth, *Primitive Economics of the New Zealand Maori* (New York, E. P. Dutton, 1919), 162, 167.

83   Firth, *Art and Life in New Guinea,* 31. See also Driver, *Indians of North America,* 176; Robert Goldwater, Introduction to the *Art of Oceania, Africa and the Americas,* from the Museum of Primitive Art, pages unnumbered.

84   Skeat, *Wild Tribes of the Malay Peninsula,* 470-471.

85   Semon, *In the Australian Bush,* 327, 329.

86   Boas, "Decorative Art of the North Pacific Coast," *loc. cit.,* 307.

87   *Theory of the Leisure Class,* 308-309.

88   Linton and Wingert, "Arts of the South Seas," in *Anthropology and Art,* edited by Otten, 385.

89   Firth, *Primitive Economics of the Maori,* 154.

90   Trowell, *African and Oceanic Art,* 16.

91   Adrian A. Gerbands, "Art as an Element of Culture in Africa," in *Anthropology and Art,* edited by Otten, 369, 376.

92   Neverman, *African and Oceanic Art,* 206, 213.

93   Bunzel, *Zuni Ritual Poetry, loc. cit.,* 847-848.

94   Farb, *Indians of North America,* 110.

95   Karsten, *South American Indians*, 215-217.

96   Leuzinger, *Africa.The Art of the Negro Peoples*, 28. In Dionysian frenzy all differences between god and man tend to disappear. Whoever leads the dance becomes god. Girard, *Violence and the Sacred*, 128. Not conscious of acting a major part in a drama, the shaman became, in his own mind, the very thing which he worshipped. The audience, because it had been properly manipulated, accepted the same illusion. La Barre, *Ghost Dance*, 320.

97   *Patterns of Culture*, 79-81.

98   See textual material associated with footnotes 17, 18 and 19 of this chapter.

99   Benedict, *Patterns of Culture*, 158-160.

100   *Cubeo*, 247.

101   *Ibid.*, 215, 236, 247, 249.

102   *The Birth of Tragedy or Hellenism and Pessimism*, translated by William A. Haussmann (London, T.N. Fullis, 1910), 26-32.

103   Reichel-Dolmatoff, *Amazonian Cosmos*, 171.

104   Nietsche, *Birth of Tragedy*, 61, 67-68.

105   Benedict, *Patterns of Culture*, 84-85. Jamake Highwater claimed that the peyote cults assumed popularity only after 1850 and as a means of individual escape from tribal humiliation at the hands of the white man. *Primal Mind*, 84-85.

106   Benedict, *Patterns of Culture*, 81-82.

107   *Ibid.*, 90-91.

108   *Zuni Ritual Poetry, loc. cit.*, 898-899. Also see Highwater, *Primal Mind*, 161, 166.

109   *Mornings in Mexico* (New York, Alfred A. Knopf, 1927), 141-179.

110   *Patterns of Culture*, 91-92.

111   Lawrence, *Mornings in Mexico*, 154, 171.

112   *Ibid.*, 150-151, 173, 176-177.

113   *Reflections on the French Revolution* with Introduction ... by Russell Kirk (New Rochelle, New York, Arlington House, no date), 108-110.

114   *Dances of Anáhuac*, 174, 177, 188, 191.

115   G. C. Valliant, *Aztecs of Mexico. Origin, Rise and Fall of the Aztec Nation* (Garden City, New York, Doubleday, 1947), 64, 155-156.

116   Bernal, *Mexico Before Cortes*, 115-116.

117   Sir Clements Markham, *Incas of Peru*, 104; Second Part of *The Chronicle of Peru* by Piedro de Cieza de Leon, 83-84.

118   Kluckholn and Leighton, *Navaho*, 213-221.

119   Douglas and D'Harnoncourt, *Indian Art of the United States*, 28-29.

120   *Eagle, Jaguar and Serpent*, 232.

121   Belkis Acar, "Yuncü Nomad Weaving in the Bahkesir Region of Western Turkey," 27-31 in *Yörük. The Nomadic Weaving Tradition of the Middle East*, edited by Anthony Landreau (Pittsburg, Pennsylvania, Museum of Art, Carnegie Institute, 1978), 31.

122   Ralph S. Yohe, "'Gone to the Yayla,' Rugs of the Yörük Triangle," 36-39 in *ibid.*, 39.

123   *Africa and the Africans*, 149-150.

124   "Northwest Coast Indian Art," 318-340 in *Anthropology and Art*, edited by Otten, 325, 336-337.

125   Driver, *Indians of North America*, 348; Covarrubias, *Eagle, Jaguar and Serpent*, 179. Made of wood, an artificial whale might appear carrying a Jonah who had just experienced a supernatural experience at the bottom of the sea. Franz Boas, "Literature, Music and the Dance," 589-608 in *General Anthropology*, edited by Boas (New York, D. C. Heath, 1938), 607.

126   Pettitt, *Primitive Education*, 109.

127   Covarrubias, *Eagle, Jaguar and Serpent*, 94, 115.

128   Firth, *Art in New Guinea*, 32.

129   Anthony N. Landreau "Introduction: the Yörüks and Their Weaving," 11-16 in *Yörük. The Nomadic Weaving Tradition of the Middle East*, edited by Anthony Landreau, 11.

130   Boas, "Decorative Art of the North Pacific Coast," in *Golden Age of American Anthropology*, edited by Mead and Bunzel, 306.

131   Roy Sieber, "The Arts and Their Changing Function," 203-211 in *Anthropology and Art*, edited by Otten, 209.

132   Firth, *Art in New Guinea*, 32.

133   Bunzel, *Pueblo Potter*, 38, 58, 78.

134   Landreau "Introduction: The Yörüks and Their Weaving," *loc. cit.*, 11.

135   David Black and Clive Loveless, *Rugs of the Wandering Baluchi* (Washington, D.C., Textile Museum, 1976), 29.

136   George O'Bannon, "Baluchi Rugs," 62-64 in *Yörük. The Nomadic Weaving Tradition of the Middle East*, edited by Landreau, 64.

137   Ralph S. Yohe, "Gone to the Yayla," "Rugs of the Yörük Triangle," 36-39 in *Yoruk. The Nomadic Weaving Tradition of the Middle East*, edited by Landreau, 36.

138   Bunzel, *Pueblo Potters*, 88.

139   Covarrubias, *Eagle, Jaguar and Serpent*, 234.

Chapter IX

THE CULTURE CLASH:
Ideology vs. Technology

If the primitive's social aspirations could be defined, one would have to begin with the primacy of the group over the individual, spiritually as well as physically. Outside this charmed circle, an individual life was deprived of meaning. In Western history, we had a similar model, an Aristotelian and Catholic one, prior to the Renaissance. By contrast, the white man's conquest in modern times brought with it an emphasis upon individual rights and freedoms. This was a Lockean and Protestant model, dominate in the Renaissance and afterwards. Everywhere imposed upon the native, it caused the splendid outburst by Black Elk. He lamented the death of the sacred tree, the collapse of the tribe's center of gravity and the breaking of the nation's hoop, its magic circle which bound one with all and all with one.

Certain disclaimers must be made at the outset. We have no intention of making a complete analysis of the culture clash because it is too extensive a subject matter, far beyond our competence to explain here. First, we decline to cover ground long since adequately portrayed as to how the West first conquered, or imposed itself upon native populations by shot and shell. Neither are we concerned how this initial triumph was sustained over long decades by arrogant and unsympathetic colonial administrations. That kind of material has been included in classes in imperialism for over fifty years.[1] Nor are we prepared to delineate the complete range of native reactions to the conquest itself. Native depopulation is one such omission, whether it was due to the introduction of the white man's diseases, his alcohol or clothing,[2] or simply to a loss of will to live and propagate as a subjugated people.[3] In one form or another, this happened virtually everywhere and frequently in quite a dramatic fashion.

Let us begin with the central question of how effective the Christian idea of the Trinity, or the message of Christ himself, proved in combating or eroding the native's faith in his own gods or his own Trinity. The West would like to believe that it was our natural superiority of our religion, and not because of science and technology, which led to the adoption of Christianity by the native. Victory alone is not enough for us. We like to cap it with ethical and moral principles. We need to feel the universe itself is on our side because we merit it. Our problem however, is this: if the Christian message proved effective, why, and if not, why not? Assuming a dichotomy between idea and matter, or the spoken word and the deed itself, let us pose a second query. If Christianity proved ineffective in undermining the native belief systems, was technology itself, or the essence of matter and deed, any more effective? If so, why, and with what outcome for the tribe itself? Is it, for example, possible that the customary eagerness with which the native accepted the white man's superior technology invariably resulted in the destruction of tribal values, as deplored by Black Elk? Is it possible that both the white man and the conquered native allowed materialism to triumph over idealism?

Scholars of the culture clash between the imperialistic white man and the aborigine understand that the latter, as long as he was politically and militarily free, was independent of the Trinity of Father, Son and Holy Ghost. To put the matter differently, Christian doctrine and dogma, alone and without any of the coercive paraphernalia of civilization, was unable to undermine the pagan and heathen world. The word itself was inadequate.

The reaction of the American Indian may help us to understand why the word, the Gospel, which we in the Christian world had been taught to believe was so powerful and compelling, actually proved so weak and unavailing against ideological pagan strongholds. When Atahuallpa, the Inca, had the doctrine of the Trinity explained to him, his response was, because the Christian believed in three gods in one and one in three, he was that man who believed in four gods.[4] When in 1710, a Swedish missionary attempted to persuade the Susquehana or Conestoga Indians that, unless they converted to Christianity, they were doomed to hell because of "original sin," one of their chieftains rejected the invitation. He did so on the ground that a people who behaved so anti-socially as the white man could not have a religion worth the virtuous man's borrowing.[5] In 1805, the Seneca Indian, Red Jacket, declared in effect that the white man's profession of belief in Christ was far less important than whether he was a good neighbor or not. A bad man was someone who coveted Indian lands or who lied, stole or cheated them out of their rights. The fact that the same man attended church on Sunday and could perfectly recite the Nicene Creed was irrelevant to him.[6]

The traditional behavior of early Christian missionaries among the American Indian was fairly summarized. The Indian patiently listened as they spoke of their religion and mythology, and tried to learn something about the white man's history and national character. When the Indian in turn tried to explain his sacred beliefs the missionaries got angry, insisting that they were mere superstitions.[7] Dr. Charles Eastman, famous Sioux physician, told a similar tale concerning Christian creation and the origin of Indian maize. When the missionary showed disgust, declaring that he told the Indian the truth and that the latter had responded with falsehood, the Indian was astonished. He protested the lack of politeness and courtesy on the part of the white man. We believed your story, he concluded, so why did you not believe ours?[8]

Such displays of Christian intolerance naturally terminated possible learning experiences. As Masse Hadjo, a Sioux, declared, if the Indian's Messiah ever did come to earth, he would never attempt to force the white man to accept him, as the white had done.[9] The root of the difficulty was this. Like Martin Luther, the missionaries assumed, until a man received the only true faith at the hands of the Lord, the Christian variety, he could not perform good acts. As Luther concluded, a bad or sick tree could not bear good fruits.[10] On the contrary, the Indian appeared as a true behaviorist, judging a stranger first by the quality of his actions. If these were good, the Indian was willing to accept the postulate that the man had a good religion. If so, he would be curious to learn about it. If not, not. Two American Indians summarized beautifully the native view of the white man following the betrayal of the Supreme Court decision in Worcester v. Georgia, in 1832, and the Trail of Tears with the Cherokee exodus. Despite the white's obvious piety, and professed devotion to his God of Love, he was one of little faith and even less honor. How else was one man to judge fairly the worth and quality of another if not by his overt actions as compared with his stated ideals?[11]

In these reactions there were three basic themes: 1) The central theological doctrines of the Trinity were fuzzy and almost impossible to comprehend 2) The intolerance of Christian missionaries made an exchange of frank views very difficult and 3) The hypocrisy of the white man, who preached a God of Love but actually worshipped one of Greed, made a mockery of true religious feelings.

If the description in earlier chapters of the intricate beauty, symmetry and harmony of the Trinity of the primitive seemed fairly accurate, it helps to understand why he was not attracted by the Father, Son and Holy Ghost theme. He already had a religion which was quite meaningful and emotionally satisfactory to him. He saw no reasons for voluntary and drastic change.

Beyond this, there was always the tribe itself. It is imperative that we have some idea of the transcendent importance to the primitive. The tribe was a super person which endured forever while individuals came from the womb and went to the grave. It had both a reality and a destiny which transcended earthly limitations. Its members were all such close kinsmen as to literally be brother and sister together and thus ineligible to marry. Within such an extended family group the conception of Thomas Hobbes of a state of nature as a perpetual state of war of man against man was ridiculous. To use force and violence against fellow clansmen was to employ it against self, a mortal sin and one certain to call forth ancestral wrath.[12] Within this context it should be relatively easy to understand why, if the tribe itself approved of the individual, he did not have any cause to worry about his fate in the afterlife. He never thought about individual salvation in the same sense that Christians have habitually done. He never thought about it apart from that of the tribe. He in effect already had the salvation Christians were trying to dispense to him. It had come to him from the hands of the tribe itself.[13]

On the contrary, it was the deed, not the word, which historically inundated the primitive world almost overnight. That deed came as a consequence of the white man's mastery of the material world. While sailing in the Hawaiian islands in the late eighteenth century, Captain Cook discovered the natives valued small nails and bits of iron more than any other commodity. By 1840, tools had completely replaced native ones in tilling the soil of New Zealand. Twenty years later steel tools were everywhere to be seen in the hands of the Maori.[14] When the European explorers of the late nineteenth and early twentieth century penetrated the Amazon jungle, they expected the natives to want beads and mirrors. Instead they clamored after practical tools like metal knives, scissors, axes, tin plates and cups.[15] Much later, when encountering the Siriono in the tropical rain forests of Bolivia, Allan Holmberg noted that his party was immediately bombarded with pleas for tools, especially machetes.[16] In North America, Crazy Horse lamented that his contemporaries so lusted after the hardware of the trader they tried to exchange their daughters for it.[17] In the early nineteen forties, many aborigines for the first time were drawn to the mission at the edge of the Great Victorian desert in Australia. They had heard so many fascinating stories about the white man's tinned and canned food, so superior in taste to the small lizard of the terrain. It was also much easier to capture.[18] Everywhere the story was the same or almost identical. Technology seduced the primitive everywhere. The iron kettle, or the unbreakable kitchen utensils of the trader, had indisputable advantages over pottery as did the steel axe over the stone one and matches over a fire-drill. Cotton cloth was likewise valued over clothes made from bark as was wool over an animal's hide.[19] So lustful were the natives for the white man's tools that in the mid-twentieth century one explorer was reported killed in New Guinea because he injudiciously displayed steel axes too soon to strangers.[20]

Two accounts, diametrically opposed to one another, best reveal the terrific impact which technology immediately had upon the native. Upon the apparent discovery of a stone age tribe, the Tasaday, in the Philippine rain forest in 1971, Westerners wanted to do a good deed. Each male was given a steel axe, but one axe was left over. The distributors of the largesse urged the last man to take the extra axe but he refused. The male tribal equality and the social structure were more important to him than was individual greed. Meanwhile, Westerners were baffled that such a simple act could undermine tribal customs and traditions.[21] The other story is sadder because males in the Yir Yoront tribe of Australia did not control the new situation. In the old days rare stone axes were possessed only by male heads of the family. When younger males or women wanted one they had to appeal to the authority figure. The Christian missions upset the status cart overnight when they issued steel axes to younger men and women and even to children of the Yir Yoront. This led to confusion compounded in age, sex and status roles. The old men immediately lost their power and younger men and women were quickly emancipated. The result was social chaos, an immediate forerunner to the complete collapse of the tribe itself.[22]

In the final analysis, ideologies, such as a sound conservatism, rest upon their ability to explain the realities of life, such as social or tribal structure and ecology. The introduction of Western technology had unforeseen and devastating effects upon both.

In the case of the North American Indian we have many illustrations of the damage done to the social structure by the adoption of the white man's technology. The initial displacement of a primitive device by the white man's fabrication seemed simple enough. However, Catch-22 was that the tribe was unable to reproduce the new equipment. It was dependent upon the trader to bring more of the same. To obtain these the tribe had to trade what the white man wanted, such as furs. As trapping became primary for the first time so the magical beliefs and practices of the tribe had to change suddenly to accommodate. The entire tribal behavioral system of procedure was affected.[23] Among the Eskimos the adoption of the rifle led to a decreased reliance upon communal hunting because the caribou could now be killed by one man. That single change jarred tribal values to the core.[24] The Cree Indian degenerated into a simple parasite for the white trader as he gave up hunting to devote full time to trapping.[25] Using the white man's horse and gun, and dependent on his lusts for furs and pelts, the Shoshone proceeded to exterminate the bison in the Great Basin. They then moved east to the Rockies embarked on the same senseless mission.[26] When the trader's profits dropped with the decline of the fur and pelt supply, he moved on. The ex-hunter was left with an exotic skill which neither supported him in his local terrain nor supplied him with a foreign market.[27] Nor were the especially enterprising women unaffected. While Crazy Horse boasted that his grandmother's pottery was sought after by many tribes, he at the same time bemoaned the fact that currently no women in the tribe could make a simple cooking pot. The trader had destroyed her traditional skills, so vital in a subsistence economy.[28] Thus, the loss of these skills led to further deterioration of the old social order and the quality of life it once sustained.

My co-author felt the above paragraphs showed that anthropologists were in effect blaming the victims for succumbing to human greed, for more material things and an easier life. Our objective, of course, was to describe a system, or a process, one which was unquestionably based upon the greed of the white trader. That of the victor is always easy to detect while that of the loser in a conflict is apt to be obscured. His will did not prevail. If greed exists, and it certainly does, and if it is a vice as we all agree, this emotion belongs to humanity itself. We may, however, all be greedy for different things. Certainly, if in straightened economic circumstances, we would all be easy prey for the pitchman who could demonstrate that, at the same time he could reduce our work load while enhancing our creature comforts. Only village idiots, or holy men, are exempt from such temptations. The primitive was not.

In the Pacific, a similar process occurred and with much the same impact upon social structure. The recognized superiority of Western tools, and their quick adoption by the Maori, led to the creation of a new set of cultural values. He abandoned his old handicraft skills and worked at trades and occupations dictated by the white so he could obtain money to buy the lusted-for products. Life became topsy-turvy. Materials which were of little value in the old days, like pearl shell and copra in the Pacific islands and flax fibre and kauri gum in New Zealand, suddenly became the chief labor preoccupation. The native quickly absorbed the capitalistic idea of working neither for the love of it, nor of developing skills which pleasured the craftsman. Now it was for a willingness to labor long and hard at unpleasant tasks to gain something pleasant off the job, like material comforts, status symbols and such.[29] The best illustration of this principle, with the worst effects on the social structure of the tribe, was produced when native males were persuaded or forced into absentee labor situations for long periods of time. In Tikopian males an intense nostalgia set in, whether it was men sent into plantation labor elsewhere, or young lads sent away to school. The results were monumentally disastrous to all concerned.[30] An identical reaction occurred in Africa. Money could not compensate the community for the loss of the communal labor rendered in the past by the displaced worker.[31] Add to this the grievous losses experienced by the families of the men concerned and one can begin to calculate the harm done to the social structure.

The introduction of Western technology likewise abruptly and sharply impacted upon the native ecology. In Hawaii the combination of the white man's greed for sandalwood, and the introduction of cattle by Captain Vancouver, was responsible for the destruction of valuable forests which shaped a traditional way of life.[32] After rich mineral deposits were discovered under the home of a New Guinea tribe, the white man's enterprise soon produced a situation where the natives consumed his beer in the day time and slept in his prefabricated huts at night.[33] As the New Zealand native opted for the white man's hardware, including weapons, he had to exchange flax fibre in return. In order to do this he had to abandon his traditional living upon healthy high ground for low in order to grow the flax. This fact produced a radical alteration in hygenic conditions. He now had to labor incessantly in an unhealthy terrain.[34] The most disastrous effects were generally produced when whole tribes were forced to move into new and different terrains and take up new occupations. Tribal disintegration followed after the Ik, a mountain people in Uganda, were forcibly transformed into an agricultural people at a much lower altitude. A similar disaster happened when the pygmies were moved out of the rain forest into model villages in an agricultural setting. Moral as well as physical disintegration occurred on both the individual and tribal level.[35] The same adverse consequences occurred when governments around the Persian Gulf attempted to make nomads settle down into an agricultural and sedentary economy.[36] All of this enables us better to understand and sympathize with the lament of Crazy Horse. The white man built a railroad, destroyed the buffalo, and confined the Indian to a reservation. He would distribute Christian largesse on one side of a line in the Great Plains and death to the Indian on the other.[37]

However, there was an even more terrible price to be paid by the native. That was the inevitable by-product of a feeling of inferiority. Scholars noted the prevalence of that assumption in the Pacific.[38] Two American Indians bluntly acknowledged it. Always in awe of the white man's technology, Vine Deloria, Jr. asserted, this fact seemed to imply that his god was more powerful than were those of the native.[39] When still a Sioux Indian, Charles Eastman believed the white man's mastery of technology was the equivalent of the supernatural.[40] These assumptions profoundly shook tribal self-confidence, so necessary as a life-giving force. The process of social and psychological disintegration on a universal scale was best explained by F.S.C. Northrop. At worst, armies and their military technology merely broke heads. It required foreign ethics and religion to complete the debacle by capturing the imagination and loyalty of the native after he lost faith in his own religious and value systems. Not until this voluntary surrender occurred could the native culture be destroyed.[41] When, however, both the Tenetehara Indian and the Brazilian recognized the superiority of the white man, the Indian often being ashamed of his heritage, the process was complete for all practical purposes.[42] However, in the United States, the process itself might continue to grind out several unfortunate types of natives. All suffered in one way or the other from deprivation of a traditional culture or heritage.[43]

These principles make apparent the reasons for the universal reluctance of the primitive to accept Western cultural ideas while at the same time immediately adopting technological innovations. The Navaho accentuated their own ceremonials and rituals to strengthen their resistance to the temptation to adopt the white man's religion and life style.[44] The Cherokees of Southeastern United States were unusually successful at this.[45] Unfortunately, for most primitive tribes it proved virtually impossible to adopt the one without accepting the ideological baggage which accompanied it. The material apparatus of the new civilization was the first feature to be adopted by the native. Secondly, he absorbed the technical process of the production of the apparatus itself. Finally, he succumbed to the new beliefs and institutions of the conqueror.[46]

Confronted by sudden and repeated frustrations from the occupying power, native conservatism exploded. Everywhere the monk, the priest, the missionary served as the flying wedge for the intrusion of the white man's way of life. This was Christianity, as modified by individualism, nationalism, industrialism, capitalism, and science. Everywhere the shaman or medicine man was the inevitable target of the attack force. It was understood that, until that figure was undermined or overthrown, native allegiance to Christianity was suspect.[47] The most immediate and efficacious way to do this was through superior Western medical care and techniques. This once again proved to the native that the white man's god was more powerful.[48] Once established anywhere, the Christian missionary was equally bent upon changing both belief and behavior. In Hawaii it resembled an ecclesiastical despotism. The behavior of the missionaries reminds one of the Puritan ministers during the Commonwealth period in England. They were determined to weed out the social sins of the Stuarts which rested upon games, festivities, dances, theatricals, and, of course, alcohol.[49] In return the natives in Hawaii were given only the solace of the Bible, the Meetin' House, the prayer circle and occasionally a very somber tea party.[50] In British Africa one noted the prevalence of the unconscious assumption that the Christian always behaved like a Victorian English gentleman. Therefore, any strange and exotic institution would have to be extirpated if Christianity

were to flourish there.[51] The Christian missionary was both a late arrival
and an alien to Africa, full of preconceived ideas of racial, cultural and
religious superiority. It was he who encouraged his wards to imitate his
behavior at all times. The less African they became, the more Christian they
became.[52] No wonder the African regarded the Christian missionary as the
energy source for the obliteration of cherished customs.[53]

Once the native center of gravity collapsed, the law of centrifugal
force took over, spinning out what amounted to a complete and sudden
social revolution. Nothing better illustrates this than the actions of the
natives of Manus in the Admiralty islands off New Guinea in 1946 at Peré.
Almost overnight the natives discarded everything previously held sacred:
name taboos, customs of childbirth, puberty, marriage, native ornaments,
dress, houses and customs. Fathers lost control not only of the marriages of
their daughters but of their early sex life as well. Likewise they lost control
over the occupation and working place of their sons. This destruction was
done in the name of human dignity.[54] To the historian it sounds much like
the assault of the eighteenth century Enlightenment upon the Medieval
restraints of Church, State and Guild.[55]

One of the most dramatic accounts of how easily, completely and
abruptly technology broke the centuries-old hold of tradition concerned the
Fore people in the interior of New Guinea. The drama opened with the
completion of a single, steep and rough jeep road from the coast to the high
interior. This road allowed for the influx of technological magic as well as
foot traffic of the young to the outside world. New people, new goods and
ideas flowed in while young men walked out for the first time to strange
schools, jobs and ways of life. When they returned, they brought back exotic
ideas, and goods like coffee. The traditionally segregated huts for men and
women were abandoned and single houses built after the white man's
fashion. The family's children became of primary importance rather than
tribal children. Women began to wear blouses, preventing ease of access of
the breast for the youngster in their arms. This occasioned domestic scenes
of frustration previously unknown. So quickly did the sacred life of their
forefathers disappear, and a Western style take its place, that the culture
shock was highly visible. It took the form of individual amnesia. Some

persons could no longer recall the old customs and traditions, even though they had participated only a few years before.[56]

While these accounts were more dramatic than most, they nevertheless typify the quick dissolution of native ways, or the internal revolution of manners and mores which followed the white man's thrust. Invariably the women and the younger men were the first to defect. The old men struggled to maintain the ways of the ancestors.[57] This was not only because primitive societies gave positions of power to older men, but because they were the custodians of the ancient gods themselves and of their shrines. On the contrary young men and women seemingly had little to lose but inequality. Women were frequently induced to abandon the native faith because Christian medical missionaries proved much more efficacious in prenatal care, childbirth and rearing. That may help explain the Anang Ibibio women in Africa who openly marched around the villages singing hymns, burning sacred symbols and ridiculing the old ways.[58] Invariably younger men welcomed the invasion of Western technology because of job prospects, whatever the distance from the old locale. Money earned meant presumed access to transistor radios, bicycles, fancy clothes and perhaps even motor cars.[59]

The surrender itself, however, was not complete until the old men themselves despaired and cut the tribe adrift from its past. Everywhere, one suspects, the situation was much the same as with the Nandi where the council of old men quickly lost caste and influence.[60] A typical outcome occurred among the Iatmul people of the Sepik river region of New Guinea at Tambunam. There one day the old men decided not to pass on their sacred knowledge to younger men, although they themselves remained faithful to the ways of their fathers.[61] In much the same fashion the Kraho males of the tropical forest of Brazil decided, since their children must live in a white man's world, it would be better for all concerned if they dressed, looked and acted like him.[62] It was Charles Eastman's own Indian father who, following the dark days of the repression of the Sioux in the Civil War, advised his son to learn the white man's ways. This was better for the defeated power than to strangle culturally while confined to a reservation.[63]

Christian schools were the chosen instrument for the indoctrination of the young in Western thought and ways. If they were not universally successful in their cultural conversion tactics, they did unfit their charges for native life. Wherever the old priestly class had schools and temples, as at Cuzco and Mexico City, the Spanish monks instinctively rooted them out to destroy the native Higher Learning. This made a Christian and godly life possible.[64] This was a persistent pattern of behavior for all whites, regardless of nationality. Only the young were truly malleable. Sometimes, however, the natives welcomed the white man's tutelage. When Margaret Mead returned to Tambunam, New Guinea, in 1968, she was told by a village elder how, in 1953, he led a procession of 195 children, boys and girls, to the new mission school. The elders had decided their children should not learn about a dead past which could only handicap them in the future.[65] Consciously or unconsciously, such schools immediately became propoganda instruments for sharp and vast cultural change. Throughout Africa, Christian schools not only taught literacy, theology and morality, but new ways of expression and the principles of bureaucracy. It was consciously designed to produce a new kind of African and, superficially at least, seemed highly successful.[66] Among the Pakot people in East Africa, where circumcision was a "must" for manhood, mission schools preached the obliteration of such customs.[67] In Guatemala, however, the cultural schooling devices were less than successful. While the boys were withdrawn early by the fathers, because the school did not teach agriculture, prize girl students soon forgot Spanish after graduation.[68]

Vine Deloria, Jr.'s objection to white instruction of the Indian was a profound one. The white attempted to teach the Indian a trade or a craft but, as a consequence of his entire approach, the student lost his native faith in both the tribal nature of religious experience and his mysterious and transcendent gods.[69] This was an inevitable development since, if the Hopi experience were typical, the white never took Indian religious mysticism seriously.[70] Following his education by the white, the Plains Indian returned to the reservation with little learning in English but much cultural alienation.[71] One also noted adverse sociological consequences for the young Manus girls eager to be educated by whites in the Pacific. The exodus from the village caused a sharp population decline. Those girls returning home after this exotic experience found themselves regarded as unmarriagable because they were "damaged goods."[72] Among the Alaskan Eskimo, girls educated in high school were thereafter dependent upon the white man's consumer goods without being able to make enough money to pay for them in old locales. Therefore, they emigrated to the larger cities of Alaska, remote from their old homes.[73]

Francis Huxley fairly summarized the plight of the young natives who were anxious to become white because they were convinced of the inadequacy of their own provincial background. They tried to emulate the life style of the Brazilian without an understanding of the values which lay behind them. At the same time they were scornful of their own inherited values. Naturally, they ended up in a kind of limbo, without any understandable values or morality.[74] In sum, it was education at the white man's schools, compulsory or not, which broke the loyalty of native children both to their pueblo and way of life.[75]

While it is difficult to capsulate the native dilemma brought about by the culture clash, it is probably fair to say that everywhere history and tradition left him completely unprepared when the white man forced individualism and a money economy upon him. Africa was a typical case. There the Western insistence upon individualism collided with the age-old emphasis upon the extended family with its intricate network of social duties and obligations. It resulted in the latter's immediate disadvantage.[76] Among the Bantus the introduction of the white man's farming, and particularly mining, produced an urban society almost overnight. It turned a simple and innocent culture into one which resembled Sodom and Gomorrah.[77] Success in life was no longer judged by the native to come as a result of tribal approval of socially acceptable virtues displayed by the individual. Now it was solely dependent upon individual economic effort. As a consequence, the new fear prevalent in Baganda society was not that of the foreigner, but rather a suspicion that one's neighbor plotted to take advantage of or exploit him.[78] Sacking the old communal way of life with its subsistence economy for the highly impersonal money economy of the white brought the immediate illusion of freedom and opportunity. However, the dream often soured as the native showed an incapacity to handle money as did the rational Victorian bourgeois. He was often conned into sacrificing a month's wages for some object of little worth.[79] The same laments were heard in the New World. In Chile, a native might even dispose of his land while intoxicated, a catastrophe unheard of in the old days. This was because of the white man's monopoly on the sale of liquor. For this the native would part with most anything when he had a strong craving for drink.[80] And drunkenness occured as an integral pattern of his demoralization.[81]

Everywhere the perceptive native deplored the erosion of the old social values, particularly the decay of generosity and social concern. Primitive peoples generally felt an individual was entitled to food and the other necessities of life regardless of whether one was currently a producer of them.[82] This meant skilled hunters shared their quarry with the rest of the community. However, when a society left the hunting stage, the values based upon that kind of culture soon eroded. There was a profound difference between sharing game the individual had slaughtered and dividing up a relief check or something from the white man determined on a scale of his own values.[83] But, even when on the Osage reservation, Gray Bird was loath to abandon the old idea of sharing with the widows and orphans. Although his catch was much lighter when he arrived in the bosom of his immediate family, his heart sang with joy. Conversely, when he sneaked past the widow's home with his catch intact his heart felt heavy with sorrow. To be an Indian was to think with one's heart, not one's head.[84] Finally, when Red Cloud was told he must now be and act like the white man, he knew what the situation called for. Forget the wisdom of your ancestors, he opined. Lay up food for yourself and ignore the hungry. When your new house is built, and your storehouse full, look around for a neighbor you can plunder.[85]

This entire disastrous process appeared to proceed at a considerably faster pace the more primitive the society was;[86] likewise, it seemed to encounter less resistence in agricultural ones than in the nomadic variety.[87] The mobility of the latter not only gave them a cultural autonomy,[88] but oftentimes provided a means of escape when a new predator arrived on the scene.[89]

While technology remarkably accelerated native surrender to the white man, the latter was also considerably assisted by a universal behavioral impulse on the part of the conquered. It was the conservative theorist, Thomas Hobbes, who allowed the only valid reason for revolution against one's sovereign would be the latter's failure to protect his subjects against an external foe.[90] Likewise, military defeat, sudden and complete, was a valid reason for the primitive to abandon his gods. Considering the assumption the gods make powerful war medicine, it was natural, before the coming of the white man to Africa, for the loser to accept the religion of the victor. At least he would add his god to their panoply of gods.[91] In this way the defeated power borrowed strength at an apparently very low interest rate.[92] In recent times we have seen how a completely defeated power tends voluntarily to ape the conquerer's ways. For example, as Vichy France immediately sought to emulate its conquerer, Nazi Germany,[93] so Japan later did the same for its American victor.[94]

In addition, when the victor was intolerant of any opposition in a religious sense, it is easy to see why, on the surface at least, Christianity was the only religious doctrine among the aborigine following the white man's conquest. Spanish religious fanaticism in the Philippines caused their priests to regard all native manuscripts as works of the Devil. One in Southern Luzon bragged about the destruction of three hundred such documents.[95] In Tikopia, the intolerance of Christian missionaries was due to a pseudo-Christian compulsion to make others conform to their standards of behavior, regardless of the adverse effect they might have upon the native. The big complaint of the native was the missionary's opposition to any observance of native ritual. This despite the fact it demonstrably served the same purpose as Judaic or Christian prayer, notably individual and community welfare.[96] Similar behavior in the New World caused the collapse, almost over-night, of the fragile priestly cultures of the Inca, the Maya and the Aztec. Only the native culture of hearth and home remained undisturbed.[97] In the American Southwest the partnership of priest and military presido was commonplace. In California the lives of the conquered Indians were turned topsy-turvy. The small nomadic bands were forced to live in compounds where the sexes were carefully segregated but former tribal enemies were not. Thus the entire physical, social and moral atmosphere was changed within a generation. The Indian was required to change with it, or be hunted down like a wild animal. The explanation was simple. Spanish monks insisted on nothing less than total conversion to Christianity. That meant the blotting out of any individual or tribal customs which hinted at opposition to it.[98]

The initial shock of the cultural impact in Maya Yucatan, under the direction of Bishop Diego de Landa in the mid-sixteenth century, contained all the familiar elements of enslavement, raiding, resettlement, forced conversions,[99] and book burning.[100] But later developments introduced the much-needed element of compensation. Recalled to Spain in 1568 for his overzealous religious measures, he wrote a book in defense of his own actions. It contained an account of his efforts to determine the Maya alphabet. However, it was not until 1952 that scholars realized the bishop had provided an essential key to Maya writing of both the Classic and Postclassic periods.[101]

One should not make the mistake of assuming that such religious and racial intolerance was restricted to Latin and Catholic missionaries. A typical instance of WASP intolerance occurred in 1894 at New Oraibi on the Hopi reservation. When the Hostiles, or the traditionalist faction of the Hopi Indians, refused to send their children to the white man's school, Federal troops were ordered to invade the homes, seize the children and imprison the offending adults. Nineteen of the latter were incarcerated for eighteen months.[102] This coercive policy was continued for the next half century with miserable outcomes for all. While the children lost faith in their own religion and culture, they failed to acquire any respect for that of the conquerer. As a consequence, their lack of conviction made their ineffectiveness particularly felt when they participated in tribal councils.[103]

In North Africa in the Thirties, Italians were intolerant of the strange customs of the Bedouins. "Because they lived in tents without most of the goods the peasant, and even more the townspeople regarded as signs of civilization the Italians spoke of them as barbarians, little better than beasts, and treated them accordingly."[104] Convinced they could not break the Bedouin solidarity down without the total destruction of their tribal and kinship systems, the Italians launched a systematic attack upon both. By law, individual ownership was to supercede 'patriarchial agriculture' and tribal and lineage ownership of wells was abolished. "The epoch of the clans is about to pass forever in these provinces."[105]

Even in recent times, the efforts of Christian missionaries, both Catholic and Protestant, were dedicated to the destruction of native customs and values and the substitution of their own. Jean-Paul Dumont told how the process ultimately worked against the Panare of Venezuela who tenaciously clung to tradition.[106] Whereas the Catholic clergy tried to work the miracle of change overnight, regardless of social consequences and even morality, the Protestant effort was more subtle. It slowly but deeply penetrated the culture it sought to efface.[107] The first significant signs of the waning of the old values was observed in the play of children. When he first arrived, they played with toy blow guns. However, by the time he departed, they were using make-believe trucks and airplanes instead. Thus, they were in the process of internalizing values which were foreign to their own culture and experiencing that of the West, if only in their imagination. It demonstrated a cultural vulnerability, a beginning of the end.[108]

The process of the culture clash as just described is predictable under the deductive law of cultural dominance. By the terms of this law cultural predominance flows toward that power which has technical predominance. That occurs because it expands at the expense of competing powers which possess less technological know-how.[109]

Imagine, wrote my co-author, that space aliens came to confront us in both war and peace with a whole new technology, one vastly superior to ours. Since much of our daily life is built around work organizations and work roles, imagine the destructive impact upon both our economy and culture. Because we always worshipped technological efficiency, and because our own apparatus is now obviously discredited, our society would instantly be disorganized and mass alienation discernable. It would be difficult, if not impossible, to discover an organized will and capacity to resist immediate and drastic change. The only plausible analogy which comes to mind is the complete and sudden reversal of behavior by the Japanese in August, 1945, following the command of their Emperor to surrender to General MacArthur.

What the conquering white did not grasp, however, was the primitive frequently borrowed that which he did not understand. It was probably because eventually he could make it his own by coming up with a product that was unique. It bore little relationship to a world doctrine like Christianity. The borrowing society attempts to emulate an exotic pattern of life, or belief system, without an understanding of its original cultural context. The new life-style, or belief, is then received into the old culture stripped of most, if not all, of the elements which originally gave it life and verve. Therefore, it can easily be manipulated to conform with the beliefs and customs of the borrowing tribe.[110]

Even more self-defeating on the part of the conqueror was the supposition that his particular truth, Christianity, could everywhere be imposed overnight without any consideration of highly different pasts, customs and religious beliefs. One theological system could not universally be substituted for a multitude of religious beliefs, all of which in the past had been highly effective on a comparatively small scale. Crucial questions were not addressed because they were not even thought of, as the Melanesian experience demonstrated. "How adequately is the Christian (and especially the Protestant) 'God the Father' suited to adopt a 'maternal' role? How inextricably is monotheism tied to rationalist individualism? Do the New Caledonian categories of male 'power' and female 'life' make sense in a modern context? ... Finally, is there not a fundamental contradiction between a single, transcendent God and the plenitude of relations -esthetic, social, religious, ecological - that [Maurice] Leenhardt recognized as elemental?"[111]

What this meant was that Christian conversions throughout the world were more apparent than real. Christians among the Anang Ibibio of Southeastern Nigeria appeared typical. Many natives accepted Christianity without rejecting their traditional religious beliefs.[112] Perhaps as a consequence, they were not only baffled by the doctrine of the Trinity, but unable to grasp the significance of Christ's death on the cross.[113] As a result of their selectivity in borrowing, African religions in the modern world continued to flourish. This occurred despite Moslem efforts of a thousand years and the almost frenetic Christian activity since the period 1850-1870.[114] Likewise, there was an unwillingness of the old gods to die in

Tikopia and the superficiality of Christianity in the island.[115] Despite the unrelenting pressure of Christian missionaries since the seventeenth century, the religion of the Tentehara Indians in Brazil appeared less modified from pre-conquest days than any other institution.[116] An American aborigine deplored the moral bankruptcy of the white man's policy which marked the period when the Indian was not allowed to be an Indian, but yet could not become a white man. With freedom of religious choice given the Indian since 1934, it was not surprising Christianity has been in a state of decline. Tribal religions and customs revived.[117] After several centuries of Christian conquest, the Guatemalan village of Chimalteco was surprisingly free of Catholic influence. There were no private confessions, no marriages in the church and, most surprising, the mass itself was considered unimportant.[118]

Conversely, even if the doctrine of a religion is understood and accepted, it is by no means likely the new doctrine will be followed emotionally and spontaneously. That is because of the old, culturally conditioned emotions, feelings and reflexes shaped and guided by the native doctrine or faith. The best instrument for the evoking of emotion is art, and the means for the conditioning of new habits is ceremonial and communal ritual. It is probably fair, therefore, to conclude that, while the Catholic Church might be pretty well equipped to meet such a challenge, Protestant churches rooted in Calvinism would be abysmally prepared.[119]

It was religious and social behavior such as this which prompted the observation that it seemed to fortify the principle of evolutionists: successful adaptation occurs when a form undergoes the smallest possible change which, at the same time, permits an effective response to an environmental disturbance.[120] Finally, one must single out that element of native revenge against the white conqueror for his sudden uprooting and inevitable tribal disorder or "organizational sabotage." For example, forty years after a New Guinea tribe had been forcibly removed from the interior highlands to the coast, its members were still ignorant of fishing, swimming, and the art of making canoes.[121]

Thus, while primitive ideologies appeared impervious to the Christian one, they proved quite vulnerable to technology in the form of tools, goods, food, medicine and, finally, to the military organization and weapons system of Western man. And, not surprisingly, where Christianity came in the wake of technological conquest, its universal elements were blurred in the process and parochialism eventually triumphed.

There was, however, one additional pragmatic reason for native defection from its gods. That was when the heavens no longer responded to man's universal appeal: "Give us this day our daily bread." Naturally, this process took much longer to occur because the believer ordinarily was slow to lose the faith. For a people to be deprived of its gods was in effect for it to be projected back into a state of nature. There a naive folk had to live in a frighteningly impersonal world, full of the unpredictable, capricious and tragic. That, of course, was why cosmology, ritual and art had made their initial appearance, at least in an organized form. They substituted certainty for uncertainty and order for mere flux. At any rate, the tribes which lost this heavenly favor, or those which were losers in the Darwinian struggle for survival, left few physical traces and no chronicles. Instead they left mystery in their wake. After two hundred years of a sedentary life, the artistic Mimbreños Indians of the American Southwest left their settlements to walk off the face of the earth.[122] Unscientific farming and declining food yields among the Mayans in the sixth century A.D. may have caused their priesthood to report that the gods desired a great exodus or migration. The priests did this in order to check a general religious decline.[123] The perpetual and deepening water crisis at Machu Picchu, the pre-Incan civilization at 12,000 feet, must have precipitated a like situation when it was finally apparent that migration was the only tribal alternative.[124] This was always a great leap into the unknown.

When, for whatever reason, the local gods died, it liberated the individual from an authoritarian system, as Franz Boas insisted. For him change, evolution and progress were possible.[125] My co-author felt this contention was another illustration of cultural blindness. Were not, he asked, Catholicism and certain brands of Protestantism equally authoritarian? One suspects Boas knew this. He was content to point out the collapse of a native belief system liberated the individual from *that* brand of authoritarianism.

Yet, for the tribe it made for the kind of a tragedy which would bring a tear to the eye of a passing stranger, assuming he were both perceptive and compassionate. It was a sad and wretched day when, after the Indian religions and languages had been proscribed on the reservation, the old men sold or gave the tribe's sacred bundle to the state museum. It was received as a mere curiosity.[126] Equally touching were the pathetic efforts of the Australian aborigine in Echo Island off Cape Arnheim in 1958. He openly displayed his most precious ritual boards to the soon indifferent white in the vain hope the latter would give something of equal value.[127] Even where the native profited temporarily in a materialistic sense as a consequence of contact with the white man, he at the same time suffered the death of the soul. The greater the false prosperity the white man brought to the Great Plains, the more once-sacred things were offered for sale by the Indian to his own kind. As tribal wealth continued to spiral upwards, the price for sacred bundles followed in a faithful - or rather faithless -manner.[128] It is hard to avoid the conclusion that when the local gods die, their people die likewise. It is not that life, or activity itself, ceases. This obviously intensifies. It is just that, while individual souls may be saved, the collective soul is obviously lost. No one expressed this any better than Black Elk. He lamented the fact that white intrusion had caused the death of the sacred tree, the collapse of the tribe's center of gravity, and the dismemberment of the nation's hoop, its magic circle which bound one with all and all with one.[129] It was no doubt a similar feeling among the people of Manus. Some forty odd years after their sudden conversion to Western ways, it caused them to revive old dances, songs, oratory and costumes. The West, it seemed, could provide a revolution as concerned technology and a life tempo in a new world market. It could not warm the soul as did the old culture. Margaret Mead thought this a happy mix.[130]

Time now to follow the lead of Weston La Barre. He described in fascinating detail the world-wide and historical tendency for disintegrating societies in social deprivation and trauma to resort to their Ghost Dance.[131] He likened this to the reaction of the individual ego when customary stimulation is quickly and extensively withdrawn and the personality suffers severe depression. To conquer the sense of isolation, he peoples this void with paranoid projections of his own making.[132] This is the kind of eerie experience sought for by the Indian of North American hunting tribes in their celebrated vision quest. The adolescent went out alone to a remote and isolated spot to seek a supernatural experience. After long fasting, which radically altered the physical state of his body, and much prayer in which he displayed himself as a helpless child at the knee of an almighty power, he might obtain such a vision. This vision or power he used to direct the rest of his life.[133] It was also the kind of experience associated with mountains, deserts, open seas, frozen wastes and the like, which afford a monotonous landscape and thus avoided offering the subject different and diverting sensations. White explorers experienced such hallucinations at both the North and South polar regions. Perhaps the classic example was of Captain Joshua Slocum who sailed around the world alone at the turn of the century. Once in a storm in the South Atlantic, when he lay helpless in his bunk, the pilot of Columbus' *Pinta* took over and did an expert job. He returned to give additional help when it was essential.[134] Our concern, however, is not with historical implications on a global level but limited instead to primitive despair which induced the Ghost Dance of the Plains Indians of 1890 and the Oriental cargo cults of the twentieth century.

While the West categorized the Ghost Dance as the triumph of the irrational, the primitive believed human will could magically command events in nature, provided the ritual was correct.[135] Science looks to the same outer world as does the believer in magic, but it seeks to dominate by an understanding of the impersonal principles or laws which make it operate as it does. Religion differs from both in that man, despairing of his control over this world, seeks a supernatural power or powers which does control it in order to bend the knee and worship it. He does this in the hope that power will then be shared between the worshipped and the worshippers. It was the age-old theme: the forces of history were unavailing before the returning hero or god. The very meaning of the word messiah designated someone who came to rearrange events, or to end human history.[136]

A most curious mixture of the traditional elements of native magic and the white man's religion, the Ghost Dance of the Plains Indians of 1890 showed man's irrational mental capacity to substitute a brave new world for one tired, corrupt and depraved. Hunters had suffered a Paradise Lost, or those days when the Plains were open and vast and populated by great herds of buffalo. Now they were at the mercy of the white who built the Iron Horse, destroyed the buffalo and penned the Indian up in ever smaller and smaller prisons, reservations. There he suffered both disease and boredom. But he had time to ponder his fate. Somehow he had sinned against the gods and the white man had been dispatched by them for appropriate punishment. Heavenly signs now indicated that time for sorrow and weeping were over and the day of deliverance was at hand. Provided all tribes danced the Ghost Dance in a prescribed way, and each warrior carried a white feather which would lift him into the new world, this would compel the miracle. Dancing would protect the warrior both from the white man's bullets and his diseases. A new messiah would appear. A new skin would slide over the earth, burying the white man's world and ushering in Paradise Regained. Departed warriors and chiefs would accompany new trees and buffalo herds. All this the ancient gods were prepared to deliver provided their sons paid them the proper respect through the prescribed rituals of the Ghost Dance.[137]

On the other side of the world the cargo cults of the twentieth century manifested the same grievous sense of loss, as well as the same naive belief that a demonstrated sense of will could magically wipe out an undesired world and usher in a new and perfect society. It also highlighted the old longing of the native for the white man's technology while retaining his familiar ideology. Technology itself was mysterious. It showed up in boats in New Guinea and elsewhere in Melansia only after the black man worked long and hard to produce gold and copra and the white man stopped sipping his whiskey and soda long enough to scribble a few words on paper. God and copra slipped off the edge of the world to the West. In its place came guns, machines, radios and what-not which made the white man so powerful. While black youngsters worked at several places in the Far East, none had witnessed the manufacture of these mysterious goods. In a world where no fabrication occurred without the necessary addition of magic to make it effective, it was relatively easy to deduce these wonderful goods were being processed in the world of the native dead, somewhere to the West. However, these goods were unfortunately intercepted by the predatory white. The answer clearly lay in ritualistic behavior. If only the blacks would cease the long and arduous manual labor dictated by the white and emulate his ease around the conference and coffee tables, or the liquor cabinet, then the goods would come to their rightful heirs, the natives themselves. Unfortunately, this was the prelude to social and economic disaster.[138]

Other authorities declared that even sterner measures were demanded of the natives by the prophets. First of all, they had to demonstrate their faith in the future by physically destroying the present. They were to do this by the destruction of all the property they had, not only of European origin but their own, including pigs and gardens.[139] After tearing up their fields and slaughtering their pigs, the natives often spent several days on beaches awaiting the new cargoes from Heaven.[140]

Vittoria Lanternari aptly described the Melanesian cargo cults as an eclectic mix of pagan magic and Christian miracle. The common desire to efface an evil world and usher in a pristine one supposedly occurs at the same time as the resurrection of that society's dead and a revival of its traditional value system. "Often the chiliastic myth, or myth of the millenium, involves the coming of the Messiah in human form, whose redemptive action is to be the fulfillment of society's hope that the traditional ways of life can be restored. The Messiah, regarded as the re-creator of the world, is usually the personification of some national hero whose return has long been awaited, or of the ancestor who formed the cultural lineage, either Adam or Jesus Christ."[141]

At the same time, however, the cargo cults invariably reflect the tremendous influence of the white man's technology upon the native mind. The day of theological judgment is accompanied by the arrival of cargo ships from the West, all of whose contents are earmarked by their ancestors, or ghosts, for the native population. It represents a dramatic reversal of the usual earthly procedure: To him who hath shall be given, to him who hath not, shall be taken away.[142] Paradise is social justice as an oppressed agrarian people conceives it.[143] It is no accident that their conquerors taught them well. They came bringing both religious evangelism and a plethora of heretofore unknown goods.[144]

In the view of the objective set forth at the beginning of this chapter, namely the effect of Christian doctrine, dogma and technology upon the native at the outset of the culture clash, one need not in time go past the Ghost Dances. Naturally, native reactions do not end there. Indeed, there is no end, only a continual evolution, or the sort of thing Margaret Mead kept discovering with relation to technology as she returned again and again to Manus in the Admiralty islands off New Guinea.[145] While the California Indian never assimilated Christian ethics, because they were so contrary to his own, Christianity of a sort could be superimposed upon primitive variety and in time successfully incorporated within it.[146] Finally, one has been uncomfortably aware of the elusive causal factor raised by Charles Wagley with regard to the different fates of the Tentehara and Tapirapé Indians. The problem he rightly called attention to was the intriguing one of why the Tentehara Indians, after several hundred years of contact with the white man, seemed to be doing so well, population-wise, whereas the Tapirapé were threatened with virtual extermination after a rather brief encounter. Perhaps, as he suggests, it was because the Jesuits shielded their protégés, the Tentehara, for a long time, thereby dulling the culture shock, whereas the Tapirapé were exposed to it all at once.[147] What eventually happens, however, to a cultural mix clearly lies outside our area of concern.

To sum up, as one examines the basic values of the two conflicting groups, the reason for the distress and anguish of the conquered is quite obvious. It involved the great social and psychological distance between the Aristotelian notion of the primacy of a growing and evolving biological organism, or social order, as opposed to the Lockean idea of society as nothing more than the result of legal contracts between separate and independent atomic substances or personalities.

A careful reading of Aristotle's *Politics* leads to the conviction that, when he postulated the ideal state, he was in reality describing the typical underpinings of the primitive social order. For example, he insisted the social group existed before either the individual or the family and its welfare was the ultimate reality. With relation to its ecology, ideal social order should have less population than both territory and resources, thus insuring material blessings for all. Population should also be small and manageable, its numbers being manipulated through eugenic selection of the newly-born.[148] As we have seen these were the principle characteristics of primitive cultures. When they were violated, it was not long before the group was victimized by Malthusian pressures, or the law of diminishing returns, or both simultaneously.

No one, it appears, has done a better job of analyzing Lockean man than has F.S.C. Northrop. Locke's conceptualization of the primacy of the separate and independent individual, or atomic particle, was based on the new physics of Galileo and Newton. There was no religious or social tie between him and his fellows that was not the result of contractual needs of that individual organism. His social obligations extended no further than his legal concessions. His property was his own by virtue of the fact that it was the result of his own labors while in a state of nature. The state itself had been called into being for the purpose of protecting that property. Therefore, the state might not make demands on it, either because economic needs of the sovereign or those of the multitudes. Intellect, not passion, was stressed. Consequently, the rational man emerged. He looked at the world scene of suffering and despair with some disinterest, rather than with concern and compassion. The source of good and evil in the world was rooted in the individual. He, not society, was responsible for his economic well-being and for the crime which might follow as a consequence of his own incapacity to cope with that individual responsibility.[149] In religious matters Lockean man employed the intellect in reading, preaching and listening. On the contrary, he was highly suspicious of the emotional and intuitive approach. This accounted for the Protestant suppression in the sixteenth and seventeenth centuries of stained glass windows, incense, bells, rich vestments, elaborate rituals and all such things which were not specifically mentioned in the New Testament. They seemed to seduce man sensually and artistically, rather than appealing to him through the word or the idea.[150] On the contrary, one may say of the primitive what others did of the devotees of the great religions of the Orient. If one were to take away all art from religion, there would not be much of the edifice remaining.[151]

The greatest culture clash of all between the primitive mind and the civilized Christian occurred when the missionary, ignoring the aesthetic or artistic component, was entirely preoccupied with preaching the word of the

Gospels. He was fanatically devoted in both thought and deed to modern Western principles of individualism. Just as it was not possible for any of the followers of the four great religions of the East to abandon their religion for Christianity without that deed undermining their entire culture pattern, so the same situation obtained for the primitive.[152] It now becomes obvious why he had to be coerced or seduced into the rejection of the religion of his ancestors. The tragedy was compounded when he discovered what his white conqueror offered in its stead lacked the same spiritual comfort as did his traditional religion. He was condemned to living between two highly different worlds without belonging to either.[153]

To sum up, the price primitive peoples pay for being seduced or conquered by white civilization is that a once homogeneous culture is transformed into a schizophrenic one. Take the case of the fierce Asmat tribe of New Guinea. Its homogeneous character was entirely based on the practice of headhunting. When that was forcibly suppressed by the Dutch and later the new Indonesian government, the whole traditional fabric of society disintegrated almost overnight.[154] But while the native carpenter seemed contented, even happy, wielding the white man's tools, the one who retained the bow and arrow was alienated and forlorn.[155] That this is not merely a transitory phase is indicated by reference to the Aymara Indians in the mountainous region of Lake Titicaca, descendents of those conquered in the early sixteenth century. Not only does the native traditionally regard the white with suspicion and half-suppressed hostility,[156] but, despite nominal membership in the Catholic Church, a great many hate that institution as much as the white race which forced it upon them.[157]

In our opinion no author did a better job than Leslie Marmon Silko in displaying the bitterness, the frustration and the alienation which descended on a once happy primitive people as a consequence of their military and cultural degradation at the hands of the white man. It focused on a small group of young Pueblos whose tragedy was that they fought in World War II in defense of a land already lost, already stolen from them. Their most sacred values had been openly scoffed at in their schools where the teacher pointed out the contrary "truth" contained in their science text. Their war-time hopes of acceptance and racial equality quickly evaporated when "business as usual" was resumed after the conflict. On the reservation itself there was little besides drought, misery, hunger and poverty. Off it, the atmosphere was suffused with public contempt, labor exploitation and police brutality. Alcoholism and violence appeared the only safety valves for pent-up emotions. As one might expect, the latter was turned by the Indian against himself with tragic consequences. Meanwhile, the attitude of the whites seemed to be that such deviant behavior merely fulfilled one's expectations. As for the white man himself, his discovery of the atomic bomb merely capped his compulsive role as destroyer of both man and nature.[158]

The so-called economic miracle of modern Brazil certainly ploughed both under. The trans-Amazonian highway cut both the terrain and tribes in two. Village life was terminated and the survivors from a dying culture were forced into a life of beggary on the part of the men and prostitution on that of the womenfolk.[159]

In retrospect, David Bidney would be quite justified in citing Tom, Jeff and me as good examples of romantic, cultural relativists. We no longer believe, as did nineteenth century anthropologists, that it is either wise or virtuous to attempt to impose ethnocentric absolutes upon those with entirely different cultural backgrounds and social needs. When that happens, the results have been uniformly disastrous involving the loss of tribal self-respect and the will to live. Even when given more time and good counsel, primitive peoples demonstrated a seeming inability to understand or appreciate Western values when applied to their daily lives. Therefore, they should be encouraged to develop the potential of their own culture which has a relative value equal to our own. Since the days of Melville J. Herskovits, younger anthropologists have gravitated to this theory. However, Bidney now believes it should be superseded by a world anthropological endeavor, through the study of comparative cultures, to arrive at a set of moral and cultural norms capable of universal application. Hopefully, this should help safeguard against local tyrannies.[160]

Since World War II, however, the perennial, the wrenching, the wearying violations of Human Rights by both the Communist and non-Communist blocks throughout the world have left the perceptive observer wondering whether there is any realism devoid of despair.

Footnotes

1   Perhaps the classic analysis of the essentially exploitative, even parasitic, character of European imperialism in colonial areas is contained in a book first published in 1902 by John Hobson, entitled *Imperialism: a Study* (London, George Allen & Unwin, reprinted 1954). Especially pertinent is the chapter entitled "Imperialism and the Lower Races," 223-284.

2   S. M Lambert, "The Depopulation of Pacific Races," 42 pp. (Honolulu, Hawaii, published by the Museum, 1934), 36-37; Semon, *In the Australian Bush*, 22. In Australia, for example, the aborigines had no prior opportunity to evolve a biological immunity or resistence from the diseases of the white man, so that initial mortality rates were very high. Birdsell, "Local Group Composition," in *Current Anthropology*, vol. 11, No. 2, April, 1970, 117. Although the Chukchee was a sturdy Siberian tribe, it proved an easy victim for new and strange diseases brought by the white man. Waldemar Bogoras, "The Chukchee," in *Golden Age of American Anthropology*, edited by Mead and Bunzel, 322. Part of the problem, in the Far East at least, was that the native shared clothing, received from the white man, with many of his fellows. Spencer and Gillen, *Northern Tribes of Central Australia*, 17-18. During the voyage of the *Beagle* at the southern tip of South America, Darwin noted the same practice among the family and friends of Jemmy Button as they divested him of clothing and possessions brought from England. *Voyage of the Beagle*, 215-218. Dietary effects, diseases, social and genetic factors were deemed the most deadly agents introduced among the California Indians. S.F. Cook, *Conflict Between the California Indian and White Civilization*, 7, 13. See also Firth, *Primitive Economics of the Maori*, 452 and Sandoz, *Crazy Horse*, 285.

3   In Australia the natives blamed the sheer presence of the white man for their population reverses. Because he was there, the native males could not obtain the proper mental and spiritual equilibrium and thus not the right dreams for producing children. Bjerre, *Last Cannibals*, 37-38. According to Clark Wissler, the beginning step in the subjugation of a conquered people is to remove it from its own physical environment. The new and strange surroundings invariably produce a feeling of nostalgia. In a primitive society anything which seriously disturbs the inner peace of the group tends to increase the death rate. For example, half the Cherokees died on the way to Oklahoma from Georgia. "The Conflict and Survival of Cultures," in *Golden Age of American Anthropology*, edited by Mead and Bunzel, 598. See also Ralph Linton, "Marquesan Culture," in *Individual and His Society*, edited by Kardiner, 137; W.H.R. Rivers, "Psychological Factor," in *Essays on the Depopulation of Melanesia* (Cambridge, England, Cambridge University Press, 1922), 104; Matthew W. Stirling, "Vanishing Cultures Mirror the Yesterdays of Man," 8-35 in *Vanishing Peoples of the Earth*, 11.

4   Means, *Fall of the Inca Empire*, 32.

5   A Conestoga Chief, "We Find the Christians Depraved," 253-254 in *Literature of the American Indian*, edited by Sanders and Peak, 254.

6   "Red Jacket to the Missionary," 270-273 in *ibid.*, 272.

7   Vine Deloria, Jr., "An Open Letter to the Heads of the Christian Churches in

America, 400-407 in *ibid.*, 403.

8 Deloria, Jr., *God is Red*, 99.

9 "A Letter to the editor of the Chicago Tribune, 1890," 357-358 in *Literature of the American Indian*, edited by Sanders and Peak, 357.

10 "Treatise on Christian Liberty," 301-348 in *Works of Martin Luther, With Introduction and Notes*. The Philadelphia Edition, 6 vols. (Philadelphia, Muhlenberg Press, 1915), II, 331.

11 Thomas E. Sanders and Walter W. Peak, "Anguished, Angry and Articulate," 445-451 in *Literature of the American Indian*, edited by Sanders and Peak, 446. In a similar fashion on the other side of the world in the Australian desert, the Walbiri rejected Christianity because it preached the doctrine of the brotherhood of man while allowing racial prejudice of the worst sort. Meggitt, *Desert People*, 331-332.

12 Marshall D. Sahlins, "Tribesmen in History and Anthropology," 194-211 in *Concept off the Primitive*, edited by Montagu, 209.

13 Highwater, *Primal Mind*, 169, 171. "... *each Bemba person* is so totally and thoroughly socialized that there is virtually no individual self-consciousness." Maxwell, *Bemba*, 151-152. "From the standpoint of the social unit, the broken-off individual is simply nothing - waste." Campbell, *Hero with a Thousand Faces*, 383.

14 James Cook, "The Discovery of the Hawaiian Islands," 1-10 in *A Hawaiian Reader*, edited by A. Grove Day and Carl Stroven (New York, Appleton-Century-Crofts, 1959), 2; Firth, *Primitive Economics of the Maori*, 461.

15 Weltfish, *Origins of Art*, 47-49.

16 *Nomads of the Long Bow*, 266.

17 Sandoz, *Crazy Horse*, 54.

18 Catherine and Ronald M. Berndt, "Australian Aborigines," in *Vanishing Peoples of the Earth*, 127.

19 Daniel R. Gross, "Ecology and Acculturation Among the Native People of Brazil," 1043-1050 in *Science*, vol. 206, No. 4422, November 30, 1979, 1049.

20 E. T. Gilliard, "New Guinea's Rare Birds and Stone Age Men," 421-488 in *National Geographic*, vol. 103, April, 1953, 453.

21 Peter Farb, *Humankind* (Boston, Houghton Mifflin, 1978), 98. Although my co-author counseled against the use of any material on the Tasadays, because of the possible hoax, I assume the responsibility for its inclusion. First, the act itself is so typical of primitives. Second, I have a considerable respect for Peter Farb. And third, since he was not one of the scholarly "discoverers" of the tribe, it tends to show the anthropological fraternity itself accepted the original account.

22   Lariston Sharp, "Steel Axes for Stone Age Australians," 346-352 in *Readings in Anthropology*, edited by Jennings and Hoebel, 3rd edition (1972), 351-352. Also see the same author's "Technological Innovation and Culture Change. An Australian Case," 84-94 in *Cultural and Social Anthropology*, edited by Peter Hammond (1964), 89, 91.

23   Clark Wissler, "The Conflict and Survival of Cultures," in *Golden Age of American Anthropology*, edited by Mead and Bunzel, 593.

24   Sayce, *Primitive Arts and Crafts*, 196. The breakdown of a taboo may cause an entire culture to collapse. Wissler, "The Conflict and Survival of Cultures," *loc. cit.*, 600.

25   Farb, *Indians of North America*, 117.

26   *Ibid.*, 31.

27   Mowat, *People of the Deer*, 50, 74. The trader's aim was always to maximize profits within a short time and move on. *Ibid.*, 38-39. This was an old problem and one which haunted British administrators prior to the Revolutionary War. *The Appalachian Indian Frontier. The Second Atkin Report and Plan 1755*, edited and with an introduction by Wilbur R. Jacobs (Lincoln, University of Nebraska Press, 1967), 12, 23, 25-26. The same feeling of exploitation at the hands of the trader was still being echoed in modern times by a stone age tribe living on the Surinam-Brazilian border. The first white trader contacted had taken all their monkey teeth bracelets with which they did not wish to part, as well as various stone implements needed for survival. Of course he had given compensation in the form of modern artifacts but neglected to give instruction in their care and usage. As a result, the tribe felt defrauded. It was presently travelling westward toward arrow cane fields so that it could ward off further incursions by the white man. Ivan L. Schoen, "Contact with the Stone Age," 10-18 in *Natural History* vol. 77, No. 1, January, 1969, 14.

28   Sandoz, *Crazy Horse*, 54. See also Farb, *Indians of North America*, 117-118.

29   Firth, *Primitive Economics of the Maori*, 444-445.

30   Dorothy Lee, *Freedom and Culture*, 34.

31   Muir, *African People in the Twentieth Century*, 5.

32   E. H. Bryan, Jr., "Nature's Balance in Hawaii," 269-275 in *Ancient Hawaiian Civilization*, edited by Handy, *et al*, 5.

33   Clarke and Hindley, *Challenge of the Primitives*, 10.

34   Firth, *Primitive Economics of the Maori*, 477.

35   Turnbull, *Mountain People*, 280-281; Turnbull, *Forest People*, 259-260.

36   Frederik Barth, "Herdsmen of Southeast Asia," 63-84 in *Cultural and Social Anthropology*, edited by Peter B. Hammond (New York, Macmillian, 1964), 64.

37   Sandoz, *Crazy Horse*, 215, 390.

38   According to W. H. R. Rivers, it was the white man's technology which made the Melanesian regard him as a person superior to himself. Bartlett, *Psychology and Primitive Culture*, 144.

39   *God is Red*, 252.

40   *Indian Boyhood*, 186.

41   *Meeting of East and West*, 22.

42   Wagley, *Tentehara Indians*, 176.

43   Clyde Warrior, "Which One are You? Five Types of YoungIndians," 521-523 in *Literature of the American Indian*, edited by Sanders and Peak, 521-522.

44   Kluckholn and Leighton, *Navaho*, 235-236.

45   Alexander Lesser, "The Right Not to Assimilate," 583-593 in *Readings in Anthropology*, 2 vols., edited by Fried, *Cultural Anthropology*, II, 586.

46   Firth, *Primitive Economics of the Maori*, 473.

47   Cook, *Conflict Between the California Indians and White Civilization*, 145-147.

48   John C. Messenger, Jr., "Religious Acculturation among the Anang Ibibio," in *Continuity and Change in African Cultures*, edited by Bascom and Herskovits, 294. With every cure by Western medicine, native confidence in their shaman or medicine man was severely shaken. Mischa Titiev, *Araucanian Culture in Transition*, 147.

49   See Godfrey Davies, *The Early Stuarts, 1603-1660* (Oxford, England, Clarendon Press, 1949), 301-312; Maurice Ashley, *England in the Seventeenth Century* (London, Penguin Books, Cox and Lyman, 1962), 108.

50   James J. Jarves, "Between Heathenism and Missionaryism," 69-81 in *Hawaiian Reader*, 74-75.

51   Muir, *An African People in the Twentieth Century*, 263-264.

52   E. A. Ayandele, "External Influence on African Society," 133-148 in *Africa in the Nineteenth and Twentieth Centuries. A Handbook for Teachers and Students*, edited by Joseph C. Anene and Godfrey N. Brown (London, Ibadan University Press and Nelson & Son, 1968), 135.

53   Gray, "The Missionary Factor in East Africa," 458-471 in *ibid.*, 469.

54   Mead, (Return to Manus, 1953), in *Letters from the Field*, 248.

55   See the Declaration of the Rights of Man passed in the National Assembly August 27, 1789, 60-61 in *The Quest for a Principle of Authority in Europe, 1715-Present*, edited by Thomas C. Mendenhall *et al* (New York, Holt, Rinehart and Winston, 1948); "Chapelier to the National Assembly," in *ibid.*, 62-63.

56   E. Richard Sorenson, "Growing Up as a Fore, is to be 'in-touch' and 'free,'" 107-115 in *Smithsonian*, vol. 8, No. 2, May, 1977, 110-114.

57   The earliest Spaniards in the New World noticed a sharp difference between the receptivity of the young to the Christian faith and the reluctance of the older generations to abandon the traditional one. *Travels of Piedro de Cieza de Leon*. First Part, 182.

58   Messenger, Jr., "Religious Acculturation among the Anang Ibibio," *loc. cit.*, 288, 297.

59   Catherine H. and Ronald M. Berndt, "Australian Aborigines," in *Vanishing Peoples of the Earth*, 232-233.

60   Huntingford, *Nandi*, 118.

61   Margaret Mead, "A Letter from Tambunam," 22-26 in *Redbook*, vol. 131, No. 4, August, 1968, 26.

62   Schultz, "Indians of Central Brazil," in *Vanishing Peoples of the Earth*, 161.

63   *Indian Boyhood*, 190.

64   C. C. Griffin, "The Significance of Native Indian Culture in Hispanic America," 104-123 in *Concerning Latin American Culture* ...., edited by C. C. Griffin (New York, Columbia University Press, 1944), 111.

65   "A Letter from Tambunam," *loc. cit.*, 22.

66   Bohannan, *Africa and the Africans*, 234-235.

67   Schneider, "Pakot Resistence to Change," in *Continuity and Change in African Culture*, edited by Bascom and Herskovits, 159.

68   Charles Wagley, *The Social and Religious Life of a Guatemalan Village*, 1-150 in *American Anthropologist*, vol. 51, No. 4, Part 2, October, 1949, 31.

69   *God is Red*, 259-260.

70   Waters, *Book of the Hope*, xii-xiii.

71   Margaret Mead, "What I Learned from Three Cultures: The Lost, the Gentle and the Fierce," 40-47 in *Redbook*, vol. 140, No. 3, January, 1973, 42.

72   Mead, "Return to Manus, 1953," in *Letters from the Field*, 271.

73   Fred A. Milan, "The Indomitable Eskimo. Master of a Frozen World," 132-151, in *Vanishing Peoples of the Earth*, 150.

74   *Affable Savages*, 94.

75   Leslie A. White, *Acoma Indians*, in *47th Annual Report of the Bureau of American*

Ethnology to the Secretary of the Smithsonian (1932), 56. By 1967, for example, when almost a thousand Hopi children were voluntarily attending white schools on the reservation, and hundreds at his school off it, the old people claimed that farming and herding were dying as they died. Now people bought groceries at stores and children preferred jobs in town. The one concession the young made was a willingness to participate in native rituals. Arthur P. Miller, Jr., "Hopis: 'The Peaceful Ones' Confront the Twentieth Century," in *Vanishing Peoples,* 182. In New Guinea, Asmat girls kept attending the mission school at Erma long after they were supposed to be at home getting married, as previously arranged for by contract. When they did return, many refused to honor their parents' word. No longer, lamented one baffled father, do the girls have a maidenly reserve. Instead they are shameless, unprincipled and disobedient. Father Alphonse Sowada, "New Guinea's Fierce Asmat," in *Vanishing Peoples of the Earth,* 197.

76   W. E. F. Ward, "Colonial Rule in West Africa," 308-325 in *Africa in Nineteenth and Twentieth Centuries,* edited by Anene and Brown, 309.

77   Ayundale, "External Influence on African Society," *loc. cit.,* 146.

78   Muir, *An African People in the Twentieth Century,* 276.

79   *Ibid.,* 6-7.

80   Titiev, *Araucanian Culture in Transition,* 143.

81   Kluckholn, *Navaho,* 295, 320.

82   Wissler, "Conflict and Survival of Cultures," *loc. cit.,* 593.

83   Erickson, *Childhood and Society,* 129.

84   John Joseph Matthews (Osage), "The Indian Agent Visits Gray Bird," 424-431 in *Literature of the American Indian,* edited by Sanders and Peek, 429.

85   Deloria, Jr., *God Is Red,* 204.

86   Rivers, *History of Melanesian Society,* II, 293-294.

87   Schneider, "Pakot Resistence to Change," *loc. cit.,* 164-165: Gulliver, *Family Herds,* 1.

88   Lawrence Krader, "The Ecology of Nomadic Pastorals," 499-510 in *International Social Science Journal,* vol. 11 (1959), 509.

89   Frederick Barth, *Nomads of South Persia. The Basserai Tribe of the Khamseh Confederacy* (New York, Humanities Press, 1961), 126, Owen Lattimore, *Inner Asian Frontiers of China* (New York, Capitol Publishing and American Geographical Society, 1951), 209-210.

90   *Leviathan* (London, J. M. Dent, 1940), 177-178.

91   Herskovits, *Myth of the Negro Past* (Boston, Beacon Press, 1958), 72. The same

practice prevailed when the Christians arrived. "... the Christian doctrine has been accepted only to the extent that the natives believe it to be an instrument of magical power or *mana*. They believe European civilization has prevailed only because of its secret powers of magic and because of the greater mana the white man is endowed with." Vittorio Lanternari, *The Religions of the Oppressed. A Study of Modern Messianic Cults.* Translated from the Italian by Lisa Sergic (New York, Alfred A. Knopf, 1963), 318.

92   Messenger, Jr., "Religious Acculturation Among the Anang Ibibio," *loc. cit.*, 290.

93   Alexander Werth, *The Twilight of France, 1933-1940* (New York, Harper, 1942), 356; William L. Shirer, *The Collapse of the Third Republic. An Inquiry into the Fall of France in 1940* (New York, Simon and Schuster, 1969), 909; Léon Marchal, *Vichy. Two Years of Deception* (New York, Macmillan, 1943), 68-71.

94   Edwin C. Reischauer, *Japan Past and Present*, 3rd edition revised (New York, Alfred A. Knopf, 1967), 204; Mamoru Shigemitsu, *Japan and Her Destiny. My Struggle for Peace* (New York, E. P. Dutton, 1958), 377; *Reminiscences. General of the Army Douglas MacArthur* (New York, McGraw-Hill, 1964), 310.

95   O. Otley Beyer, "The Philippines Before Magellan. I. The Hindus of Malayasia," 861-892 in *Asia*, vol. 21 (1921), 861. This openly expressed contempt for the native Higher Learning was apparently part of a well-conceived plot to remake the cultural complex. This not only involved conversion to Christianity but to a Spanish way of life as well. This necessitated the relocation of scattered tribes in remote and mountainous areas of the Philippines, such as the Igorots. They were moved to lowland communities with an exclusive dependence upon agriculture. Here they could be reached not only by the clergy but by the tax collector and the police. William Henry Scott, *The Discovery of the Igorots. Spanish Contacts with the Pagans of Northern Luzon* (Quezon City, Philippines, New Day Publications, 1974), 75.

96   Firth, *We, the Tikopia*, 44, 376.

97   Griffin, "Native Indian Culture," in *Concerning Latin American Culture*, edited by Griffin, 111.

98   Sherburne Cook, *Conflict Between the California Indian and White Civilization*, 9, 87, 145-146.

99   Shele and Miller, *Blood of Kings*, 31.

100   Because, according to Bishop Landa, the great number of Maya writings contained only "superstition and lies of the devil, we burned them all, which they regretted to an amazing degree, and which caused them much affliction." *Ibid.*, 56.

101   *Ibid.*, 31.

102   Frank Waters, *Book of the Hopi* (New York, Viking, 1963), 289, 292. Clark Wissler gave us an excellent clue as to what motivated such tragic circumstances. Christian Indians of reservations frequently informed on pagan Indians, petitioning the whites to suppress their ceremonies. This illustrates the general principle that a new convert to any cause is distinguished for his hostility to the belief he just abandoned. "The

Conflict and Survival of Cultures," in *Golden Age of American Anthropology*, edited by Mead and Bunzel, 599-600.

103　　*Book of the Hopi*, 330-331. The same material is contained on page 402 of the same book as published by Ballantine Books of New York in 1963. A less pessimistic long-range view was that of Jamake Highwater. While the white man's boarding schools were disruptive of tribal life, and sometimes brutal and insensitive to the emotional needs of its students, they nevertheless failed to eradicate native languages, religions and customs. Indeed, they unconsciously united the Indian by giving him a common language with which to protest this cultural imperialism. *Primal Mind*, 11-12.

104　　E. E. Evans-Pritchard, *The Samusi of Cyrenaica* (London, Clarendon Press, Oxford University Press, 1973), 196.

105　　*Ibid.*, 208.

106　　*The Headman and I. Ambiguity and Ambiance in the Field-working Experience* (Austin, University of Texas Press, 1978), 196. A typical native response to Jesuit attempts to alter religious behavior patterns among Hindus was that of a native Brahman. He and his people were interested in all religions, but they did not like outsiders coming for the purpose of changing the traditional ways and beliefs. Bernard Delfendahl, "On Anthropologists versus Missionaries," *Current Anthropology*, vol. 22, No. 1, February 1981, 89.

107　　Dumont, *Headman and I*, 183-184. The Protestant invasion of Catholic territory in Melanesia made for Christian hostility toward other Christians. Only outwardly were relations "officially correct." A hot rivalry for native souls was launched. James Clifford, *Person and Myth. Maurice Leenhardt in the Melanesian World* (Berkeley, University of California Press, 1982), 32.

108　　Dumont, *Headman and I*, 196-197.

109　　Sahlins, *Tribesmen*, 2.

110　　Ralph Linton, *Tree of Culture* (New York, Alfred A. Knopf, 1955), 44-45. Raymond Firth argued that no extraneous culture could successfully be imposed upon a people, but would remain as a superficial element only. The adoption of any new trait from an alien folk would follow only after it had been rendered in harmony with the entire culture complex. In effect the new element was submerged among the old. *Primitive Economics of the Maori*, 444. Robert Morrison MacIver called this trait the conservative impulse, one maintained even when a people was borrowing from the outside world. "Social Causation and Change," 121-138 in *Twentieth Century Sociology*, edited by Georges Gurvitch and Wilbert E. Moore (New York, Philosophical Library, 1945), 122. For example, when Catholicism was imposed on the Yakui Indians of the Southwest, the new idea was thoroughly assimilated into preexistent ritual forms and thus neutralized. Highwater, *Primal Mind*, 145.

111　　Clifford, *Person and Myth*, 221.

112　　Simon Ottenberg, "Ibo Receptivity of Change," 130-143 in *Continuity and Change in African Cultures*, edited by Bascom and Herskovits, 139. "... the so-called 'conversions' are more apparent than real, touching only the surface of native belief and never reaching into their true religious life. These are facts which many enlightened missionaries willingly admit. ... most of the natives preserve their fundamental beliefs and their traditional religions; their ancient rituals are performed or remembered in hiding, ready to be resumed in the open as soon as the opportunity arises...." Lanternari, *Religions of the Oppressed*, 16-17.

113   Messenger, Jr., "Religious Acculturation Among the Anang Ibibio," in *Continuity and Change in African Cultures*, 291.

114   Melville J. Herskovits and William R. Bascom, "The Problem of Stability and Change in African Cultures," 1-14 in *ibid.*, 3, 5-6.

115   Raymond Firth, "Studying and Restudying Tikopia," 142-158 in *Readings in Anthropology*, 2 vols. edited by Fried, *Cultural Anthropology*, II, 147.

116   Wagley, *Tentehara Indians*, 173.

117   Deloria, Jr., *God Is Red*, 259, 261, 270-271.

118   Wagley, "Economics of a Guatemalan Village," 1-85 in *Supplement to American Anthropologist*, vol. 43, No. 3, Part 3, Number 58, 1941, 16; Wagley, "Social and Religious Life of a Guatemalan Village," 1-150 in *American Anthropologist*, vol. 51, No. 4, Part 2, October, 1949, 50.

119   Northrop, *Meeting of East and West*, 485. To Sherburne Cook, it was no accident that Catholicism was almost universally effective among primitive peoples. Its skilled and knowledgeable missionaries could teach a simple dogma to a simple folk; its entire creed could be visually dramatized so as to capture primitive hearts and minds. *Conflict Between the California Indian and White Civilization*, 146-147.

120   Gross, "Ecology and Acculturation among the Native Peoples of Brazil," *loc. cit.*, 1048-1049. Sherburne Cook applied the same principle in a different way. According to classical theory, when an environment changes, species must either undergo parallel changes for survival purposes or perish. In general, however, the older the culture, the more exactly adapted to the environment, and the genetically stable it is, the more difficult it is going to be to come up readily with the required changes and on time. Unfortunately for them the California Indians belonged to this type. *Conflict Between the California Indians and White Civilization*, 9.

121   Marshall D. Sahlins, "Culture and Environment: the Study of Cultural Ecology," 132-147 in *Horizons of Culture*, edited by Tax, 141.

122   Weltfish, *Origins of Art*, 96. To Weston La Barre, religion was meaningless unless it was understood as the persistence of both awe of the Father and the desire for *mana* which comes from him. *Ghost Dance*, 15. An excellent illustration of this generalization occurred among the Ibibio tribe following its conversion to Christianity by Christian spiritualist churches, like the Seventh Day Adventists. The new religion suffered, however, when the extravagent materialistic promises missionaries made to the natives did not materialize. Their Holy Spirit proved no more effective in producing good crops than did the old shamans and their gods. Locusts and crop failures in 1936-1937 contributed to the

revival of the old religious faiths. Messenger, Jr., "Religious Acculturation among the Anang Ibibio," *loc. cit.*, 289.

123   Thomas Gann and J. Eric Thompson, *The History of the Mayas from the Earliest Times to the Present Day* (New York, Scribner's, 1931), 60-66. A more complicated explanation for the collapse of Maya civilization was given by T. Patrick Culbert. The ceremonial elite spent too much money on administrative and religious buildings and ritual which resulted in malnutrition and disease for the working and productive members of the society. There were no technological nor social innovations to blunt the adverse impact. In brief, the small aristocratic elite proved technologically inadequate to cope with the complex and unstable conditions of a partly urbanized population of some five millions of people. It was, however, a combination of factors, rather than a single one, which eventually caused the collapse and the radical emigration, i.e., trade disruptions, social unrest, disease, and agricultural difficulties. *The Classic Maya Collapse* (Albuquerque, University of New Mexico Press, 1973), 490-491.

124   Hiram Bingham, *In the Wonderland of Peru*, 387-573 in *National Geographic*, Vol. 24, No. 4, April, 1913, 456-457. Elsewhere Bingham alluded to the fact that Machu Picchu was built in the midst of great granite deposits and, consequently, there was little arable land around it at any time. It was always a sacred city. When its inhabitants conquered Cuzco and the rich valleys around it, it probably made no sense to continue to eke out an existence at Machu Picchu. "The Story of Machu Picchu. The Peruvian Expeditions of the National Geographic Society and Yale University," 172-186 in *National Geographic*, vol. 27, January-June, 1915, 176, 179.

125   *Anthropology and Modern Life with a New Introduction by Ruth Bunzel* (New York, W. W. Norton, 1962), 163-164; Frederick J. Teggart, *Theory and Processes of History* (Berkeley and Los Angeles, University of California Press, 1960), 272.

126   Deloria, Jr., *God Is Red*, 248.

127   Catherine H. and Ronald Berndt, "Australian Aborigines: Blending Past and Present," in *Vanishing Peoples of the Earth*, 114, 122, 124.

128   Farb, *Indians of North America*, 127.

129   *Black Elk Speaks*, 276. For similar fates among the Blackfeet and Shoshoni Indians, see George Bird Grinnel, "The Disappearance of the Buffalo," 148-150 in *Golden Age of American Anthropology*, edited by Mead and Bunzel, 149; Farb, *Indians of North America*, 32.

130   "Return to Manus," 60-69 in *Natural History*, vol. 85, No. 6, June-July, 1976, 68-69.

131   *Ghost Dance*, 55, 349.

132   *Ibid.*, 51-52.

133   *Ibid.*, 133. After the coming of the horse to the Great Plains, the Sun Dance was devised to do for the entire tribe what the vision quest had done earlier for the individual. *Ibid.*, 135.

134   *Ibid.*, 53-54.

135   *Ibid.*, 222; La Barre, "Studies of Crisis Cults," in *Current Anthropology*, vol. 12, No. 1, February, 1971, 11.

136   La Barre, *Ghost Dance*, 113; "Crisis Cults," *loc. cit.*, 18.

137   La Barre, *Ghost Dance*, 41, 229-230, 232. See also Weltfish, *The Lost Universe with a closing chapter in 'The Universe Regained* (New York, Basic Books, 1965), 446-447. This was an old belief by religious man. The Hebrew Feast of the Tabernacle was dominated by the idea that the desired outcome would automatically result from the rite itself, provided it were correctly and properly performed. This explains the primary importance of the material facets of the ceremony. Durkheim, *The Elementary Forms of Religious Life*, 35. Because, however, of the subsequent massacre of the Ghost Dancers at Wounded Knee, South Dakota in 1890, Indians have never fully recovered a crucial aspect of their old world view. Highwater, *Primal Mind*, "Prelude," xii.

138   La Barre, *Ghost Dance*, 41; Firth, *Tikopia. Ritual and Belief*, ft. 157.

139   Gillian Gillison, "Fertility Rites in a New Guinea Village," in *National Geographic*, vol. 152, No. 1, July, 1977, 138-139; Mead, "Return to Manus," in *Letters from the Field*, July 2, 1953, 247.

140   Bjerre, *Last Cannibals*, 180-182.

141   Lanternari, *Religions of the Oppressed*, 303.

142   *Ibid.*, 202-203, 207-209.

143   *Ibid.*, 229-230. "The abundance of messianic and prophetic cults among agrarian populations and the almost total absence of them among tribes which live by ordinary hunting is an interesting and by no means accidental fact." Tradition has shallow roots among peoples who do not live on the land but are constantly moving in search of prey. Australia, for example, the home of the hunter was a sterile soil for prophets, spiritual fathers of the cargo cults. Likewise, they were devoid of traditional rites such as the worship of the dead or offering them first fruits. *Ibid.*, 222.

144   *Ibid.*, 229-230.

145   Mead was at Manus when the sudden cultural upheaval occurred in 1928. She returned in 1953 and again in 1971 and 1975. In the interim nothing had stabilized. All was in continual flux. See Mead, Peré Village, July 23, 1975 in *Letters from the Field*, 323-324.

146   Cook, *Conflict Between the Californian Indian and White Civilization*, 153.

147   "Cultural Influences on Population: A Comparison of Two Tupi Tribes," 268-280 in *Environmental and Cultural Behaviour*, edited by Vayada, 270-271; Wagley, *The Tentehara Indians*, 178. See also Shapiro, "The Tapirapé During the Era of Reconstruction," in *Brazil, Anthropological Prospect*, edited by Margolis and Carter, 63-65. To Weston La Barre, it is cases like that of the Tapirapé Indians which makes an almost ideal situation

for a study of culture clash. The suddenness of the contact provides a shock. The vast cultural differences between the native and the interloper insures a dramatic interaction. The visible transformation worked among the conquered affords an excellent opportunity for studies of cultural innovation and change. "Crisis Cults," *loc. cit.*, 3.

148   *Aristotle. Politics and Poetics,* translated by Benjamin Jowett and S. H. Butcher (New York, Heritage Press, 1964), xvii. 7-9.

149   *Meeting of East and West,* 72-97 *passim.*

150   Protestant churches have always been frightened at the prospect of using art to further religious purposes. They preferred to use the intellect rather than the senses. *Ibid.,* 37, 92.

151   *Ibid.,* 334-335.

152   *Ibid.,* 430-431.

153   Sapir, *Selected Writings,* 318.

154   Father Alphonso Sowada, "New Guinea's Fierce Asmat," in *Vanishing Peoples of the Earth,* 192.

155   *Ibid.,* 202.

156   La Barre, *The Ayamara Indians,* 1-250 in *American Anthropologist,* vol. 50, No. 1, Part 3, January, 1948, 39.

157   *Ibid.,* 171.

158   *Ceremony* (New York, Viking Press, 1977), 262 pages.

159   Luiz R. B. Mott, "Indigenous Anthropology and Brazilian Indians," 112-120 in *Indigenous Anthropology in Non-Western Countries,* 113.

160   "The Concept of Value in Modern Anthropology," 682-689 in *Anthropology Today. An Encyclopedic Inventory.* Prepared under the Chairmanship of A. L. Kroeber (Chicago, University of Chicago PRess, 1953), 697-698.

Chapter X

MEANING FOR THE WEST:
Introduction

In the development of anthropology it was not uncommon for researchers to encounter a people on one side of a mountain who proclaimed themselves "people," and then added that those on the other side were "unpeople."

Anthropologists, of course, were unable to detect any physical differences and few, if any, crucial cultural ones. They were, in short, the same people.

At the same time, however, these anthropologists often failed to challenge assumptions about our own racial and cultural superiority. Thus, they left uncorrected the fallacy that "we alone are people."

When examining assumptions as to our own superiority, and its peculiar, even unique, cultural aspects, we shall attempt to do this as if we were anthropologists dissecting an alien culture.

"For example, the Native American Cheyennes refer to themselves by a term that means 'The Human Beings'; no one else is a 'human being' in their eyes." Dimen-

Schein, The Anthropological Imagination, 37-38.

While we made two separate and distinct efforts to analyze the reaction of the modern, as well as the primitive, in a single volume, we eventually became aware the product would be too bulky. This would impair its readability. Accordingly, we decided to offer as volume one that portion restricted to the primitive and the supernatural. Meanwhile, we would revise, as volume two, that section exclusively devoted to the loss of vitality experienced by Christianity in the twentieth century, as well as by the two chief exponents of the idea of progress, communism and the so-called peaceful, democratic and industrialized state.

In this concluding chapter, therefore, we can do little more than suggest the hypotheses assumed in the forthcoming volume.

The first of two basic ways of viewing the primitive vis-à-vis the West is, by stressing the vast differences between the two, to document the superiority one felt at the outset. Over the centuries this feeling of superiority was pervasive throughout our cultural complex; it was, curiously enough, based upon two essentially different notions, the sacred idea of Providence and the secular one of progress.

Before dissecting each, however, it is necessary - as my co-author observed - to note the social functions performed by these assumptions: 1) It gave a justification for the exploitation of the human and natural resources of the Third World 2) In reality, it fortified our psychological security, i.e., it is one thing to advance a reason for our actions and another to believe in it implicitly and 3) Out of the first two emerged our sense of mission, or our calling to make the half-devil, half-child over in our own self-image.

It was the idea of Providence which proclaimed the revolutionary idea of God in history. Its essence was that God became man in the person of Jesus, suffered and died for humanity, and His Resurrection contained a promise of immortality for it. This intrusion of the Christ into the historical process provided history with its central point. It effaced the curse God placed on the human race because of the sin of Adam and Eve. It made the rest of human history meaningful as it strained toward the Redemption, the

Second Coming and the Day of Judgment. However pervasive sin and evil, they could not prevent the ultimate triumph of the Good. Jesus, therefore, may - from a Christian viewpoint - be seen as the Lord of History.[1]

Nevertheless, one must enter certain reservations about this supposed redemption of humanity. As Mircea Eliade observed, this was not meant to be a cosmic regeneration of a collective or the human race. Only the chosen would survive or those who, faced with worldly temptations, remained true to the Kingdom of Heaven.[2] Even this generalization can be refined. From the first century A.D., the Christian Church never ceased to proclaim the only way for human salvation was through a professed belief in Jesus as the Christ. That meant only a very small portion of humanity could qualify. It not only excluded believers of all other religions, including Hebrews of which Jesus was one, but all those who lived and died without coming into contact with Christ or the Christian message. It did, of course, always act as a spur to the evangelical movement of world conversion to Christianity. This may have been its chief purpose.[3]

The second notion was the secular idea of progress. Like its Western counterpart, communism came into being only with the decline of faith in the Christian mythology; it substituted one kind of optimism for another. The idea of progress, observed J. B. Bury, was based on an interpretation of history representing man as slowly advancing in a definite and desirable direction. It inferred that this progress would continue indefinitely. Further, as a prime consideration, a condition of general or mass happiness would ultimately be enjoyed. This, of course, would justify the whole process. Otherwise the direction would not be desirable. This movement was a necessary outcome of the valued properties of man himself, or his marvelously adaptive intellectual and social nature. Here was the clearest rejection of the Christian notion of the inherent sinfulness of man and his helplessness to change his nature, or to save himself without God's Grace. In brief, this philosophy lay outside the mercy of Divine Will. Otherwise the idea of progress would deteriorate into another version of the idea of Providence which Christians had already exploited into a philosophy of history. This idea of progress, probably reached its zenith in the last part of the nineteenth century and the first of the twentieth. [4]

At the same time one must take note of the insistence by Robert A. Nisbet that, concomitant with the growth of the idea of progress, there were many profound minds in Europe which rejected the notion as childish. The reaction to the naiveties of progress, which many thought the end result of the two world wars, a terrible depression and the growth of totalitarianism, had been anticipated since the eighteenth century. One notes the pessimism of such thinkers as Hume, Bonald, de Tocqueville and Burckhardt.[5]

Regardless of the sharp ideological differences between the two doctrines, they re-inforced each other at one crucial juncture: the white man possessed a monopoly of truth, and even virtue, and the only way for the non-white to share in these blessings was through the conqueror's good offices.

Among scholars the idea of cultural superiority persisted, being based apparently on the concept of progress or Christianity. Writing late in 1931, Charles A. Beard confessed his belief that, judged by intellectual as well as physical standards, there had been a fantastic improvement within humanity since primitive times. It was history which clearly revealed the chasm between the primitive and the best of the modern social orders.[6] It was the cosmopolitan historian, Arnold Toynbee, shortly after World War II, who declared while paganism could accomplish the soul's salvation, it was at the same time clearly inferior to Christianity in the latter's ability to shed spiritual illumination and grace.[7] We cite the case of a couple of historians merely to show anthropologists were not the sole champions of cultural imperialism. A preoccupation with their natural subject matter afforded more unconscious opportunities to display it.

Thus these two ideas - Christianity and the idea of progress - were used as justification for the reduction, even obliteration, of primitive and pagan beliefs and customs everywhere.

Our investigation, on the contrary, begins by considering the primitive as part of homo sapiens. This approach suggests psychological kinships of belief and action between the primitive and modern variety, especially in the realm of cosmology, ritual and art. It is the contemplation of these facets of Western life which chip away at the feeling of superiority, a stumbling block in any attempt to understand the primitive. Better understanding is the first step in the comprehension of man himself. To hold up the mirror to the primitive is to see a dim reflection of ourselves.

A second area of concern, equally important, is to examine the modern. Here we focus on the question of what has happened -since the obliteration of primitives on a global scale - to the universality of beliefs in our own culture as regards both Christianity and the idea of progress. The latter concept was also adopted by the Soviet Union. It buttressed the idea that man was master of his own fate. Accordingly, we not only trace the dissipation of beliefs in these separate ideologies but attempt to account for the waning process.

When writing, it became apparent one must devote separate chapters to modern art, cosmology and ritual. Unlike the other two, art was comparatively free from outside intellectual attacks. Art was convulsed by an internal revolution of its most able and imaginative artists. Its outcome bore a product, conveniently termed abstract art, which had a remarkable resemblance to that of primitive art. That episode made it unique.

The second of these chapters investigates the assumption that, from a cosmological viewpoint, Christianity had a monopoly on Ultimate Truth. Since the sixteenth century, this assumption was seriously eroded by both science and history. This alienation ultimately forced Christian and Protestant scholars to shift emphasis from a stress on the historical Jesus to a mythological one. While successful, it marred the idea of the uniqueness or actuality of the Christian assertion, i.e., For God so loved the world He sent his only begotten Son. Since, as Peter Berger observed, the resurrection of Christ could no longer be regarded as an event which actually happened in historical time, it was somehow transferred to a life of its own in the consciousness of the believer.[8] This caused a sudden and dramatic break with the Church's past of almost two thousand years. Its powerful and compelling message had been built upon the certainty of the historical birth, crucifixion and resurrection of Jesus.[9] It was bound to introduce the principle of uncertainty where there had been none before.

When one turns to an examination of modern homo sapiens, and secular critiques, it is necessary to make a distinction between Catholic ritual man and the Protestant variety. Parallels of belief in magic and mystery between Catholic Christianity and pagan cults were legion. The Protestant Revolution of the sixteenth and seventeenth centuries challenged the old Catholic idea of the world as life within a sort of enchanted forest. Ritual - the Seven Sacraments - was regarded as the magic key, not only to survival, but to the good life itself and thus Salvation.[10] Furthermore, and as a consequence of the nineteenth century triumph of science and technology over Christian theology and mysticism, there arose two competing notions - that of Marxist communism and the so-called peaceful, democratic and industrialized state. Both faiths were the product of the human perfectability school, designed to supply emotional substitutes for the religious one supplanted. The late agonies suffered by the Catholic Church, since the Sixties and to the present, were in large measure an ultimate consequence of the erosion of an authoritarian church in a sea of free thought and criticism. Following the battering from the left and the center, the Church recently suffered many casualities from the radical right. Protestant fundamentalist churches made many recruiting inroads. This was particularly true among youths seeking a more personalized religion or one which made them the center of religious concerns rather than the priest or the altar.

Protestantism, which began with a distrust in ritual and a belief that science merely revealed the wonders of God,[11] floundered in the modern world over the concept of Evolution. True, in the twentieth century, urban liberal Christians maintained the old alliance with science while at the same time originating a compatible Social Gospel. It concerned an obliteration of poverty and a general Christian reconstruction of the social order.[12] But, more important, fundamentalist Protestants declared science the enemy in the Scopes trial of the Twenties.[13] They have not ceased their animosity. Instead of advocating traditional liberty of conscience, these right-wing religious groups zealously substituted social compulsion: no abortions, compulsory prayer in public schools, oaths of allegiance to the flag, increased church and ministerial authority and, in the case of Southern Baptists, dismissal of suspect liberals, or even moderates, in theological seminaries and overseas missions. Contrary to the Social Gospel movement, which stresses societal sins of an industrial nature, Protestant fundamentalists were blind to these. They were preoccupied with individual sins. They had a long history of attacks against alcohol, tobacco, dancing, card playing, the theater, adultery, fornication and other questionable pleasures of the flesh. At the same time they would substitute a ritual of their own, they paint a picture of the universe which contains magic, mysticism and authority.[14] These were the very ideas attacked by the Protestant Reformation of the sixteenth and seventeenth centuries. Thus it is that both the Catholic Church on the one hand and the fundamentalists and pentacostals on the other offer a picture of the interaction of gods and men which is in essential harmony with the primitive and pre-Christian. No wonder it is an impossible task to generalize accurately the meaning of twentieth century American Protestantism.[15]

It became obvious at this point that the logic of the situation demanded an analysis of the ideological, or mythological pretensions and historical outcomes for both the communism of Karl Marx and that of the so-called peaceful, democratic and industrialized state. Not only had each system no tolerance for alleged backward peoples in their sphere of influence, but they were also the secular challengers of Christianity. Soviet Russia and the United States were accepted as the natural prototypes for each.

The first of two scholarly aims was to investigate the prevalence of the magical and mystical elements of these societies. Each was supposedly without them because of a superficial dedication to science, technology and rationality. With the West, it is the same as with the primitive. When man faces simple and predictable tasks, such as striking a match, polishing his boots, turning on a light switch, or having his car motor tuned up, he characteristically does these things without any regard for ritual and magic.

However, as soon as he enters the gray area of uncertainty, or when affairs become chancey or dicey with a high risk of loss of either life or fortune, he behaves as does the primitive. When fishing in a safe lagoon, noted Bronislaw Malinowski, the primitive dispensed with ritual and magic but, before embarking on the high seas to fish, he invariably used them.[16] Sixty years ago, Alexander Goldenweiser said much the same thing of the modern. Belief in magic and superstition was proportionate to the degree that one's occupation or profession was in the control of unforseeable events. He stressed gamblers. We put at least equal emphasis upon professional athletes. A typical instance occurred when Pittsburgh Steeler quarterback, Terry Bradshaw, threw a last-minute desperation pass which, touched by an opposing player, flew into the prayerful hands of Franco Harris.His ensuing touchdown won the game and launched the Steeler dynasty of the Seventies. The play itself, appropriately enough, was subsequently called "The Immaculate Reception." Both Goldenweiser and we sensed public willingness, even eagerness, to allow an aura of magic to hover over the head of the modern physician. Both recognized in Christianity an exercise in magic. Goldenweiser thought this belief in magic united men of all ages, whether early, primitive or modern and supposedly civilized. He called it the "common-human element."[17] On the contrary, it was precisely because the Kimberley women of Western Australia were serenely confident of their ability and skills to track down wild honey and the iguana for food they never troubled to develop any magic to help them at their trade.[18]

A second purpose is to examine what happened to the mythological pretensions of each system in the light of harsh historical reality. For an outsider, it takes little time to discover that Soviet Russia early and consistently failed to deliver on its key promises of bread and freedom. The system itself has to be rejected for these reasons. In any examination of how history has dealt with the ideological pretensions of the peaceful, democratic and industrialized state, it is equally natural and fair that the examiner take the role of an outsider. The academic rationale for the criticism of one's own social order was postulated and practiced by the most able historians of Greece and Rome, notably Thucydides and Polybius.[19]

As soon as one assumes such a stance, he is apt to discover the tripod of the peaceful, democratic and efficient industrialized state is a bit rickety. First of all, the expansive nature of our industrialized system, when confronted by the challenge of world communism, weakened any serious commitment to peace on our part. It was considered mere appeasement.[20]

The closer one peered at our supposedly democratic system, the more fissures one discovered. While a myriad of voices proclaim us a democracy, there is little agreement as to what constitutes one. We resorted to an operational definition by Thomas Jefferson to resolve the dilemma. He stressed the necessity for an independent, informed and active electorate. It must not be deceived by its governors. This negates the preconditions for a democracy. The most recent elections of 1986 and 1988, however, reveal a miserable performance. While much more money was spent than ever before, the real issues were glossed over. Meanwhile, negative and malicious campaigning hit new highs. In 1988, the electorate responded with the greatest indifference and absenteeism from the ballot box since the "Keep Cool with Coolidge campaign of 1924."[21] The final element in this tragedy was that it occurred at a time when communism was on the verge of collapse in the Soviet Union and eastern Europe. The democratic cry of free and fair elections seems an empty one if the vacuum created by the absence of force is immediately filled by the influence of money and property.[22] This is always in the hands of a minority[23] which has never distinguished itself as being democratic in a Jeffersonian sense. Indeed, de Tocqueville regarded the then new minority of industrial-financial elite as a grave threat to the idea of democracy and social justice.[24] Perceptive modern experts apparently share the same misgivings.[25]

The industrialized system itself is responsible for many defects in democratic society. We mention only one here, the dehumanization of the worker and his or her alienation from work. This occurred as a consequence of capital investment in technological innovations which, routinizing the productive process, required less work skill. The computer age has merely speeded up the process to the disadvantage of the worker. Management's privileged position falsely encourages it "to maintain profits by reducing the living standards and increasing the labor efforts of working people."[26] Nor is this system immune from relative stagnation and decay. Our own multinational corporations, devoid of patriotism when it comes to calculating profit and growth, have compounded the problem by shifting production and capitalization abroad.[27] Simultaneously, America went from a position of the world's greatest creditor to the biggest debtor with a tremendous adverse trade balance.[28] While America went through a financial orgy of mergers and leveraged buy-outs in the J. P. Morgan banking tradition,[29] Japan was quietly buying up our one-time financial and business assets.[30] Cities decayed and roads and bridges deteriorated as the infrastructure of the industrialized state was generally neglected.[31] Finally, both the United

States and Soviet Russia alternately ignored and abused the common global environment. Both treated nature as if it were an adversary, one to be subdued and reduced to a position of servitude.[32] This, of course, was the equivalent of a primitive act of hubris against the gods. From this perspective the future seems a bit gloomy for all three key facets of our social order.

While this may be a jaundiced view, and its pessimism questionable, agreement should be possible on one crucial point. If the United States were democratic, peaceful and possessed of both an efficient and benign industrial system, that would constitute a splendid argument for the perfectability of man, and for the near perfection in our own social order. Were this ideology to prevail and gain universal currency, there would be precious few mourners for the primitive here and abroad who stood in its way. It would be the best possible justification for the nineteenth century Manifest Destiny theme. It argued that our reduction of "less civilized" races and/or nations on the continent of North America and its adjacent islands was in response to the workings of the will of Providence. Our devotion to individual freedom, morality and the Protestant work ethic - the essence of virtue and the good life -was destined to prevail over the indolence and vice of the lesser breeds we encountered.[33]

However, central to our argument is that scientists and intellectuals eventually deserted the traditions of material progress. They discovered nature could and did strike back in a way which endangered homo sapiens, the very source of arrogance itself. Their recently acquired reverence for nature, and their insistence that man tailor population to its dictates, borrowed much from the traditional beliefs and knowledge of the primitive.

In so far as the public shared this environmentalist viewpoint, it weakened a basic belief in the idea of progess. This was the American dream of bigger, better and more in the years to come, always to come. Totally absent was any conception in this "business" view that, if an ever-increasing body of worms ate the same apple, it would eventually be reduced to its core and disappear.[34] Such was the falsity of the implicit assumption of the perfectability of man, resting as it invariably did in twentieth century America, upon a material base. It was the modern's belief in the magical and the mystical.

Other authorities believed our crucial social problems could not be solved merely by new scientific understandings and appropriate uses of land, sea and air. They felt the real dilemma of our social order originated in the two things of which we were most proud, freedom and its resulting diversity. First, due to emigration, the United States has a cultural and social diversity which virtually staggers the imagination. "Religions abound, and so do peoples, their beliefs, styles of worship, and moral codes," concluded Catherine L. Albanese. "Community is fragile and temporary, and estrangement probably the one thing many have in common...."[35] Further, because of the element of free choice, the core of our culture is rapidly shrinking. As a consequence, we are fast approaching the point where, as Ralph Linton observed, there are no longer enough things all agree upon to give our culture form and pattern.[36]

It is important to realize that the primitive, prior to his devastating contact with the white man, was free from such fragmenting social ills.

The great Roman emperor and philosopher, Marcus Aurelius of the third century A.D., said that by the time a man reached the age of forty, he had seen everything.[37] I, too, am reasonably confident that, as a man in his late-seventies, I have witnessed in my own lifetime, at least among thinkers, the sapping of the verve of three key myths. The fact that my two sons, Tom and Jeff, three decades younger than I, gave immediate assent to my proposition would tend to suggest this is not merely an old man's natural disillusionment.

Of these mythologies only the first is a religious one: it involves the Christ figure, whether that merely of His actual historical Resurrection, or that event coupled with the promise of His Second Coming. The outsider is apt to forget that, while to be a "proper" Christian, one *must* believe in the Resurrection of Christ and His role as Saviour, there is a basic distinction between and among Christians. It is between those who believe Christ redeems and gives everlasting life only upon an individual and private basis - presumably after death - and those who believe Christ will publicly and dramatically return to this world in order to terminate human history, to judge between sinners and saints, believers and non-believers. Thus, he will have ushered in metahistory, or something beyond history. Jesus, Peter, Paul, and the Apostles believed in the imminent return of the Christ as judge. So did St. Augustine in the fifth century A.D. With the long passage of time and His failure to return, the medieval faith apparently shifted to Christ through the vehicle of His church. The scientific revolution of the sixteenth and seventeenth century also eroded faith in the Second Coming.[38]

At present the conflict within the Christian Church is open and unabated. Fundamentalists like Billy Graham, and conservative churches like the Lutheran, Latter Day Saints, Southern Baptists, Seventh Day Adventists and the like, believe and teach in the Second Coming on Judgment Day.[39] The shifting attitude of the Presbyterian Church may be typical of main line churches. While the Second Coming was heralded in the Westminster Confession of 1642, the Presbyterian statement of 1967 was nebulous. It left the event open for individual judgment.[40] In 1922, the Anglican Church confessed, as an actual historical event, the Second Coming presented "great difficulties."[41] Likewise the theological statements in the *New Catholic Encyclopedia* are in conflict with one another.[42]

Despite this apparent concession to a humanistic concept of history - the sacking by Christian intellectuals of the myth of the Second Coming - it still leaves a great many twentieth century thinkers as doubters of the less extreme proposition of the Resurrection itself. Although questionable, it was declared to have happened only once, at Jerusalem. It no doubt made sense to his immediate followers at the time of his death that Jerusalem, and that city only, witnessed the Second Coming, and the dead tumbling from their tombs. Such a single and solitary appearance no longer makes sense on a global level with five billion souls to witness, and nobody knows how many dead. The prospective ensuing chaos is probably the reason why, in 1922, the Anglican Church confessed "great difficulties."

One suspects that in a secular and humanistic age, the more learned of Christian proponents were willing to sacrifice unnecessary miracles to maintain a certain intellectual respectability. Fundamentalists will throw no sacred baggage overboard at any time for any reason.

Furthermore, this significant shift away from ancient doctrine and dogma by the thinking man's Protestant may explain the contention of Raimundo Pannikar, the crucial doctrine of the Trinity has atrophied in a great part of Christendom.[43] Indeed, it has invaded Christian theology at the highest level. In 1984, the Rev. David Jenkins, Bishop of Durham, reportedly questioned not only the Immaculate Conception, but the Resurrection itself. Fourteen theologians of the Church of England proclaimed - in a report also sanctioned by 43 bishops - that the bishop's attempt to approach truth via reason, as well as by traditional methods, was in harmony with Anglicanism. They conceded the writing in the Gospels about the person of Jesus was less than scientific history. Their report concluded, however, that these activities merely reflected an intellectual vitality within the Church rather than a decline of faith. The report itself supposedly would be debated in July, 1987, when the full policy-making synod met at York.[44]

While the other two weakened mythologies were secular - the notion of the withering away of the communist state and the idea of progress with its implicit promise of the perfectability of man and society - all three represented the coming of the Supreme Good. Thus, they lay in the realm of the magical and the mystical.

Because of this, i.e., the blessing that may not be renounced, adherents have not hesitated to apply force to the unbeliever or the outsider, presumably for his greater good. Examples of aggression by communist Russia against its neighbors are too recent to need recapitulation. From 1870 to 1914, and even beyond, the West was just as ruthless in the subjugation of peoples in Africa and Asia in the name of Christianity and progress, or science and technology. The assumption of the superiority of color - the white race - was the third element in the colonial tripod of conquest. We have not been particularly concerned with that folk attitude in this study. However, the virtual total support of imperialism by intellectuals in the nineteenth century was in sharp contrast to twentieth century imperialism, whether in Eastern Europe, Vietnam or Afghanistan. This pronounced trend represents a societal decline in the belief in our superiority, of our destiny, and of the justification of the application of force in the support of a "noble" idea.

If, therefore, ours is presently a mythless society, as Edward Edinger concluded, it is in large measure because the Christian myth lost its luminous character and the new religious myth has not yet risen.[45] The same fate holds true for the idea of progress. Walter Schmithals arrived at a similar conclusion when observing a decline in the belief that there would be sacred intervention at the end of human history for its redemption. Simultaneously, there was a similar disillusionment in the belief that mankind would ultimately forge its own secular redemption through the law of progress. Cultural optimism was the victim on both counts. To such a people in such a plight, their own history ceases to be meaningful. Of course, one good outcome is their own culture cannot be imposed upon others as an essential part of human redemption. Nevertheless, the very collapse of historical meaning through space and time - or a sense of nihilism - may well result in an equally irrational return to the spirit of early Christians. They felt themselves standing upon the very end of time itself, anxiously awaiting the imminent return of Jesus as the Lord of History. Naturally, it was this same Christian faith in the historical reappearance of the Christ which had been crippled by ultimate outcomes of British empiricism, the eighteenth century Enlightenment and the scientific explanation of the ultimate demise of the world via enthrophy, cosmic contraction or collision, or atomic disintegration.[46]

For one who has deliberately chosen the position of an outsider to any particular culture or country, it is hard to avoid the conclusion that Christianity, communism and the democratic, peaceful state with a benign and efficient industrial system are three gods which failed the social order of the twentieth century. They may have done so by convincing their followers that their system deserves to be universalized whereas this situation never progresses further than mythology. The last named system was the kind of a democratic state which was idealized by Thorstein Veblen at the beginning of this century. It was the polar opposite of a state run by and for the leisure classes, like eighteenth century England, or that for the vested interests of business and banking, like the United States of the pre-New Deal era. Yet, at the end of this century, democracy in the United States is seriously flawed with little prospect of improvement. It has failed the test of operational definitions by both Thomas Jefferson[47] and Thorstein Veblen.[48]

Yet, if and when the average citizen loses faith in the industrial mechanisms of democracy, and even of Christianity itself, it certainly does not mean the end of the world of enchantment.[49] On the contrary, one would logically expect the revival of a great many crisis cults, authoritarian, ritualistic and mystical in nature. They are similar to those which occurred with the decay of the economic and political power of the Roman Empire and concomitant with the rise of Christianity as one such cult.[50] Harvey Cox offered a third possibility with his prediction that it would only be liberal Christian theology which would decline. This was because of its over-identification with the secular city, also in a state of decay. On the contrary, North American fundamentalism would remain healthy and exuberant for its peculiar causes of such things as restoration of prayer in public schools, the pledge of allegiance, and anti-abortion. The same could also be expected for the South American and Catholic model sponsoring social and economic reforms in behalf of the under-privileged. At any rate, in Cox's postmodern society, religion could be expected to flourish at the expense of the rational and the empirical.[51] This is precisely the point that Marvin Harris made in his illuminating chapter, "Why the Cults are Coming." It was because the rational order of the old social structure demonstrably broke down with regard to crime, unemployment, inflation, unresponsible bureaucracies in both government and big business, the decay of cities, the breakup of families, alienation from work, malfunctioning of American machines and gadgets, and a host of other misfortunes.

Unfortunately, these were unaccompanied by any rational explanation understood by the masses. Consequently, they turned greedily to magic and mysticism. They, as always, promised an easy and prompt solution. The mass popularity of the modern TV revivalist, or masters of the video cult, is a case in point. They promise to save the idea of progress - interpreted in an American sense as health, prosperity, and material possessions - via magical and supernatural means. The old and familiar combination of monetary contributions and prayer are alleged to work sudden miracles which defy rational explanation. Little time and even less effort are required. The old skin of painful and ugly life is immediately shed and a new, youthful, beautiful one stands in its place. The entire process is pitched on no higher rational and scientific ground than were the Ghost Dances on the Great Plains in 1890.[52]

None of these unpalatable religious developments could have come as much of a surprise to Wilfred Cantwell Smith. He had little respect for what men customarily call religion. Throughout history no man who has been religiously great was satisfied with the religion into which he was born.[53] He was forced to add that present Christian theology is inadequate. A considerable revision is necessary, especially for its own theologians.[54] As Christians' faith in God has weakened they have busied themselves with Christianity; and as their personal relation to Christ has virtually lapsed they have turned to religion for solace.[55]

Pondering evidence such as this, one thing seems clear. The Age of Enlightenment, which among other things produced liberal Christian theology and scientific Biblical criticism, is over. For an intellectual, whether within or without the Church, the future, where not ambiguous, promises very little.

Nevertheless, since these three Western faith systems were responsible for colonialism and imperialism throughout the world since 1492 - virtually five hundred years - their failure deprives us of any grounds for superiority over the internal system of the primitive. The latter's religion sustained and nurtured him until he was seduced by the white man's technology and overawed by weaponry. The fact that we administered these terrible blows to ourselves, as well as to him, neither alleviates the pain nor lessens the consequences.

Footnotes

1   See Lynn White, Jr., "Christian Myth and Christian History," 145-158 in *The Journal of the History of Ideas*, III (1942); Oscar Cullmann, *Christ and Time. The Primitive Christian Conception of Time and History*, translated from the German by Floyd V. Filson (Philadelphia, Westminster Press, 1964). 19-21; Reinhold Neibuhr, *Faith and History, a Comparison of Christian and Modern Views of History* (New York, Charles Scribner's Sons, 1949), 26; Paul Tillich, "History as the Problem of Our Period," *Review of Religion*, III (1939), 262.

2   *Myth and Reality*. Translated from the French by Willard R. Trask. Planned and edited by Ruth Nanda Anshen (New York, Harper and Row, 1963), 65. Calvinism was even more pessimistic and contemptuous of human nature. Of that small part of humanity which was saved, and not damned, salvation did not derive from individual merit, but from God's will and judgment. It was grounded before the world was. Max Weber, *The Protestant Ethic and the Spirit of Capitalism*. Translated by Talcott Parsons. With a Foreword by R. H. Tawney (New York, Charles Scribner's Sons, 1956), 103.

3   Although we have no historical evidence that Jesus himself ever made such a sweeping claim, the *New Testament* portrays him as denying the spiritual value of all other religions than his own: "I am the way, and the truth, and the life; no one comes to the Father, but by me." *John*, 14, 6 in *The New Covenent. Commonly Called the New Testament of Our Lord and Savior Jesus Christ*. Revised Standard Version (New York, Thomas Nelson & Sons, 1946). Christians today, as always, continue to assert the exclusive powers of the Savior, Jesus Christ. The Lausanne II International Congress of World Evangelization in Manilla issued a manifesto which concluded: "There is only one Gospel because there is only one Christ, who because of his death and Resurrection is himself the only way to salvation." "Evangelicals vote on Jews," in the Kansas City *Times*, August 19, 1989, E-4. The Grace Baptist Church of Lee's Summit, Missouri published a manifesto in the Kansas City *Times* of August 19, 1989, E-9 which declared: "The Lord Jesus Christ is the only mediator between God and man."

4   *The Idea of Progress. An Inquiry into Its Origin and Growth* (New York, Dover, 1955), 5.

5   *Social Change and History. Aspects of the Western Theory of Development* (New York, Oxford Press, 1969), 126.

6   "Introduction" to J. B. Bury, *The Idea of Progress*, xxvi, xxx.

7   *Civilization on Trial* (New York, Oxford University Press, 1949), 251.

8   *The Sacred Canopy. Elements of a Sociological Theory of Religion* (Garden City, New York, Doubleday, 1967), 166. A good example of this was afforded by Karl Barth when he said that without the resurrection of Christ, he would not be a Christian theologian. Without this event, Christianity would be but an illusion and "moral sentimentalism." The resurrection certainly has a life of its own in the consciousness of such a man. See *The Knowledge of God and the Service of God According to the Teaching of the Reformation*, translated by J. L. M. Haire and Ian Henderson (London, Hodder and

Staughton, 1938), 88.

9   Lynn White, Jr., "Christian Myth and Christian History," *loc. cit.,* 147.

10   Thus was born the spirit of rationalization and intellectualization. There were no mysterious and incalcuable forces that come into play and dominate this world. Man could by calculating and technical means perform the kinds of services previously thought the result of magic and religion. Man could not easily harbor these thoughts and at the same time conceive of life as in some sort of exchanted forest. Thus, the idea of the disenchantment of the world. Max Weber, *Essays in Sociology.* Translated, edited and with an Introduction by H. H. Gerth and C. Wright Mills (New York, Oxford Press, 1953), 139, 155.

11   Operating on this theory, the Protestant business civilization of the sixteenth and seventeenth centuries endorsed both science and technology. Robert K. Merton, "Puritanism, Pietism and Science," 574-606 in *Social Theory and Social Structure.* Revised and enlarged (Glencoe, Illinois, Free Press, 1961), 574-575.

12   Charles Howard Hopkins, *The Rise of the Social Gospel in American Protestantism, 1865-1915* (New Haven, Yale University Press, 1940), 257, 318, 320. See also Paul A. Carter, *The Decline and Revival of the Social Gospel. Social and Political Liberalism in American Protestant Churches, 1920-1940* (Ithaca, New York, Cornell University Press, 1954).

13   L. Sprague de Camp, *The Great Monkey Trial* (Garden City, New York, Doubleday, 1968), 2, 11, 328. See also the chapter entitled, "Single Combat," 369-414 in *ibid.*

14   A prominent Episcopal priest sounded this warning: "... no group... has the right to determine and then impose a moral or religious standard on society. ... Religious intolerance must not be tolerated." Peter G. Kreitler, priest at St. Matthews Episcopal church, Los Angeles Times News service, "Religious intolerance of powerful TV preachers cannot be tolerated," in the Kansas City *Times,* March 20, 1987, A-17. A church historian at a respectable southern seminary reminded us that one cannot compromise with fanatics. "By its very nature," he observed, "fundamentalism is possessed of an absolutist mentality that says: 'I am right. Therefore, only if you agree with me can you be right or Christian or saved or whatever it is that we are talking about.'" E. Richard Hinson, church history professor at the Southern Baptist Theological Seminary in Louisville, Kentucky and visiting professor in economics at Catholic University in Washington for the academic year of 1986-1987. The Washington Post, "Baptist schism may be the answer to internal fight, scholar says," in the Kansas City *Times,* April 4, 1987, C-17.

15   The preaching of Protestantism has become as empty and blank as Locke's *tabula rasa,* becoming more devoid of meaning in terms of the modern science and philosophy it "purported to accept." Northrop, *Meeting of East and West,* 93, 289. In 1925, Reinhold Niebuhr thought he understood why the institution was "so impotent ethically and why the achievements of the church so meager compared to its moral pretensions." Protestantism did not venture beyond personal loyalty to Jesus, assuming nothing more was needed for salvation. The terrible price for this ignored pertinent issues of social justice the church should have addressed. Further, preachers never seemed to realize how many of the miseries of man were caused, not by malice or evil, but by misdirected zeal and unbalanced virtues. *Leaves from the Notebook of a Tamed Cynic* (Hamden, Connecticut, The Shoe String Press, 1956), 74. At the beginning of the depression, a highly successful Protestant

cleric observed "no profession of men is so thoroughly empty of dignity and grace as that of the Protestant ministry today." Carter, *Decline and Revival of the Social Gospel*, 70.

16   *Magic, Science and Religion and Other Essays* (Garden City, New York, Doubleday, 1948), 30-31. Weston La Barre described similar practices among the Eskimos from Alaska to Greenland and for the same reasons. Land hunting in summer was within the realm of the technological competence of the Eskimo. Numerous hazards were offered in winter when fishing through the ice for sea mammals. Failure probably meant starvation. Sedna, a goddess who lived in the sea, could either provide the necessary food or deny it. Consequently, she was at the center of the ritual life of the Eskimo. *The Ghost Dance*, 25-26.

17   *Early Civilization. An Introduction to Anthropology* (New York, Alfred A. Knopf, 1922), 194-196.

18   Phyllis M. Kaberry, *Aboriginal Woman, Sacred and Profane*. Introduction by Professor A. P. Elkin (Philadelphia, The Blakiston Company, first published 1939), 17.

19   Polybius best expressed this philosophy of history. While it was proper for the average citizen to share the loves, the hates, fears and folklore of his own people, the historian was under no such obligation, but that of Truth instead. Without it, history became merely an idle tale for those seeking amusement, or patriotic fervor, but no instruction. The historian had to divorce himself psychologically and spiritually from his own kinsmen and treat them no differently than the enemy, assessing praise and blame impartially. He had to act as an honest and impartial umpire, not as a partial coach pretending meanwhile to be the umpire. *Polybius. The Histories*. With an English Translation by W. R. Paton in six vols., (New York, G. P. Putnam's Sons, 1922), I, Book One, 35-37. Thucydides was probably the first historian to do this. His own state, democratic Athens, was probably responsible for starting the Peloponnesian War. Its daring and aggression on the high seas caused the remainder of the Greek city states to fear they would fall victim to Athenian imperialism unless they made a common alliance against Athens. *History of the Peloponnesian War*, Book One, Chapter One.

20   Research tended to verify a prediction by Thorstein Veblen. Business men favor an aggressive foreign policy. When in government, they direct one which is both patriotic and warlike. "The quest for profits," he concluded, "leads to a predatory foreign policy." *The Theory of Business Enterprise* (New York, Scribner's, 1935), 391, 398. The business man's tocsin was sounded before the end of World War II by Dean Acheson, Assistant Secretary of State. To avoid another depression, America must insure foreign markets for the surplus of manufactured and agricultural goods she produced. Testimony before the Hearings on Post-War Economic Policy and Planning, Select Sub-Committee on Post-War Economic Policy and Planning, House, 78th Congress, 2nd session, 1944 in *The Pentagon Watchers. Students Report on the National Security State*, edited by Leonard S. Rodberg and Derek Shearer (Garden City, New York, Anchor Books, Doubleday and Company, 1970), 4.

21   Voter turn-out in 1988 was less than half that of the voting age population. James Q. Wilson, *The 1988 Election* (D. C. Heath, Lexington, Masachusetts, 1989), 9, 10, 13. Tom Wicker came to the same pessimistic conclusions about the low character of the election of 1986. It had a lesser voter turn-out than any campaign since 1942 when the nation was at war. "Political consultants are no asset," in the Kansas City *Star*, November

23, 1986, C-5. The Republicans, darling of the conservatives, raised five times the money the Democrats did for the election of 1986. Anthony Lewis, New York Times News Service, Boston, "Grotesque disparity in party resources," in the Kansas City *Times,* November 4, 1986, A-7. See also Washington, "Republicans spent more," in the Kansas City *Times,* February 16, 1987, B-8

22   Charles A. Beard, *The Economic Basis of Politics* (New York, Alfred A. Knopf, 1934), 39. See also Max Weber, *Selections from His Works,* with an Introduction by S. M. Miller (New York, Thomas Y. Crowell, 1968), 49.

23   "Despite sweeping claims of the democratization of ownership associated with 'People's Capitalism,' there is very little, if any, evidence of a significant widening of the concentrated ownership and control of the American corporate structure." Robert L. Heilbroner, *The Future as History* (New York, Harper and Brothers, 1960), 125.

24   "On Democracy in America" in *The People Shall Judge,* vol. 1, The Staff, Social Science 1 (Chicago, The University of Chicago Press, 1949), Second Book, 549-550.

25   "Many businessmen have begun to fear that capitalism and democracy may be incompatible in the long run." This somewhat surprising conclusion came from a couple of observers. They attended a meeting held by the Conference Board, a forum for big business leaders to exchange candid views. Paul L. Wachtel, *The Poverty of Affluence. A Psychological Portrait of the American Way of Life* (New York, Free Press, Macmillan, 1983), 267. See also Frances Fox Piven and Richard A. Cloward, *The New Class War. Reagan's Attack on the Welfare State and Its Consequences* (New York, Pantheon Books, 1982, 1-40, 125-150.

26   Pliven and Cloward, *The New Class War,* 147. Karl Marx was the first to call attention to this disturbing phenomenon. The history of industrialization, concluded Lilian Breslow, proved him correct. *Worlds of Pain. Life in the Working-Class Family* (New York, Basic Books, Inc., 1976), 159, 161. For decades the problem has not been how to produce more but rather how to consume what has been produced. In such an affluent society, the labor force becomes quite vulnerable. Richard Sennett and Jonathan Cobb, *The Hidden Injuries of Class* (New York, Alfred A. Knopf, 1972), 261. This tragedy is compounded by the fact that as a society we have yet to face the problem or, worse, even to acknowledge it. Paul L. Wachtel, *The Poverty of Affluence. A Psychological Portrait of the American Way of Life* (New York, Free Press, Macmillan, 1983), 248. Although Charles Dickens exposed human tragedies characteristically produced by the assembly line process, those same worker ills exist today. "Once deceptively dubbed 'stitcher's wrist' or 'cotton-twister's hand,' the wrist and hand injuries are now collectively known as culminative trauma disorders. The potentially crippling conditions often result from the repetition of assembly line work. Safety experts say the human toll is staggering. In general food-processing workers are stricken with repetitive motion disorders at twice the rate of those in other industries." Mike McGraw, "Thanksgiving treat a tragedy for some. Workers critical of two Missouri turkey processing plants," in the Kansas City *Star,* November 19, 1989, A-1.

27   Paul Baran and Paul Sweezy, "The Multinational Corporation and Modern Imperialism," 435-441 in *The Capitalist System. A Radical Analysis of American Society.* Written and edited by Richard C. Edwards *et al* (Englewood Cliffs, New Jersey, Prentice-Hall, Inc., 1972), 438-441; Arthur MacEwan, "Capitalist Expansion, Ideology and

Intervention," 410-420 in *ibid.*, 412. This significant economic trend becomes understandable if we postulate that, with regard to the host nation, the modern corporation is a kind of mid-nineteenth century merchant. As Adam Smith correctly anticipated, he was not really a citizen of any particular country. On the contrary, he was "as much as possible, isolated from all necessary relationships, duties and prejudices." He was thus free to calculate self-interest. As a rational man, everything he did was based upon this single principle. Tönnies, *Community and Society*, 80-81.

28   Barry Bosworth, economist for the Brookings Institute, explained: "This is a country which is on a consumption binge and is forced to borrow overseas." By the Associated Press, New York. "U.S. deficits blamed for trade lag," in the Kansas City *Star*, January 23, 1987, A-13. Kenneth McCay of the House Budget Committee agreed: "We are consuming more than we produce, borrowing more than we save." Our national plight was dramatized when he added: "... we're borrowing [since 1979] at roughly ten times the rate we're increasing our productivity." William R. Neikirk, Chicago Tribune, Washington, "'Competitiveness' a meaningless word," in the Kansas City *Star*, August 6, 1987, B-6.

29   "A leveraged buyout is a corporate acquisition financed mainly with borrowed money that is repaid with cash from the target company's cash flow or the sale of its assets." Critics think "such debt-burdened companies are more likely to fail during an economic turndown, leading to lay-offs...." New York, The Associated Press, "Buyouts affect fewer top firms," in the Kansas City *Times*, November 27, 1989, A-2. For example, look at what happened when the Campeau Corporation of Canada took over the highly successful giant, Allied Stores Incorporated. The purchase came from funds Campeau did not have but bankers did, or about four billion dollars. After the transaction, Campeau tried to pay the money back by saddling all the debt to the company it bought out. Bankers themselves are indifferent as long as their money is out at a high interest rate and returns are prompt and steady. Sidney Rutberg, Fairchild News Services, "Bargains like this are few indeed," in the Kansas City *Star*, January 20, 1987, A-4.

30   The money we send to Japan to make up for our trade deficit is reinvested by them in the United States. The Japanese buy government bonds which means they supply the money to keep our economy going while our government spends $200 billion a year more than it collects. David Nyham, Boston Globe, "Japanese investors are buying a lot more," in the Kansas City *Star*, April 14, 1987, A-9. In California, where five of the largest banks are Japanese-owned, foreign investors now own more than half of 170 banking firms. The number is 300 in New York. Tony Coelho, "The Foreign Greening of America. Outsiders Banking Moves Threaten our Ability to Compete," in the Los Angeles *Times*, March 26, 1987, Part II, 5. Sony's $3.4 billion purchase of Columbia Pictures was "the largest foreign takeover of an entertainment producer based in the United States. ... four of the five largest record companies are now foreign-owned...." Paul Farhi, Washington Post, "Tinseltown isn't all that glitters from abroad," in the Kansas City *Star*, November 26, 1989, G-1, 6. Perhaps the greatest blow to America's pride was the purchase of Rockefeller Center in New York by the Japanese. *Time*, vol. 131, No. 2, November 13, 1989, 83. In the early winter of 1989, the Perkin-Elmer Corp., unable to find an American buyer for its "state-of-the-art superconductor equipment business, was contemplating its sale to a Japanese firm. The sale would surrender the future of computer chip manufacture to the Japanese and make this country totally dependent on the Japanese for technological innovation in that field. ... We're sitting here spending our research money on missiles which we bury in the ground to scare the Russians while the Japanese and Germans, free of such burdens, seize control of the technology of the 21st century." Donald Kaul,

Tribune Media Services, "The Cold War is over, and its clear who lost - but who, really, won?" the Kansas City *Times*, December 7, 1989, A-21. As Wright Investors Service put it: "Foreign buying should not be counted on as a lasting support since a weakened dollar, a faltering economy, or declining foreign stock prices could each send foreigners for the exit." The shock to our stock market might rival that of 1929. Elizabeth Weir, Congressional Quarterly, Inc., Washington, "No dire predictions from the seers-yet," in the Kansas City *Star*, July 29, 1987, K-3. See also the New York Times, Washington, "Studies say deficits, foreign debt will linger," in the Kansas City *Times*, November 6, 1987, C-1.

31   As Lee Iacocca explained, financial rip-offs have had much to do with America's industrial decline: "I see billions of dollars tied up in new corporate debt to keep the raiders at bay while research and development goes begging. I see billions going for greenmail that ought to be building high tech factories. ... I also see a huge share of America's best management talent wasted on takeover games when it should be devoted to strengthening the industrial base of the country. But I don't see raiders creating jobs. I don't see them increasing productivity. And worst of all, I don't see them doing a thing to help America compete in the world." Lee Iacocca, Guest Columnist, in the Kansas City *Times*, January 29, 1987, C-1, 3. Recently, Tokyo informed the George Bush administration that it was critical of very high salaries paid American executives and their focus on short-term profits. These led to the curtailment of investment and modernization. "Japan asserts that costly corporate takeovers financed by mountains of 2debt have wiped out the resources needed to develop new products." Steven R. Weisman, "Japan advises U.S. to clean up its act," in the Kansas City *Times*, November 20, 1989, A-1.

32   E. F. Schumacher, *Small is Beautiful. Economics as if People Mattered* (New York, Harper and Row, 1973), 13, 137-139. William T. Blackstone delineated the major assumptions which made this terrific miscalculation possible: 1) the belief that we can exploit the environment without restriction 2) that the production of goods is more important than the people who make and use them 3) that nature will provide unlimited resources 4) we, therefore, have no obligation to future generations to preserve resources 5) the continual increases in human population are desirable and there is an inviolable right to have as many children as one pleases 6) the answer to the few questions about technology is more of the same and 7) the gross inequality in the distribution of goods and services is acceptable. "Ethics and Ecology," 16-42 in *Philosophy and the Environmental Crisis* (Athens, University of Georgia Press, 1974), 16.

33   Some exponents of Manifest Destiny and progress envisioned the annexation of Central America and, indeed, the entire continent of South America. Naturally, they were armed with contempt for persons of color, as well as non-Protestant Christians. When applied to our expansion at the expense of less civilized peoples, force was justified. It speeded up the inexorable law of progress. Finally, it was part of a providential and masterful plan in which the godly and pious should be happy to participate. See this author's "New Orleans and the Cuban Question During the Lopez Expeditions of 1849-1851. A Local Study in 'Manifest Destiny', 3-75 in *The Louisiana Historical Quarterly*, vol. 22, No. 4, October 1939 and "The Ideology of Southern Imperialism: New Orleans and the Caribbean, 1845-1860," 48-73 in *The Louisiana Historical Quarterly*, vol. 39, No. 1, January 1956.

34   Aleksandr Solzhenitsyn, *Letter to the Soviet Leaders*. Translated from the Russian by Hilary Sternberg (New York, Harper and Row, 1975), 21-26. Lévi-Strauss put the same attitude in the form of a question. Like maggots in a flour sack, who become so numerous

they poison the flour and bring on their own extinction, will man eliminate himself the same way through poisoning his environment? Interview in the New York *Times*, December 31, 196? from The Introduction, ft. 2 in *Ecology and Religion in History* edited by David and Eileen Spring (New York, Harper Torchbook, Harper and Row, 1974).

35   *America. Religions and Religion* (Belmont, California, Wadsworth Publishing Company, 1981), 370.

36   Quoted in Redfield, *Folk Culture*, 349.

37   The Roman philosopher could say this precisely because he rejected the idea of progress. Although there was continual change, history repeated itself in a cyclical way. This meant that a wise man who had attained the age of forty would have seen and understood as much as one who had lived one or two hundred years, or even forever. All things repeat the same form throughout eternity and come round the circle. He who has seen the current age has seen them all. *Marcus Aurelius and His Times. The Transition from Paganism to Christianity*. With an Introduction by Irwin Edman. Published for the Classic Club by Walter J. Black (New York, Walter J. Black, 1945), 24, 63.

38   See F. Martin, "Eschatology (In the Bible)," 524-533 in the *New Catholic Encyclopedia*, V (Washington, D.C., McGraw-Hill, 1967); M.E. Williams, "Eschatology (Theological Treatment)," 533-538 in *ibid.*, "Parousia," 1017-1018 in *The Oxford Dictionary of the Christian Church* (New York, Oxford University Press, 1958); "Particular Judgment," 1018 in *ibid.*, Kenneth Foreman, "Eschatology," 392-393 in *Twentieth Century Encyclopedia of Religious Knowledge*, editor-in-chief Lefferts A. Loetscher (Grand Rapids, Michigan, 1955).

39   Billy Graham, Kansas City *Star*, January 25, 1985, B-7. The Seventh-day Adventist view is typical of the many who hold that the final age, the "aschaton," is here. "These are the last days, this is the final phase of God's dealing with men." The Adventists place this event to occur in this generation. Forman, "Eschatology," *loc. cit.*, 392. In a strict sense, millennialism relates to a book in the Christian New Testament, the book of Revelation. This tells of a thousand year period at the end of time, one closely connected to the second coming of Jesus. Here God defeats Satan, who is chained for the next thousand years, while the believers in Jesus rule by his side. At the end of that time another great battle occurs between God and Satan who is finally eliminated. In a looser sense, however, millennialism refers to any religious affiliation "in which there is intense expectation that the end of the present world order is near." For them, the anticipated end is also a new beginning. Albanese, *America. Religions and Religion*, 275.

40   "The Westminster Confession of Faith," 77-101 in *The Proposed Book of Confessions of the Presbyterian Church in the United States of America together with related documents* (Atlanta, Georgia, Materials Distribution Service, 1976), 100-101; *The Constitution of the United Presbyterian Church in the United States of America. Part I. Book of Confession*, Second edition, 1970. Published by the Office of the General Assembly of the United Presbyterian Church in the United States of America. (Philadelphia, General Assembly of the United Presbyterian Church, 1967), 9.01 to 9.56

41   In 1922, it officially declared that, while ultimately God's purpose for man would be made manifest to all, it would be impossible to stipulate what kind of an historical event this would be. "The expectation of a single great Day of General Resurrection, considered

literally and interpreted as a kind of Final Event in the temporal order, presents great difficulties." Part III. "Eschatology," 202-220 in *Doctrine in the Church of England. The Report of the Commission on Christian Doctrine appointed by the Archbishops of Canterbury and York in 1922,* William Ebor, Chairman, (London, England, Society for the promotion of Christian Knowledge, first published 1938, re-issued 1962), 206, 211.

42   Modern Catholic doctrine apparently contains contradictory elelments. "How is it that, though man no longer looks forward to a more decisive act (Second Coming), man still groans within himself as he awaits his redemption?" F. Martin, "Eschatology (In the Bible)," *New Catholic Encyclopedia,* V, 533. Contrast that with the following statement by M. E. Williams. The recent liturgical revival "has meant a Christological approach to the last things. Just as the individual is poised between Christ's first coming at Baptism and the final coming at death, so the world is an interim period between the first and Second Coming of Christ." The Church itself will only be perfected at the end of time when the Lord comes in majesty with His angels (Second Coming). "Eschatology (Theological Treatment)," 533-538 in *New Catholic Encyclopedia,* V, 537.

43   *The Trinity and the Religious Experience of Man. Icon-Person-Mystery* (New York, Orbis Books, 1973), 6.

44   London, The Associated Press. "Questioning tenets is O.K., report says," in the Kansas City *Times,* June 8, 1987, E-8. When there was no follow-up in the public prints, I wrote the bishop and received a reply from his office. It asserted he had been misunderstood. What he said was that to be a Christian one does not have to accept stories about the Virgin Birth as historically true. "He is completely convinced of the reality of the resurrection of our Lord Jesus Christ. However, he follows the Apostle Paul's view... that the Raised Body was a transformed body and, therefore, not physically the same as his earthly body." Rebecca Jenkins, Bishop's Press Officer, Auckland Castle, Diocese of Durham, England to C. Stanley Urban, Park College, Parkville, Missouri, December 15, 1989. This means that Christians no longer have to believe two historical and fundamental tenets about the faith: 1) It was the seed of God inserted into Mary which produced the saviour-hero, Jesus and 2) It was an angel who rolled away the huge stone guarding the tomb of Jesus so that he could revisit his followers in his earthly body, one pierced by a doubting Thomas. Altogether, it enhances Christian confusion about the identity of Jesus and what happened to his "dead" body and why.

45   *The Creation of Consciousness: Jung's Myth for Modern Man* (Toronto, Inner City Books, 1984), 9-12.

46   "Eschatology," 154-161 in *Dictionary of the History of Jesus. Studies of Selected Pivotal Ideas.* Philip P. Weiner, editor-in-chief, II (New York, Charles Scribner's Sons, 1973), 160.

47   It is impossible to find Jefferson expressing the core of his political philosophy in a single paragraph. One would have to begin with his insistence on the fact that a democracy trusts the people themselves with major decisions. However, it is equally paramount that the people represent an educated, informed and active electorate. If the government lies or misrepresents factual situations to the public, the latter cannot fulfill its necessary duties. His suspicions of an absent and powerful government could in some measure be assuaged by a free press, public education and bill of rights to protect the individual from the force of law. He opposed a standing army in peacetime, as well as a

large navy which could drag the country into wars far from our shores. He certainly could not have forseen, nor likely agreed to, a large standing army in Korea, Vietnam and Germany, our national policy which resulted in and from the Cold War. Nor would he have tolerated the consequent art by government of manipulating public opinion by lying or distorting the news. Furthermore, he felt that these foreign adventures could result in a grinding public debt which not only impeded happiness but induced despair. Finally, he was a great friend of science, philosophy and the liberal arts, but suspicious of those Christian fanatics who would make all others conform to a single belief, i.e., theirs. Reason and persuasion were the only effective agents of peaceful change or reform. See *The Political Writings of Thomas Jefferson. Representative Selections.* Edited with an introduction by Edward Dumbauld (New York, the Liberal Arts Press, 1956), 37, 47-48, 68-69, 93.

48   The following excerpt was taken from an unpublished paper written some twenty years ago: "In his *Engineer and the Price System,* Veblen states his preference for a system which he hopes will replace that of the doomed free enterprise variety. It involves one in which the engineer, the economist, the technician and the laborer combine to produce to their full capacity the best product at the cheapest cost. It is one in which the machine is servant to man and one in which man has been inculcated with a natural cause and effect philosophy, itself derived from a long observation of the way in which the machine works. This new system necessarily disposes of the old anthropomorphic concept of the universe which is always twisted to mean that God intends for the Establishment to govern and for the governed to submit. It also eliminates the eighteenth century Natural Rights concept which argued that a man could do with his own what he willed, including shutting down a factory and locking out a labor force. But it is essential for any modern revolutionary to pay particular attention to Veblen's insistence that any revolution aimed at the economic sector has to provide immediately a system which works better than that cast aside. Merely to destroy or paralyze an on-going economic system is to introduce irrationality and chaos." (C. Stanley Urben, "Veblen's Analysis of American Capitalism," 9 pp., Park College, 4 May 1970), 7.

49   Kathleen Agena, "The Return of Enchantment," 67-80 in The New York *Times* Magazine, November 27, 1983.

50   Weston La Barre, *The Ghost Dance. Origins of Religion.* A Delta Book (New York, Dell Publishing, 1972), 254, 349. The celebrated Russian historian, M. Rostovtzeff, arrived at much the same conclusion. See *Rome,* translated from the Russian by J. D. Duff, edited by E. J. Bickerman. Galaxy edition (New York, Oxford University Press, reprint 1967), 318, 322, 324; *The Social and Economic History of the Roman Empire,* 2 vols., I (Oxford, England, Clarendon University Press, 1963), 509, 523-524.

51   John A. Coleman, reviewer of Religion in the Secular City. Toward a Postmodern Theology, by Harvey Cox in The New York *Times* Book Review, March 4, 1984, Section 7, 1, 36-37.

52   *America Now. The Anthropology of a Changing Culture* (New York, Simon and Schuster, 1981), 141-165.

53   *The Meaning and End of Religion. A New Approach to the Religious Tradition of Mankind.* (New York, Macmillan, 1963), 129.

54   *Ibid.*, 198.

55   *Ibid.*, 34, 127.

BIBLIOGRAPHY

Books

Adams, Henry, *Mont-Saint Michel and Chartres* (Boston, Houghton Mifflin, 1904).

Albanese, Catherine L., *America. Religions and Religion* (Belmont, California, Wadsworth Publishing Company, 1981).

Allan, William, *The African Husbandman* (New York, Barnes and Noble, 1967).

Ardrey, Robert, *African Genesis. A Personal Investigation into the Animal Origins and Nature of Man* (New York, Athenum, 1961).

Arens, William, *The Man-Eating Myth. Anthropology and Anthropophagy* (New York, Oxford Press, 1979).

Aristotle. *Politics and Poetics,* translated by Benjamin Jowett and S.H. Butcher (New York, Heritage Press, 1964).

Ashley, Maurice, *England in the Seventeenth Century* (London, Penguin Books, Cox and Lyman, 1962).

Aurelius, Marcus, *Marcus Aurelius and His Times. The Transition from Paganism to Christianity*. With an Introduction by Irwin Edman. Published for the Classic Club by Walter J. Black (New York, Walter J. Black, 1945).

Barth, Frederick, *Nomads of South Persia. The Basserai Tribe of the Khamseh Confederacy* (New York, Humanities Press, 1961).

Barth, Karl, *The Knowledge of God and the Service of God According to the Teaching of the Reformation,* translated by J.L.M. Haire and Ian Henderson (London, Hodder and Stoughton, 1938).

Bartlett, F.C., *Psychology and Primitive Culture* (Westport, Connecticut, Greenwood Press, reprint of 1923 edition, 1970).

Beard, Charles A., *The Economic Basis of Politics* (New York, Alfred A. Knopf, 1934).

Beard, Charles A., *Economic Origins of Jeffersonian Democracy* (New York, Macmillan, 1915).

Benedict, Laura Watson, *Bagobo Ceremonial, Magic and Myth* (New York, Annals of New York Academy of Sciences, 1916-1917).

Benedict, Ruth, *Patterns of Culture* (Boston, Houghton Mifflin, 1959); also (New York, Mentor Book, New American Library of World Literature, 1960).

Berger, Peter, *The Sacred Canopy. Elements of a Sociological Theory of Religion* (Garden City, New York, Doubleday, 1967).

Bernal, Ignacio, *Mexico Before Cortez: Art, History, Legend* (Garden City, New York, Doubleday, 1963).

Bettelheim, Bruno, *Symbolic Wounds. Puberty Rites and the Envious Male* (Glencoe, Illinois, Free Press, 1954).

Bidney, David, *Theoretical Anthropology* (New York, Columbia University Press, 1953).

Bingham, Hiram, "In the Wonderland of Peru," 387-573 in *National Geographic,* vol. 24, No. 4, April 1913.

Birdsell, J.B., *Human Evolution. An Introduction to the New Physical Anthropology* (Chicago, Rand McNally, 1972).

Birket-Smith, Major, *Primitive Man and His Ways. Patterns of Life in Some Native Societies* (Cleveland and New York, World Publishing Company, 1957).

Bjerre, Jens, *The Last Cannibals*. Translated from the Danish by Estrid Bannister (New York, William Morrow, 1957).

Black, David and Loveless, Clive, *Rugs of the Wandering Baluchi* (Washington, D.C., Textile Museum, 1976).

Black Elk Speaks. Being the Life Story of a Holy Man of the Oglala Sioux, as told through John G. Neihardt (Lincoln, University of Nebraska Press, 1961).

Boas, Franz, *Anthropology and Modern Life with a New Introduction by Ruth Bunzel* (New York, W.W. Norton, 1962).

Boas, Franz, editor, *General Anthropology* (New York, D.C. Heath, 1938).

Bohannan, Paul, *Africa and the Africans*. Published for the American Museum of Natural History (Garden City, New York, Natural History Press, 1964).

Brandon, William, *The American Heritage Book of Indians* (New York, Simon and Schuster, 1961).

Brentjes, Burchard, *African Rock Art* (New York, Clarkson N. Potter, 1965).

Briggs, Lloyd Cabot, *Tribes of the Sahara* (Cambridge, Harvard University Press, 1960).

Brodine, Virginia, *Air Pollution* (Harcourt Press, 1973).

Brown, Lester R., *The Twenty-Ninth Day. Accommodating Human Needs and Numbers to the Earth's Resources* (New York, W.W. Norton, 1978).

Brown, Norman O., *Life Against Death. The Psychoanalytical Meaning of History* (Middletown, Connecticut, Wesleyan University Press, 1959).

Bunzel, Ruth, "Zuni Ritual Poetry," 611-835 in *Forty-Seventh Annual Report of the Bureau of American Ethnology to the Secretary of the Smithsonian Institute, 1929-1930* (Washington, D.C. Government Printing Office, 1932).

Bunzel, Ruth, *The Pueblo Potter. A Study of Creative Imagination in Primitive Art* (New York, AMS Press, 1969).

Breslow, Lillian, *Worlds of Pain. Life in the Working Class Family* (New York, Basic Books, 1976).

Burke, Edmund, *Reflections on the French Revolution* ... with an Introduction by Russell Kirk (New Rochelle, New York, Arlington House, no date).

Burke, Kenneth, *Permanence and Change* (New York, New Republic and Co., 1935).

Bury, J.B., *The Idea of Progress. An Inquiry into Its Origin and Growth* (New York, Dover Publications, 1955).

Campbell, Joseph, *The Hero with a Thousand Faces* (New York, Pantheon Books, Bollingen Series, vol. 17, 1961).

Carter, Paul, *The Decline and Revival of the Social Gospel. Social and Political Liberalism in American Protestant Churches, 1920-1940* (Ithaca, New York, Cornell Univesity Press, 1954).

Charney, Desiré, *The Ancient Cities of the New World. Being Voyages and Explorations in Mexico and Central America from 1857-1882* (New York, Harper, 1887).

Childe, V. Gordon, *What Happened in History*. With a New Foreword by Professor Graham Clark (Baltimore, Maryland, Penguin Books, 1967).

Clarke, Robin and Hindley, Geoffrey, *Challenge of the Primitives* (New York, McGraw-Hill, 1975).

Clifford, James, *The Predicament of Culture. Twentieth Century Ethnography, Literature and Art* (Cambridge, Massachusetts, Cambridge University Press, 1988).

Clifford, James, *Person and Myth. Maurice Leenhardt in the Melanesian World* (Berkeley, University of California Press, 1982).

Cohen, Mark Nathan, *Health and the Rise of Civilization* (New Haven, Yale University Press, 1989.

Cole, Fay Cooper, *The Wild Tribes of Davao District, Mindanao*. Anthropological Series No. 12 (Chicago, Field Museum of Natural History, 1913).

Commoner, Barry, editor, *Radioactive Contamination*, Virginia Brodine, Consulting Editor in Environmental Issue Series. Scientist's Institute for Public Information (New York, Harcourt Brace and Jovanovich, 1975).

Cook, S.F., *Conflict Between the Californian Indian and White Civilization*, 4 vols. Ibero-Americana (Berkeley, California, University of California Press, 1943), I *The Indian versus the Spanish Mission*.

Covarrubias, Miguel, *The Eagle, the Jaguar, and the Serpent, Indian Art of the Americas* .... (New York, Alfred A. Knopf, 1954).

Culbert, T. Patrick, *The Classic Maya Collapse* (Albuquerque, University of New Mexico Press, 1973).

Cullman, Oscar, *Christ and Time. The Primitive Christian Concept of Time and History*, translated from the German by Floyd V. Filson (Philadelphia, Westminster Press, 1964).

Curtis, Edward S., *The North American Indian*, 20 vols. (New York, Edward S. Curtis, 1924).

Daly, Mary, *Gyn/Ecology. The Metaphysics of Radical Feminism* (Boston, Beacon Press, 1978).

Dark, Philip J.C., *Bush Negro Art. An African Art in the Americas* (New York, St. Martins Press, 1973).

Darwin, Charles, *Journal of Researches into the Geology and Natural History of the Various Countries Visited during the Voyage of H. M. S. Beagle Round the World* (New York, E. P. Dutton, 1912).

Davies, Godfrey, *The Early Stuarts, 1603-1660* (Oxford, England, Clarendon Press, 1949).

Davis, W. Jackson, *The Seventh Year. Industrial Civilization in Transition* (New York, W. W. Norton, 1979).

Day, Martin S., *The Many Meanings of Myth* (Lanham, Maryland, The University Press of America, 1984).

de Camp, L. Sprague, *The Great Monkey Trial* (Garden City, New York, Doubleday, 1968).

Deloria, Vine Jr., *God is Red* (New York, Grosset & Dunlap, 1973).

de Tocqueville, Alexis, "On Democracy in America" in *The People Shall Judge,* The Staff, Social Science 1 (Chicago, University of Chicago Press, 1949), I.

De Waal Malefijit, Annemarie, *Images of Man. A History of Anthropological Thought* (New York, Alfred A. Knopf, 1974).

Diemen-Schen, Muriel, *The Anthropological Imagination* (New York, McGraw-Hill, 1977).

Dornan, S. S., *Pygmies and Bushmen of the Kalahari* (London, Seeley, Service, 1925).

Douglas, Frederic H. and D'Harnoncourt, René, *Indian Art of the United States* (New York, Museum of Modern Art, 1941).

Driberg, J. H., *People of the Small Arrow* (New York, Payson & Clarke, 1930).

Driberg, J. H., *The Savage as he really is* (London, George Routledge, 1929).

Driver, Harold E., *Indians of North America* (Chicago, University of Chicago Press, 1966).

Dumont, Jean-Paul, *The Headman and I. Ambiguity and Ambivalence in the Fieldworking Experience* (Austin, Texas, University of Texas Press, 1978).

Durkheim, Emilé, *The Elementary Forms of Religious Life.* Translated from the French by Joseph Ward Swain (New York, Free Press, 1915. London, George Allen & Unwin Ltd.).

Durkheim, Emilé, *Incest. The Nature and Origin of the Taboo*. Translated by Edward Sagarin (New York, Lyle Stuart, Inc., 1963).

Durkheim, Emilé, *Selections from His Work* with an Introduction and Commentaries by George Simpson (New York, Thomas Y. Crowell, 1969).

Durkheim, Emilé and Mauss, Marcel, *Primitive Classification* (Chicago, University of Chicago Press, 1963).

Eastman, Charles, *Indian Boyhood*. (Greenwich, Connecticut, Fawcett Publication, 1972).

Edinger, Edward, *The Creation of Consciousness: Jung's Myth for Modern Man* (Toronto, Canada, Inner City Books, 1984).

Eliade, Mircea, *Myth and Reality*. Translated from the French by Willard R. Trask. Planned and edited by Ruth Nanda Anshen (New York, Harper and Row, 1963).

Eliade, Mircea, *The Myth of the Eternal Return*. Translated from the French by Willard R. Trask. Bollingen Series, vol. 46 (New York, Pantheon Books, 1954).

Eliade, Mircea, *Myths, Dreams and Mysteries. The Encounter between Contemporary Faiths and Archaic Realities*. Translated by Philip Mairet (New York, Harper & Brothers, 1960).

Eliade, Mircea, *The Sacred and the Profane. The Nature of Religion*. Translated from the French by Willard R. Trask (New York, Harper and Row, 1959).

Ellis, Albert, *The Origins and Development of the Incest Taboo* (New York, Lyle Stuart Inc., 1963).

Erikson, Erich, *Childhood and Society* (New York, W. W. Norton, 1950).

Euripides, *Medea, Hippolytus, The Bacchae,* translated by Phillip Vallcott (New York, The Heritage Press, 1963).

Evans-Pritchard, E. E., *The Position of Women in Primitive Societies and Other Essays* (New York, Free Press, 1965).

Evans-Pritchard, E. E., *The Samusi of Cyrenaica* (London, Clarendon Press, Oxford University Press, 1973).

Evans-Pritchard, E. E., *Social Anthropology and Other Essays* (New York, Free Press, 1962).

Fabian, Johannes, *Time and the Other. How Anthropology Makes Its Object* (New York, Columbia University Press, 1983).

Farb, Peter, *Man's Rise to Civilization as Shown by the Indians of North America from Primeval Times to the Coming of the Industrial State* (New York, E. P. Dutton, 1968).

Farb, Peter, *Humankind* (Boston, Houghton Mifflin, 1978).

Firth, Raymond, *Art and Life in New Guinea* (New York, AMS Press, 1976).

Firth, Raymond, *Primitive Economics of the New Zealand Maori* (New York, E. P. Dutton, 1929).

Firth, Raymond, *Tikopia, Ritual and Belief* (Boston, Beacon Press, 1965, 1967).

Firth, Raymond, *We, the Tikopia. A Sociological Study of Kinship in Primitive Polynesia* (Boston, Beacon Press, 1965).

Fortes, Meyer and Evans-Pritchard, E. E., editors, *African Political Systems* (New York, Oxford University Press, 1966).

Fortes, Meyer, editor, *Social Structure Studies presented to Radcliffe-Brown* (New York, Russell and Russell, 1963).

Frazer, Sir James George, *The Golden Bough*, 12 vols. *The Magic Art and the Evolution of Kings* (New York, Macmillan, 1935), I.

Freud, Sigmund, *Civilization and Its Discontents* (London, Hogarth Press, 1957).

Fried, Morton H., *Readings in Anthropology*, 2 vols., *Physical Anthropology, Linguistics, and Archaeology*, vol. I (New York, Thomas Crowell, 1968).

Fried, Morton H., *Readings in Anthropology*, 2 vols., *Cultural Anthropology*, vol. II (New York, Thomas Y. Crowell, 1968).

Gann, Thomas and Thompson, J. Eric, *The History of the Mayas from the Earliest Times to the Present Day* (New York, Scribner's, 1931).

Garcia, L. P. and Perello, E. R., editors, *Prehistoric Art of the Western Mediterranean and the Sahara*. Viking Fund Publications in Anthropology No. 39 (New York, Wenner-Gren Foundation for Anthropological Research, Inc., 1954).

Geertz, Clifford, *The Interpretation of Cultures. Selected Essays* (New York, Basic Books, 1973).

Geertz, Clifford, *Local Knowledge. Further Essays in Interpretative Anthropology* (New York, Basic Books, 1983).

Girard, René, *Violence and the Sacred*, translated by Patrick Gregory

(Baltimore, Johns Hopkins University Press, 1977).

Goldenweiser, Alexander A., *Early Civilization. An Introduction to Anthropology* (New York, Alfred A. Knopf, 1922).

Goldman, Irving, *The Cubeo Indians of the Northwest Amazon,* Illinois Studies in Anthropology, No. 2 (Urbana, University of Illinois Press, 1963).

Goldwater, Robert, Introduction to the *Art of Oceania, Africa and the Americas,* from the Museum of Primitive Art (Greenwich, Connecticut, The Metropolitan Museum of Art, distributed by the New York Graphic Society, 1969).

Griffin, C. C., editor. *Concerning Latin American Culture.* Papers Read at Byrdcliffe, Woodstock, New York, August 1939 (New York, Columbia University Press, 1944).

Gulliver, P. H., *The Family Herds. A Study of Two Pastoral Tribes in East Africa, the Jie and Turkana* (Westport, Connecticut, Negro University Press, 1970).

Guthrie, A. B., Jr., *Fair Land, Fair Land* (Boston, Houghton Mifflin, 1982).

Hall, Edward C., *Beyond Culture* (Garden City, New York, Anchor Books, Anchor Press, 1977).

Hallpike, C. R., *The Foundations of Primitive Thought* (Oxford, England, Clarendon Press, 1979).

Hammond, Peter B., *Cultural and Social Anthropology. Selected Readings* (New York, Macmillan, 1964).

Hammond, Peter B., *Cultural and Social Anthropology. Introductory Readings in Ethnology,* 2nd edition (New York, Macmillan, 1975). First edition, 1964.

Harris, Marvin, *America Now. The Anthropology of a Changing Culture* (New York, Simon and Schuster, 1981).

Heilbronner, Robert L., *The Future as History* (New York, Harper and Brothers, 1960).

Herskovits, Melville J., *Man and His Works. The Science of Cultural Anthropology* (New York, Alfred A. Knopf, 1964).

Herskovits, Melville J., *The Economic Life of Primitive Peoples* (New York, Alfred A. Knopf, 1940).

Herskovits, Melville J., *Myth of the Negro Past* (Boston, Beacon Press, 1958).

Highwater, Jamake, *The Primal Mind. Vision and Reality in Indian America* (New York, Harper and Row, 1981).

Hinsley, C. M., Jr. *Savages and Scientists: The Smithsonian Institution and the Development of American Anthropology, 1846-1910* (Washington, D. C., Smithsonian Institute Press, 1981).

Hobbes, Thomas, *Leviathan* (London, J. M. Dent, 1940).

Hobson, John, *Imperialism: a Study* (London, George Allen & Unwin, reprinted 1954).

Holmberg, Allan R., *Nomads of the Long Bow. The Siriono of Northern Bolivia* (Garden City, New York, The Natural History Press, 1969).

Hopkins, Charles Howard, *The Rise of the Social Gospel in American Protestantism, 1865-1915* (New Haven, Yale University Press, 1940).

Housego, Jenny, *Tribal Rugs. An Introduction to the Weaving of the Tribes of Iran* (New York, Van Nostrand and Reinhold, 1978).

Hudson, Charles, *The Southeastern Indians* (Knoxville, University of Tennessee Press, 1976).

Hugh-Jones, Christine, *From the Milk River: Spatial and Temporal Processes in Northwest Amazonia* (London, Cambridge University Press, 1979).

Humboldt, Alexander von, *The Life Travels and Books of ..* with an Introduction by Bayard Taylor (New York, Rudd and Carleton, 1959).

Huntington, G. W. B., *Nandi of Kenya: Tribal Control in Pastoral Society* (London, Routledge and Kegan Paul, 1953).

Huxley, Francis, *Affable Savages* (New York, Viking Press, 1957).

Jacobs, Wilbur R., edited and with an introduction by, *The Appalachian Indian Frontier. The Second Atkin Report and Plan 1755* (Lincoln, Nebraska, University of Nebraska Press, 1967).

Jefferson, Thomas, *The Political Writings of Thomas Jefferson. Representative Selections*. Edited with an introduction by Edward Dumbauld (New York, The Liberal Arts Press, 1956).

Jennings, Jesse D. and Hoebel, E. Adamson, editors, *Readings in Anthropology,* 3rd edition (New York, McGraw-Hill, 1972).

Kaberry, Phyllis M., *Aboriginal Women. Sacred and Profane*. (Introduction by Professor A. P. Elkin (Philadelphia, The Blakiston Company, first published 1939).

Kardiner, Abram, editor, *The Individual and His Society. The Psychodynamics of Primitive Social Organization* (New York, Columbia University Press, 1947).

Karsten, Rafael, *The Civilization of the South American Indian. With Special Reference to Magic and Religion* (New York, Alfred A. Knopf, 1926).

Kluckholn, Clyde, *Navaho Witchcraft* (Boston, Beacon Press, 1944).

Kluckholn, Clyde and Leighton, Dorothea, *The Navaho*. The Natural History Library (New York, Doubleday, 1962).

Krieger, Herbert W., *Peoples of the Philippines*. War Background Studies, No. 4, November 1912 (Washington, D. C., Smithsonian Institute, 1912).

Kuper, Adam, *Kalahari Village Politics. An African Democracy* (London, Cambridge University Press, 1970).

Kroeber, A. L., *Cultural and Natural Areas of Native North America*. University of California Publications in American Archaeology and Ethnology, vol. 38 (Berkeley, University of California Press, 1939). Republished by the same press in 1953 and 1963.

La Barre, Weston, "Aymara Indians of the Lake Titicaca Plateau of Bolivia," 1-250 in *American Anthropologist,* vol. 50, No. 1, Part 2, January 1948.

La Barre, Weston, *Culture in Context. Selected Writings* (Durham, North Carolina, Duke University Press, 1980).

La Barre, Weston, *Ghost Dance. Origins of Religion* (Garden City, New York, Doubleday, 1970).

Landreau, Anthony N., editor, *Yoruk. The Nomadic Weaving Tradition of the Middle East* (Pittsburgh, Pennsylvania, Museum of Art, Carnegie Institute, 1978).

Lanternari, Vittorio, *The Religions of the Oppressed. A Study of Modern Messianic Cults*. Translated from the Italian by Lisa Sergio (New York, Alfred A. Knopf, 1963).

Lattimore, Owen, *Inner Asian Frontiers of China* (New York, Capitol Publishing and American Geographical Society, 1951).

Lawrence, D. H., *Mornings in Mexico* (New York, Alfred A. Knopf, 1927).

Leakey, Richard and Lewin, Roger, *People of the Lake. Mankind and Its Beginnings*. (Garden City, New York, Anchor Press, Doubleday, 1978).

Lee, Dorothy D., *Freedom and Culture* (New York, A Spectrum Book, Prentice-Hall, 1958).

Leighton, Dorothea and Kluckholn, Clyde, *Children of the People* (Cambridge, Massachusetts, Harvard University Press, 1947).

Léon-Portilla, Miguel, *Aztec Thought and Culture, a Study of the Nahuatl Mind* (Norman, Oklahoma, University of Oklahoma Press, 1963).

Lett, James, *The Human Enterprise. A Critical Introduction to Anthropological Theory* (Boulder, Colorado, Westview Press, 1987).

Leuzinger, Elsy, *Africa. The Art of the Negro Peoples* (New York, McGraw-Hill, 1960).

Lévi-Strauss, Claude, *Savage Mind* (Chicago, University of Chicago Press, 1966).

Lévi-Strauss, Claude, *Structural Anthropology,* translated from the French by Claire Jacobson and Brooke Grundfest Schoepf (New York, Basic Books, 1963).

Lévi-Strauss, Claude, *Triste Tropique* (Paris, France, Plon Library, 1955).

Lewin, Roger, *Bones of Contention. Controversies in the Search for Human Origins* (New York, Simon and Schuster, 1987).

Lewis, I. M., *A Pastoral Democracy. a Study of Pastoralism and Politics Among the Northern Somali of the Horn of Africa* (New York, International African Institute, Oxford University Press, 1961).

Linton, Ralph, *Tree of Culture* (New York, Alfred A. Knopf, 1955).

Linton, Ralph, "Marquesan Culture," 137-250 in *The Individual and His Society. The Psychodynamics of a Primitive Social Organization* (New York, Columbia University Press, 1947).

Loewen, Jacob A., *Selections from the Writings of Jacob A. Loewen. Cultural and Human Values: Christian Interpretation in Anthropological Perspective* (South Pasadena, California, William Carey Library, no date).

Lowie, Robert, *Selected Papers in Anthropology* (Berkeley, University of California Press, 1960).

Lowie, Robert H., *Indians of the Plains.* American Museum Science Books (Garden City, New York. The Natural History Press, 1963).

MacArthur, Douglas, *Reminiscences, General of the Army ....* (New York, McGraw-Hill, 1964).

McCaull, Julian, editor, *Water Pollution* (New York, Harcourt Brace and Javanovich, 1974).

Malinowski, Bronislaw, *Argonauts of the Western Pacific. An Account of Native Enterprise and Adventure in the Archapelagoes of Melanesia and New Guinea* (London, Routledge & Kegan, 1966).

Malinowski, Bronislaw, *Magic, Science and Religion and Other Essays* (Garden City, New York, Doubleday, 1948).

Malinowski, Bronislaw, *Sex and Repression in Savage Society* (New York, Harcourt Brace, 1927).

Malinowski, Bronislaw, *The Sexual Life of Savages in Northwestern Melanesia....* 2 vols. (London, George Routledge, 1929), I.

Manners, Robert A. and Kaplan, David, editors, *Theory in Anthropology. A Sourcebook* (Chicago, Aldine, 1968).

Mannheim, Karl, *Ideology and Utopia. An Introduction to the Sociology of Knowledge* (New York, Harcourt-Brace, 1940).

Marchal, Léon, *Vichy. Two Years of Deception* (New York, Macmillan, 1943).

Marcham, Frederick George, *A History of England* (New York, Macmillan, 1950).

Marcus, George E. and Fischer, Michael M. J., *Anthropology as a Cultural Critique. An Experimental Moment in the Human Sciences* (Chicago, University of Chicago Press, 1986).

Margolis, Maxine L. and Carter, William E., editors, *Brazil. Anthropological Prospect. Essays in Honor of Charles Wagley* (New York, Columbia University Press, 1979).

Maringer, Johannes and Bandi, Hans Georg, *Art in the Ice Age. Spanish Levant Art, Arctic Art* (New York, Frederick A. Prager, 1953).

Markham, Sir Clements, editor, *Chronicle of Peru by Pedro de Cieza de Leon* (Originally published by the Hakluyt Society and reprinted by Burt Franklin, No. 33 and 68, New York, 1883).

Markham, Sir Clements, *The Incas of Peru*. Second Part of the *Chronicle of Peru by Piedro de Cieza de Leon* (New York, E. P. Dutton, 1911).

Martí, Samuel and Kurath, Gertrude P., *Dances of the Anahuac. The Choreography and Music of Precortesian Dances*. Viking Fund Publication in Anthropology No. 38 (New York, Wenner-Gren Foundation for Anthropological Research, 1964).

Mather, Cotton, *Diary of (1681-1709)*, 2 vols. (New York, Frederick Unger, 1911), I.

Maxwell, Kevin B., *Bemba Myth and Ritual. The Impact of Literacy on an Oral Culture* (New York, Peter Lang, 1983).

Mead, Margaret, *Letters from the Field, 1925-1975*. Planned and edited by Ruth Nanda Anshen (New York, Harper and Row, 1977).

Mead, Margaret, *Sex and Temperament in Three Primitive Societies, From the South Seas* (New York, William Morrow, 1948).

Means, Phillip, *Fall of the Inca Empire and Spanish Rule in Peru* (New York, Scribner's Sons, 1932).

Meggitt, M. J., *Desert People. A Study of the Walbiri Aborigines of Central Australia* (Chicago, University of Chicago Press, 1962).

Montagu, Ashley, *Anthropology and Human Nature* (Boston, Porter Sergent, 1957).

Montagu, Ashley, editor, *The Concept of the Primitive* (New York, Free Press, 1968).

Montagu, Ashley, editor, *Man and Aggression* (New York, Oxford Press, 1968).

Morgan, Lewis, *Ancient Society,* edited by Leslie A. White (Cambridge, Massachusetts, Harvard University Press, 1964).

Mowat, Farley, *People of the Deer* (New York, Pyramid Books, 1952).

Muir, L. P., *African People in the Twentieth Century* (New York, Russell & Russell, 1965).

Mulvaney, John Derek, *The Prehistory of Australia* (New York, Praeger Press, 1969).

Nance, John, *The Gentle Tasaday. A Stone Age People in the Philippine Rain Forest.* Foreword by Charles A. Lindburgh (New York, Harcourt Brace Jovanovich, 1975).

Niebuhr, Reinhold, *Faith and History, a Comparison of Christian and Modern Views of History* (New York, Charles Scribner's Sons, 1949).

Niebuhr, Reinhold, *Leaves from the Notebook of a Tamed Cynic* (Hamden, Connecticut, The Shoestring Press, 1956).

Nietsche, Frederick, *The Birth of Tragedy or Hellinism and Pessimism,* translated by William A. Haussmann (London, T. N. Fullis, 1910).

294

Nisbet, Robert A., *Social Change and History. Aspects of the Western Theory of Development* (New York, Oxford Press, 1969).

Northrop, F. S. C., *The Meeting of East and West. An Inquiry Concerning Understanding* (New York, Macmillan, 1946).

Otten, Charlotte, *Anthropology and Art. Readings in Cross-Cultural Aesthetics* (Garden City, New York, Natural History Press, 1971).

Otto, Rudolph, *The Idea of the Holy. An Inquiry into the non-rational factor in the idea of the divine and its relation to the rational.* Translated by John W. Harvey (London, Oxford University Press, 1946).

Pandian, Jacob, *Anthropology and the Western Tradition* (Prospect Heights, Illinois, Waveland Press, 1985).

Pannikkar, Raimundo, *The Trinity and the Religious Experience of Man. Icon-Person-Mystery* (New York, Orbis Books, 1973).

Parson, Elsie Clews, "Isleta, New Mexico," 193-466 in *47th Annual Report of the Bureau of American Ethnology to the Secretary of the Smithsonian Institute, 1929-1930* (Washington, D. C., Smithsonian Institute, 1932).

Pedersen, Johs., *Israel. Its Life and Culture,* 2 vols. (London, Oxford University Press, 1963).

Pentagon Watchers. Students Report on the National Security State, edited by Leonard S. Rodberg and Derek Shearer (Garden City, New York, Anchor Books, Doubleday, 1970).

Pettitt, George A., *Primitive Education in North America.* California University in American Archaeology and Ethnology, vol. 43, No. 1 (Berkeley, University of California Press, 1946).

Pivan, Frances Fox and Cloward, Richard A., *The New Class War. Reagan's Attack on the Welfare State and Its Consequences* (New York, Pantheon Books, 1982).

Polybius, *The Histories.* With an English Translation by W. R. Paton in six volumes (New York, G. P. Putnam's Sons, 1922), I.

Poulik, Josef, *Prehistoric Art ... Up to Roman Times,* translated by R. F. Samsour (London, Spring Books, no publication date).

Powell, T. G. E., *Prehistoric Art* (New York, Frederick A. Praeger, 1966).

Prescott, William, *History of the Conquest of Peru,* 2 vols. (Boston, Phillips, Samson & Co., 1856), I.

Prescott, William, *History of the Conquest of Mexico* in 3 vols. (New York,

Harper and Brothers, 1849), I.

Quatrafages, Armand de, *The Pygmies,* translated by Frederick Starr (New York, Negro University Press, reprint, 1969).

Radcliffe-Brown, A. R., *Andaman Islanders. A Study in Social Anthropology* (London, Cambridge University Press, 1922).

Radcliffe-Brown, A. R., *Structure and Function in Primitive Society* (New York, Free Press, 1952).

Radin, Paul, *The World of Primitive Man* (New York, Henry Schuman, 1953).

Radin, Paul, *The Autobiography of a Winnebago Indian* (New York, Dover Publishing, 1963).

Rattray, R. S., *The Tribes of Ashanti Hinterlands* (Oxford, England, Clarendon Press, 1969).

Redfield, Robert, *The Folk Culture of Yucatan* (Chicago, University of Chicago Press, 1942).

Redfield, Robert, *The Primitive World and Its Transformation* (Ithaca, Cornell University Press, 1953).

Reichel-Dolmatoff, Gerardo, *Amazonian Cosmos. The Sexual and Religious Symbolism of the Tukano Indians* (Chicago, University of Chicago Press, 1971).

Reischauer, Edwin C., *Japan Past and Present,* 3rd edition revised (New York, Alfred A. Knopf, 1967).

Rivers, W. H. R., *Essays on the Depopulation of Melanesia* (Cambridge, England, Cambridge University Press, 1922).

Rivers, W. H. R., *Medicine, Magic and Religion* (New York, Harcourt Brace, 1927).

Rivers, W. H. R., *History of Melanesian Society,* 2 vols. (Cambridge, England, Cambridge University Press, 1914), I. (Reprinted in Osterhout N. B., The Netherlands, Anthrop Publishing, 1968).

Rivers, W. H. R., *Social Organization* (New York, A. A. Knopf, 1924). Reprinted in London, Dawsons of Pall Mall, 1968.

Rostovtzeff, M., *Rome,* translated from the Russian by J. D. Duff, edited by E. J. Bickerman. Galaxy edition (New York, Oxford University Press, reprint 1967).

Rostovtzeff, M., *The Social and Economic History of the Roman Empire,* 2 vols. (Oxford, England, Clarendon University Press, 1963), I.

Rubin, Jonathan, *The Barking Deer* (New York, George Brazillier, 1974).

Sahlins, Marshall D., *Tribesman* (Englewood Cliffs, New Jersey, Prentice-Hall, 1968).

Sanders, Thomas E. and Peek, Walter, W., *Literature of the American Indian* (Beverly Hills, California, Glencoe Press, 1973).

Sandoz, Mari, *Crazy Horse. The Strange Man of the Oglalas* (Lincoln, University of Nebraska Press, 1962).

Sapir, Edward, *Selected Writings of Edward Sapir in Language, Culture and Personality,* edited by David C. Mandelbaum (Berkeley, University of California Press, 1949).

Sayce, R. U., *Primitive Arts and Crafts. An Introduction to the Study of Material Culture* (New York, Biblio and Tannan, 1963).

Schele, Linda and Miller, Mary E., *The Blood of Kings. Dynasty and Ritual in Maya Art* (Fort Worth, Texas, Kimbell Art Museum, 1986).

Schumacher, E. F., *Small is Beautiful. Economics as if People Mattered* (New York, Harper and Row, 1973).

Scott, William Henry, *The Discovery of the Igorots. Spanish Contacts with the Pagans of Northern Luzon* (Quezon City, Philippines, New Day Publications, 1974).

Semon, Richard, *In the Australian Bush and on the Coast of the Coral Sea* (New York, Macmillan, 1899).

Sennett, Richard and Cobb, Jonathan, *The Hidden Injuries of Class* (New York, Alfred A. Knopf, 1972).

Service, Elman R., *The Hunters.* Foundations of Modern Anthropology Series (Englewood Cliffs, New Jersey, Prentice-Hall, 1966).

Service, Elman R., *A Profile of Primitive Culture* (New York, Harper, 1958).

Shigemitsu, Mamoru, *Japan and Her Destiny. My Struggle for Peace* (New York, E. P. Dutton, 1958).

Shirer, William L., *The Collapse of the Third Republic. An Inquiry into the Fall of France in 1940* (New York, Simon and Schuster, 1969).

Silko, Leslie Marmon, *Ceremony* (New York, Viking Press, 1977).

Smith, Goldwin, *A History of England* (New York, Charles Scribner's Sons, 1949).

Smith, Wilfred Cantwell, *The Meaning and End of Religion. A New Approach to the Religious Tradition of Mankind* (New York, Macmillan, 1963).

Solzhenitsyn, Aleksandr, *Letters to the Soviet Leaders*. Translated from the Russian by Hilary Sternberg (New York, Harper and Row, 1975).

Sophocles, *The Tragedies of....,* translated by E. H. Plumptree (New York, George Routledge, no date).

Spencer, Baldwin and Gillen, F. J., *The Northern Tribes of Central Australia* (New York, Macmillan, 1904).

Spencer, Robert F., *The North Alaskan Eskimo. A Study in Ecology and Society* (Washington, D. C., Bureau of American Ethnology, Smithsonian Institute, 1959). Republished in 1969.

Steffens, Lincoln, *Autobiography* (New York, Literary Guild, 1931).

Stern, Philip M., *The Oppenheimer Case: Security on Trial* (New York, Harper and Row, 1969).

Stites, Raymond S., *The Arts and Man* (New York, McGraw-Hill, 1940).

Tax, Sol, editor, *Horizons of Anthropology* (Chicago, Aldine Publishing Co., 1964).

Taylor, Henry Osborn, *The Classic Heritage of the Middle Ages* (New York, Harper Torchback, Harper and Row, 1958).

Teggart, Frederick J., *Theory and Processes of History* (Berkeley and Los Angeles, University of California Press, 1960).

Theal, George C., *The Yellow and Dark-Skinned People of Africa South of the Zambeisi* (New York, Negro Universities Press, 1910).

Thompson, J. Eric, *The Rise and Fall of Maya Civilization* (Norman, Oklahoma, University of Oklahoma Press, 1955).

Thompson, Laura and Joseph, Alice, *The Hopi Way,* with a Foreword by John Collier, Commissioner of Indian Affairs (Chicago, University of Chicago Press, 1944).

Thucydides, *The Complete Writings of the Peloponnesian War*. The unabridged Crawley translation with an introduction by Joseph Gavarse (New York, Modern Library, 1934).

Titiev, Mischa, *Araucanian Culture in Transition* from the Museum of Anthropology (Ann Arbor, Michigan, University of Michigan Press, 1951).

Toynbee, Arnold, *Civilization on Trial* (New York, Oxford University Press, 1949).

Trowell, Margaret and Neverman, Hans, *African and Oceanic Art* (New York, Henry N. Abrams, 1968).

Turnbull, Colin M., *The Mountain People* (New York, Simon & Schuster, 1972).

Turnbull, Colin M., *The Forest People. A Study of the Pygmies of the Congo. Clarion Book* (New York, Simon and Schuster, 1961).

Turner, Victor, *The Ritual Process: Structure and Anti-Structure* (Chicago, Aldine Press, 1969).

Tylor, E. B., *Primitive Cultures. Researches into the Development of Mythology, Philosophy, Religion, Language and Custom,* 2 vols. (New York, Henry Holt, 1889).

Valliant, George C., *Aztecs of Mexico. Origin, Rise and Fall of the Aztec Nation* (Garden City, New York, Doubleday, 1947).

Van Der Post, Laurens, *The Lost World of the Kalahari* (New York, William Morrow, 1958). (Republished in New York, Harcourt-Brace, 1977).

Vayada, A. P., editor, *Environmental and Cultural Behavior. Ecological Studies in Cultural Anthropology.* American Museum Source Books in Anthropology (Garden City, New York, Natural History Press, 1969).

van Gennep, Arnold, *The Rites of Passage,* translated by M. B. Vizedom and G. L. Caffee. Introduction by Solon T. Kimball (Chicago, University of Chicago Press, 1960).

Veblen, Thorstein, *The Theory of Business Enterprise* (New York, Scribner's Sons, 1935).

Veblen, Thorstein, *Theory of the Leisure Class* (New York, The Modern Library, Random House, 1934).

von Hagen, Wolfgang, *The Ancient Sun Kingdom of the Americas* (Cleveland and New York, World Publishing Co., 1961).

von Hagen, Wolfgang, "The Tsatchela Indians of Western Ecuador"in *Indian Notes and Monographs No. 51.* Museum of the American Indian (New York, Heye Foundation, 1939).

von Humboldt, Alexander, *The Life Travels and Books of.* Introduction by Bayard Taylor (New York, Rudd and Charleton, 1859).

Vonnegut, Kurt, *Palm Sunday. An Autobiographical Collage* (New York, Delacourte Press, 1981).

Von Rad, Gerhard, *Genesis, a Commentary.* The Old Testament Library

(Philadelphia, Pennsylvania, The Westminster Press, 1972).

Wachtel, Paul L., *The Poverty of Affluence. A Psychological Portrait of the American Way of Life* (New York, Free Press, Macmillan, 1983).

Wagley, Charles, "The Social and Religious Life of a Guatemalan Village," 1-150 in *America Anthropologist,* vol. 51, No. 4, Part 2, October 1949.

Wagley, Charles and Galváo, *The Tentehara Indians of Brazil. A Culture in Transition* (New York, Columbia University Press, 1949).

Wagley, Charles, *Welcome of Tears. The Tapirapé Indians of Central Brazil* (New York, Oxford University Press, 1977).

Wassing, René S., *African Art. Its Background and Traditions* (New York, Henry Abrams, 1968).

Waters, Frank, *Book of the Hopi* (New York, Viking Press, 1963). (Also published in New York, Ballantine Books, 1963).

Weber, Max, *Ancient Judaism*. Translated and edited by Hans H. Gerth and Don Martindale (Glencoe, Illinois, The Free Press, 1952).

Weber, Max, *Essays in Sociology*. Translated and Edited and with an Introduction by Hans H. Gerth and C. Wright Mills (New York, Oxford Press, 1953).

Weber, Max, *The Protestant Ethic and the Spirit of Capitalism*. Translated by Talcott Parsons. With a Foreword by R. J. Tawney (New York, Scribner's Sons, 1956).

Weber, Max, *Selections from His Works* with an Introduction by S. M. Miller (New York, Thomas Y. Crowell, 1968).

Weber, Max, *The Sociology of Religion*. Translated by Ephraim Fischoff. Introduction by Talcott Parsons (Boston, Beacon Press, 1963).

Welch, Galbraith, *Africa. Before They Came* (Norman, Oklahoma, University of Oklahoma Press, 1963).

Weltfish, Gene, *The Lost Universe with a Closing Chapter in 'The Universe Regained'* (New York, Basic Books, 1965).

Weltfish, Gene, *The Origins of Art* (Indianapolis, Indiana, Bobbs-Merrill, 1953).

Werth, Alexander, *The Twilight of France, 1933-1940* (New York, Harper, 1942).

White, Leslie A., "The Acomo Indians," 23-192 in *47th Annual Report of* the Bureau of Ethnology to the Secretary of the Smithsonian Institute, Washington, 1929-1930 (Washington, D. C., Smithsonian Institute, 1932).

Willett, Frank, African Art. An Introduction (New York, Frederick A. Praeger, 1971).

Williams, Thomas Rhys, The Dusan. A North Borneo Society (New York, Henry Holt, 1965).

Wilson, James Q., The 1988 Election (Lexington, Massachusetts, D. C., Heath, 1989).

Wingert, Paul, Primitive Art. Its Transition and Styles (New York, Oxford University Press, 1962).

Wingert, Paul, The Tsimshian Indians and Their Arts. The Tsimshian Indians and Their Neighbors (Seattle, University of Washington Press, no date).

Wissler, Clark, The American Indian. An Introduction to the Anthropology of the New World (New York, Oxford University Press, 1922).

Wissler, Clark, The Relation of Nature to Man in Aboriginal America (Originally published in New York by the Oxford University Press, 1926 and later reprinted in New York by AMS Press).

Wolf, Eric, Anthropology (Englewood Cliffs, New Jersey, Prentice-Hall, 1964).

Articles

Acar, Belkis, "Yuncü Nomad Weaving in the Bahkesir Region of Western Turkey," 27-31 in Yörük. The Nomadic Weaving Tradition of the Middle East, edited by Anthony Landreau (Pittsburgh, Pennsylvania, Museum of Art, Carnegie Institute, 1978).

Adams, Robert M., "The Origins of Agriculture," 120-131 in Horizons of Anthropology, edited by Sol Tax (Chicago, Aldine Press, 1964).

Agena, Kathleen, "The Return of Enchantment," 67-80 in The New York Times Magazine, November 27, 1983.

Albrecht, William A., "Physical, Chemical and Biochemical Changes in the Soil Community," 395-418 in Man's Impact on the Environment, edited by Thomas R. Detwyler (New York, McGraw-Hill, 1971).

Asad, Talal, "Anthropological conceptions of religion: reflections on Geertz," 237-259 in Man. The Journal of the Royal Anthropological

Society, vol. 18, No. 2, June 1983.

Asad, Talal, "Anthropology and the Analysis of Ideology," 607-627 in *Man. The Journal of the Royal Anthropological Institute,* vol. 14, No. 4, December 1979.

Asad, Talal, "A Comment on the Idea of Non-Western Anthropology," 284-287 in *Indigeneous Anthropology in Non-Western Countries,* edited by Hussein Fahim (Durham, North Carolina, Carolina Academic Press, 1982).

Ayandele, E. A., "External Influence on African Society," 133-148 in *Africa in the Nineteenth and Twentieth Centuries. A Hand-book for Teachers and Students,* edited by Joseph C. Anene and Godfrey N. Brown (London, Ibadan University Press and Nelson & Son, 1968).

Baran, Paul and Sweezy, Paul, "The Multinational Corporation and Modern Imperialism," 435-441 in *The Capitalist System. A Radical Analysis of American Society.* Written and edited by Richard C. Edwards *et al* (Englewood Cliffs, New Jersey, Prentice-Hall, Inc., 1972).

Barnard, Alan, "Hunting and Gathering Societies. Fourth International Conference," 234-236 in *Current Anthropology,* vol. 28, April 1987.

Barnes, J. A., "Social Science in India: Colonial Import, Indigeneous Product or Universal Truth," 19-34 in *Indigeneous Anthropology in Non-Western Countries,* edited by Hussein Fahim (Durham, North Carolina, Carolina Academic Press, 1982).

Barth, Frederick, "Herdsmen of Southeast Asia," 63-84 in *Cultural and Social Anthropology,* edited by Peter H. Hammond (New York, Macmillan, 1964).

Bartholomew, George A. and Birdsell, Joseph B., "Ecology and Proto-hominids," 481-498 in *American Anthropologist,* vol. 55, No. 4, October 1953.

Bateson, Gregory, "An Old Temple and a New Myth," 291-307 in *Djawa* (Weltevreden, Java), vol. 17, 1937.

Bateson, Gregory, "Bali: The Value of a Steady State," 35-53 in *Social Structure. Studies presented to A. R. Radcliffe-Brown,* edited by Meyer Fortes (New York, Russell & Russell, 1963).

Beard, Charles A., "Introduction" to J. B. Bury, *The Idea of Progress. An Inquiry into Its Origin and Growth* (New York, Dover, 1955).

Beatty, John, "Taking Issue with Lorenz on the Ute," 111-115 in *Man and Aggression,* edited by Ashley Montagu (New York, Oxford Press, 1968).

Benedict, Ruth, "Religion," 627-665 in *General Anthropology,* edited by

Franz Boas (New York, D. C. Heath, 1938).

Berndt, Catherine H. and Ronald M., "Australian Aborigines: Blending Past and Present," 114-131 in *Vanishing Peoples of the Earth* (Washington, D. C., National Geographic, 1968, 1971).

Berndt, Catherine, "The Concept of the Primitive," 7-31 in *The Concept of the Primitive,* edited by Ashley Montagu (New York, Free Press, 1968).

Beyea, Jan and von Hippel, Frank, "Containment of a Reactor Meltdown," 52-61 in *Bulletin of the Atomic Scientist,* August-September, 1982.

Beyer, O. Otley, "The Philippines Before Magellan, I. The Hindus of Malaysia," 861-892 in *Asia,* vol. 21, 1921.

Bidney, David, "The Concept of Value in Modern Anthropology," 682-689 in *Anthropology Today. An Encyclopedic Inventory.* Prepared under the Chairmanship of A. L. Kroeber (Chicago, University of Chicago Press, 1953).

Bingham, Hiram, "The Story of Machu Picchu. The Peruvian Expeditions of the National Geographic Society and Yale University," 172-176 in *National Geographic,* vol. 27, January-June, 1915.

Birdsell, Joseph *et al,* "A Basic Demographic Unit," 337-356 in *Current Anthropology,* vol. 14, No. 4, October, 1973.

Birdsell, Joseph B., "Local Group Competition among the Australian Aborigines: a Critique of the Evidence from Fieldwork Conducted Since 1930," 115-142 in *Current Anthropology,* vol. 11, No. 2, April, 1970.

Blackstone, William T., "Ethics and Ecology," 16-42 in *Philosophy and the Environmental Crisis* (Athens, University of Georgia Press, 1974).

Blumer, Max, "Oil Pollution in the Ocean," 295-301 in *Man's Impact on the Environment,* edited by Thomas R. Detwyler (New York, McGraw-Hill, 1971).

Boas, Franz, "Decorative Art of the North Pacific Coast," 305-317 in *The Golden Age of American Anthropology,* edited by Margaret Mead and Ruth Bunzel (New York, George Braziller, 1960).

Boas, Franz, "Literature, Music and the Dance," 589-608 in *General Anthropology,* edited by Franz Boas (New York, D. C. Heath, 1938).

Boas, Franz, "The Mental Traits of Primitive Man," 404-412 in *The Golden Age of American Anthropology,* edited by Margaret Mead and Ruth Bunzel (New York, George Braziller, 1960).

Bogoras, Waldemar, "The Chukchee," 320-330 in *The Golden Age of American Anthropology*, edited by Margaret Mead and Ruth Bunzel (New York, George Braziller, 1960).

Bohannan, Paul, "An Artist and Critic in an African Society," 738-745 in *Readings in Anthropology*, 2 vols., Edited by Morton H. Fried, *Cultural Anthropology*, II (New York, Thomas Crowell, 1968).

Bohannan, Paul, "The Impact of Money on an African Subsistence Economy," 467-474 in *Readings in Anthropology*, 3rd edition, edited by Jessee D. Jennings and E. Adamson Hoebel (New York, McGraw-Hall, 1972).

Boulding, Kenneth, "Where Are We Going If Anywhere? A Look at Post-Civilization," 368-374 in *Readings in Anthropology*, edited by Jessee D. Jennings and E. Adamson Hoebel, 3rd edition (New York, McGraw-Hill, 1972.

Bryan, E. H., Jr., "Nature's Balance in Hawaii," 269-275 in *Ancient Hawaiian Civilization*, A series of lectures delivered at the Kamehameha Schools, edited by A. S. C. Handy *et al* (Reprinted Tokyo, Japan, Charles E. Tuttle, Publisher, 1975).

Caldwell, John, Pat and Bruce, "Anthropology and Demography," 25-3 in *Current Anthropology*, vol. 28, No. 1, February, 1987.

Carpenter, Edmund, "The Eskimo Artist," 163-171 in *Anthropology and Art. Readings in Cross-Cultural Aesthetics*, edited by Charlotte Otten (Garden City, New York, Natural History Press, 1971).

Carrighar, "War is Not in Our Genes," 37-50 in *Man and Aggression*, edited by Ashley Montagu (New York, Oxford Press, 1968).

Chagnon, Napoleon A., "Yanomamö," 141-186 in *Primitive Worlds. People Lost in Time* (Washington, D. C., National Geographic, 1973).

Chagnon, Napoleon A., "Yanomamö - The Fierce People," 22-31 in *Natural History*, vol. 76, No. 1, January, 1967.

Coe, Michael, "Preface," to *The Blood of Kings. Dynasty and Ritual in Maya Art*, Linda Schele and Mary Ellen Miller (Fort Worth, Texas, Kimbell Art Museum, 1986).

Coelho, Tony, "The foreign greening of America. Outsiders banking moves threatens our ability to compete," in the Los Angeles *Times*, March 26, 1987, Part II, 5.

Coleman, John A., reviewer of *Religion in the Secular City. Toward a Postmodern Theology*, by Harvey Cox in The New York *Times* Book Review, March 4, 1984, Section 7, 1, 36-37.

304

Colson, Elizabeth, "Anthropological Dilemmas in the Late Twentieth Century," 253-262 in *Indigeneous Anthropology in Non-Western Countries*. Proceedings of a Burg Warenstein Symposium. Edited by Hussein Fahim (Durham, North Carolina, Carolina Academic Press, 1982).

Cook, James, "The Discovery of the Hawaiian Islands," 1-10 in *A Hawaiian Reader*, edited by A. Grove Day and Carl Stroven (New York, Appleton-Century-Crofts, 1959).

Cook, O. F., "Staircase Farms of the Ancients. Astounding Skill of Ancient Peruvians ....," 474-534 in *National Geographic*, vol. 29, No. 6, June, 1916.

Cooper, James Montgomery, "The Relation Between Religion and Morality in Primitive Cultures," 560-572 in *The Golden Age of American Anthropology*, edited by Margaret Mead and Ruth Bunzel (New York, George Braziller, 1960).

Crashing Thunder, "The Teachings of My Father," 229-235 in *Readings in Anthropology*, 3rd edition, edited by Jessee D. Jennings and E. Adamson Hoebel (New York, McGraw-Hill, 1972).

Danahay, Deborah Reed and Rogers, Susan Carol, "Anthropological Research in France; Problems and Research Prospects for the Study of Complex Society, Introduction," 51-55 in *Anthropological Quarterly*, vol. 60, No. 2, January-October, 1987.

Delfendahl, Bernard, "On Anthropologists versus Missionaries," *Current Anthropology*, vol. 22, No. 1, February, 1981.

Deloria, Vine, Jr., "An Open Letter to the Heads of Christian Churches in America," 400-407 in *Literature of the American Indian*, edited by Thomas E. Sanders and Walter W. Peek (Beverly Hills, California, Glencoe Press, 1973).

Denny, Walter B., "Turkman Rugs in Historical Perspective," 55-59 in *Yoruk. The Nomadic Weaving Tradition of the Middle East*, edited by Anthony Landreau (Pittsburg, Pennsylvania, Museum of Arts, Carnegie Institute, 1978).

Detwyler, Thomas R., "Summary and Prospect," 695-700 in *Man's Impact on the Environment*, edited by Thomas R. Detwyler (New York, McGraw-Hill, 1971).

Diamond, Stanley, "The Search for the Primitive," 96-147 in *The Concept of the Primitive*, edited by Ashley Montagu (New York, Free Press, 1968).

Dozier, Edward P., "The Concepts of 'Primitive' and 'Native' in Anthropology," 229-256 in *The Concept of the Primitive*, edited by

Ashley Montagu (New York, Free Press, 1968).

Drummond, Lee, "The Cultural Continuum. A Theory of Interpretative Systems," 352-374 in *Man. The Journal of the Royal Anthropological Society,* vol. 15, No. 2, June, 1980.

Drummond, Lee, "Structure and Process in the Interpretation of South American Myth: The Arawak Dog Spirit People," 842-868 in *American Anthropologist,* vol. 79, December, 1977.

Dubos, René, "Man and His Environment: Scope, Impact and Nature," 684-694 in *Man's Impact on Environment,* edited by Thomas R. Detwyler (New York, McGraw-Hill, 1971).

Dyson-Hudson, Rada and Neville, "Subsistence Herding in Uganda," 76-89 in *Scientific American,* vol. 220, February, 1969.

Eckholn, Erik, "Secrets of Maya Decoded at Last: Revealing Darker Human History," New York *Times,* May 13, 1986, C-1.

Eggan, Fred, "Some Aspects of Culture Change in the Northern Philippines," 11-18 in *American Anthropologist,* vol. 43, 1941.

Emory, Kenneth P., "Navigation," 241-249 in *Ancient Hawaiian Civilization.* A Series of Lectures delivered at the Kamehameha Schools, edited by E. S. C. Hand *et al* (Reprinted, Tokyo, Japan, Charles E. Tuttle, 1975).

Emory, Kenneth P., "Warfare," 233-240 in *Ancient Hawaiian Civilization.* A Series of Lectures delivered at the Kamehameha Schools, 1933 (Reprinted Tokyo, Japan, Charles E. Tuttle).

Evans-Pritchard, E. E., "Nuer Rules of Exogamy and Incest," 85-103 in *Social Structure. Studies Presented to A. R. Radcliffe-Brown,* edited by Meyer Fortes (New York, Russell & Russell, 1963).

Farhi, Paul, Washington Post, "Tinsel town isn't all that glitters," in the Kansas City *Star,* November 26, 1989, G-1, 6.

Firth, Raymond, "Authority and Public Opinion in Tikopia," 168-188 in *Social Structure. Studies Presented to Radcliffe-Brown* (New York, Russell and Russell, 1963).

Firth, Raymond, "Studying and Restudying Tikopia," 142-158 in *Readings in Anthropology,* 2 vols., edited by Morton H. Fried, *Cultural Anthropology,* (New York, Thomas Y. Crowell, 1968), II.

Foreman, Kenneth, "Eschatology," 392-393 in *Twentieth Century Encyclopedia of Religious Knowledge,* editor-in-chief Lefferts A. Loetscher (Grand Rapids, Michigan, Baker Book House, 1955).

Fortes, Meyer, "The Political System of the Tallensi of the Northern Territory of the Gold Coast," 239-271 in *African Political Systems,* edited by Meyer Fortes and E. E. Evans-Pritchard (New York, Oxford University Press, 1966).

Garfield, Eugene, "Anthropological Journals: What They Cite and Who Cites Them," 514-528 in *Current Anthropology,* vol. 25, No. 4, August-October 1984.

Geertz, Clifford, "Culture and Social Change: the Indonesian Case," 511-532 in *Man. The Journal of the Royal Anthropological Society,* vol. 19, No. 4, December 1984.

Geertz, Clifford, "Distinguished Lecturer: Anti-Revisionism," 263-278 in *American Anthropologist,* vol. 85, No. 2, June, 1984.

George, Katherine, "The Civilized West Looks at Primitive Africa: A Study in Ethnocentrism," 175-193 in *The Concept of the Primitive,* edited by Ashley Montagu (New York, Free Press, 1968).

Gerbands, Adrian A., "Art as an Element of Culture in Africa," 366-382 in *Anthropology and Art. Readings in Cross-Cultural Aesthetics,* edited by Charlotte M. Otten for the American Museum of Natural History (New York, Natural History Press, 1971).

Gilliard, E. T., "In the Land of the Head-Hunters," 437-486 in *National Geographic,* vol. 108, October, 1955.

Gilliard, E. T., "New Guinea's Rare Birds and Stone Age Men," 421-488 in *National Geographic,* vol. 103, April, 1953.

Gillison, Gillian, "Fertility Rites and Sorcery in a New Guinea Village," 124-146 in *National Geographic,* vol. 152, No. 1, July, 1977.

Gluckman, Max, "The Role of the Sexes in Wiko Circumcision Ceremonies," 145-167 in *Social Structure, Studies presented to Radcliffe-Brown,* edited by Meyer Fortes (New York, Russell & Russell, 1963).

Gluckman, Max, "Kingdon of the Zulu of South Africa, " 25-55 in *African Political Systems,* edited by Meyer Fortes and E. E. Evans-Pritchard (New York, Oxford University Press, 1966).

Goffman, Erving, "The Nature of Deference and Demeanor," 473-502 in *American Anthropologist,* vol. 58, 1956.

Gorer, Geoffrey, "Man Has No 'Killer' Instinct," 27-36 in *Man and Aggression,* edited by Ashley Montagu (New York, Oxford Press, 1968).

Gray, J. Patrick, "Do Women Have Higher Social Status in Hunting Societies Without High Gods?," 1121-1131 in *Social Forces. An International*

Journal of Social Research, vol. 65, No. 4, June, 1987.

Gray, J. R., "The Missionary Factor in East Africa," 458-471 in *Africa in the Nineteenth and Twentieth Centuries. A Handbook for Teachers and Students,* edited by Joseph C. Anene and Godfrey N. Brown (London, Ibadan University Press and Nelson & Son, 1968).

Gregor, Thomas, "Secrets, Exclusion and Dramatization of Man's Roles," 260-269 in *Brazil. Anthropological Prospect. Essays in Honor of Charles Wagley,* edited by Maxine L. Margolis and William E. Carter (New York, Columbia University Press, 1979).

Griffin, C. C., "The Significance of Native Indian Culture in Hispanic America," 104-123 in *Concerning Latin American Culture .... ,* edited by C. C. Griffin (New York, Columbia University Press, 1944).

Grinnel, George Bird, "The Cheyenne Indians," 139-148 in *The Golden Age of American Anthropology,* selected and edited with introduction and notes by Margaret Mead and Ruth Bunzel (New York, George Braziller, 1960).

Grinnel, George Bird, "The Disappearance of the Buffalo," 148-150 in *The Golden Age of American Anthropology,* edited by Margaret Mead and Ruth Bunzel (New York, George Braziller, 1960).

Gross, Daniel R., "A New Approach to Central Brazilian Social Organization," 321-342 in *Brazil. Anthropological Prospect. Essays in Honor of Charles Wagley,* edited by Maxine L. Margolis and William E. Carter (New York, Columbia University Press, 1979).

Gross, Daniel R., Ecology and Acculturation Among the Native People of Brazil," 1043-1050 in *Science,* vol. 206, No. 4422, November 30, 1979.

Gunther, Erna, "Northwest Coast Art," 18-40 in *Anthropology and Art. Readings in Cross-Cultural Aesthetics,* edited by Charlotte M. Otten. Published for the American Museum of Natural History (Garden City, New York, Natural History Press, 1971).

Hage, Per, "On Male Initiation and Dual Organization in New Guinea," 268-285 in *Man. The Journal of the Royal Anthropological Society,* vol. 16, No. 2, 1981.

Handy, E. S. C., "Feasts and Holidays," 61-68 in *Ancient Hawaiian Civilization.* A Series of Lectures delivered at the Kamehameha Schools, edited by A. S. C. Handy *et al,* (Reprinted, Tokyo, Japan, Charles E. Tuttle, 1975).

Handy, E. S. C., "Government and Society," 35-46 in *Ancient Hawaiian Civilization,* a Series of Lectures delivered at the Kamehameha

Schools, 1933. (Reprinted, Tokyo, Japan, Charles E. Tuttle, 1975).

Harding, Jim, "Three Mile Island. Three Years After," 20-23 in *Sierra*, March-April, 1982.

Harris, Marvin, "Yanamamö and the Cause for War in Band and Village Societies," 121-132 in *Brazil. Anthropological Prospect, Essays in Honor of Charles Wagley*, edited by Maxine L. Margolis and William E. Carter (New York, Columbia University Press, 1979).

Herskovits, Melville, "Before the Machine," 201-214 in *Readings in Anthropology*, 2 vols., edited by Morton H. Fried, *Cultural Anthropology* (New York, Thomas Y. Crowell, 1968), II.

Herskovits, Melville J. and Bascom, William R., "The Problem of Stability and Change in African Cultures," 1-14 in *Continuity and Change in African Cultures*, edited by William E. Bascom and Melville J. Herskovits (Chicago, University of Chicago Press, 1962).

Hope, Christine A. and Stover, Ronald G., "Gender Status, Monotheism, and Social Complexity: Response to Gray," 1132-1138 in *Social Forces. An International Journal of Social Research Associated with the Southern Sociological Society*, vol. 65, No. 4, June, 1987.

Horton, Robin, "Ritual Man in Africa," 651-673 in *Readings in Anthropology*, 2 vols., edited by Morton H. Fried, *Cultural Anthropology* (New York, Thomas Y. Crowell, 1968), II.

Hsü, Francis L. K., "Rethinking the Concept 'Primitive'," 32-63 in *The Concept of the Primitive*, edited by Ashley Montagu (New York, Free Press, 1968).

Iacocca, Lee, Guest Columnist in the Kansas City *Times*, January 29, 1987, C-1.

Jacobsen, Thorkild and Adams, Robert M., "Salt and Silt in Ancient Mesopotamian Agriculture," 383-394 in *Man's Impact on Environment*, edited by Thomas R. Detwyler (New York, McGraw-Hill, 1971).

Jarves, James J., "Between Heathenism and Missionarism," 69-81 in *Hawaiian Reader*, edited by A. Grove Day and Carl Stroven (New York, Appleton Century Crofts, 1959).

Johnson, William Weber, "Two new exhibitions explore the dark mysteries of the Maya," 39-49 in *Smithsonian*, vol. 17, No. 2, May, 1986.

Karathedoris, Stephen, "From Social to Cultural Systems and Beyond: Twenty Years After, 'Religion as a Cultural System'," 53-94 in *Soundings. An Interdisciplinary Journal*, vol. 81, No. 1, 1988.

Kashoki, Mubanga, "Indigeneous Scholarship in African Universities: the Human Factor," 35-51 in *Indigenous Anthropology in Non-Western Countries,* edited by Hussein Fahim (Durham, North Carolina, Carolina Academic Press, 1982).

Kaul, Donald, Tribune Media Services, "The Cold War is over and its clear who lost - but who, really, won?" in the Kansas City *Times,* December 7, 1989, A-21.

Kehoe, Alice B., "Revisionist Anthropology: Aboriginal North America," 503-517 in *Current Anthropology,* vol. 22, No. 5, October, 1981.

Kelman, Herbert C., "A Changing Social Science for a Changing World; a Social Psychologist's Perspective," 269-283 in *Indigenous Anthropology in Non-Western Countries,* edited by Hussein Fahim (Durham, North Carolina, Carolina Academic Press, 1982).

Kipling, Rudyard, "The White Man's Burden," 292-293 in *The Quest for a Principle of Authority in Europe, 1715 to the Present. Select Problems in Historical Interpretation,* edited by Mendenhall *et al* (New York, Holt, Rinehart and Winston, 1948).

Kirk, Malcolm, "Journey into Stone Age New Guinea," 568-592 in *National Geographic,* vol. 135, April, 1969.

Knight, Chris, "Lévi-Strauss and the Dragon: Mythologies reconsidered in to the light of an Australian Aboriginal Myth," 21-50 in *Man. The Journal of the Royal Anthropological Institute,* vol. 18, No. 1, March, 1983.

Koentjaraningrat, "Anthropology in Developing Countries," 176-192 in *Indigenous Anthropology in Non-Western Countries,* edited by Hussein Fahim (Durham, North Carolina, Carolina Academic Press, 1982).

Krader, Lawrence, "The Ecology of Nomadic Pastorals," 499-510 in *International Social Science Journal,* vol. 11, 1959.

La Barre, Weston, "Materials for a History of Studies of Crisis Cults, a Bibliographical Essay," 3-44 in *Current Anthropology,* vol. 12, No. 1, February, 1971.

Lambert, S. M., "The Depopulation of Pacific Races," 42 pages (Honolulu, Hawaii, published by the Museum, 1934).

Landreau, Anthony N., "Introduction: the Yoruks and Their Weaving," 11-16 in *Yoruk. The Nomadic Weaving Tradition of the Middle East,* edited by Anthony N. Landreau (Pittsburgh, Pennsylvania, Museum of Art, Carnegie Institute, 1978).

Lattimore, Owen D., "The Frontier in History," 374-386 in *Theory in*

Anthropology. A Source Book, edited by Robert A. Manners and David Kaplan (Chicago, Aldine, 1968).

Leo, John, "Bursting the South Sea Bubble," 68-70 in *Time,* February 14, 1983.

Lesser, Alexander, "The Right Not to Assimilate," 583-593 in *Readings in Anthropology,* 2 vols. *Cultural Anthropology,* edited by Morton F. Fried (New York, Thomas Crowell, 1968), II.

Levine, Morton R., "Prehistoric Art and Ideology," 708-724 in *Readings in Anthropology,* 2 vols., edited by Morton H. Fried, *Cultural Anthropology* (New York, Crowell, 1968), II.

Lévi-Strauss, Claude, interview in the New York Times, December 31, 1969 from the Introduction, ft. 2 in *Ecology and Religion in History,* edited by David and Eileen Spring (New York, Harper Torchback, Harper and Row, 1974).

Lévi-Strauss, Claude, "Social Structure," 524-553 in *Anthropology Today. An Encyclopedic Inventory.* Prepared under the chairman-ship of A. L. Kroeber (Chicago, University of Chicago Press, 1953).

Lewis, Anthony, New York Times News Service, Boston, "Grotesque disparity in party resources," in the Kansas City *Times,* February 16, 1987, B-8.

Linton, Ralph, "Analysis of Tanala Culture," 291-351 in *Individual and His Society, The Psychodynamics of Primitive Social Organization,* edited by Abram Kardiner (New York, Columbia University Press, 1947).

Linton, Ralph and Wingert, Paul, Introduction from "Arts of the South Seas," 383-404 in *Anthropology and Art. Readings in Cross-Cultural Aesthetics,* edited by Charlotte Otten (Garden City, New York, Natural History Press, 1971).

Livingston, Frank B., "Human Populations," 60-70 in *Horizons of Anthropology,* edited by Sol Tax (Chicago, Aldine Press, 1964).

Lowie, Robert H., "The Crow Indians," 362-376 in *The Golden Age of American Anthropology,* edited by Margaret Mead and Ruth Bunzel (New York, George Braziller, 1960).

Lugard, F. D., "The Rise of Our East African Empire," 291-292 in *The Quest of a Principle of Authority in Europe, 1715 to the Present. Select Problems in Historical Interpretation,* edited by Thomas C. Mendenhall *et al* (New York, Holt, Rinehart and Winston, 1948).

Luther, Martin, "Treatise on Christian Liberty," 301-348 in *Works of Martin Luther with Introduction and Notes.* The Philadelphia edition, 6 vols. (Philadelphia, Pennsylvania, Muhlenberg Press, 1915), II.

McGraw, Mike, "Thanksgiving treat a tragedy for some. Workers critical of two Missouri turkey processing plants," in the Kansas City *Star,* November 19, 1989, A-1.

McIntyre, Loren, "The Lost Empire of the Incas," 729-787 in *National Geographic,* vol. 144, No. 6, December, 1973.

MacIver, Robert Morrison, "Social Causation and Change," 121-138 in *Twentieth Century Sociology,* edited by Georges Gurvitch and Wilbert E. Moore (New York, Philosophical Library, 1945).

MacLeish, Kenneth, "Stone Age Cavemen of Mindanao," 219-249 in *National Geographic,* vol. 142, No. 2, August, 1972.

Madan, T. N., "Indigenous Anthropology in Non-Western Countries: An Overview," 263-268 in *Indigenous Anthropology in Non-Western Countries,* edited by Hussein Fahim (Durham, North Carolina, Carolina Academic Press, 1982).

Marcus, George E., "The Predicaments of Business Dynasties as Critical Perspectives on the American Middle-Class Family," 169-177 in *Anthropology as Cultural Critique. An Experimental Moment in the Human Sciences,* edited by George E. Marcus and Michael M. J. Fischer (Chicago, University of Chicago Press, 1986).

Margolies, Luise, "Problems of Anthropological Revolution in Latin America," 451-452 in *Current Anthropology,* Vol. 23, No. 4, August, 1982.

Martin, F., "Eschatology (In the Bible)," 524-533 in the *New Catholic Encyclopedia,* V Washington, D. C., McGraw-Hill, 1967).

Matthews, John Joseph (Osage), "The Indian Agent Visits Gray Bird," 424-431 in *Literature of the American Indian,* edited by Thomas E. Sanders and Walter W. Peek (Beverly Hills, California, Glencoe Press, 1973).

Matthews, Washington, "The Night Chant: A Navaho Ceremony," 220-226 in *The Golden Age of American Anthropology,* edited by Margaret Mead and Ruth Bunzel (New York, George Braziller, 1960).

Matthiessen, Peter, "The Death of Weake," 53-60 in *Harpers,* vol. 225, October, 1962.

Mead, Margaret, "The Arapesh of New Guinea," 20-50 in *Cooperation and Competition among Primitive Peoples,* edited by Margaret Mead (New York, McGraw-Hill, 1937).

Mead, Margaret, "A Letter from Tambunam," 22-26 in *Redbook,* vol. 131, No. 4, August, 1968.

312

Mead, Margaret and Bunzel, Ruth, "The Mental Traits of Primitive Man," 404-412 in *The Golden Age of American Anthropology,* edited by Margaret Mead and Ruth Bunzel (New York, George Braziller, 1960).

Mead, Margaret, "The Mountain-Dwelling Arapesh," 3-166 in *From the South Seas. Studies of Adolescence and Sex in Primitive Societies,* edited by Margaret Mead, (New York, William Morrow, 1939).

Mead, Margaret, "Return to Manus," 60-69 in *Natural History,* vol. 85, No. 6, June-July, 1976.

Mead, Margaret, "What I Learned from Three Cultures, The Lost, the Gentle and the Fierce," 40-47 in *Redbook,* vol. 140, No. 3, January, 1973.

Means, Philip A., "The Incas: Empire Builders of the Andes," 225-264 in *National Geographic,* vol. 83, No. 1, January, 1938.

Meggers, Betty J., "Environmental Limitation to the Development of Culture," 19-45 in *Environments of Man,* edited by Jack B. Bresler (Menlo Park, California, Addison-Wesley Publishing Company, 1968).

Merton, Robert K., "Puritanism, Pietism and Science," 574-606 in *Social Theory and Social Structure.* Revised and enlarged (Glencoe, Illinois, Free Press, 1961).

Messenger, John C., Jr., "Religious Acculturation among the Anang Ibibio," 279-299 in *Continuity and Change in African Cultures,* edited by William R. Bascom and Melville J. Herskovits (Chicago, University of Chicago Press, 1962).

Milan, Fred A., "The Indomitable Eskimo. Master of a Frozen World," 132-151 in V*anishing Peoples of the Earth* (Washington, D. C., National Geographic, 1971).

Miller, Arthur P., Jr., "Hopis: 'The Peaceful Ones' Confront the Twentieth Century," 170-184 in V*anishing Peoples of the Earth* (Washington, D. C., National Geographic, 1971).

Miner, Horace, "Body Ritual among the Nacirema," Reprinted from *American Anthropologist,* vol. 58 (1956) 503-507 in *Students and Society,* edited by Jerome Rabow (Pacific Palisades, California, Goodyear Publishing, 1972).

Montagu, Ashley, "The Concept of 'Primitive' and Related Anthropological Terms: A Study in the Systematics of Confusion," 148-168 in *The Concept of the Primitive,* edited by Ashley Montagu (New York, Free Press, 1968).

Montagu, Ashley, "The Fallacy of the 'Primitive,'" 1-6 in *The Concept of the Primitive*, edited by Ashley Montagu (New York, Free Press, 1968).

Montagu, Ashley, "Primitive Art," 169-174 in *The Concept of the Primitive*, edited by Ashley Montagu (New York, Free Press, 1968).

Mooney, James, "The Ghost Dance Religion," 257-274 in *The Golden Age of American Anthropology*, edited by Margaret Mead and Ruth Bunzel (New York, George Braziller, 1960).

Morales, F. Melina, "The Building of Tenochtitian," 753-766 in *National Geographic*, vol. 158, No. 6, December, 1980.

Morauta, Louis, "Indigenous Anthropology in Papua New Guinea," 561-576 in *Current Anthropology*, vol. 20, No. 3, September, 1979.

Morley, Sylvanus G., "Yucatan, Home of the Gifted Maya," 591-644 in *National Geographic*, vol. 70, No. 5, November, 1936.

Mott, Luiz R. B., "Indigenous Anthropology and the Brazilian Indian," 112-120 in *Indigenous Anthropology in Non-Western Countries*, edited by Hussein Fahim (Durham, North Carolina, Carolina Academic Press, 1982).

Mountford, Charles P., "Earth's Most Primitive People. A Journey with the Aborigines of Central Australia," 89-102 in *National Geographic*, vol. 89, No. 1, 1946.

Murphy, Robert F., "Social Structure and Sexual Antagonism," 89-98 in *Southwestern Journal of Anthropology*, vol. 15, 1959.

Mydans, Seth, "The Tasaday Revisited: A Hoax or a Social Change at Work," New York Times, May 13, 1986, C-3.

Mynatt, F. R., "Nuclear Reactor Safety Research Since Three Mile Island," 131-135 in *Science*, vol. 216, No. 4542, April 9, 1982.

Nadel, S. F., "On Social Structure," 220-228 in *Theory in Anthropology. A Source Book*, edited by Robert Manners and David Kaplan (Chicago, Aldine Press, 1968).

Naderi, Nader Afshar, "Some Considerations Regarding Anthropological Dilemmas," 242-249 in *Indigenous Anthropology in Non-Western Countries*, edited by Hussein Fahim (Durham, North Carolina, Carolina Academic Press, 1982).

Neikirk, William R., Chicago Tribune, Washington, "'Competitiveness' a meaningless word," in the Kansas City *Star*, August 6, 1987, B-6.

Newman, Philip, "Sorcery, Religion and Man," 21-29 in *Natural History*, vol. 71, February, 1962.

Nyham, David, Boston Globe, "Japanese investors are buying a lot more," in the Kansas City *Star,* April 14, 1987, A-9.

O'Bannon, George, "Baluchi Rugs," 62-64 in *Yoruk. The Nomadic Weaving Tradition of the Middle East,* edited by Anthony N. Landreau (Pittsburgh, Pennsylvania, Museum of Art, Carnegie Institute, 1978).

Oberg, K., "The Kingdom of the Ankele in Uganda," 121-162 in *African Political Systems,* edited by Meyer Fortes and E. E. Evans-Pritchard (New York, Oxford University Press, 1966).

Ottenberg, Simon, "Ibo Receptivity to Change," 130-143 in *Continuity and Change in African Cultures,* edited by William R. Bascom and Melville J. Herskovits (Chicago, University of Chicago Press, 1962).

Paine, Robert, "Animals as Capital: Comparisons Among Northern Nomadic Hunters and Herders," 157-170 in "Comparative Studies of Nomadism and Pastoralism," [104-210] edited by Philip Salzman in *Anthropological Quarterly,* vol. 44, 1971.

Pettitt, George A., "The Vision Quest and the Guardian Spirit," 265-271 in *Readings in Anthropology,* 3rd edition, edited by Jessee D. Jennings and E. Adamson Hobel (New York, McGraw-Hill, 1972).

Rappaport, Roy A., "Ritual Regulation of Environmental Relations Among a New Guinea People," 181-201 in *Environmental and Cultural Behavior. Ecological Studies in Cultural Anthropology,* edited by A. P. Vayada (Garden City, New York, Natural History Press, 1969).

Redfield, Robert, "Art and the Icon," 39-65 in *Anthropology and Art. Readings in Cross-Cultural Aesthetics,* edited by Charlotte Otten (Garden City, New York, Natural History Press, 1971).

Richards, Audrey L., "The Political Systems of the Bemba Tribe in Northeastern Rhodesia," 83-120 in *African Political Systems,* edited by Meyer Fortes and E. E. Evans-Pritchard (New York, Oxford University Press, 1966).

Ross, Marc Howard, "The Limits to Social Structure: Social Structural and Psychocultural Explanations for Political Conflict and Violence," 171-176 in *Anthropological Quarterly,* vol. 59, No. 4, October, 1986.

Roth, Julius A., "Ritual and Magic in the Control of Contagion," 310-314 in *American Sociological Review,* vol. 22, 1957.

Ruthberg, Sidney, Fairchild News Services, "Bargains like this are few indeed," in the Kansas City S*tar,* January 20, 1987, A-4.

Sahlins, Marshall D., "Culture and Environment: the Study of Cultural Ecology," 132-147 in *Horizons of Culture,* edited by Sol Tax (Chicago, Aldine Press, 1964).

Sahlins, Marshall D., "Tribesmen in History and Anthropology," 194-211 in *Concept of the Primitive,* edited by Ashley Montagu (New York, Free Press, 1968).

Salzman, Phillip, editor, "Comparative Studies in Nomadism and Pastoralism," 104-210 in *Anthropological Quarterly,* vol. 44, 1970-1971.

Salzman, Phillip Carl, "Is Traditional Fieldwork Outmoded," 528-583 in *Current Anthropology,* vol. 27, No. 5, December, 1986.

Sanders, Thomas E. and Peek, Walter W., "Anguished, Angry and Articulate," 445-451 in *Literature of the American Indian,* edited by Thomas E. Sanders and Walter W. Peek (Beverly Hills, California, Glencoe Press, 1973).

Schmithals, Walter, "Eschatology," 154-161 in *Dictionary of the History of Jesus. Studies of Selected Pivotal Ideas.* Philip P. Weiner, editor-in-chief, (New York, Charles Scribner's Sons, 1973), II.

Schneider, Harold K., "Pakot Resistance to Change,"144-167 in *Continuity and Change in African Culture,* edited by William R. Bascom and Melville J. Herskovits (Chicago, University of Chicago Press, 1962).

Schoen, Ivan L., "Contact with the Stone Age," 10-18 in *Natural History,* vol. 77, No. 1, January, 1969.

Schultz, Harald, "The Waura. Brazilian Indians of the Hidden Xingu," 130-152 in *National Geographic,* vol. 129, No. 1, January, 1966.

Schultz, Vilma Chiara, "Indians of Central Brazil: A Struggle to Survive," 152-169 in_*Vanishing Peoples of the Earth* (Washington D. C., National Geographic, 1971).

Shapiro, Judith, "The Tapirapé During the Era of Reconstruction," 61-85 in *Brazil. Anthropological Prospect. Essays in Honor of Charles Wagley,* edited by M. L. Margolis and William E. Carter (New York, Columbia University Press, 1979).

Sharp, Lariston, "Steel Axes for Stone Age Australians," 346-352 in *Readings in Anthropology,* 3rd edition, edited by Jessee D. Jennings and E. Adamson Hoebel (New York, McGraw-Hill, 1972).

Sharp, Lariston, "Technological Innovation and Culture Change: An Australian Case," 84-93 in *Cultural and Social Anthropology. Select Readings,* edited by Peter Hammond (New York, Macmillan, 1964).

Sieber, Roy, "The Arts and Their Changing Function," 203-211 in *Anthropology and Art. Readings in Cross-Cultural Aesthetics,* edited by Charlotte Otten (Garden City, New York, Natural History Press, 1971).

Skeat, W. W., "Wild Tribes of the Malay Peninsula," 463-476 in *Smithsonian Institute Annual Reports, 1902* (Washington, D. C., Smithsonian Institute, 1902).

Sörbö, Gunnar M., "Anthropology at Home and Abroad: A Discussion of Epistemological and Ethical Issues," 152-163 in *Indigenous Anthropology in Non-Western Countries,* edited by Hussein Fahim (Durham, North Carolina, Carolina Academic Press, 1982).

Sorenson, Richard E., "Growing Up as a Fore is to be 'in-touch' and 'free'," 107-115 in *Smithsonian,* vol. 8, No. 2, May, 1977.

Sorenson, Richard E., "Mbotgate," 33-56 in *Primitive Worlds. People Lost in Time* (Washington, D. C., National Geographic, 1973).

Sowada, Father Alphonse, "New Guinea's Fierce Asmat: a Heritage of Head-Hunting," 186-203 in *Vanishing Peoples of the Earth* (Washington, D. C., National Geographic, 1971).

Spaulding, Albert C., "Distinguished Lectures; Archaeology and Anthropology," 263-271 in *American Anthropologist,* vol. 90, No. 2, June, 1988.

Steinem, Gloria, "If Men Could Menstruate," 337-340 in *Outrageous Acts and Everyday Rebellions* (New York, Holt, Rinehart and Winston, 1983).

Steward, Julian and Faron, Louis C., "The Nomadic Hunters and Gatherers: The Chono, Alacaluf, and Others," 43-53 in *Cultural and Social Anthropology. Selected Readings,* edited by Peter B. Hammond (New York, Macmillan, 1965).

Steward, Julian H., "The Development of Early Civilizations," 640-657 in *Readings in Anthropology, 2 vols., edited by Morton Fried, Physical Anthropology, Linguistics, and Archaeology,* (New York, Thomas Crowell, 1968), I.

Stirling, Matthew W., "Vanishing Cultures Mirror the Yesterdays of Man," 8-35 in *Vanishing Peoples of the Earth* (Washington, D. C., National Geographic, 1968).

Stranahan, Susan Q., "Three Mile Island. It's Worse than You Think," 54-57 plus in *Science Digest,* vol. 93, No. 6, June, 1985.

Strathern, Marilyn, "Out of Context: the Pervasive Fictions of Anthropology," 251-281 in *Current Anthropology,* vol. 28, No. 3, June, 1987.

Sweet, Louise, "Camel Pastoralism in North Arabia," 157-180 in *Environmental and Cultural Behavior. Ecological Studies in Cultural Anthropology,* edited by A. P. Vayada. Published by the Museum of Natural History (New York, Natural History Press, 1969).

Tax, Sol, "Primitive Man vs. Homo Sapiens," 81-95 in *Concept of the Primitive,* edited by Ashley Montagu (New York, Free Press, 1968).

Tax, Sol, "'Primitive' Peoples," 64-80 in *The Concept of the Primitive,* edited by Ashley Montagu (New York, Free Press, 1968).

Testart, Alain, "Game-Sharing Systems and Kinship Systems Among Hunter-Gatherers," 287-304 in *Man. The Journal of the Royal Anthropological Institute,* vol. 22, June, 1987.

Testart, Alain, "Some Major Problems in the Social Anthropology of Hunter-Gatherers," 1-13 in *Current Anthropology,* vol. 29, No. 1, February, 1988.

Thomas, Elizabeth Marshall, "The Bushmen: Gentle Nomads of Africa's Harsh Kalahari," 58-75 in *Vanishing Peoples of the Earth* (Washington, D. C., National Geographic, 1971).

Thompson, Laura, "Applied Anthropology and the Development of a Science of Man," 594-616 in *Readings in Anthropology,* 2 vols. *Cultural Anthropology,* 2nd edition, edited by Morton H. Fried (New York, Thomas Y. Crowell, 1968), II.

Tillich, Paul, "History as the Problem of Our Period," *Review of Religion,* vol. 3, 1939.

Tremearne, A. J. N., "Notes on the Kagora and Other Nigerian Head-Hunters," 136-199 in *The Journal of the Royal Anthropological Institute,* vol. 43, 1912.

Ucko, Peter J. and Rosenfeld, Andrée, "Critical Analysis of Interpretations and Conclusions from Paleolithic Cave Art," 247-281 in *Anthropology and Art. Readings in Cross-Cultural Aesthetics,* edited by Charlotte Otten (Garden City, New York, Natural History Press, 1971).

Urban, C. Stanley, "The Ideology of Southern Imperialism: New Orleans and the Caribbean, 1845-1860," 48-73 in *The Louisiana Historical Quarterly,* vol. 39, No. 1, January 1956.

Urban, C. Stanley, "New Orleans and the Cuban Question During the Lopez Expeditions of 1849-1851. A Local Study in 'Manifest Destiny'," 3-75 in *The Louisiana Historical Quarterly,* vol. 22, No. 4, October 1939.

Urban, C. Stanley, "Veblen's Analysis of American Capitalism," 9 pp., 4 May 1970, Park College, Parkville, Missouri.

318

Wagley, Charles, "Cultural Influences on Population: a Comparison of Two Tupi Tribes," 268-280 in *Environmental and Cultural Behavior. Ecological Studies in Cultural Anthropology,* edited by Andrew P. Vayada (New York, Natural History Press, 1969).

Wagley, Charles, "Economics of a Guatemalan Village," 1-85 in *Supplement to American Anthropologist,* vol. 43, No. 3, Part 3, 1941.

Wagley, Charles, "Tapirapé Shamanism," 617-635 in *Readings in Anthropology,* 2 vols. *Cultural Anthropology,* II, edited by Morton H. Fried (New York, Thomas Crowell, 1968).

Wagner, Gunter, "The Political Organization of the Bantu of Kavirondo," 197-236 in *African Political Systems,* edited by Meyer Fortes and E. E. Evans-Pritchard (New York, Oxford University Press, 1966).

Walker, J. R., "The Sun Dance of the Oglala," 377-391 in *The Golden Age of American Anthropology,* edited by Margaret Mead and Ruth Bunzel (New York, George Braziller, 1960).

Walsh, Edward J., "Three Mile Island: the Battle of Unit 1," 30-31 in *Bulletin of Atomic Scientists,* vol. 41, No. 5, May, 1985.

Ward, W. E. F., "Colonial Rule in West Africa," 308-325 in *Africa in the Nineteenth and Twentieth Centuries. A Handbook for Teachers and Students,* edited by Joseph C. Anene and Godfrey N. Brown (London, Ibadan University Press and Nelson & Son, 1968).

Warrior, Clyde, "Which One Are You? Five Types of Young Indians," 521-523 in *Literature of the American Indian,* edited by Thomas E. Sanders and Walter W. Peek (Beverly Hills, California, Glencoe Press, 1973).

Weir, Elizabeth, Congressional Quarterly, Inc., Washington, "No dire predictions from the seers - yet," in the Kansas City *Star,* July 29, 1987, K-3.

Weisman, Steven R., "Japan advises U.S. to clear up its act," in the Kansas City *Times,* November 20, 1989, A-1.

Wendt, Albert, "Three Faces of Samoa: Mead's, Freeman's and Wendt's," 10-14 in *Pacific Island Monthly,* April, 1983.

Wheatcroft, Wilson, "Tifalmin," 54-84 in *Primitive Worlds. People Lost in Time* (Washington, D. C., National Geographic, 1973).

White, Lynn, Jr., "Christian Myth and Christian History," 145-158 in *The Journal of the History of Ideas,* vol. 3, 1942.

White, Leslie, "Introduction," to *Ancient Society,* edited by Leslie A. White (Cambridge, Massachusetts, Harvard University Press, 1964).

Wichman, Juliet Rice, "Agriculture," 113-121 in *Ancient Hawaiian Civilization*. A Series of Lectures delivered at the Kamehameha Schools, edited by A. S. C. Handy *et al* (Reprinted, Tokyo, Japan, Charles E. Tuttle, Publisher, 1975).

Wicker, Tom, "Political consultants are no asset," in the Kansas City *Star*, November 23, 1986, C-5.

Williams, M. E., "Eschatology (Theological Treatment)," 533-538 in the *New Catholic Encyclopedia*, V (Washington, D. C., McGraw-Hill, 1967).

Winslow, Deborah, "Rituals of First Menstruation in Sri Lanka," 603-625 in *Man. The Journal of the Royal Anthropological Institute*, vol. 15, No. 4, December, 1980.

Wirth, Lewis, "Preface," to Karl Mannheim, *Ideology and Utopia. An Introduction to the Sociology of Knowledge* (New York, Harcourt-Brace, 1940).

Wissler, Clark, "The Conflict and Survival of Cultures," 592-601 in *The Golden Age of American Anthropology*, edited by Margaret Mead and Ruth Bunzel (New York, George Braziller, 1960).

Worcester, Dean C., "Head-Hunters of Northern Luzon," 883-930 in *National Geographic*, vol. 13, No. 9, September, 1912.

Yohe, Ralph S., "'Gone to the Yayla,' Rugs of the Yörük Triangle," 36-39 in *Yoruk. The Nomadic Weaving Tradition of the Middle East*, edited by Anthony Landreau (Pittsburg, Pennsylvania, Museum of Art, Carnegie Institute, 1978).

Unsigned Articles

The Associated Press, London, "Questioning tenets is O.K., report says," in the Kansas City *Times*, June 8, 1987, E-8.

The Associated Press, New York, "Buyouts affect fewer top firms," in the Kansas City *Times*, November 27, 1989, A-2.

By the Associated Press, New York, "U. S. deficits blamed for trade lag," in the Kansas City *Star*, January 23, 1987, A-13.

"Back from the Stone Age? An Anthropological find may be a hoax," 69 in *Newsweek*, vol. 107, May 5, 1986.

A Conestoga Chief, "We Find the Christians Depraved," 253-254 in *Literature of the American Indian*, edited by Thomas E. Sanders and Walter W. Peek (Beverly Hills, California, Glencoe Press, 1973).

320

The Constitution of the United Presbyterian Church in the United States of America. Part I. Book of Confession, Second edition, 1970. Published by the Office of the General Assembly of the United Presbyterian Church in the United States of America (Philadelphia, General Assembly of the United Presbyterian Church, 1967), 9.01 to 9.56.

"Dioxin in Missouri; Troubled Times," 60-62 in *Science News,* vol. 123, No. 4, January 22, 1983.

"Eschatology," Part III. 202-220 in *Doctrine in the Church of England. The Report of the Commission on Christian Doctrine appointed by the Archbishops of Canterbury and York in 1922, William Ebor, Chairman* (London, England, Society for the Promotion of Christian Knowledge, first published 1933, re-issued 1962).

"Evangelicals Vote on the Jews," Kansas City *Times,* August 19, 1989, E-4.

"A fresh start at Three Mile Island?," 359 in *Science News,* vol. 127, No. 23, June 8, 1985.

"A Letter to the Editor of the Chicago Tribune, 1890," 357-358 in *Literature of the American Indian,* edited by Thomas E. Sanders and Walter W. Peek (Beverly Hills, California, Glencoe Press, 1973).

Manifesto by the Grace Baptist Church of Lee's Summit in the Kansas City *Times,* August 19, 1989, E-9.

New York Times, Washington, "Studies say deficits, foreign debt will linger," in the Kansas City *Times,* November 6, 1987, C-1.

"Parousia," 1017-1018 in *The Oxford Dictionary of the Christian Church* (New York, Oxford University Press, 1958).

"Religious intolerance of powerful TV preachers cannot be tolerated," in the Kansas City *Times,* March 20, 1987, A-17.

"Summary and Prospect," 695-700 in *Man's Impact on Environment,* edited by Thomas R. Detwyler (New York, McGraw-Hill, 1971).

"TMI Restart Underway," 229 in *Science News,* vol. 128, No. 15, October 12, 1985.

"TMI Tests Trashed," 186 in *Science News,* vol. 128, No. 12, September 12, 1985.

The Washington Post, "Baptist Schism may be the answer to internal fight, scholar says," in the Kansas City *Times,* April 4, 1987, C-17.

"The Westminster Confession of Faith," 77-101 in *The Proposed Book of Confessions of the Presbyterian Church in the United States of America* together with related documents (Atlanta, Georgia, Materials Distribution Service, 1976).

Letters

Jenkins, Rebecca, Bishop's Press Officer, Auckland Castle, Diocese of Durham, England, to C. Stanley Urban, Park College, Parkville, Missouri, December 15, 1989.

Wagley, Charles, Gainsville, Florida, to Stan Urban, Park College, Parkville, Missouri, October 13, 1981, November 15, 1984.

Encyclopedias, Reference Works, Etc.

American Men of Science. A Biographical Directory. The Social and Behavioral Sciences, edited by Jaque Cattell (New York, R. R. Bowker, 1956), III.

Anthropology Today. An Encyclopedic Incentory. Prepared under the Chairmanship of A. L. Kroeber (Chicago, University of Chicago Press, 1953).

Directory of American Scholars. A Biographical Directory, edited by Jaque Cattell, 3rd edition (New York, R. R. Bowker, 1957).

The Holy Bible. Revised Standard Version Containing the Old and New Testament (New York, Thomas Nelson and Sons, 1952).

The New Covenant. Commonly Called the New Testament of Our Lord and Savior Jesus Christ. Revised Standard Version (New York, Thomas Nelson & Sons, 1946).

The New Schall-Herzog Encyclopedia of Religious Knowledge, 12 vols., edited by Samuel Macauley Jackson (New York, Funk and Wagnal, 1909), IV.

AUTHOR INDEX

Specific Citation in Text or in Explanatory Footnote

SUBJECT INDEX

A

Abraham, *quid pro quo* with Jehovah, 57-58

Absentee labor, devastates Pacific economy, 219-220

Abstract thought, relation to primitive, 72-73

Affluent society, threat to democracy and labor, 274

Alice Springs, sacred rites, 93

Anthropologists, difficulty in job description, 43-44

Anthropology: colonialism, 31-32; early restrictions, 2-4; exclusively field work, 8-9, 27; Golden Age, 35-36; link with imperialism, 5-6; subjectivity, 9

Ardrey (Robert), theory questioned, 153-154

Aristotle's *Politics,* primitive social order, 238-239

Aristotle, rejection of physical theory, 51

Art: adverse influence of West, 202-203; careers open to talent, 192; cave, 180-181; conservatism in Central Australia, 185; conservatism self-perpetuating, 188-190; danger of Western terms, 183; dominance of conservatism, 190-191; early magic, 179-180, 185; influence of environment, 192-193; Mimbres art unique, 186, 189; Northwest coast of America, 189; passion play, xi-xii, 200-201; Platonic idealism, 182-183; Polynesian freedom, 186; pride in craftsmanship, 193-194; primacy over written word, 239-240; rigidity in population cluster, 188; West African, 184-185

Artist, freedom versus technique, 201-202

Asad theory, history and religion, 75
Aztecs: architecture as religious

DATE DUE

HIGHSMITH 45-220